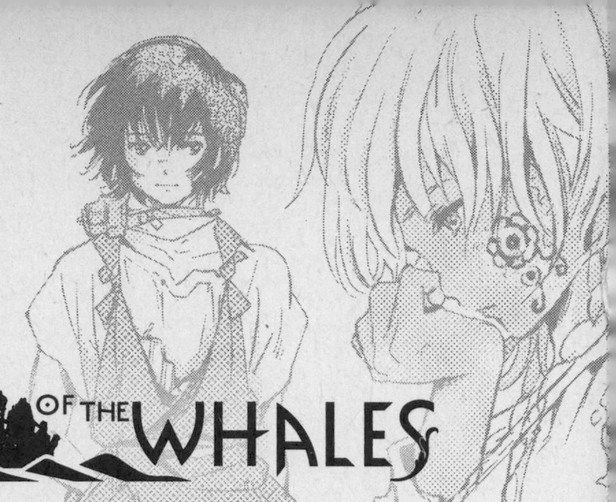

CHILDREN OF THE WHALES

Story and Art by Abi Umeda

Volume

1

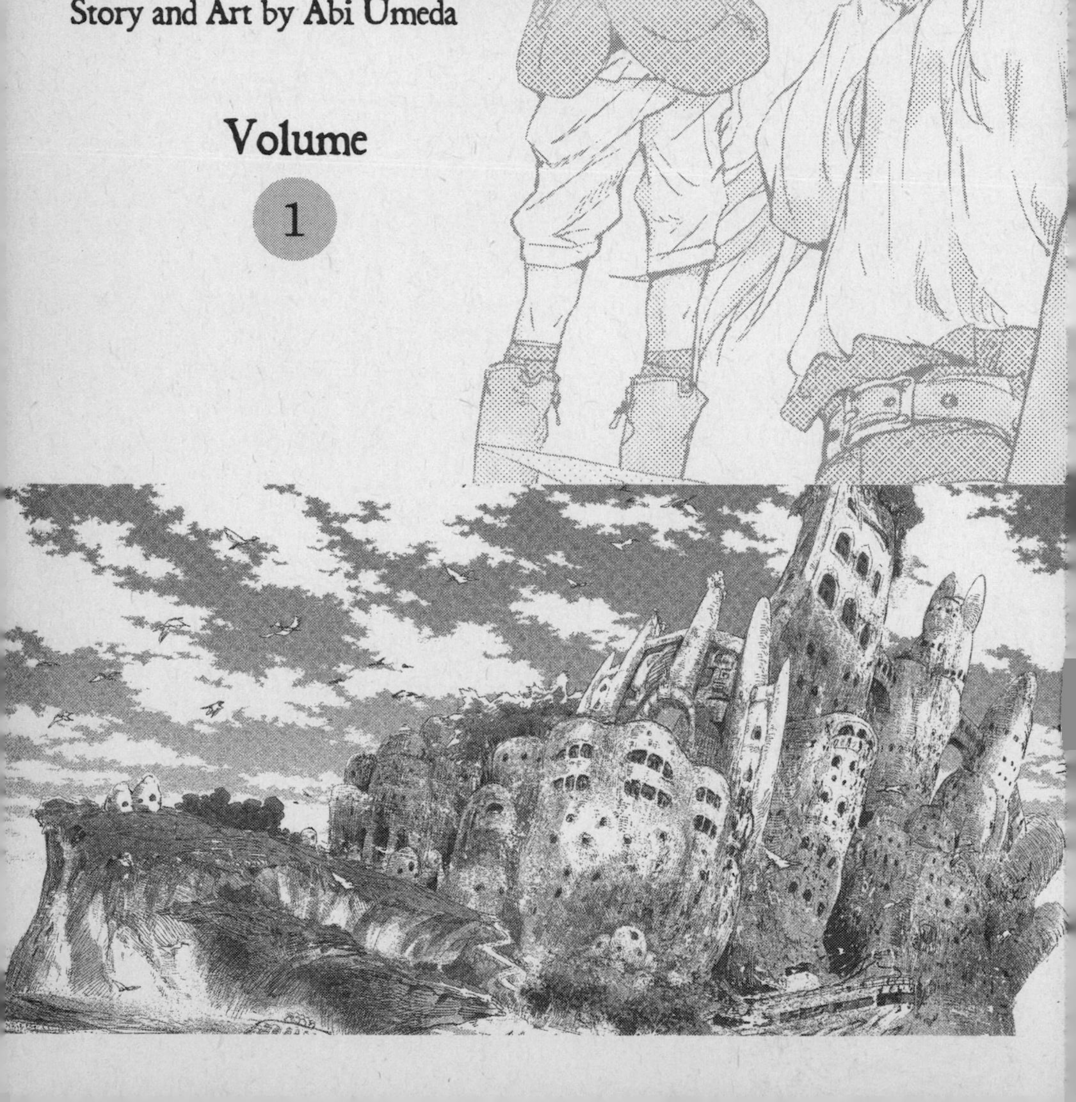

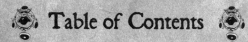 # Table of Contents

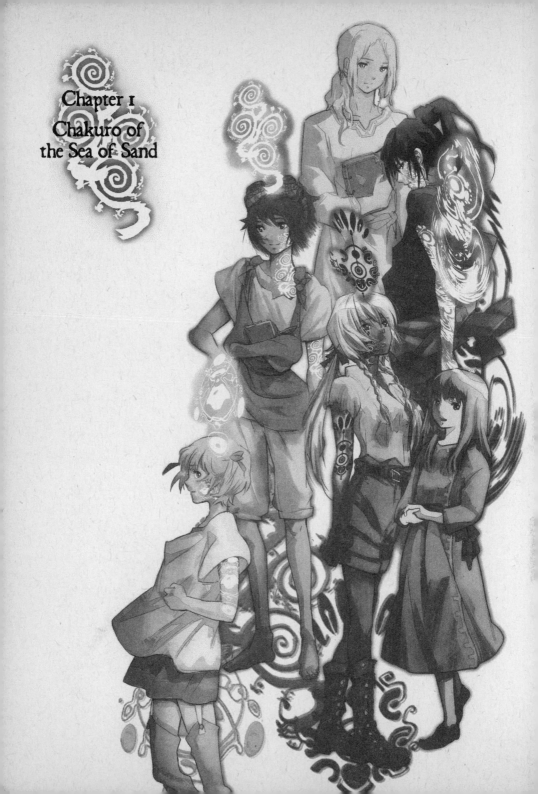

Chapter 1
Chakuro of the Sea of Sand

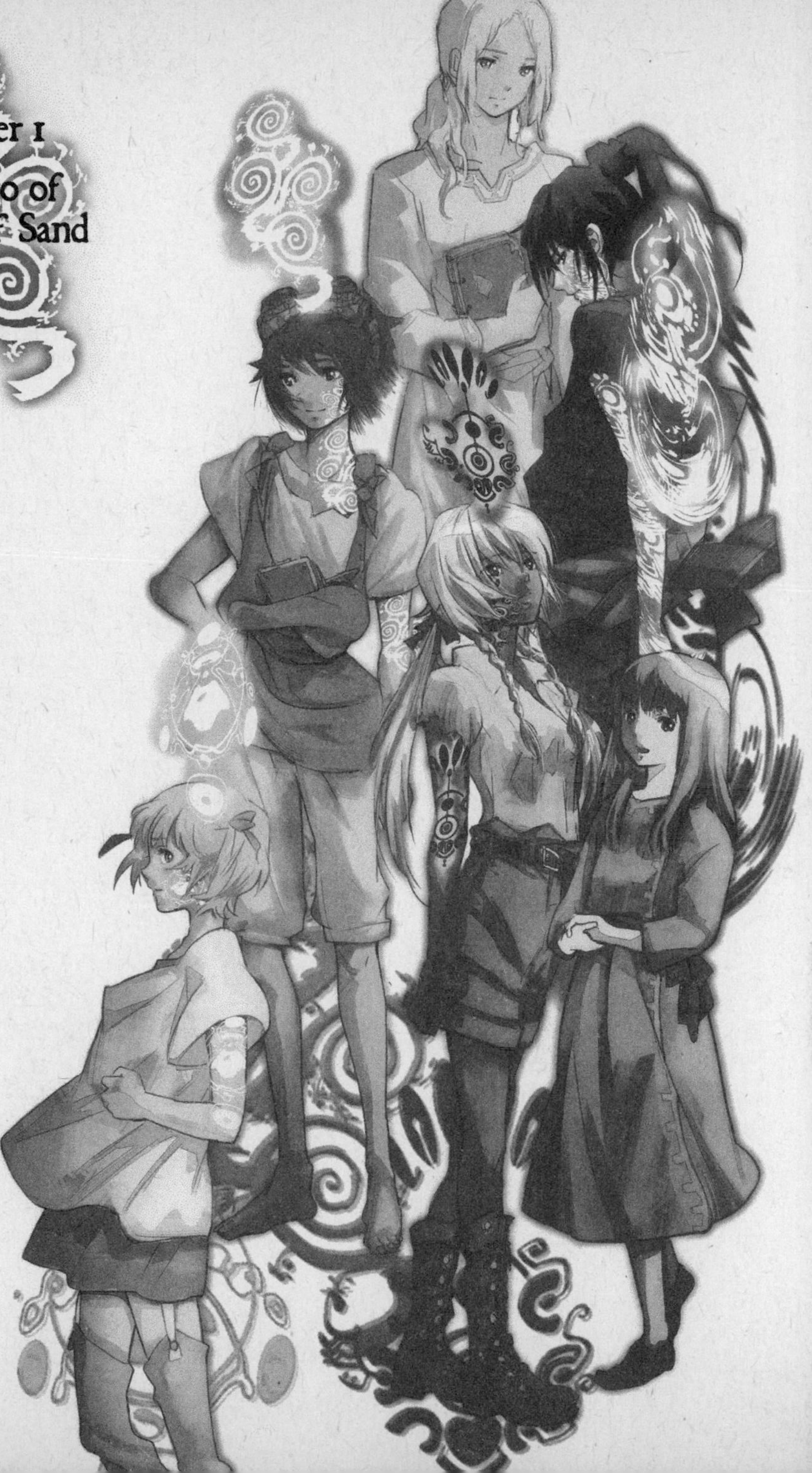

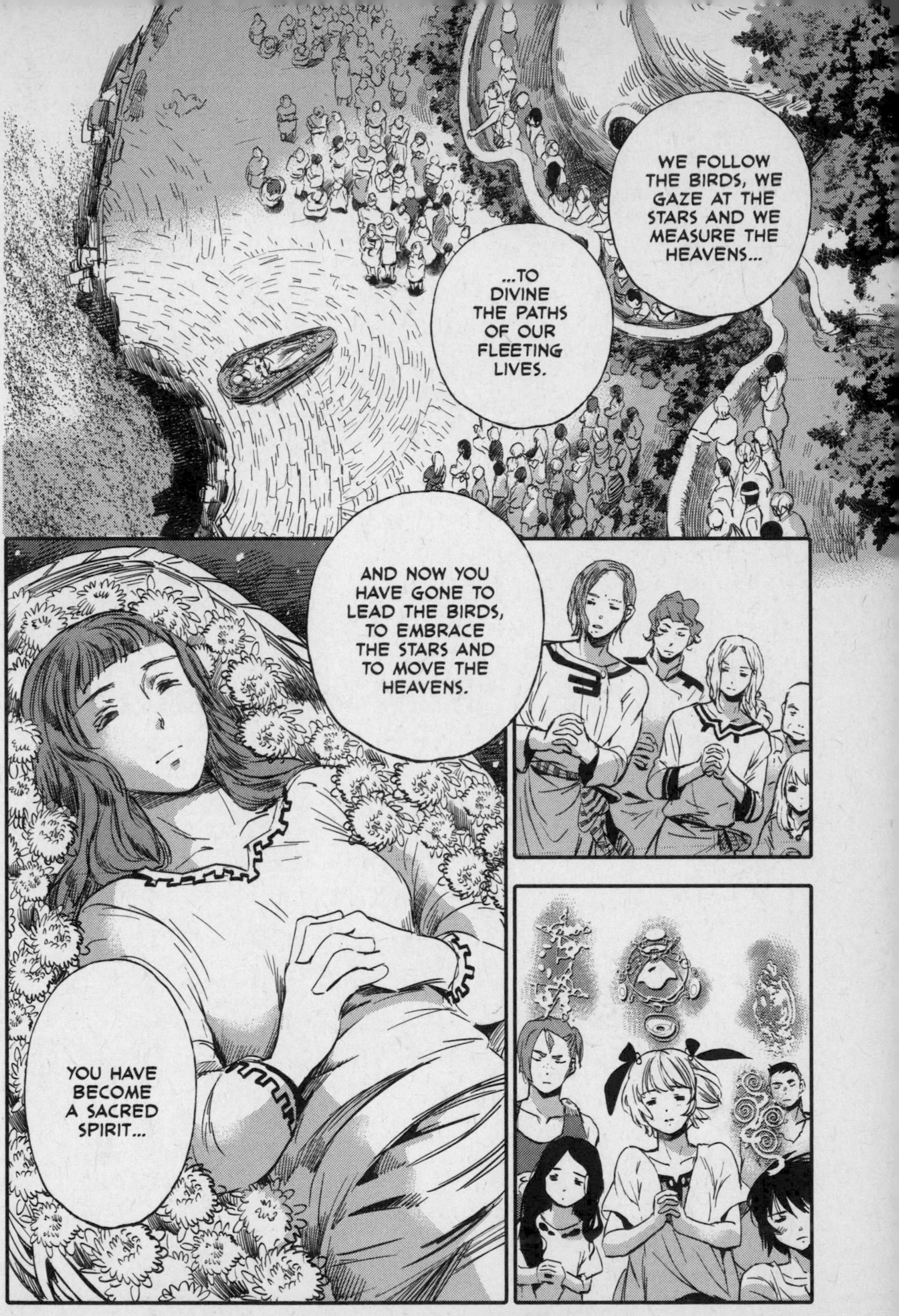
WE FOLLOW THE BIRDS, WE GAZE AT THE STARS AND WE MEASURE THE HEAVENS...
...TO DIVINE THE PATHS OF OUR FLEETING LIVES.
AND NOW YOU HAVE GONE TO LEAD THE BIRDS, TO EMBRACE THE STARS AND TO MOVE THE HEAVENS.
YOU HAVE BECOME A SACRED SPIRIT...

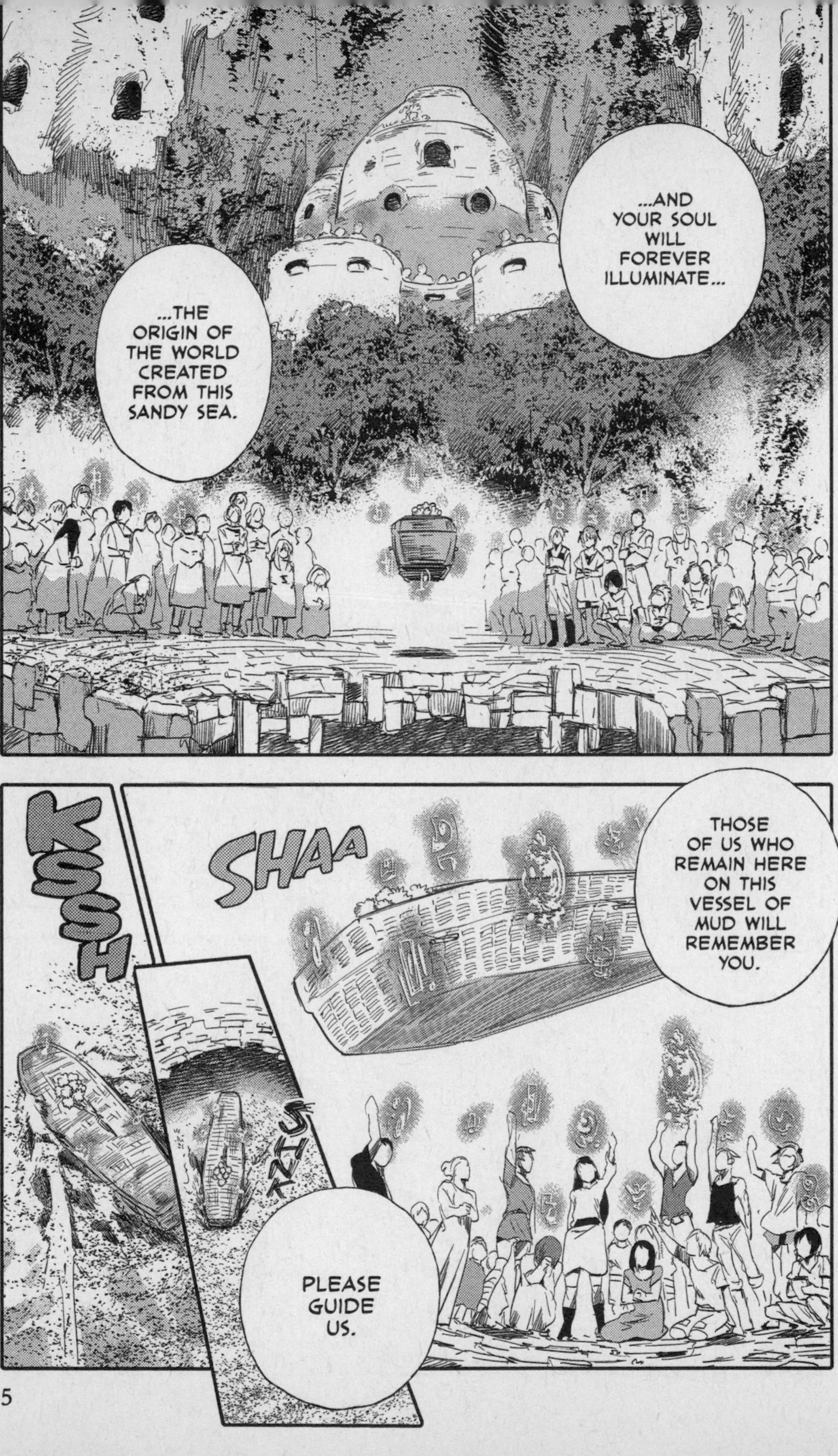
...AND YOUR SOUL WILL FOREVER ILLUMINATE...
...THE ORIGIN OF THE WORLD CREATED FROM THIS SANDY SEA.
THOSE OF US WHO REMAIN HERE ON THIS VESSEL OF MUD WILL REMEMBER YOU.
SHAA
PLEASE GUIDE US.
SHNK
KSSH

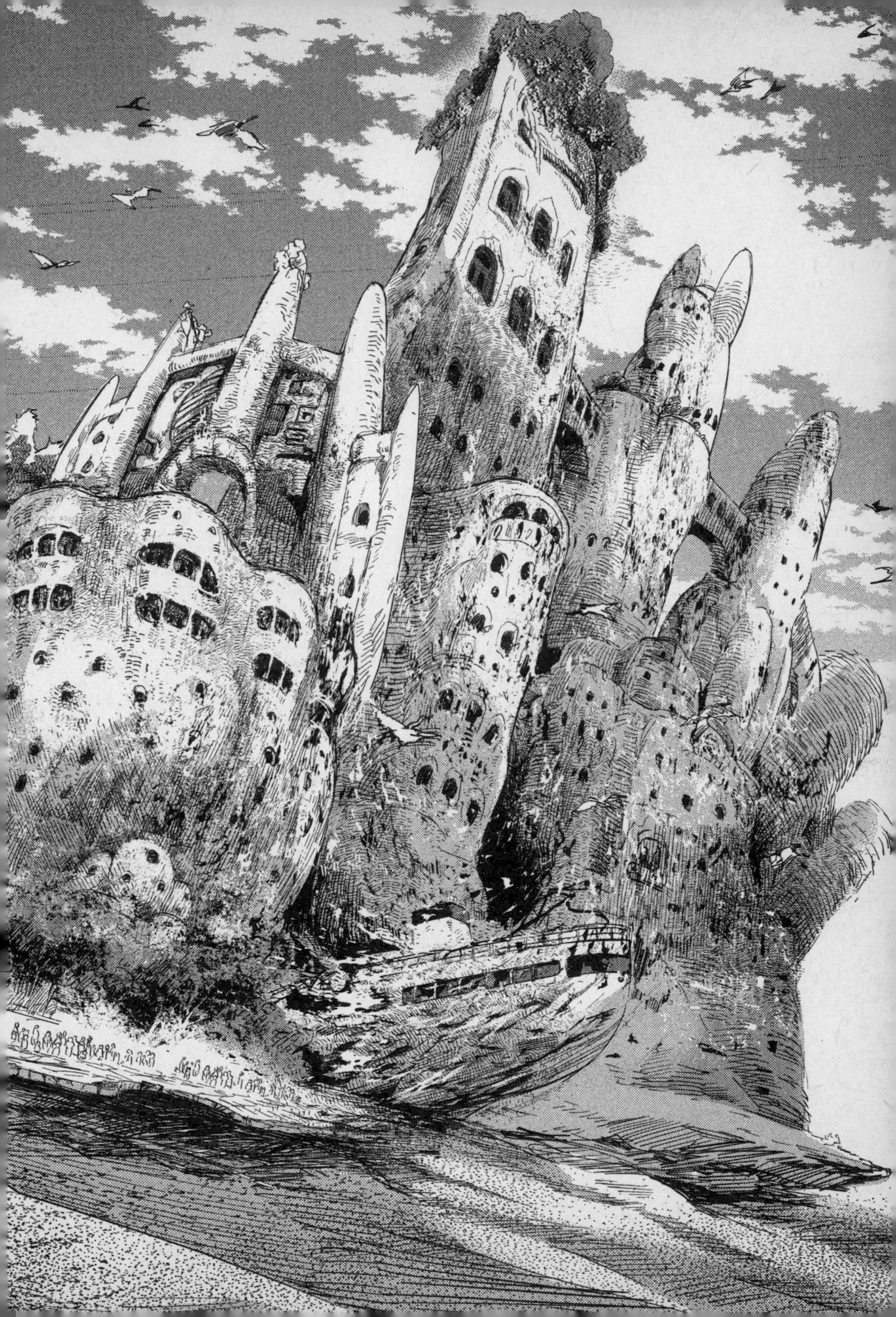

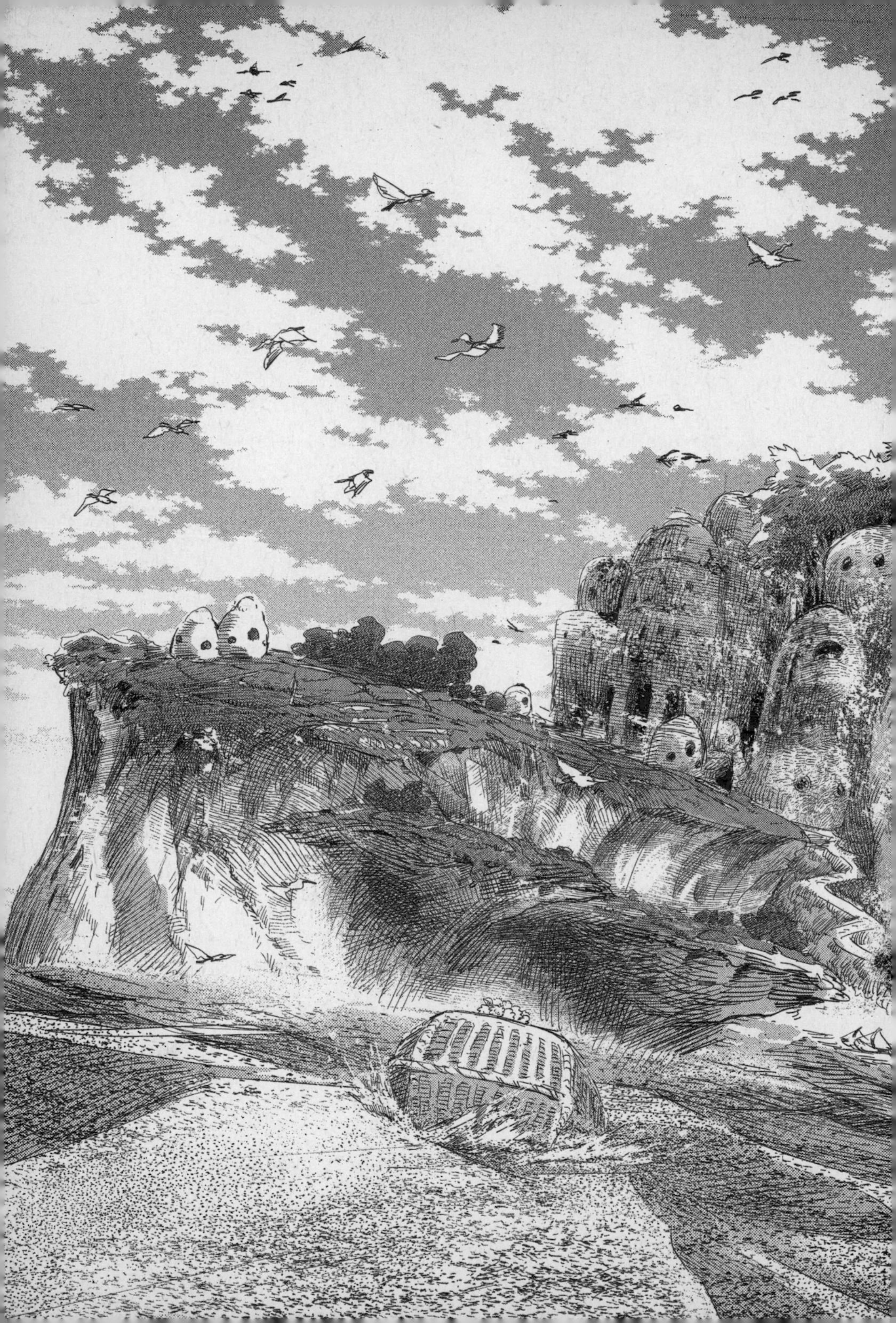

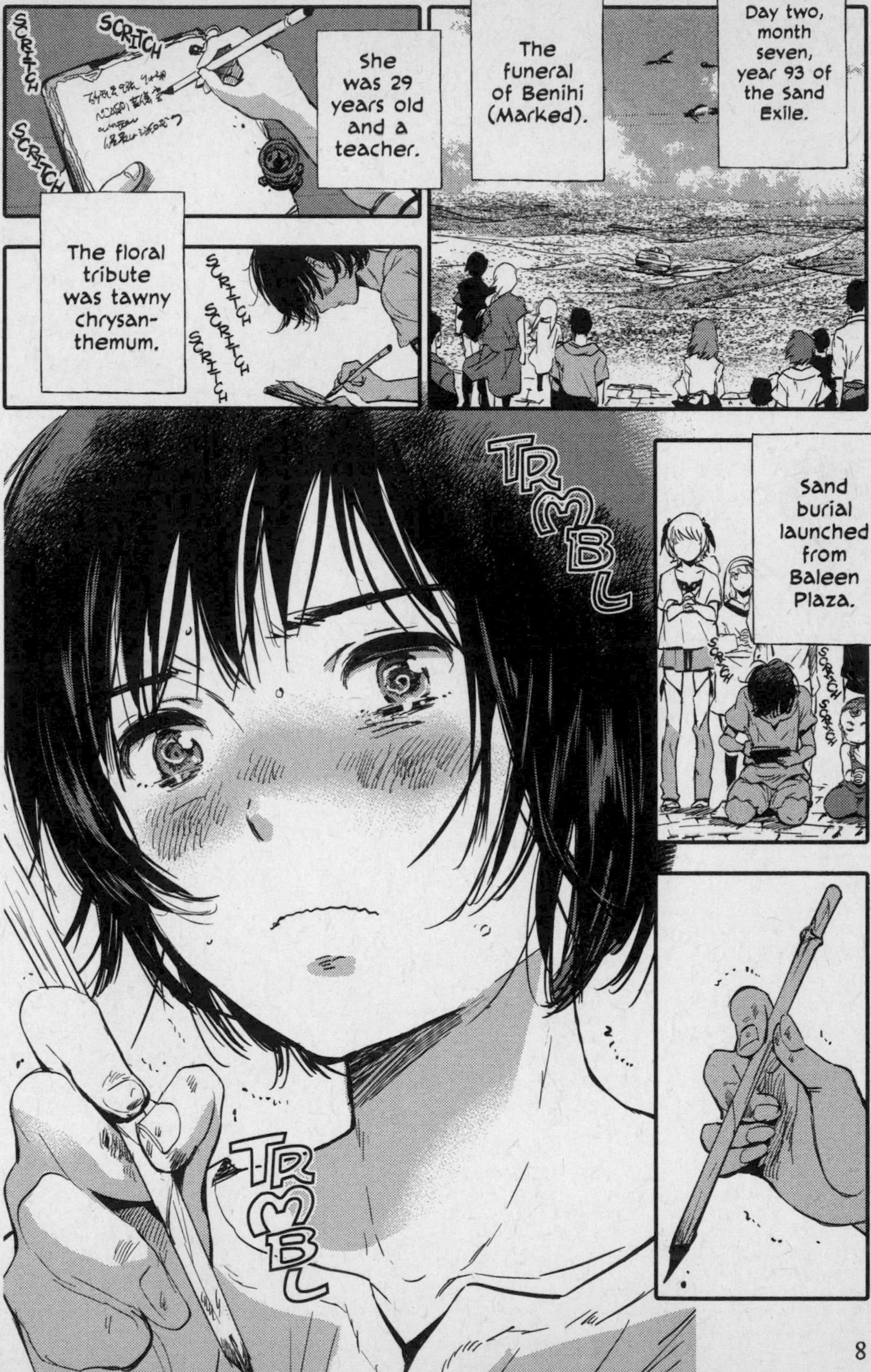
Day two, month seven, year 93 of the Sand Exile.
The funeral of Benihi (Marked).
She was 29 years old and a teacher.
SCRITCH
SCRITCH
SCRITCH
The floral tribute was tawny chrysanthemum.
SCRITCH
SCRITCH
SCRITCH
Sand burial launched from Baleen Plaza.
SCRITCH
SCRITCH
SCRITCH
TRMBL
TRMBL

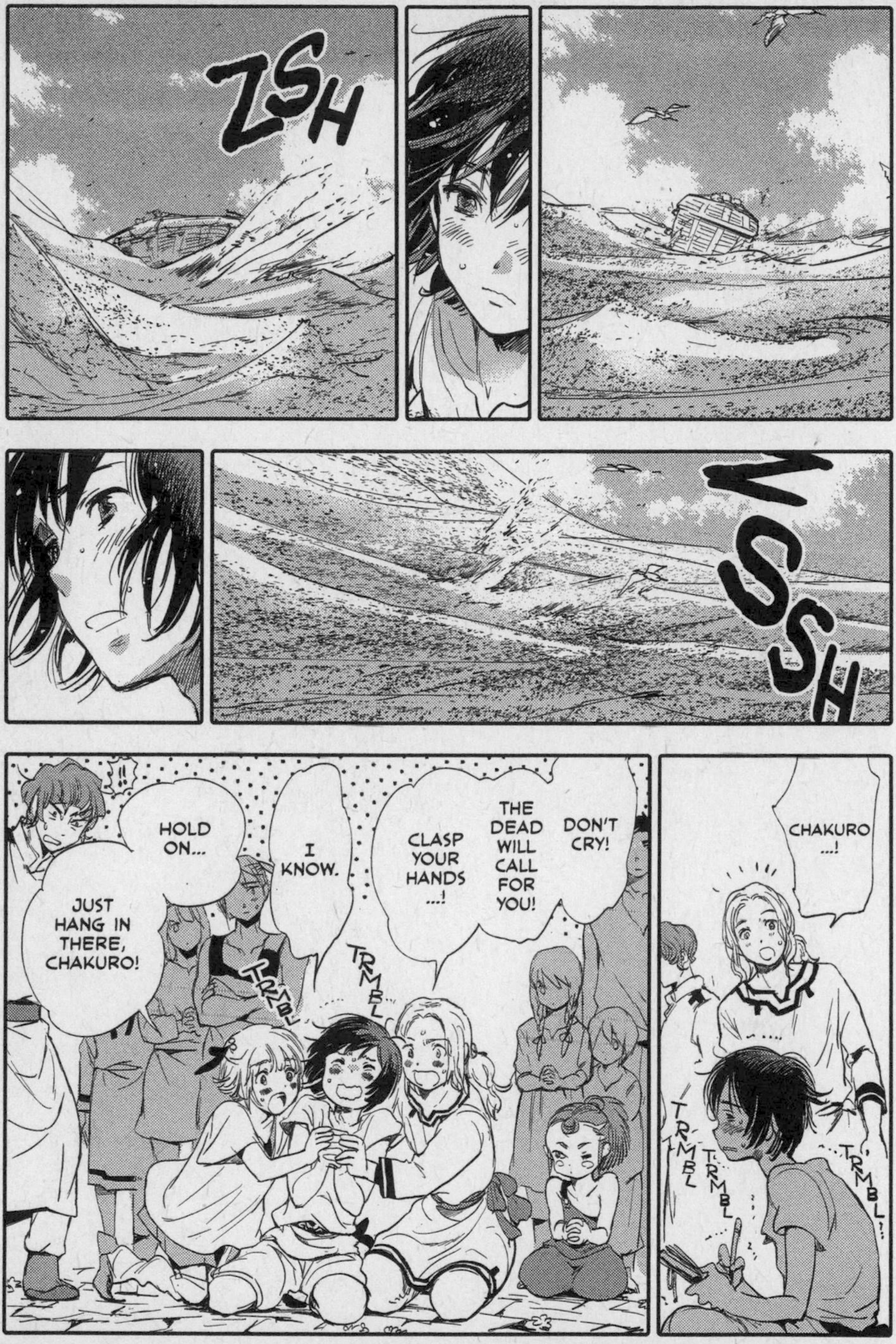
ZSH
ZSSH
CHAKURO ...!
TRMBL
TRMBL
TRMBL
DON'T CRY!
THE DEAD WILL CALL FOR YOU!
CLASP YOUR HANDS ...!
I KNOW.
HOLD ON...
JUST HANG IN THERE, CHAKURO!
!!
TRMBL
TRMBL

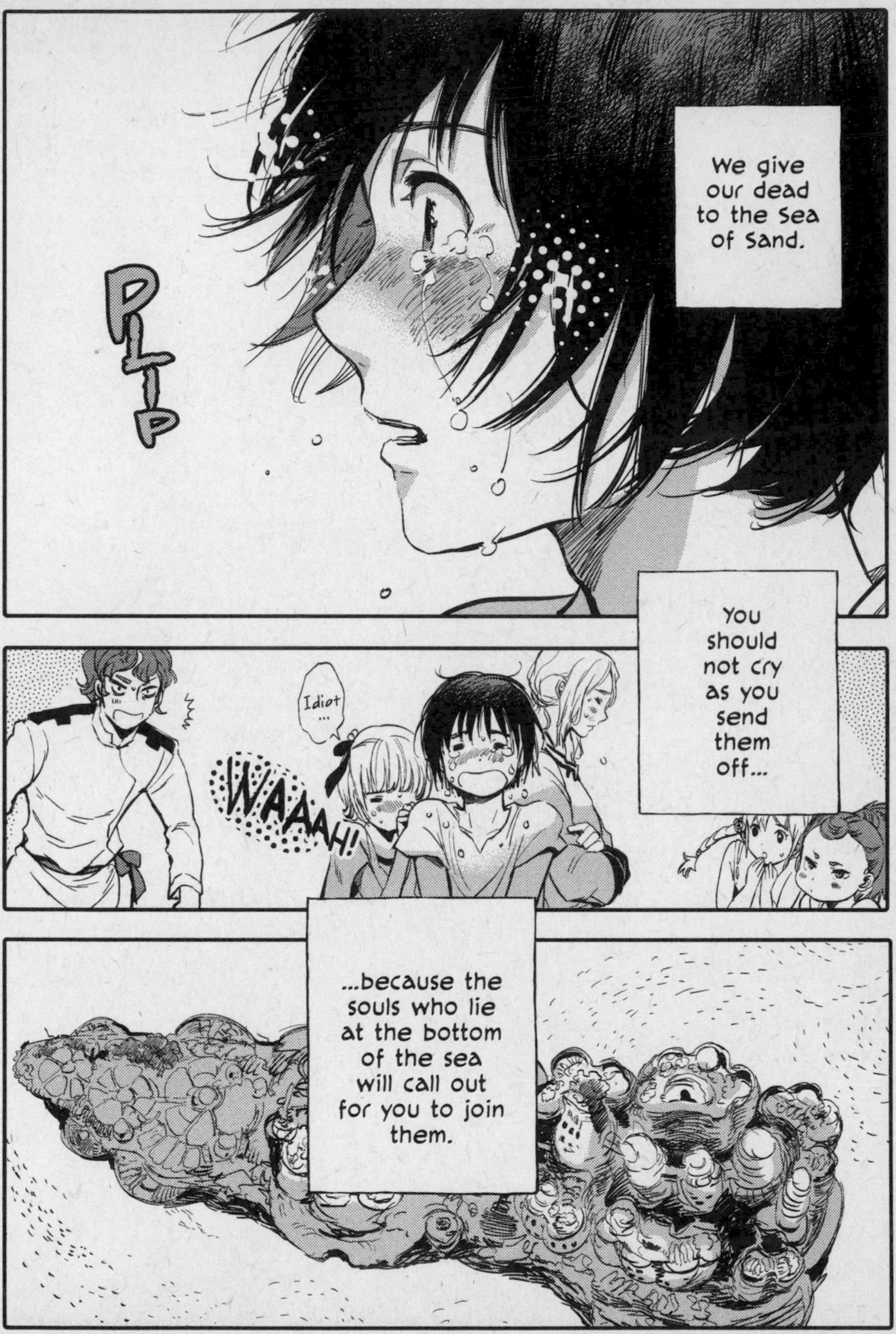
We give our dead to the Sea of Sand.
PLIP
You should not cry as you send them off...
Idiot ...
WAAAH!
...because the souls who lie at the bottom of the sea will call out for you to join them.

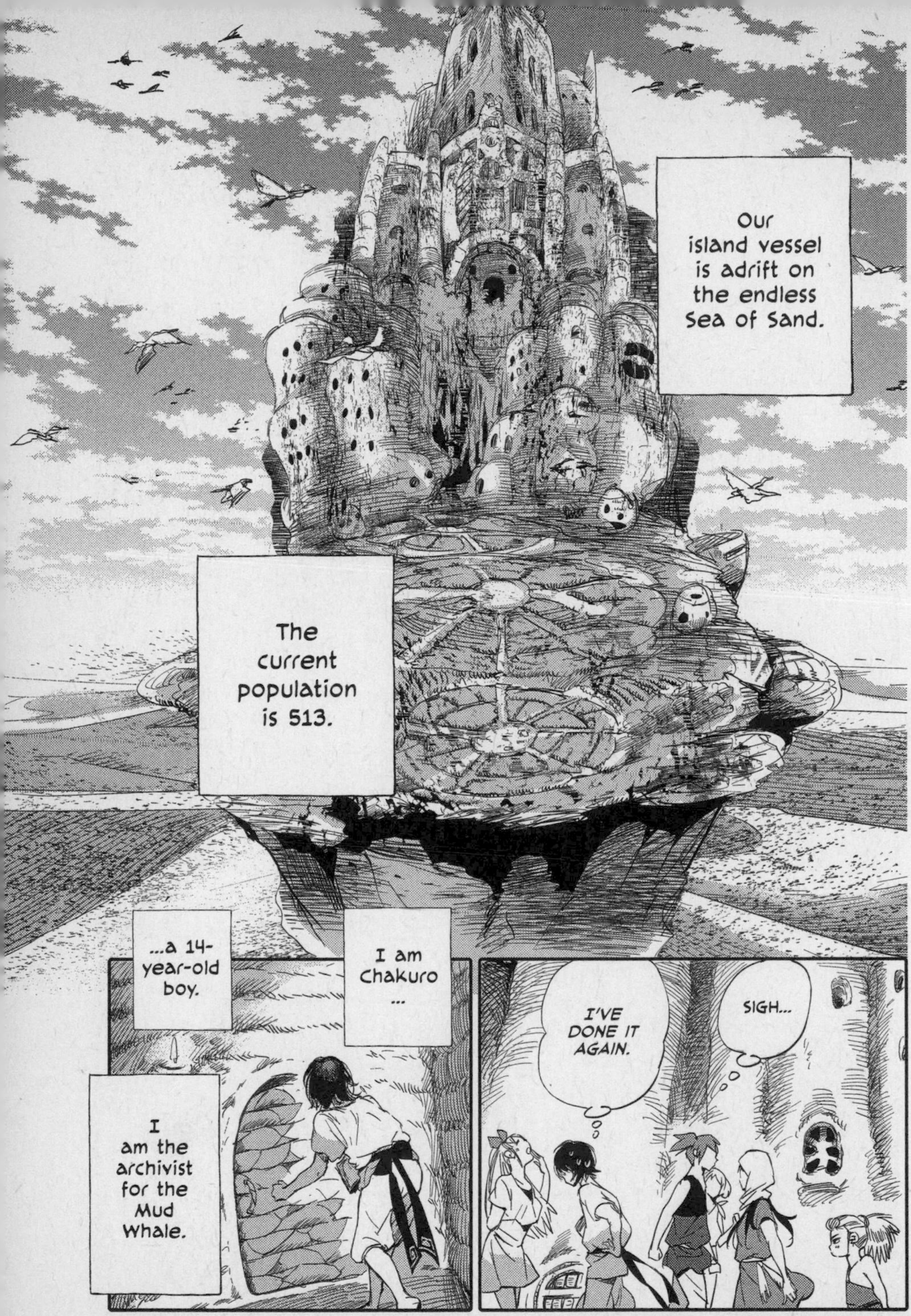
Our island vessel is adrift on the endless Sea of Sand.
The current population is 513.
SIGH...
I'VE DONE IT AGAIN.
I am Chakuro ...
...a 14-year-old boy.
I am the archivist for the Mud Whale.

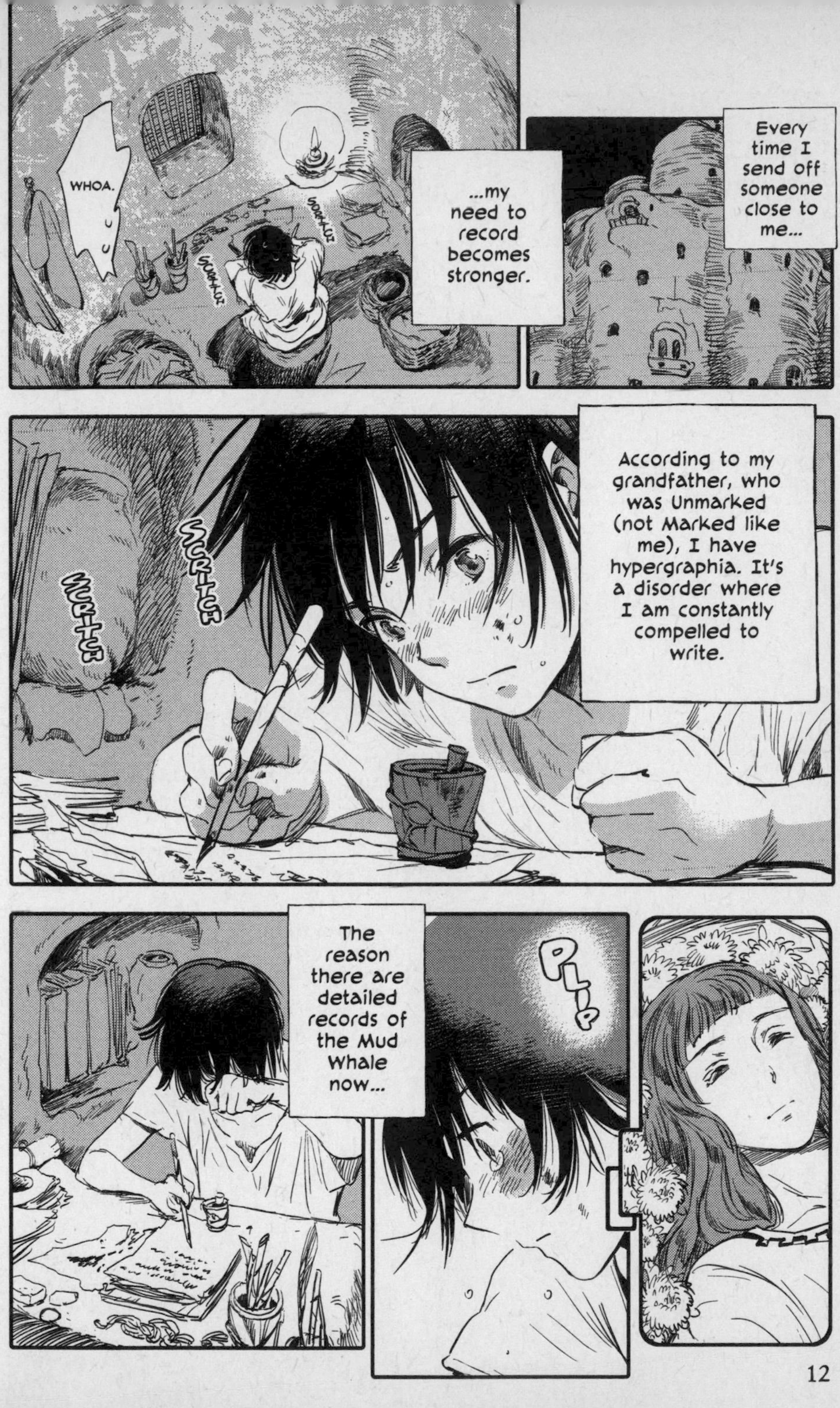
Every time I send off someone close to me...
...my need to record becomes stronger.
WHOA.
According to my grandfather, who was Unmarked (not Marked like me), I have hypergraphia. It's a disorder where I am constantly compelled to write.
SCRITCH
SCRITCH
PLIP
The reason there are detailed records of the Mud Whale now...

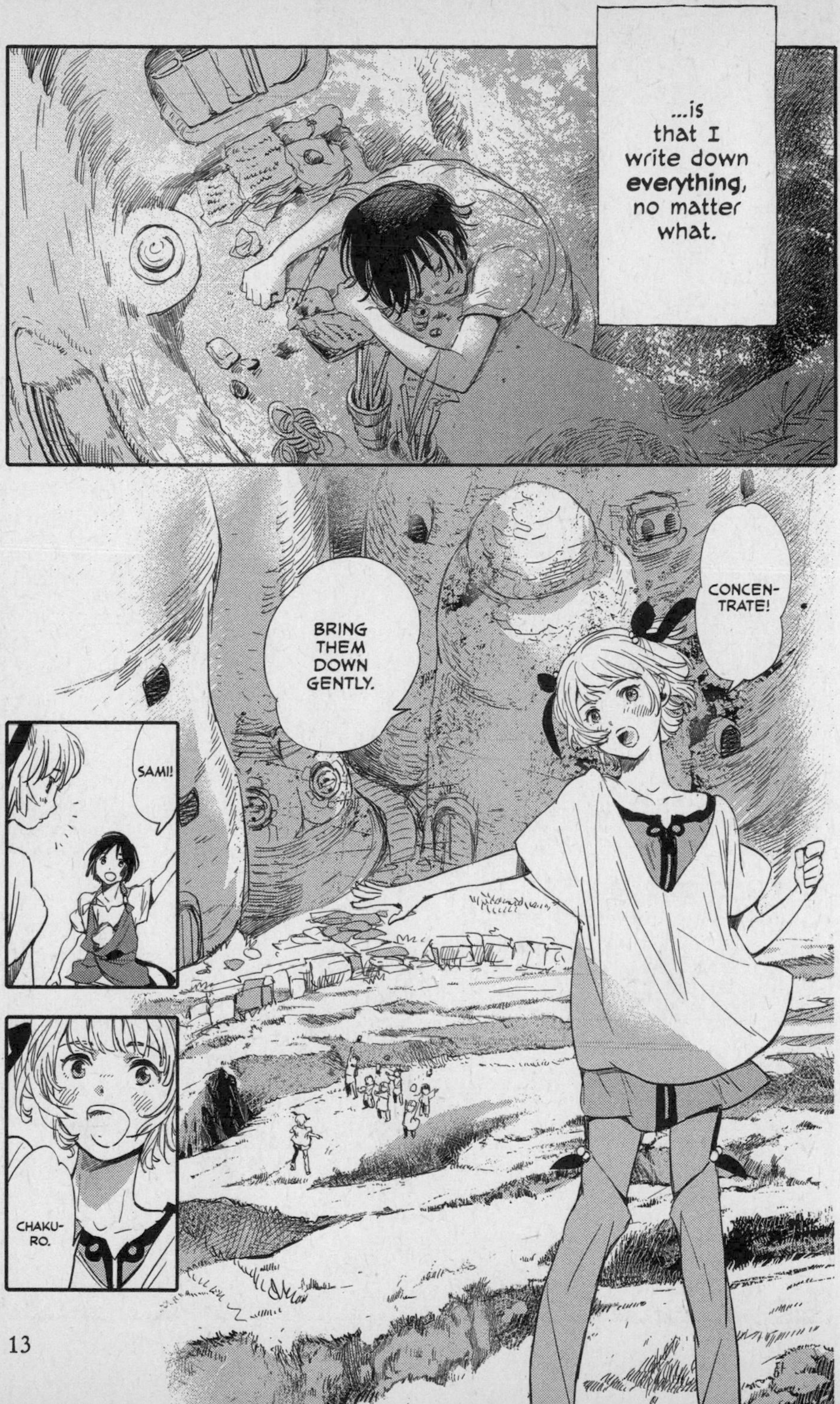
...is that I write down **everything**, no matter what.
CONCEN-TRATE!
BRING THEM DOWN GENTLY.
SAMI!
CHAKU-RO.

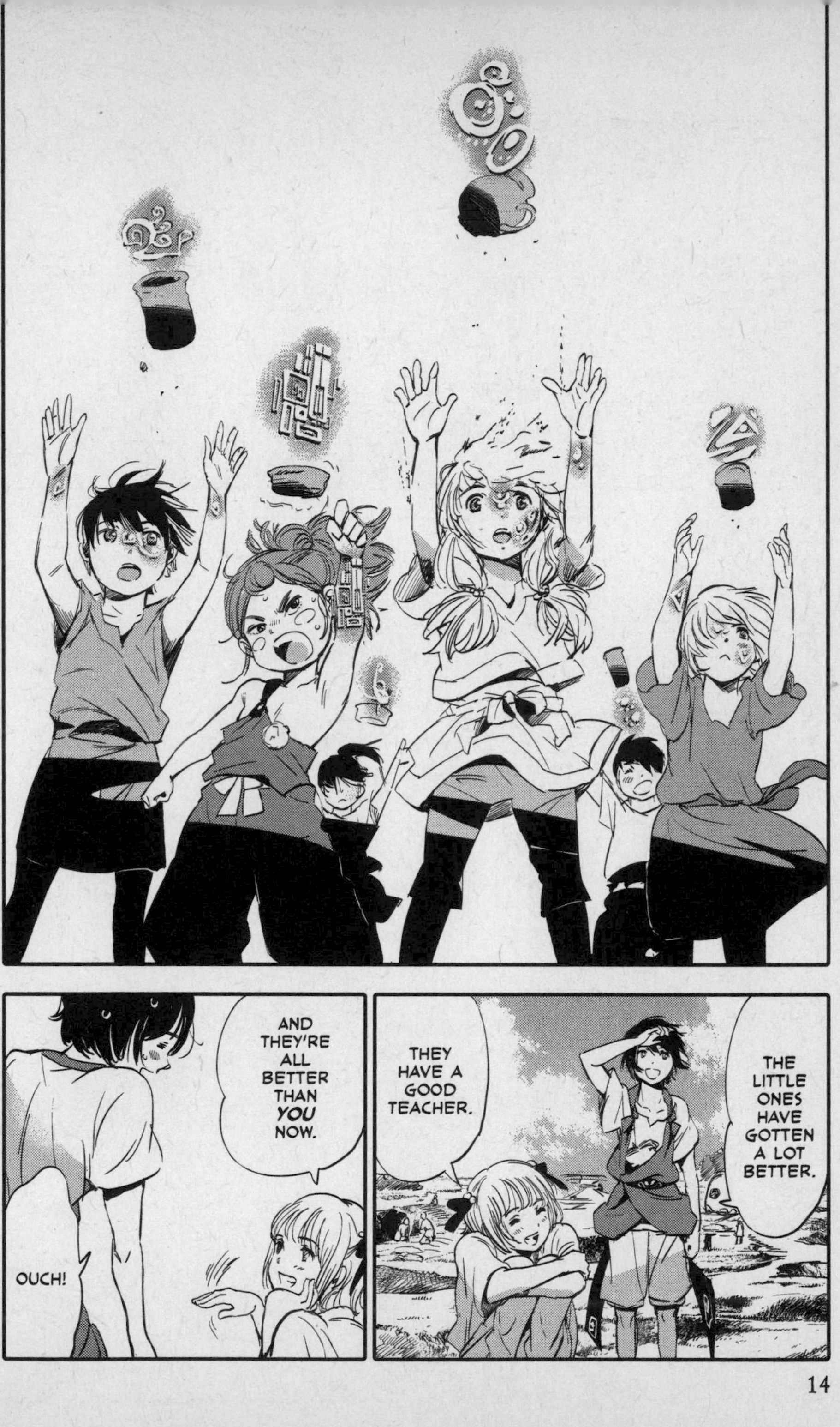
THE LITTLE ONES HAVE GOTTEN A LOT BETTER.
THEY HAVE A GOOD TEACHER.
AND THEY'RE ALL BETTER THAN *YOU* NOW.
OUCH!

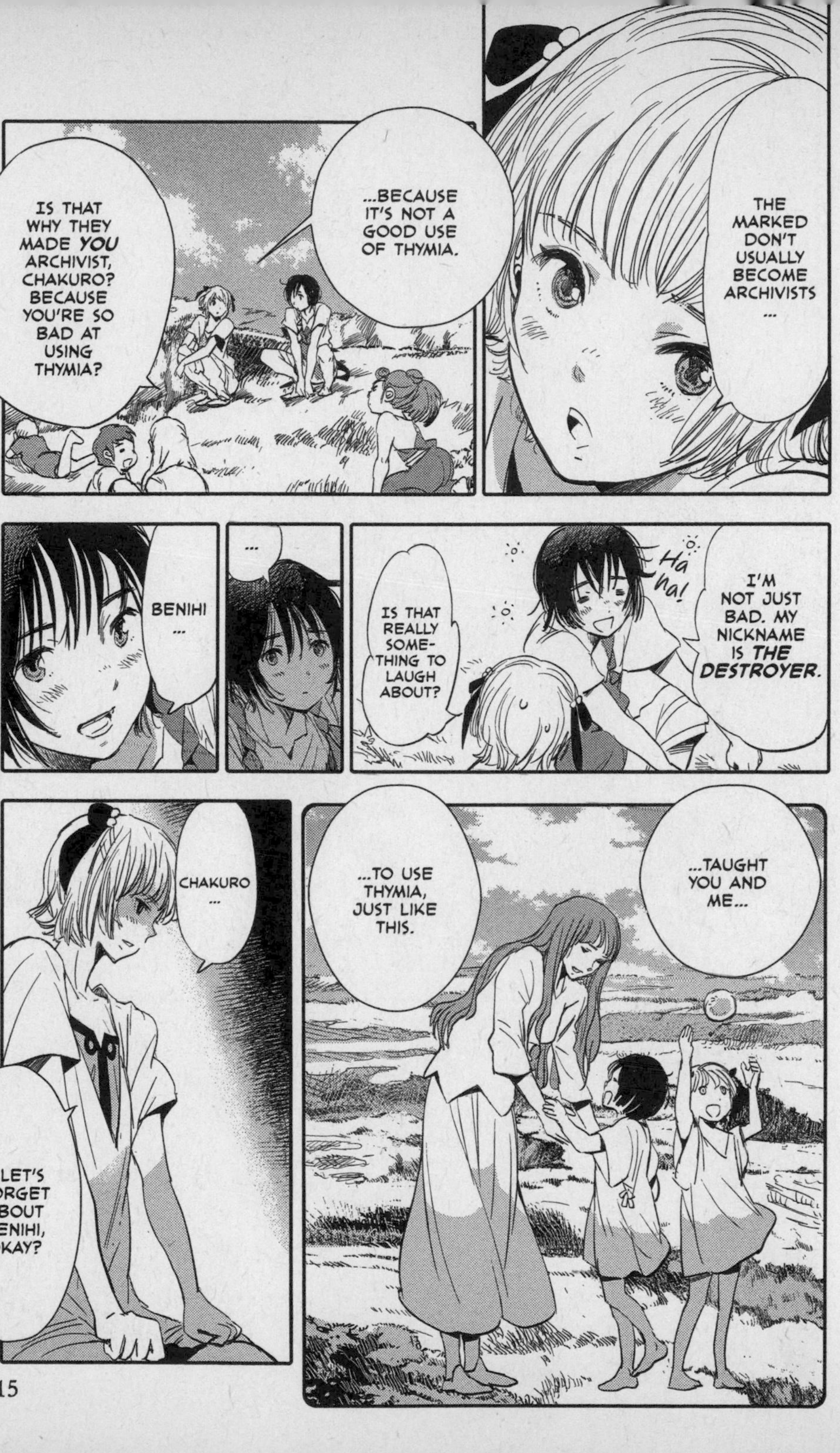
THE MARKED DON'T USUALLY BECOME ARCHIVISTS ...
...BECAUSE IT'S NOT A GOOD USE OF THYMIA.
IS THAT WHY THEY MADE *YOU* ARCHIVIST, CHAKURO? BECAUSE YOU'RE SO BAD AT USING THYMIA?
I'M NOT JUST BAD. MY NICKNAME IS *THE DESTROYER.*
Ha ha!
IS THAT REALLY SOME-THING TO LAUGH ABOUT?
...
BENIHI ...
...TAUGHT YOU AND ME...
...TO USE THYMIA, JUST LIKE THIS.
CHAKURO ...
...LET'S FORGET ABOUT BENIHI, OKAY?

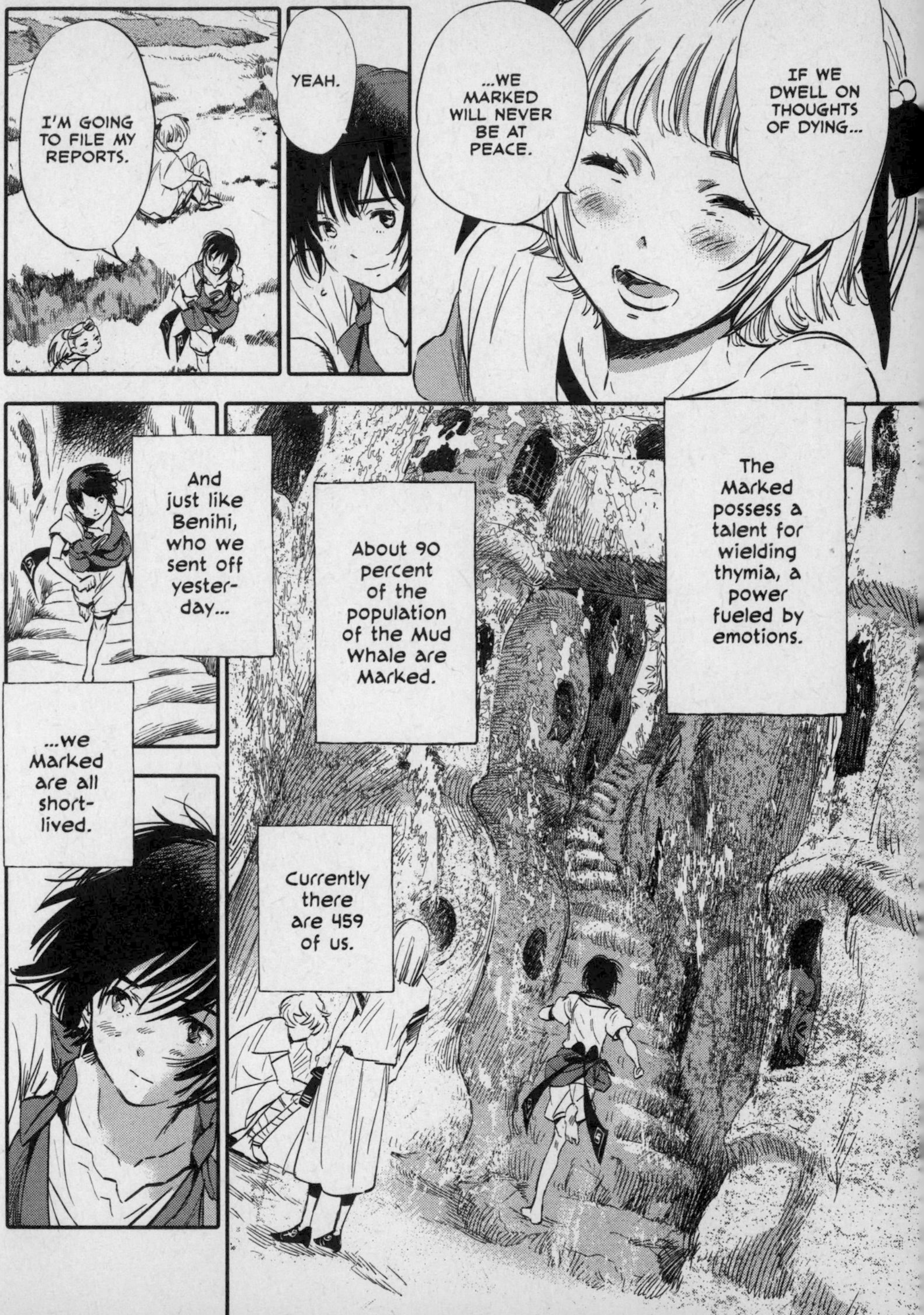
IF WE DWELL ON THOUGHTS OF DYING...
...WE MARKED WILL NEVER BE AT PEACE.
YEAH.
I'M GOING TO FILE MY REPORTS.
The Marked possess a talent for wielding thymia, a power fueled by emotions.
About 90 percent of the population of the Mud Whale are Marked.
Currently there are 459 of us.
And just like Benihi, who we sent off yesterday...
...we Marked are all short-lived.

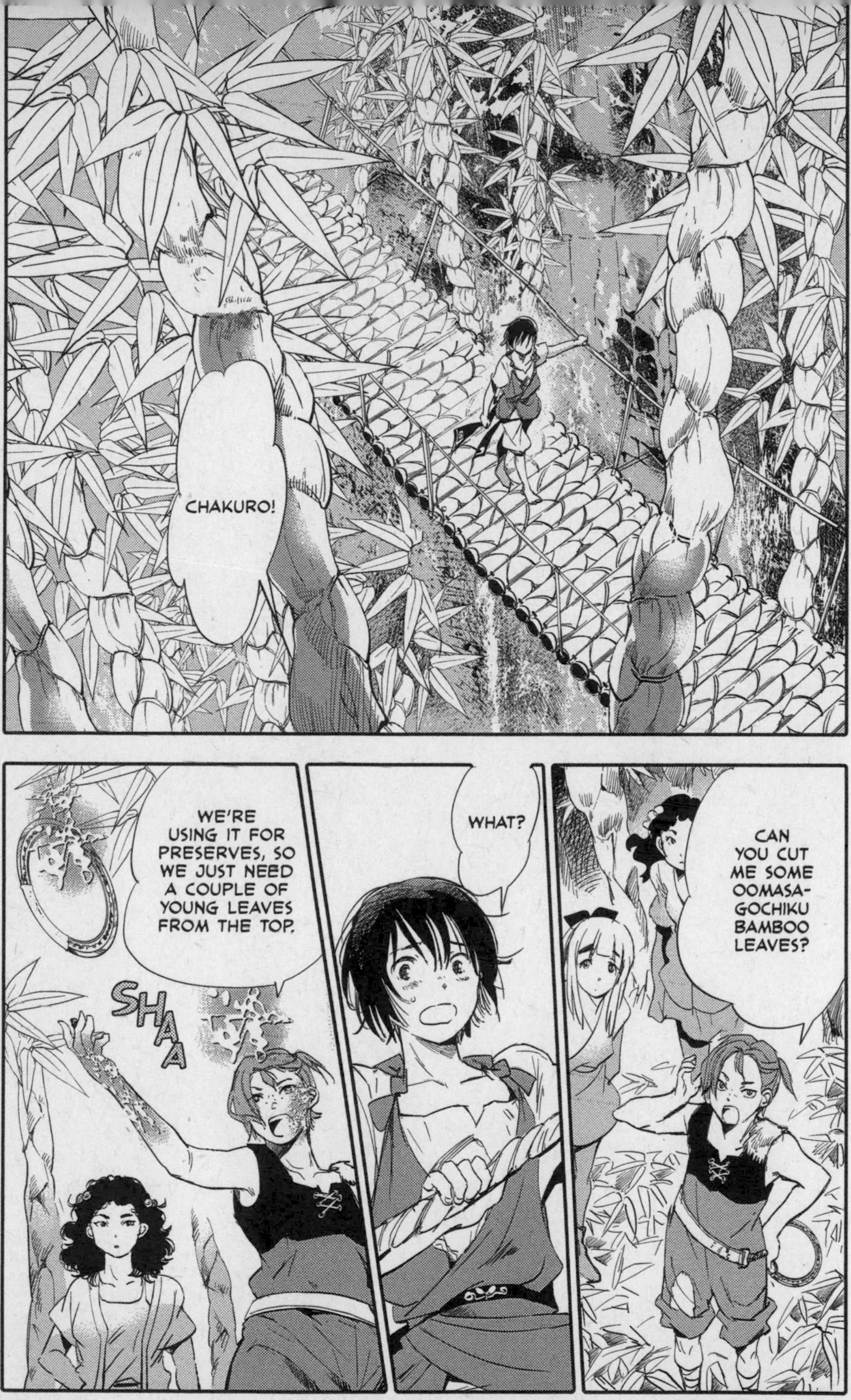
CHAKURO!
CAN YOU CUT ME SOME OOMASA-GOCHIKU BAMBOO LEAVES?
WHAT?
WE'RE USING IT FOR PRESERVES, SO WE JUST NEED A COUPLE OF YOUNG LEAVES FROM THE TOP.
SHAA

SHAK

JUST A COUPLE, JUST A COUPLE.

HUFF

POOF

SHURURU

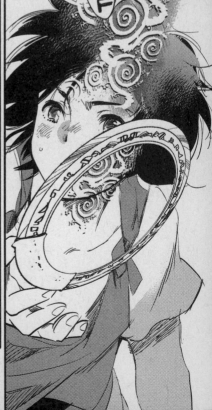

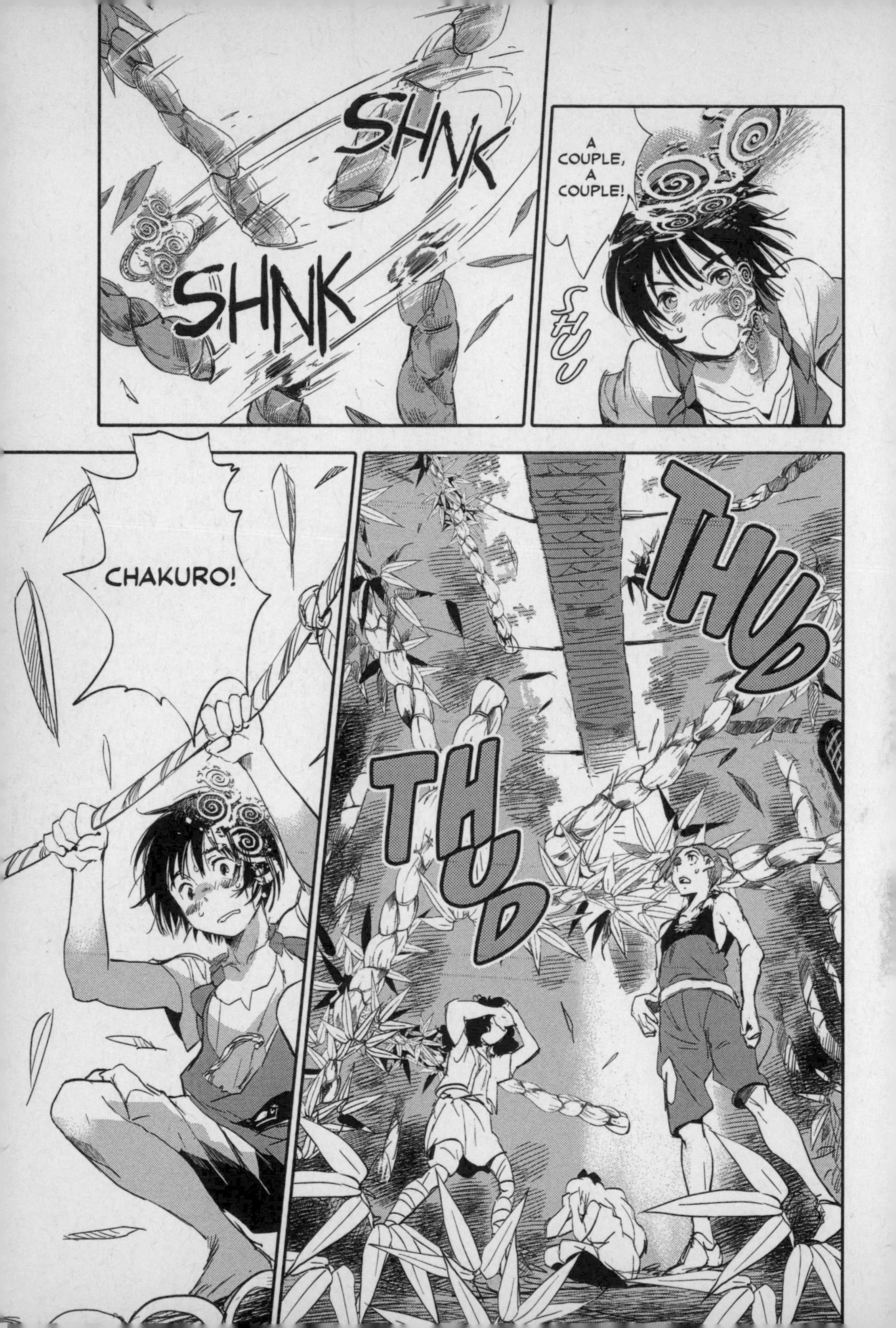
A COUPLE, A COUPLE!
SHUU
SHNK
SHNK
THUD
THUD
CHAKURO!

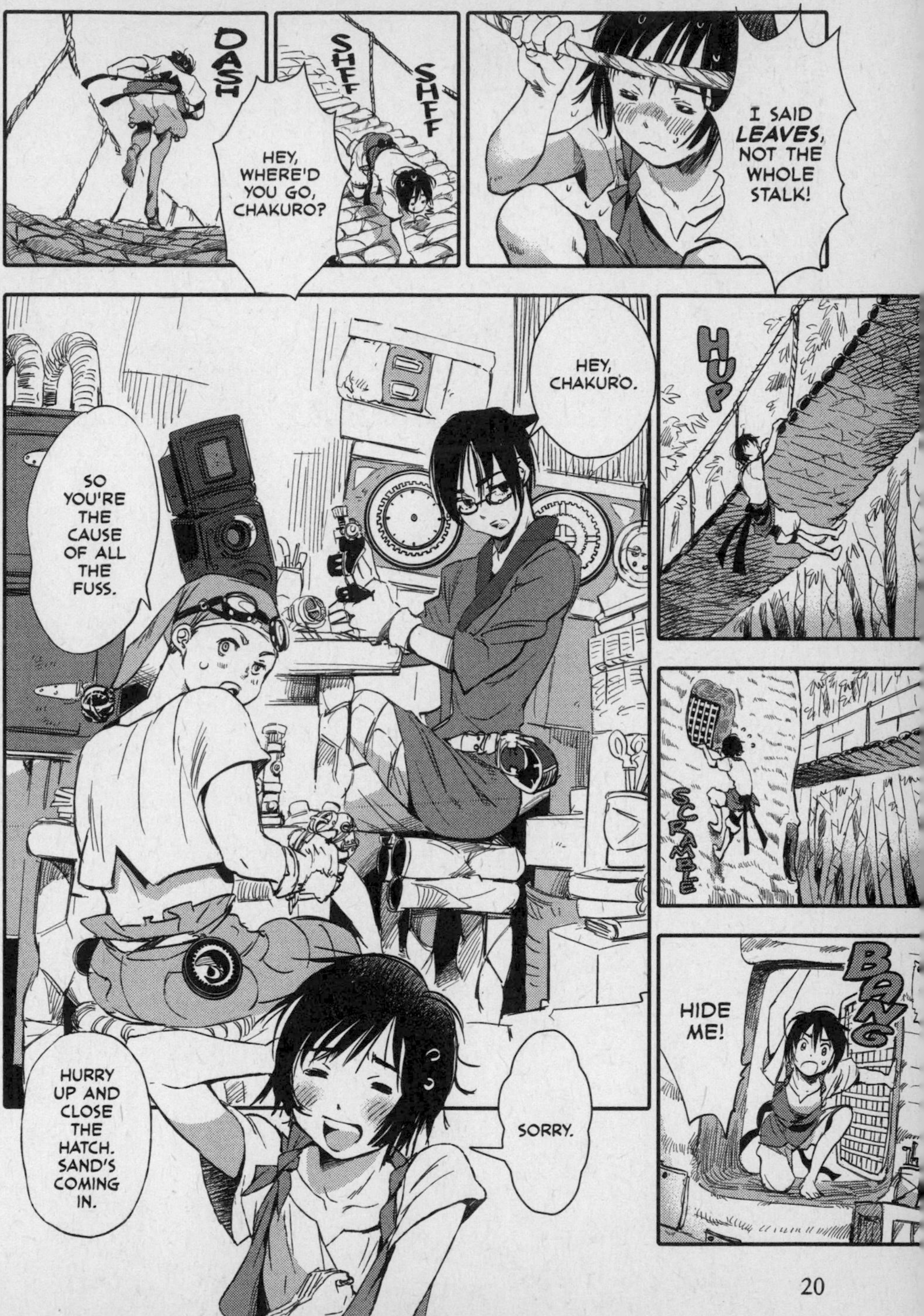
I SAID *LEAVES*, NOT THE WHOLE STALK!
SHFF
SHFF
HEY, WHERE'D YOU GO, CHAKURO?
DASH
HUP
SCRAMBLE
BANG
HIDE ME!
HEY, CHAKURO.
SO YOU'RE THE CAUSE OF ALL THE FUSS.
SORRY.
HURRY UP AND CLOSE THE HATCH. SAND'S COMING IN.

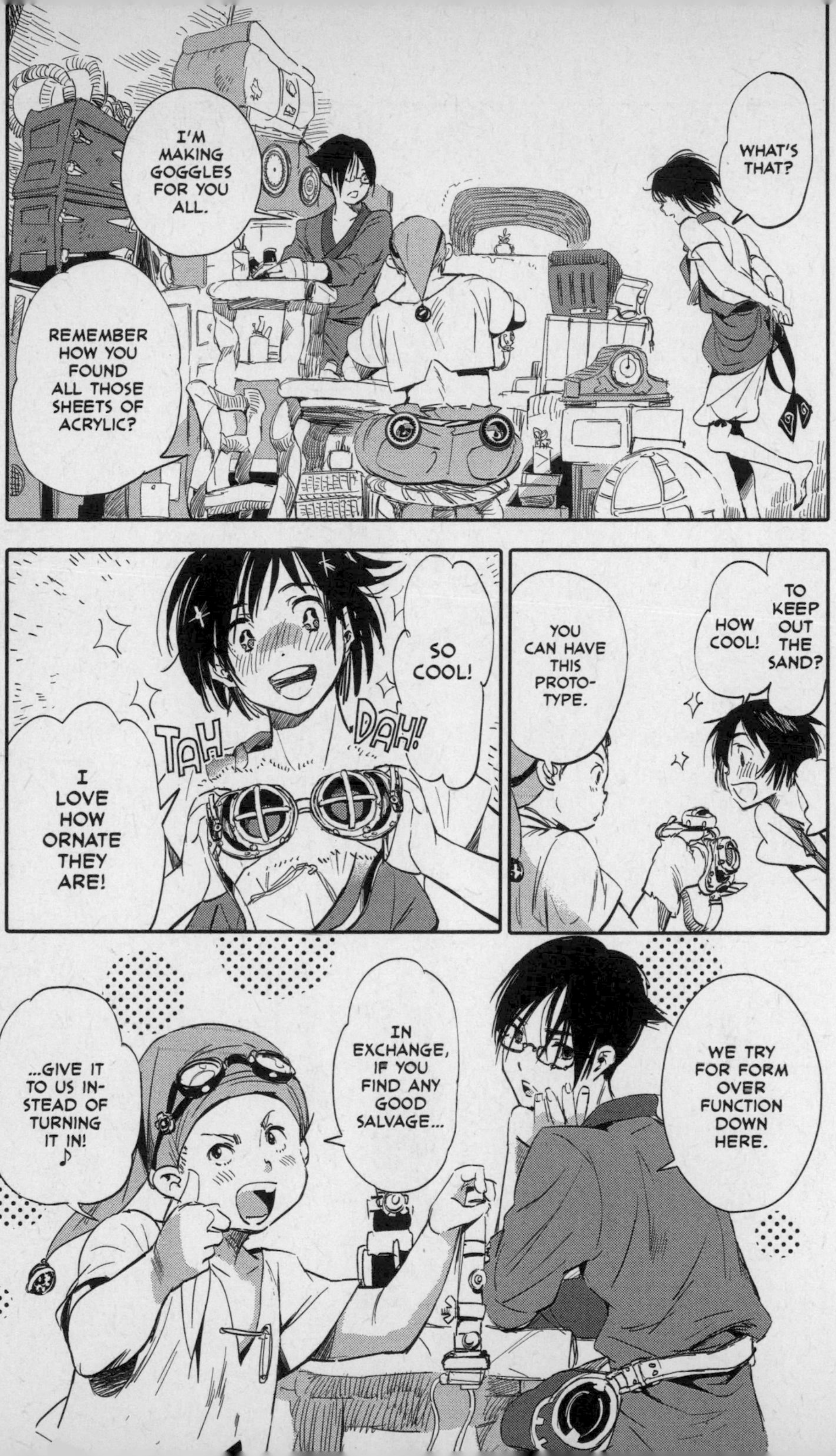
WHAT'S THAT?
I'M MAKING GOGGLES FOR YOU ALL.
REMEMBER HOW YOU FOUND ALL THOSE SHEETS OF ACRYLIC?
TO KEEP OUT THE SAND?
HOW COOL!
YOU CAN HAVE THIS PROTO-TYPE.
SO COOL!
TAH-DAH!
I LOVE HOW ORNATE THEY ARE!
WE TRY FOR FORM OVER FUNCTION DOWN HERE.
IN EXCHANGE, IF YOU FIND ANY GOOD SALVAGE...
...GIVE IT TO US IN-STEAD OF TURNING IT IN! ♪

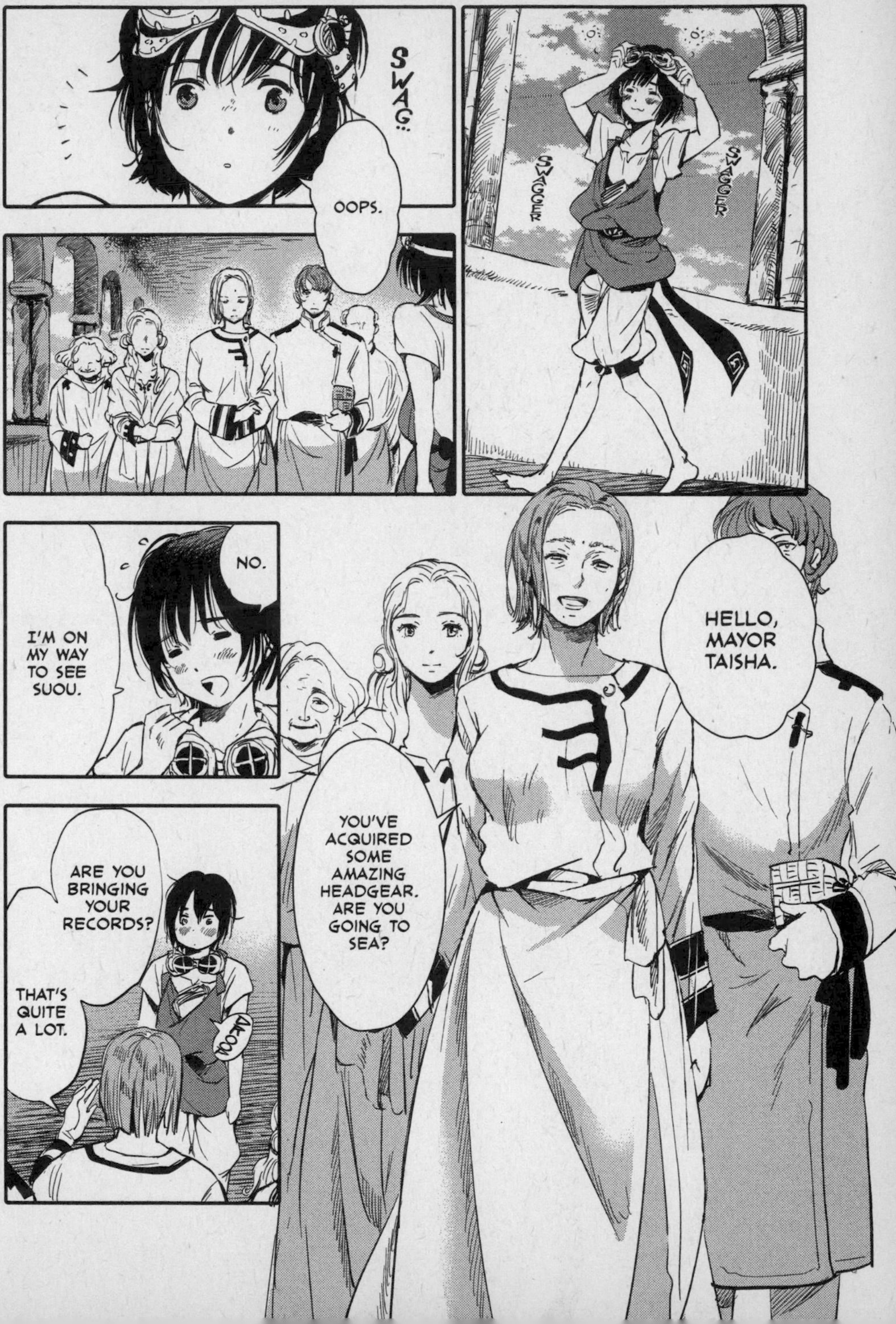
SWAGGER
SWAGGER
SWAG..
OOPS.
HELLO, MAYOR TAISHA.
YOU'VE ACQUIRED SOME AMAZING HEADGEAR. ARE YOU GOING TO SEA?
NO.
I'M ON MY WAY TO SEE SUOU.
ARE YOU BRINGING YOUR RECORDS?
THAT'S QUITE A LOT.

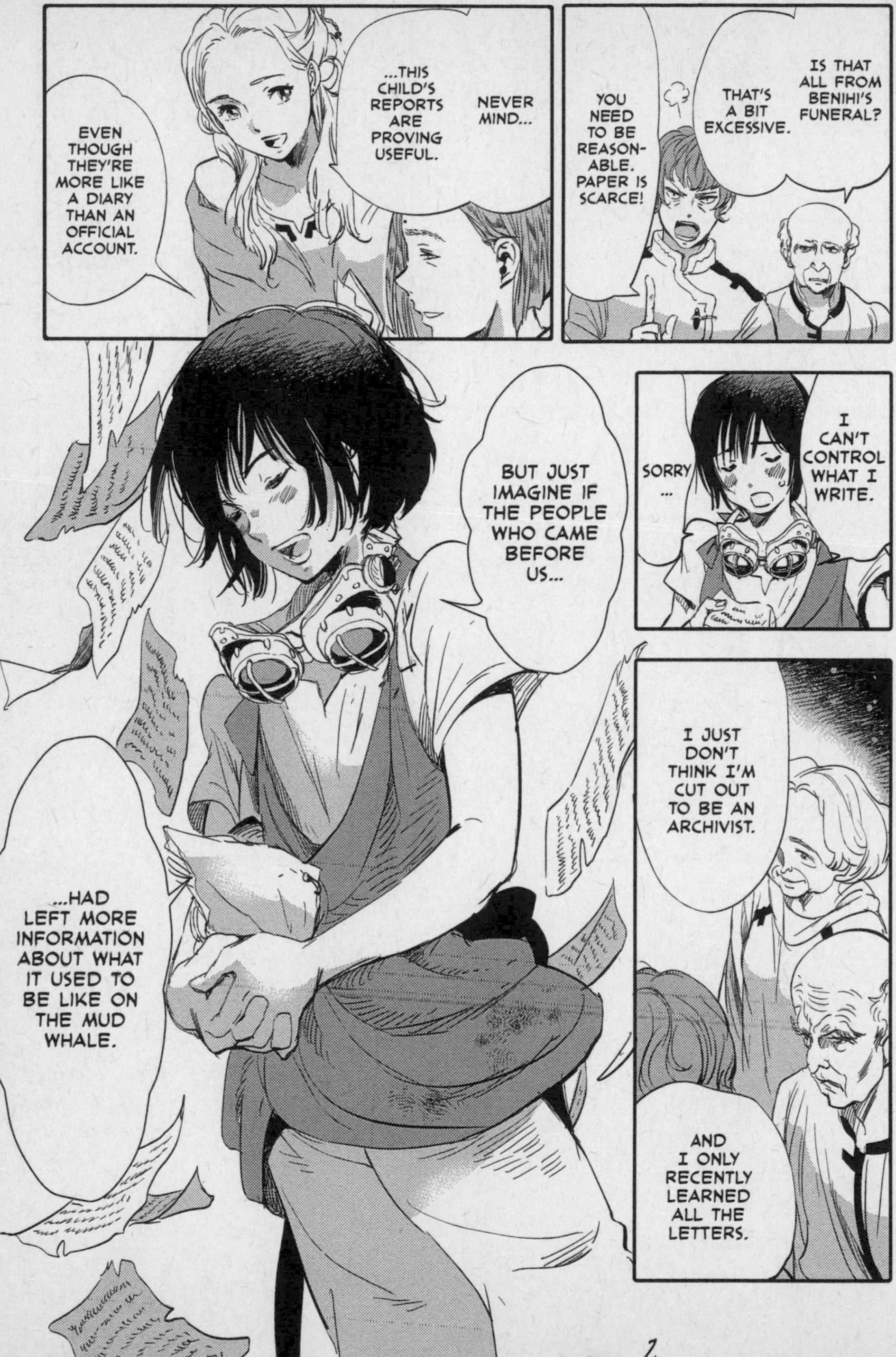
IS THAT ALL FROM BENIHI'S FUNERAL?
THAT'S A BIT EXCESSIVE.
YOU NEED TO BE REASONABLE. PAPER IS SCARCE!
NEVER MIND...
...THIS CHILD'S REPORTS ARE PROVING USEFUL.
EVEN THOUGH THEY'RE MORE LIKE A DIARY THAN AN OFFICIAL ACCOUNT.
I CAN'T CONTROL WHAT I WRITE.
SORRY...
I JUST DON'T THINK I'M CUT OUT TO BE AN ARCHIVIST.
AND I ONLY RECENTLY LEARNED ALL THE LETTERS.
BUT JUST IMAGINE IF THE PEOPLE WHO CAME BEFORE US...
...HAD LEFT MORE INFORMATION ABOUT WHAT IT USED TO BE LIKE ON THE MUD WHALE.

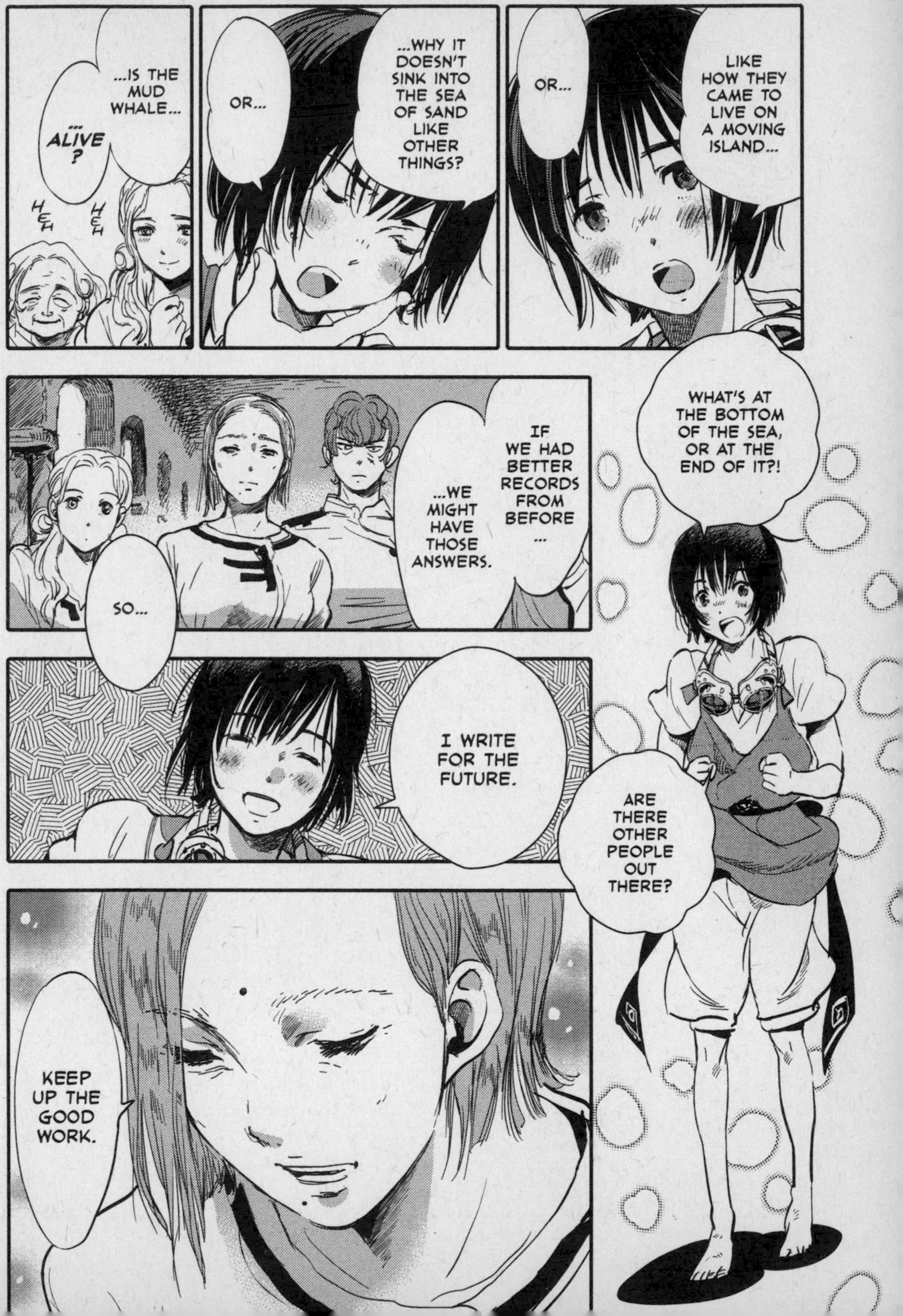
LIKE HOW THEY CAME TO LIVE ON A MOVING ISLAND...
OR...
...WHY IT DOESN'T SINK INTO THE SEA OF SAND LIKE OTHER THINGS?
OR...
...IS THE MUD WHALE...
...ALIVE?
HEH HEH
WHAT'S AT THE BOTTOM OF THE SEA, OR AT THE END OF IT?!
ARE THERE OTHER PEOPLE OUT THERE?
IF WE HAD BETTER RECORDS FROM BEFORE...
...WE MIGHT HAVE THOSE ANSWERS.
SO...
I WRITE FOR THE FUTURE.
KEEP UP THE GOOD WORK.

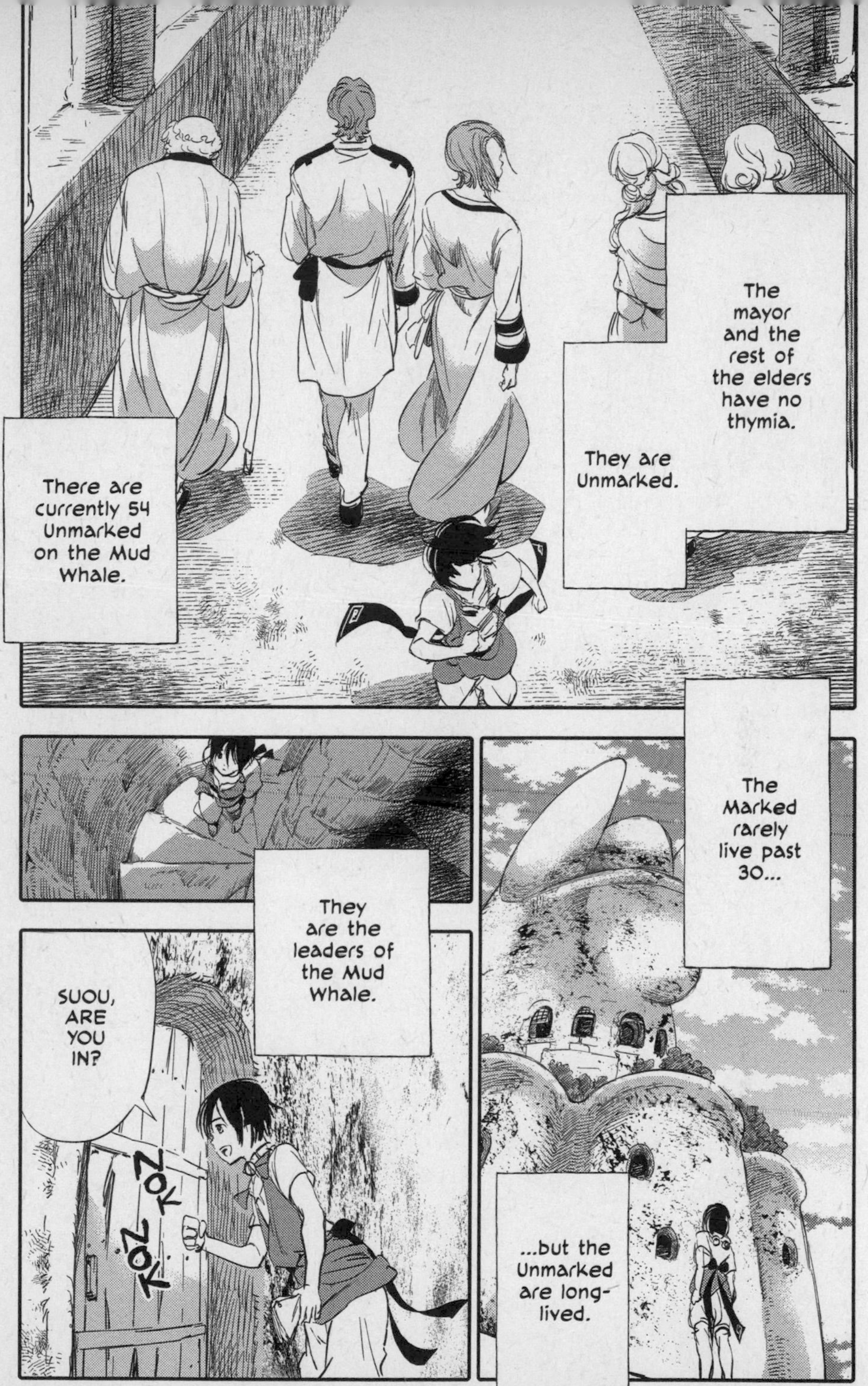
The mayor and the rest of the elders have no thymia.
They are Unmarked.
There are currently 54 Unmarked on the Mud Whale.
The Marked rarely live past 30...
...but the Unmarked are long-lived.
They are the leaders of the Mud Whale.
SUOU, ARE YOU IN?
ZOK ZOK

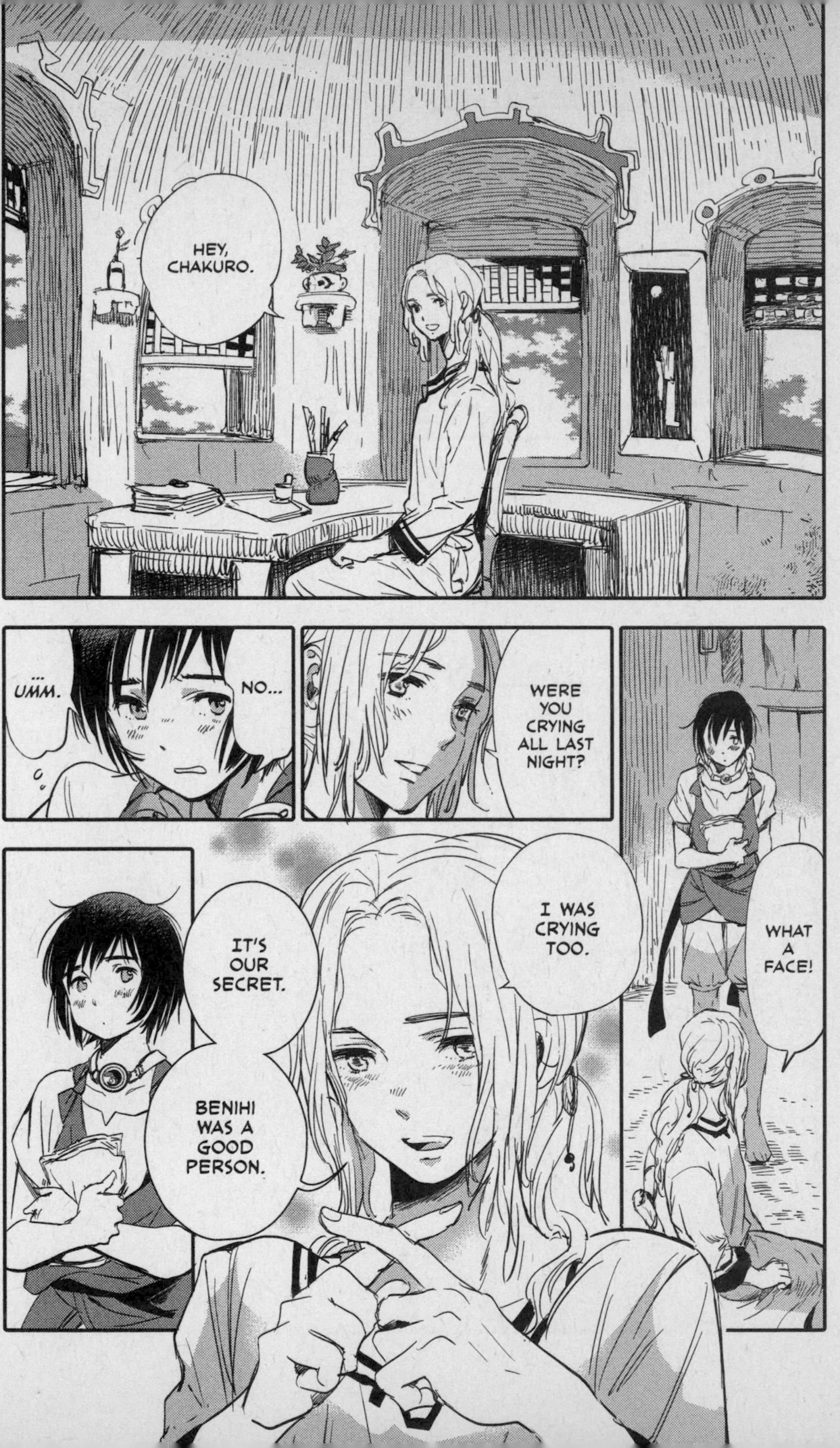
HEY, CHAKURO.
WHAT A FACE!
WERE YOU CRYING ALL LAST NIGHT?
NO...
... UMM.
I WAS CRYING TOO.
IT'S OUR SECRET.
BENIHI WAS A GOOD PERSON.

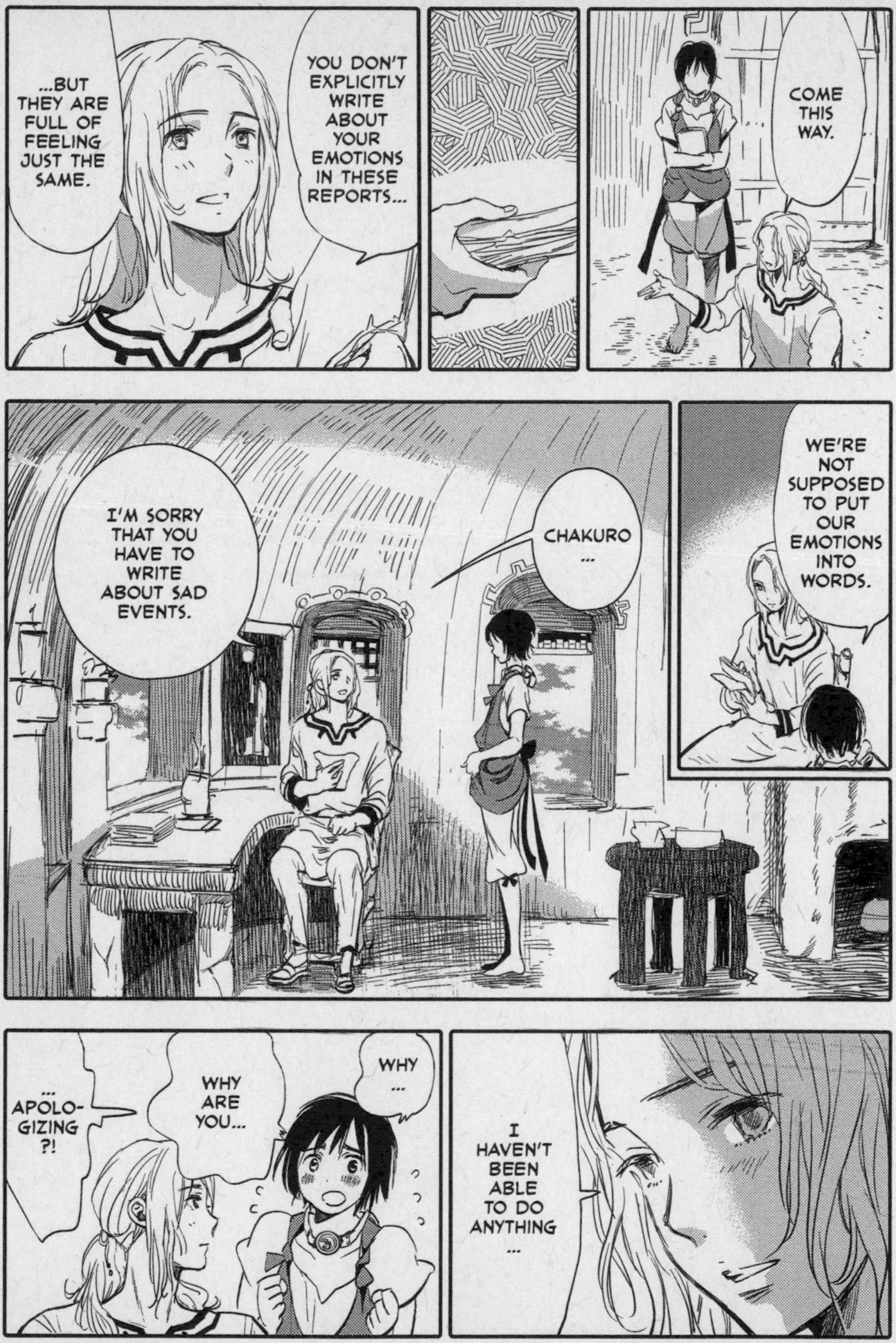
COME THIS WAY.
YOU DON'T EXPLICITLY WRITE ABOUT YOUR EMOTIONS IN THESE REPORTS...
...BUT THEY ARE FULL OF FEELING JUST THE SAME.
WE'RE NOT SUPPOSED TO PUT OUR EMOTIONS INTO WORDS.
CHAKURO ...
I'M SORRY THAT YOU HAVE TO WRITE ABOUT SAD EVENTS.
I HAVEN'T BEEN ABLE TO DO ANYTHING ...
WHY ...
WHY ARE YOU...
... APOLO-GIZING ?!

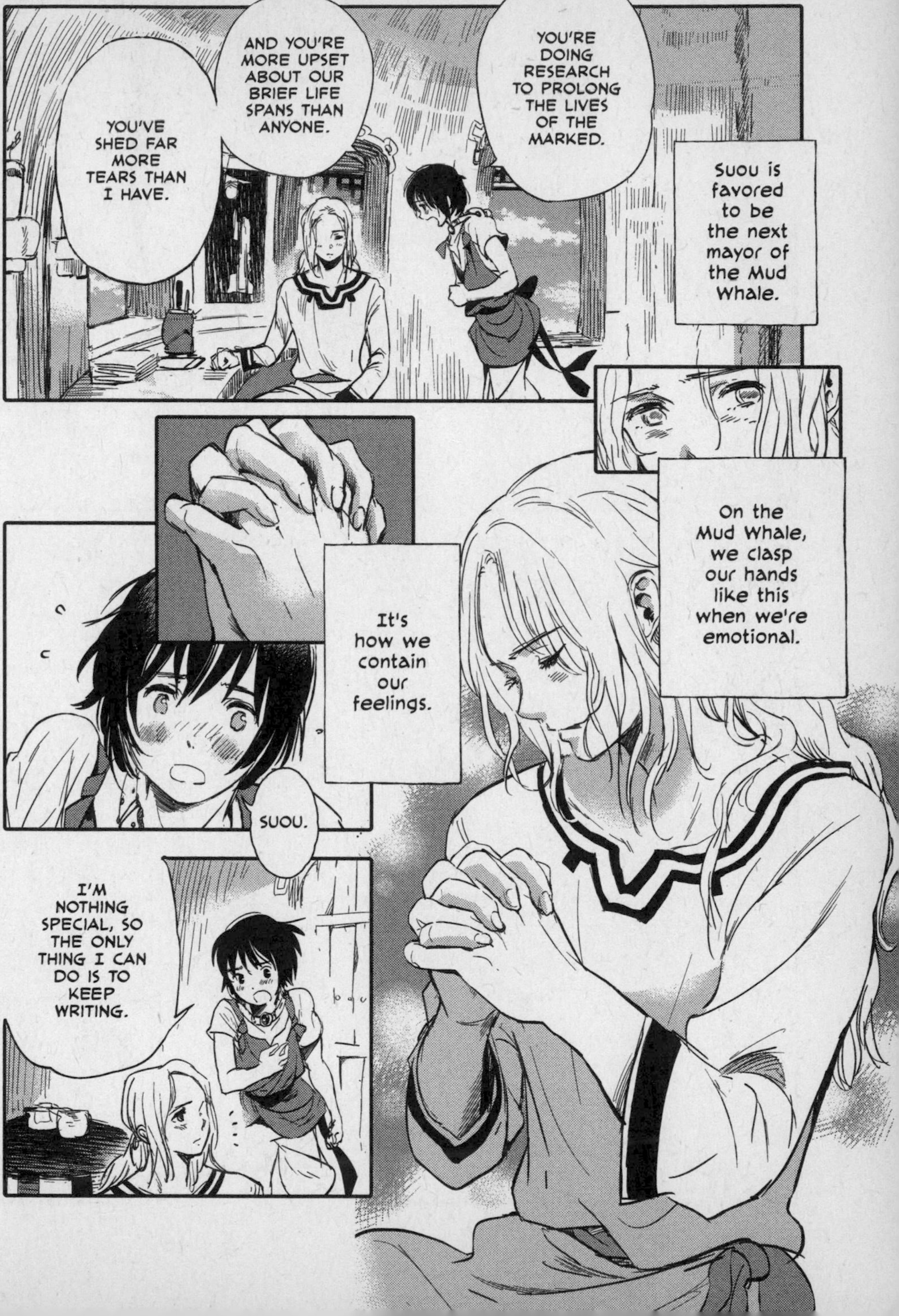
YOU'RE DOING RESEARCH TO PROLONG THE LIVES OF THE MARKED.
AND YOU'RE MORE UPSET ABOUT OUR BRIEF LIFE SPANS THAN ANYONE.
YOU'VE SHED FAR MORE TEARS THAN I HAVE.
Suou is favored to be the next mayor of the Mud Whale.
On the Mud Whale, we clasp our hands like this when we're emotional.
It's how we contain our feelings.
SUOU.
I'M NOTHING SPECIAL, SO THE ONLY THING I CAN DO IS TO KEEP WRITING.

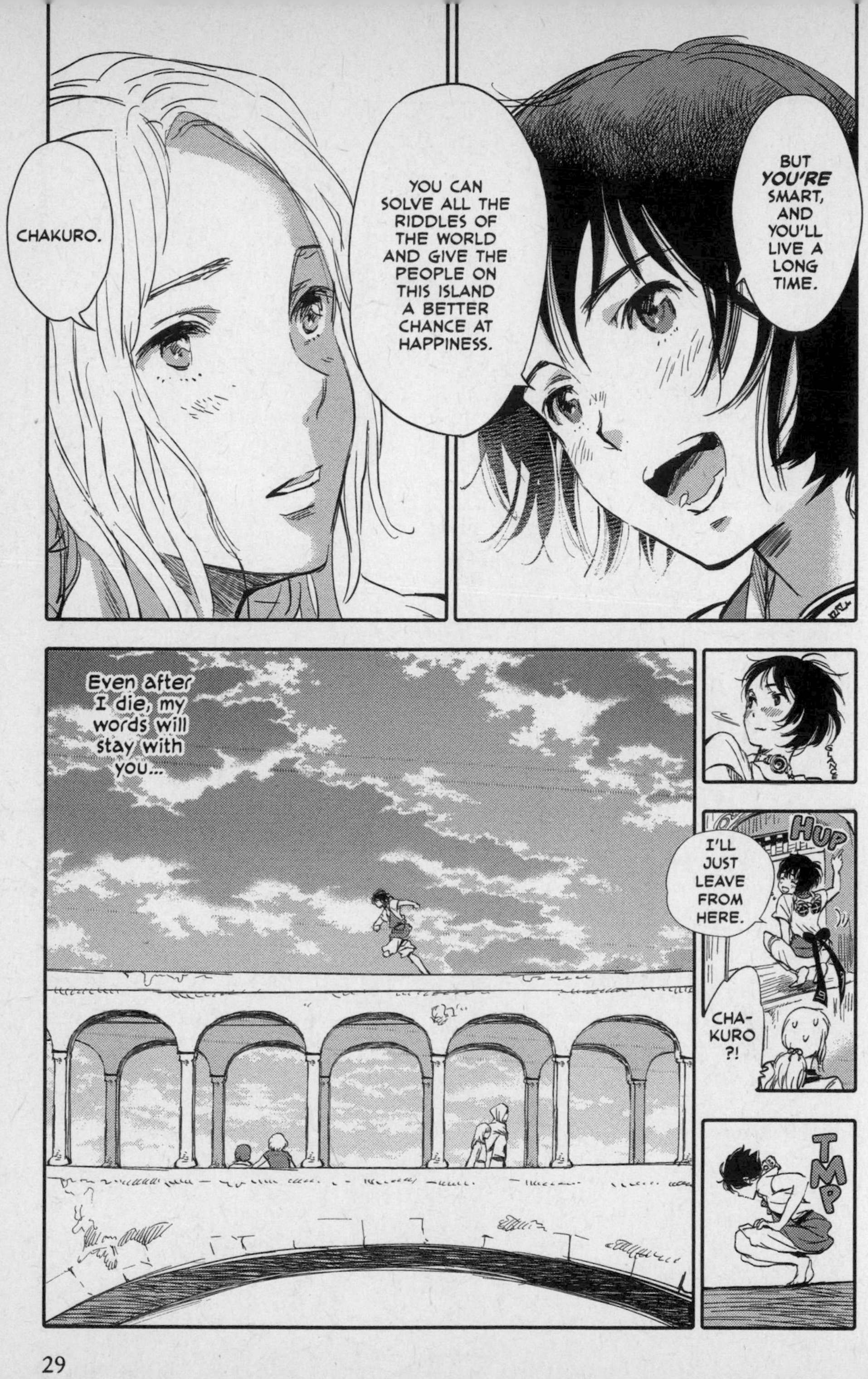
BUT *YOU'RE* SMART, AND YOU'LL LIVE A LONG TIME.
YOU CAN SOLVE ALL THE RIDDLES OF THE WORLD AND GIVE THE PEOPLE ON THIS ISLAND A BETTER CHANCE AT HAPPINESS.
CHAKURO.
GLANCE
HUP
I'LL JUST LEAVE FROM HERE.
CHA-KURO?!
TMP
Even after I die, my words will stay with you...

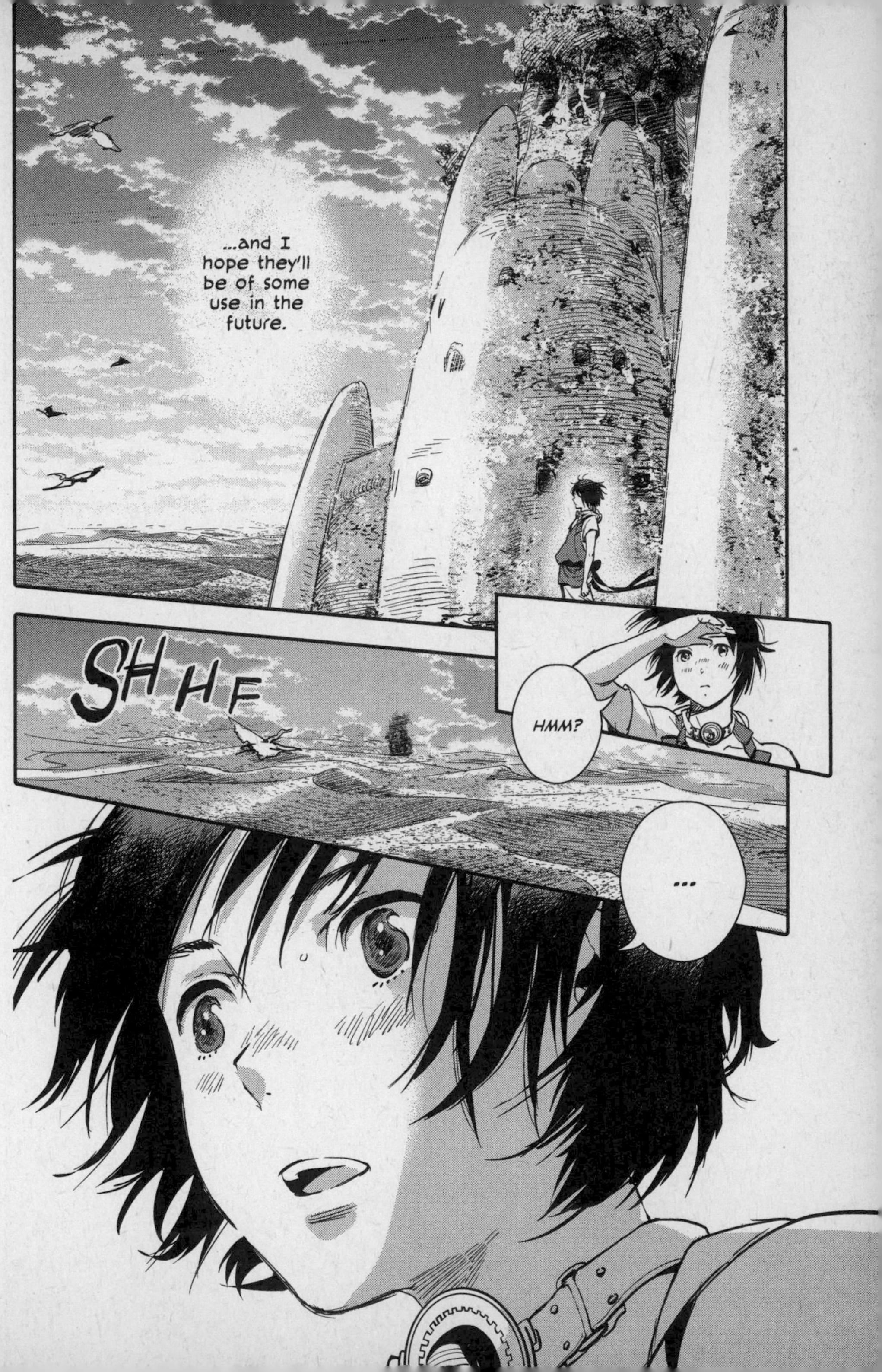
...and I hope they'll be of some use in the future.
HMM?
SHHF
...

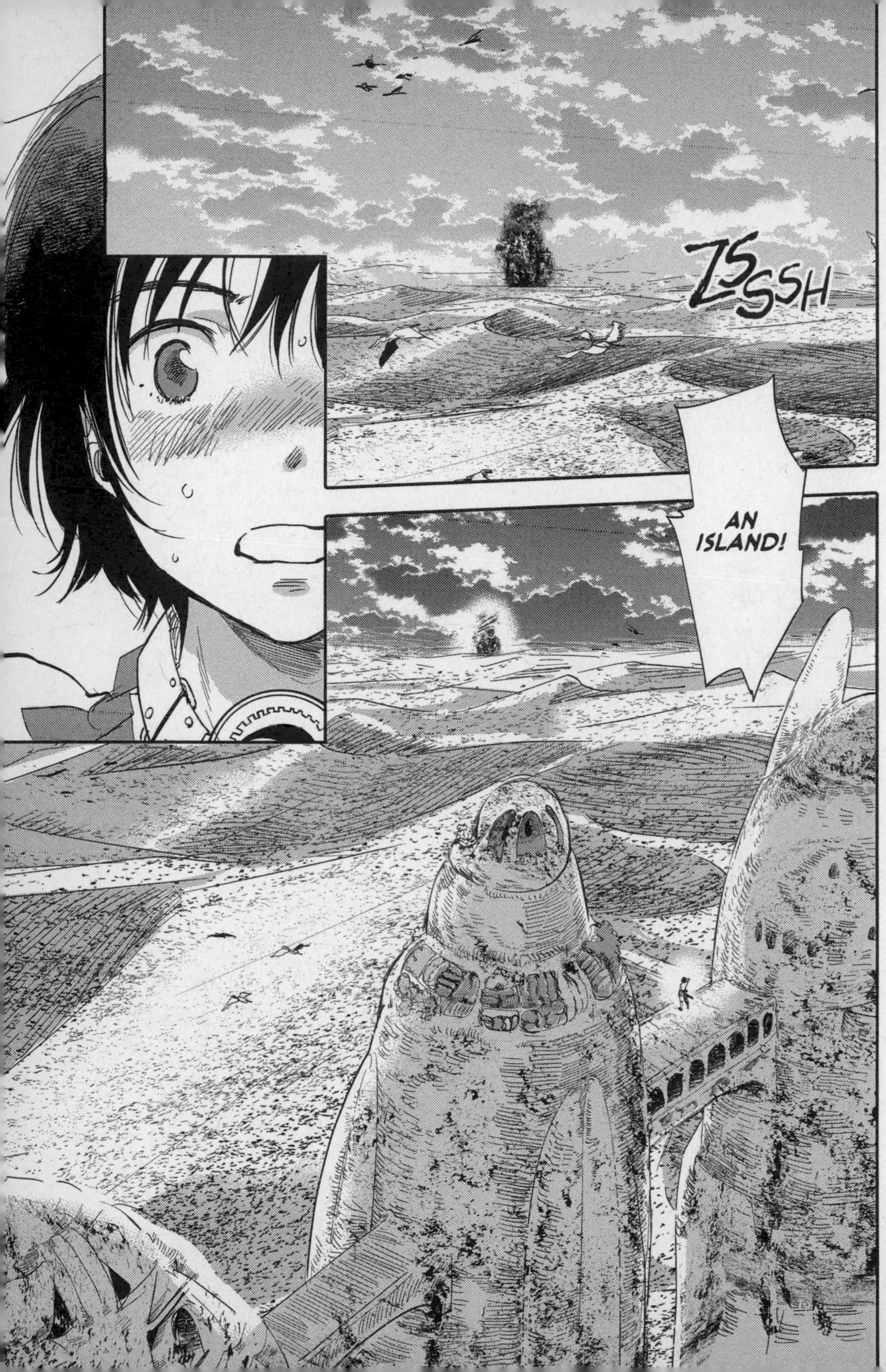
ZSSSH
AN ISLAND!

IT'S BEEN ABOUT SIX MONTHS SINCE WE LAST ENCOUN-TERED AN ISLAND.
BASED ON PREVIOUS RECORDS, WE HAVE ABOUT FIVE DAYS IN WHICH WE CAN VISIT IT TO SEARCH FOR SALVAGE.
LONGER THAN THAT AND THE DISTANCE BETWEEN US AND THAT ISLAND WILL BECOME TOO GREAT TO CROSS.
LET'S SEND A RECON-NAISSANCE TEAM TOMORROW.
IF IT'S SAFE...
...WE'LL GO BACK TO COLLECT SALVAGE.
SNEAK
SUOU, PLEASE SELECT THE TEAM BY MORNING.
ALL RIGHT.

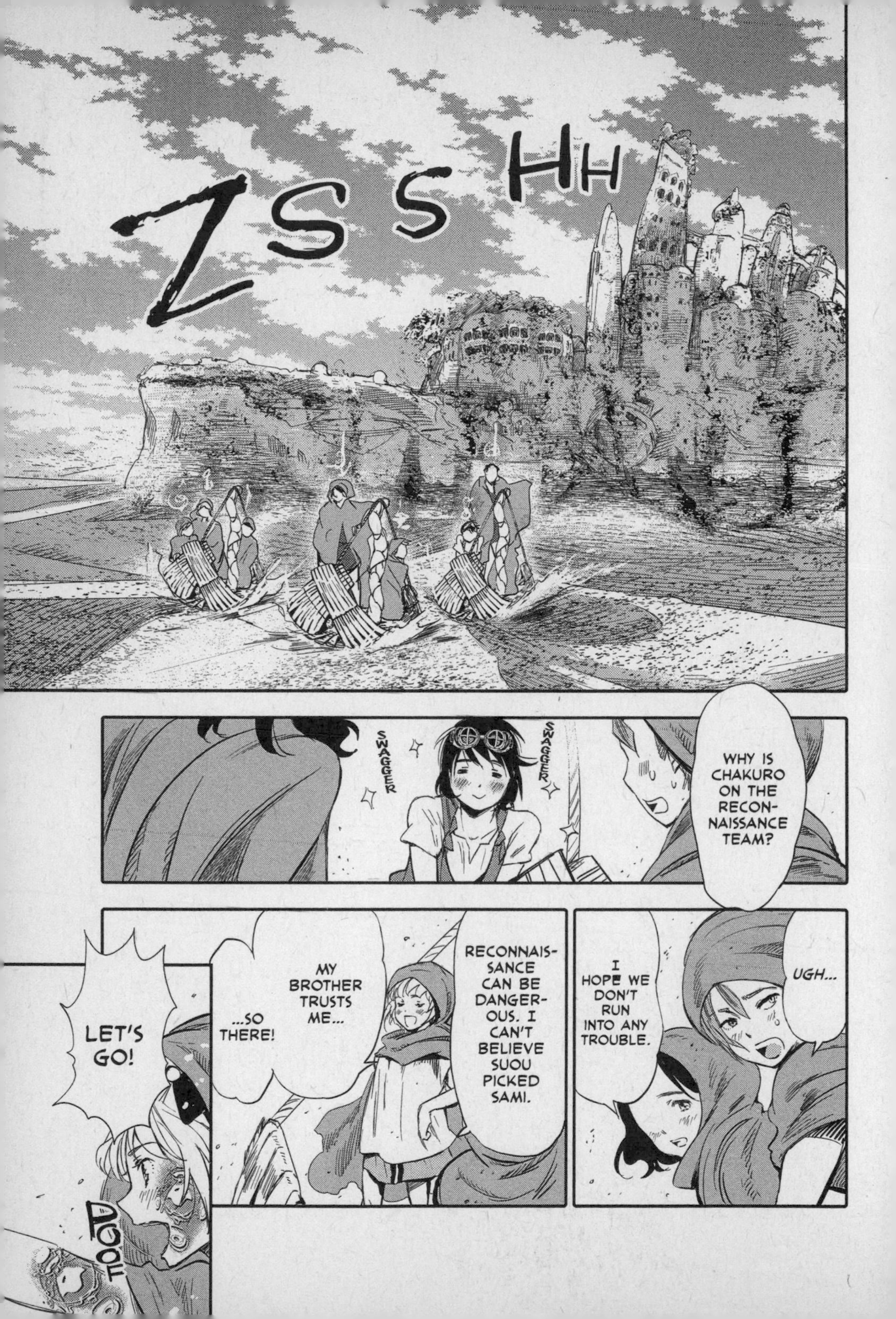
ZSSHH
WHY IS CHAKURO ON THE RECON-NAISSANCE TEAM?
SWAGGER
SWAGGER
UGH...
I HOPE WE DON'T RUN INTO ANY TROUBLE.
RECONNAIS-SANCE CAN BE DANGER-OUS. I CAN'T BELIEVE SUOU PICKED SAMI.
MY BROTHER TRUSTS ME...
...SO THERE!
LET'S GO!
TOOT

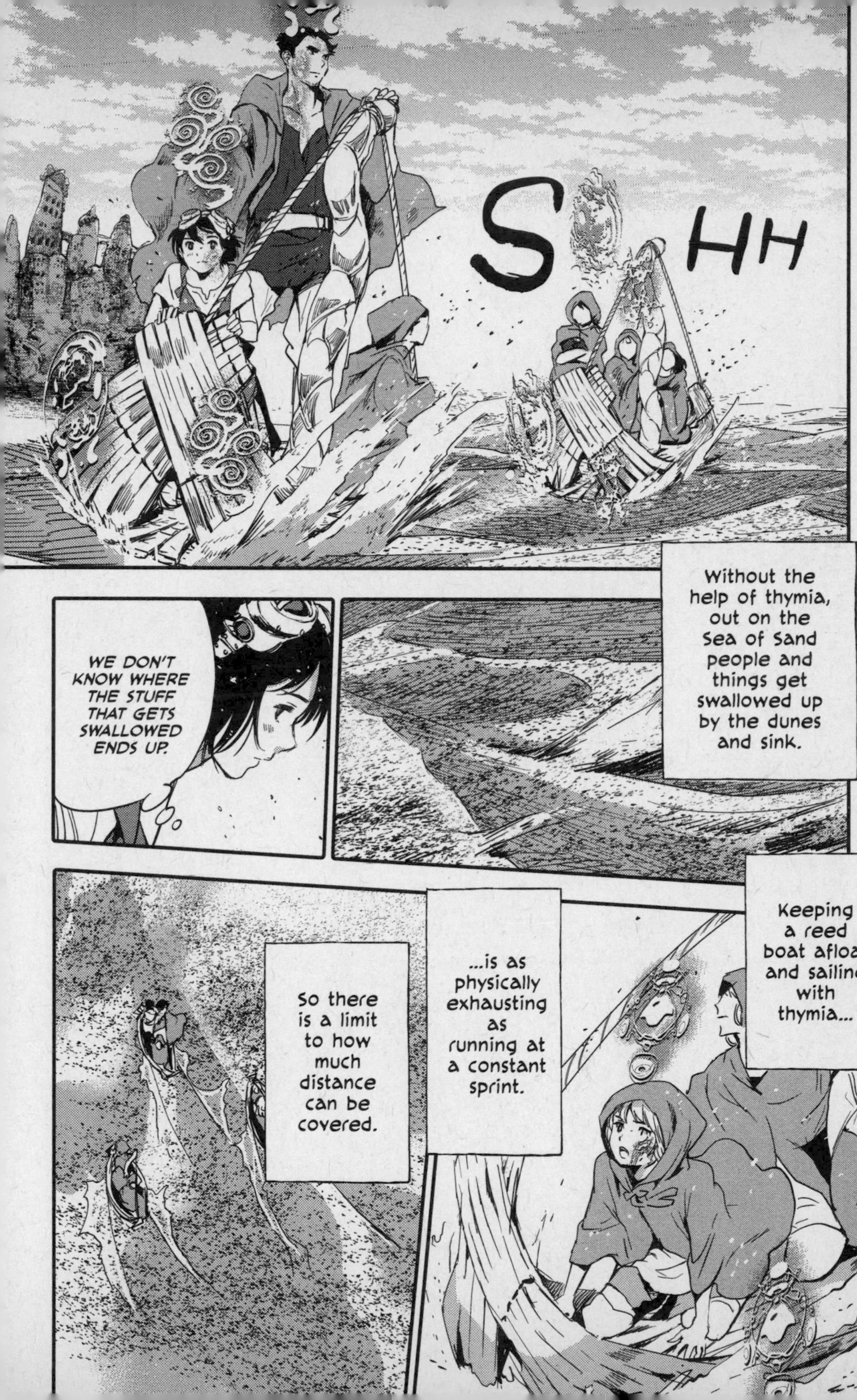
SHH
Without the help of thymia, out on the Sea of Sand people and things get swallowed up by the dunes and sink.
WE DON'T KNOW WHERE THE STUFF THAT GETS SWALLOWED ENDS UP.
Keeping a reed boat afloat and sailing with thymia...
...is as physically exhausting as running at a constant sprint.
So there is a limit to how much distance can be covered.

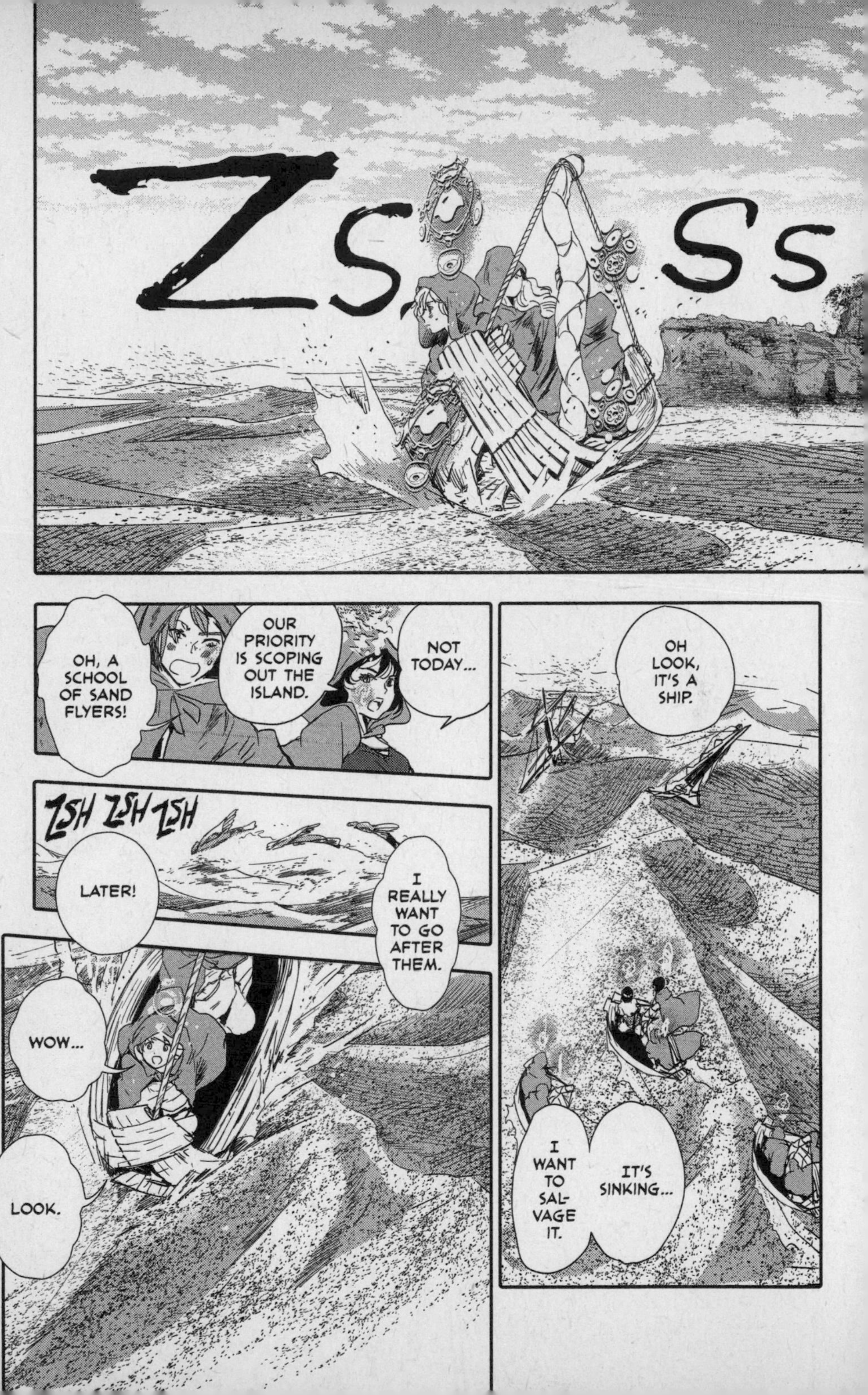
ZSSSS
OH LOOK, IT'S A SHIP.
IT'S SINKING...
I WANT TO SALVAGE IT.
NOT TODAY...
OUR PRIORITY IS SCOPING OUT THE ISLAND.
OH, A SCHOOL OF SAND FLYERS!
I REALLY WANT TO GO AFTER THEM.
LATER!
ZSH ZSH ZSH
WOW...
LOOK.

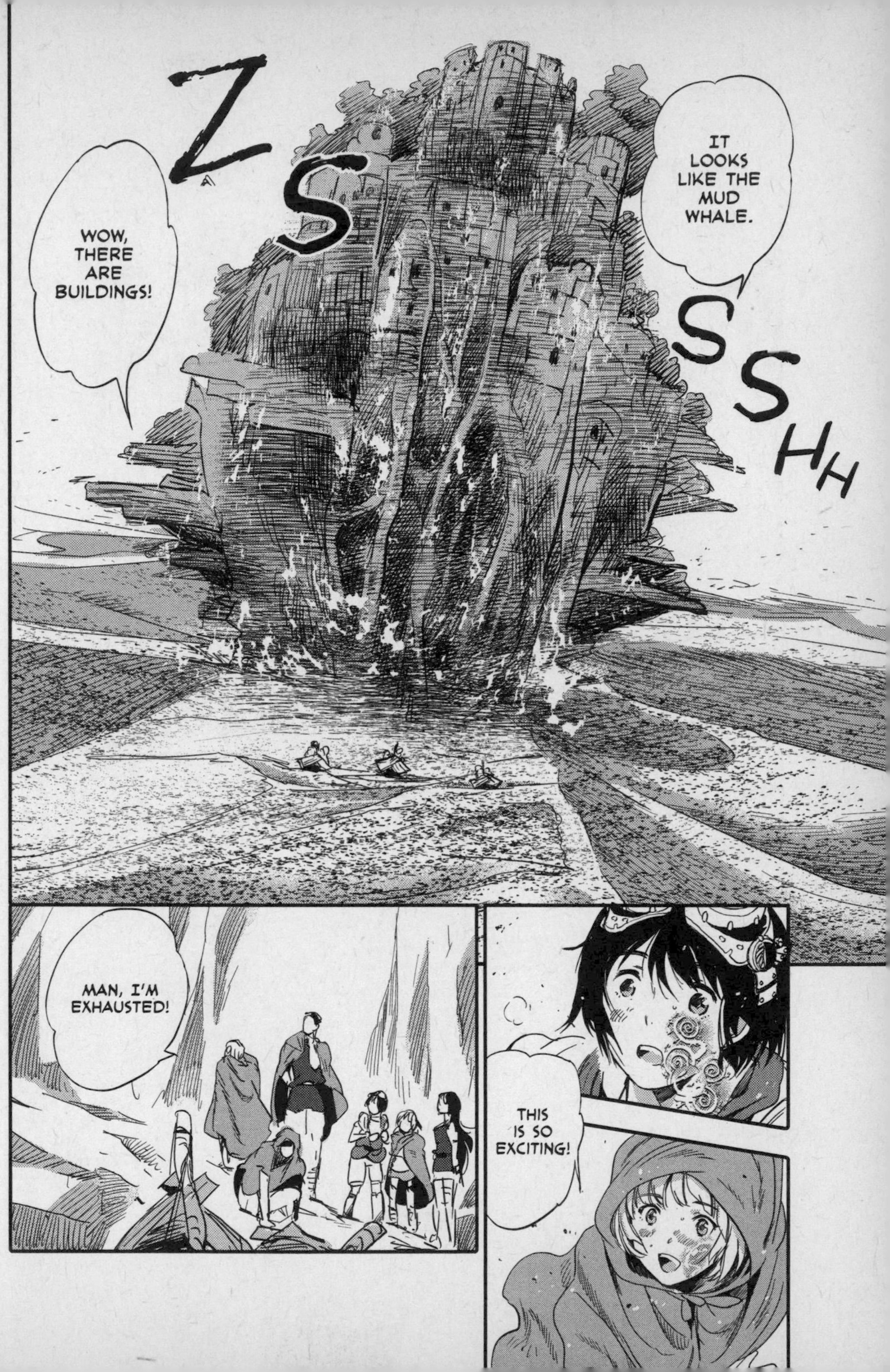
IT LOOKS LIKE THE MUD WHALE.
SSHH
ZS
WOW, THERE ARE BUILDINGS!
THIS IS SO EXCITING!
MAN, I'M EXHAUSTED!

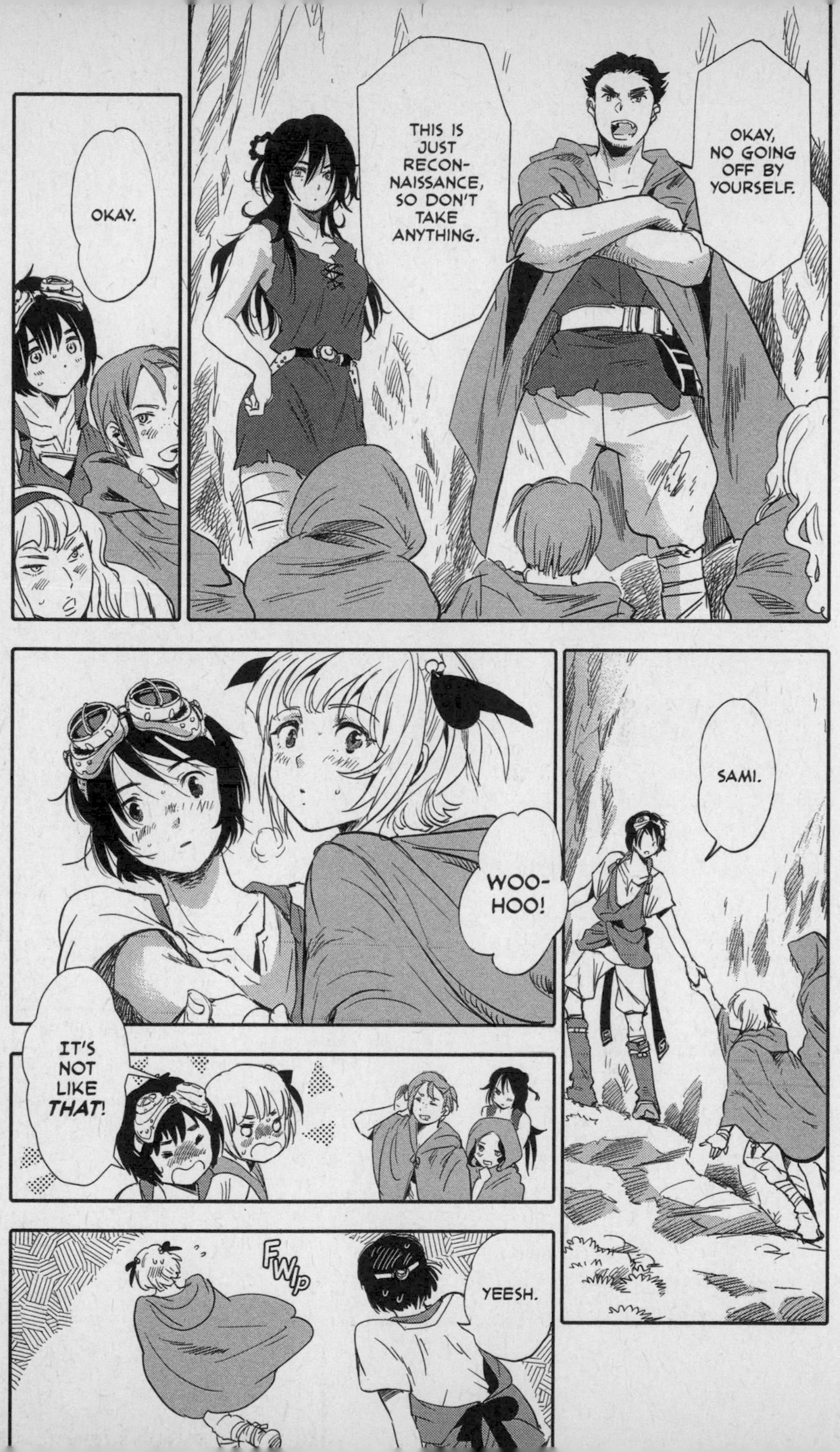
OKAY, NO GOING OFF BY YOURSELF.
THIS IS JUST RECONNAISSANCE, SO DON'T TAKE ANYTHING.
OKAY.
SAMI.
WOO-HOO!
IT'S NOT LIKE THAT!
FWIP
YEESH.

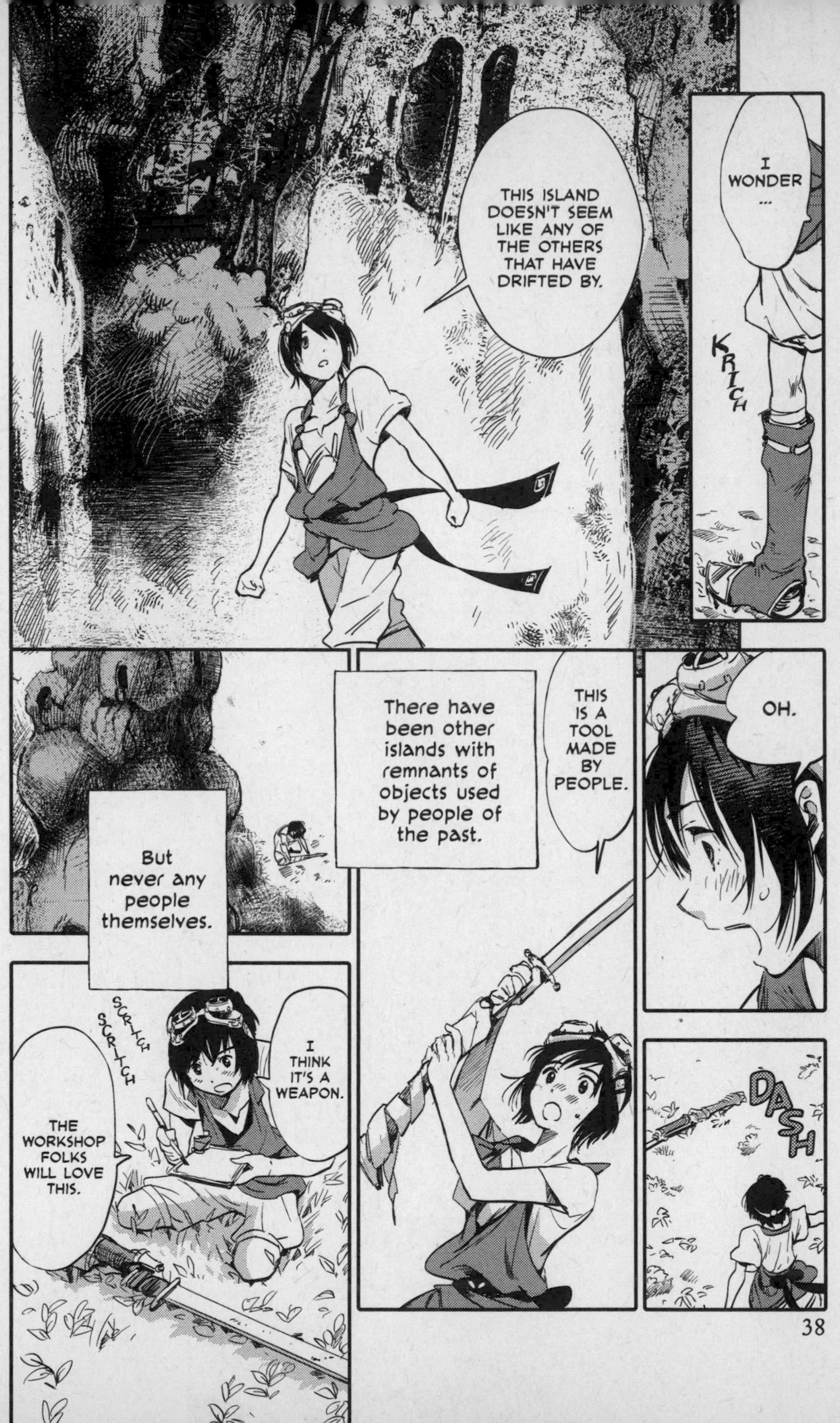
I WONDER ...
KRICH
THIS ISLAND DOESN'T SEEM LIKE ANY OF THE OTHERS THAT HAVE DRIFTED BY.
OH.
DASH
THIS IS A TOOL MADE BY PEOPLE.
There have been other islands with remnants of objects used by people of the past.
But never any people themselves.
SCRITCH SCRITCH
I THINK IT'S A WEAPON.
THE WORKSHOP FOLKS WILL LOVE THIS.

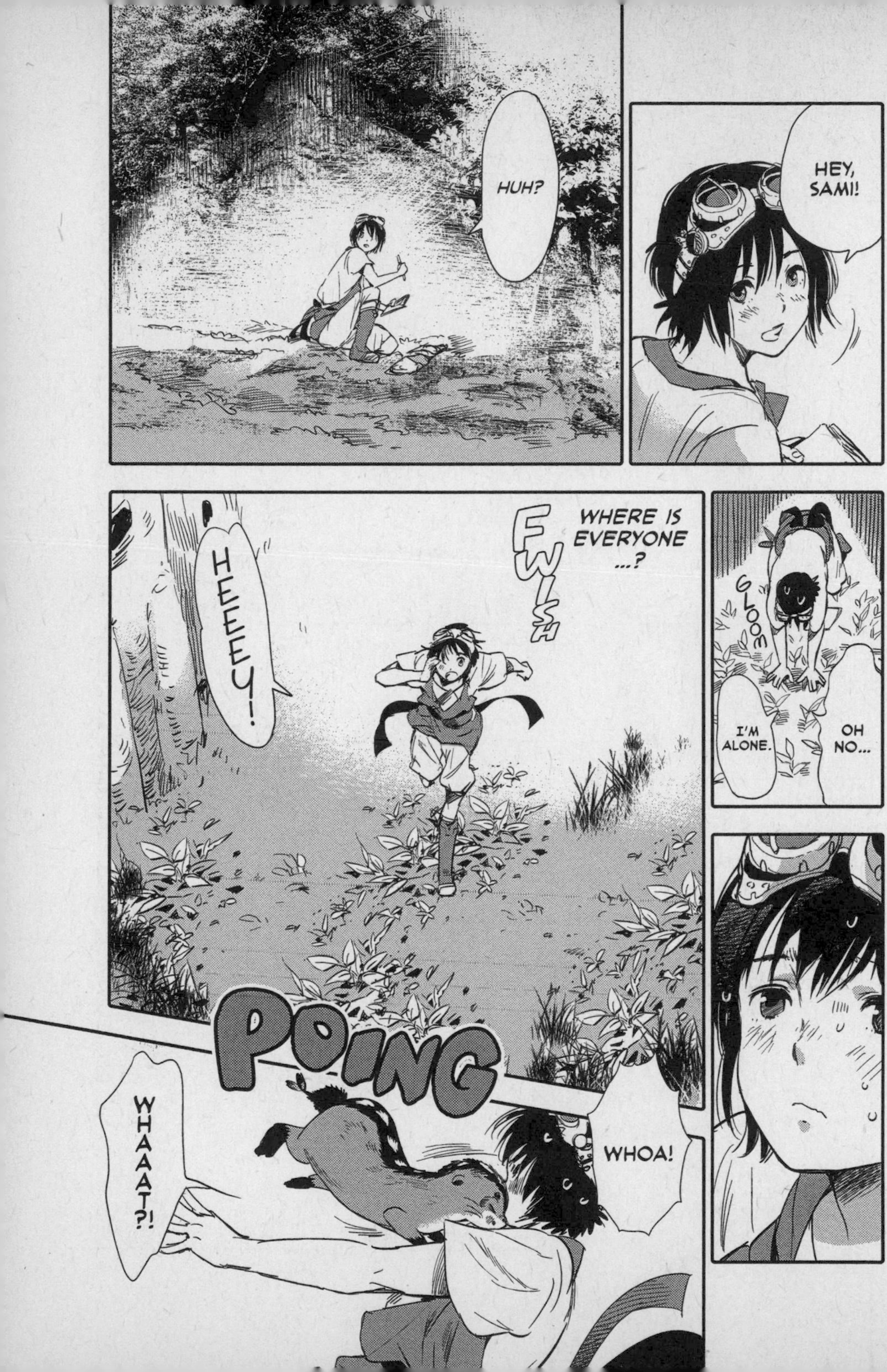
HEY, SAMI!
HUH?
GLOOM
OH NO...
I'M ALONE.
WHERE IS EVERYONE ...?
FWISH
HEEEEY!
POING
WHOA!
WHAAAT?!

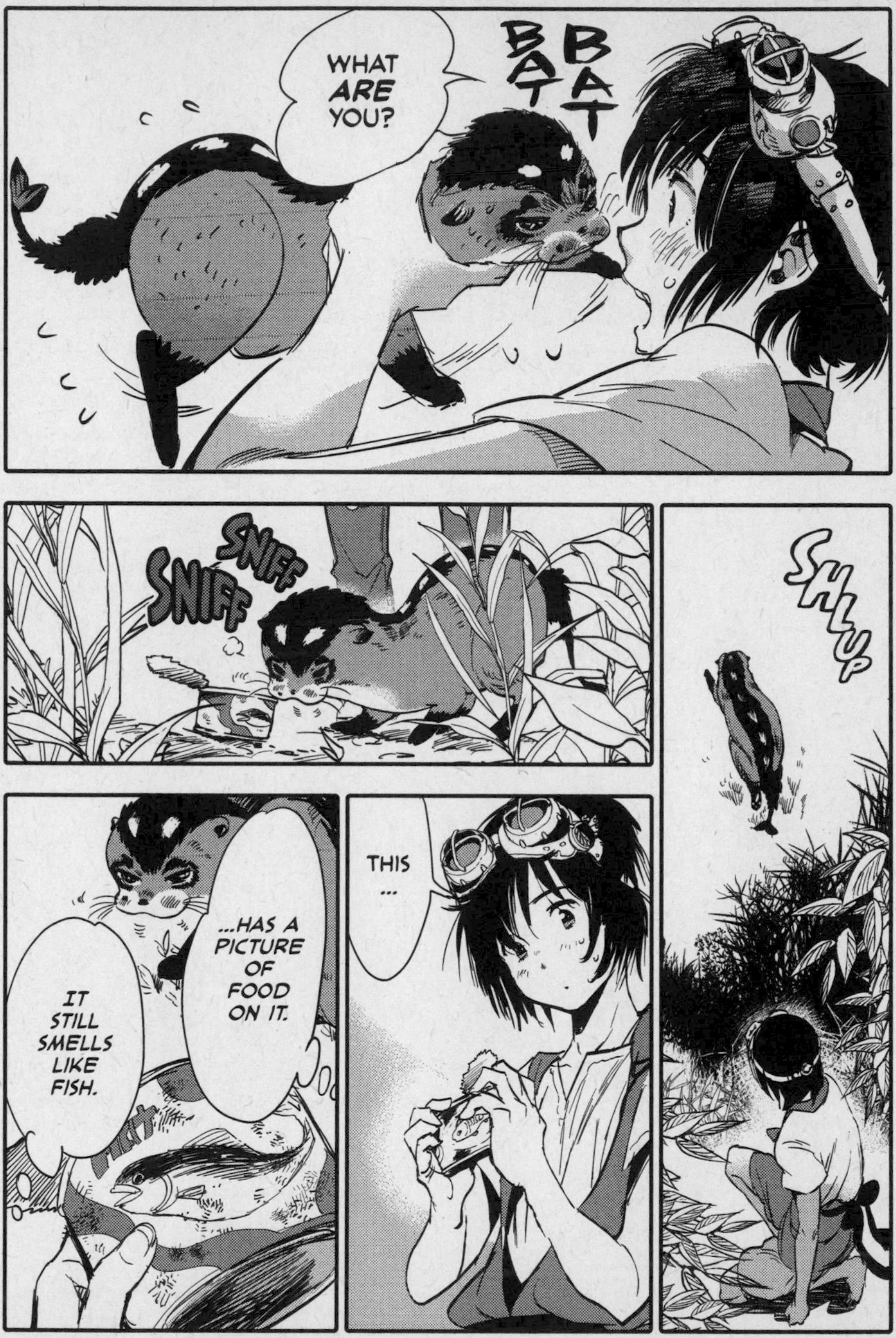
BAT BAT
WHAT ARE YOU?
SHLUP
SNIFF SNIFF
THIS ...
...HAS A PICTURE OF FOOD ON IT.
IT STILL SMELLS LIKE FISH.

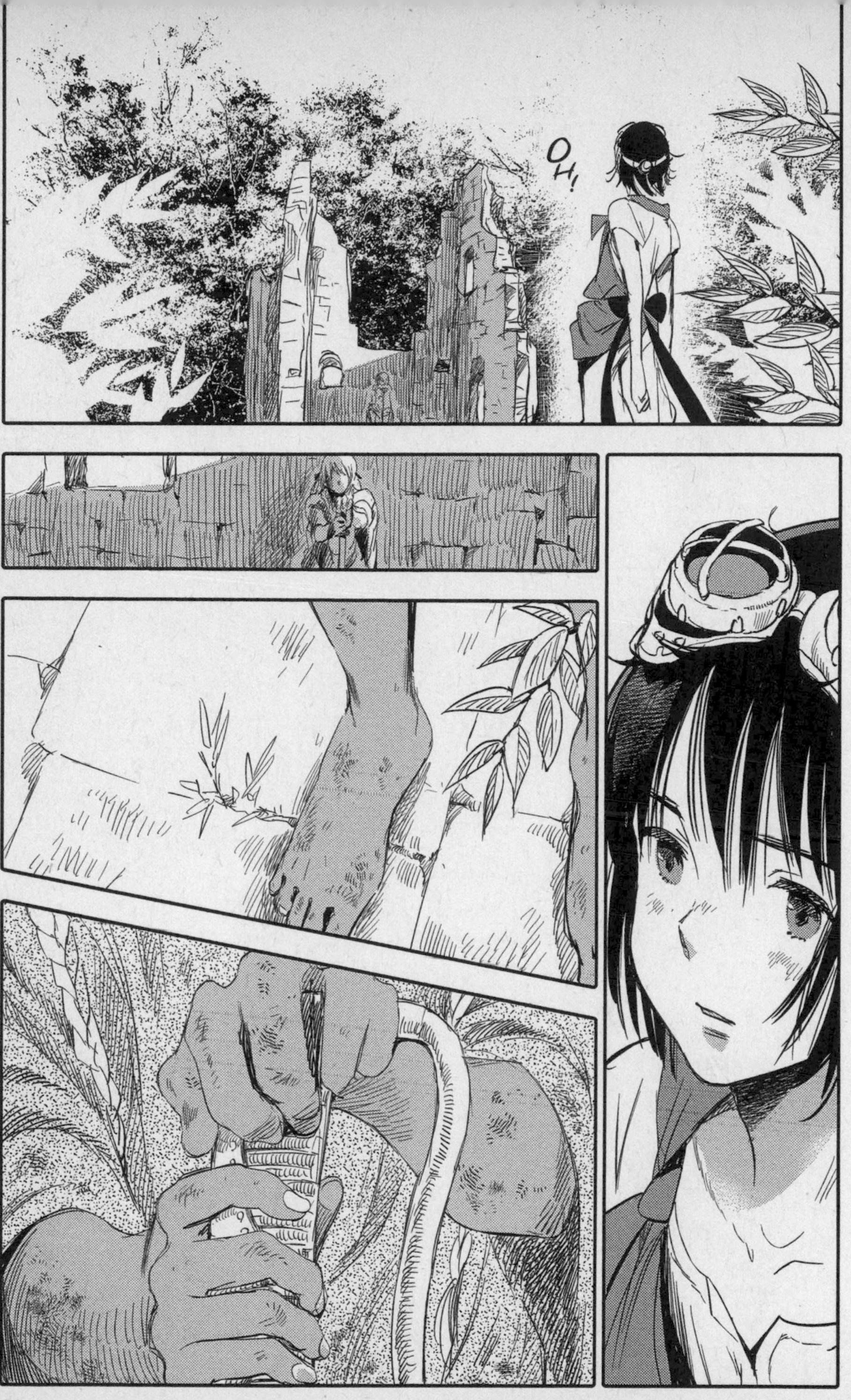
OH!

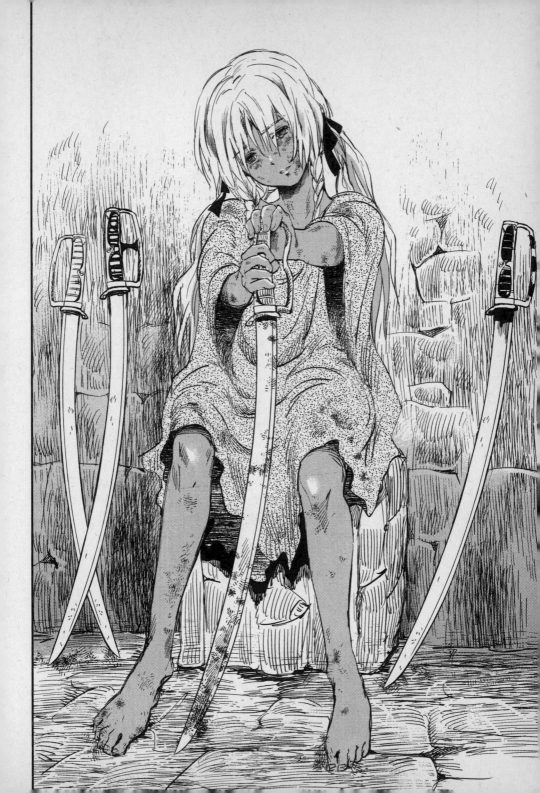

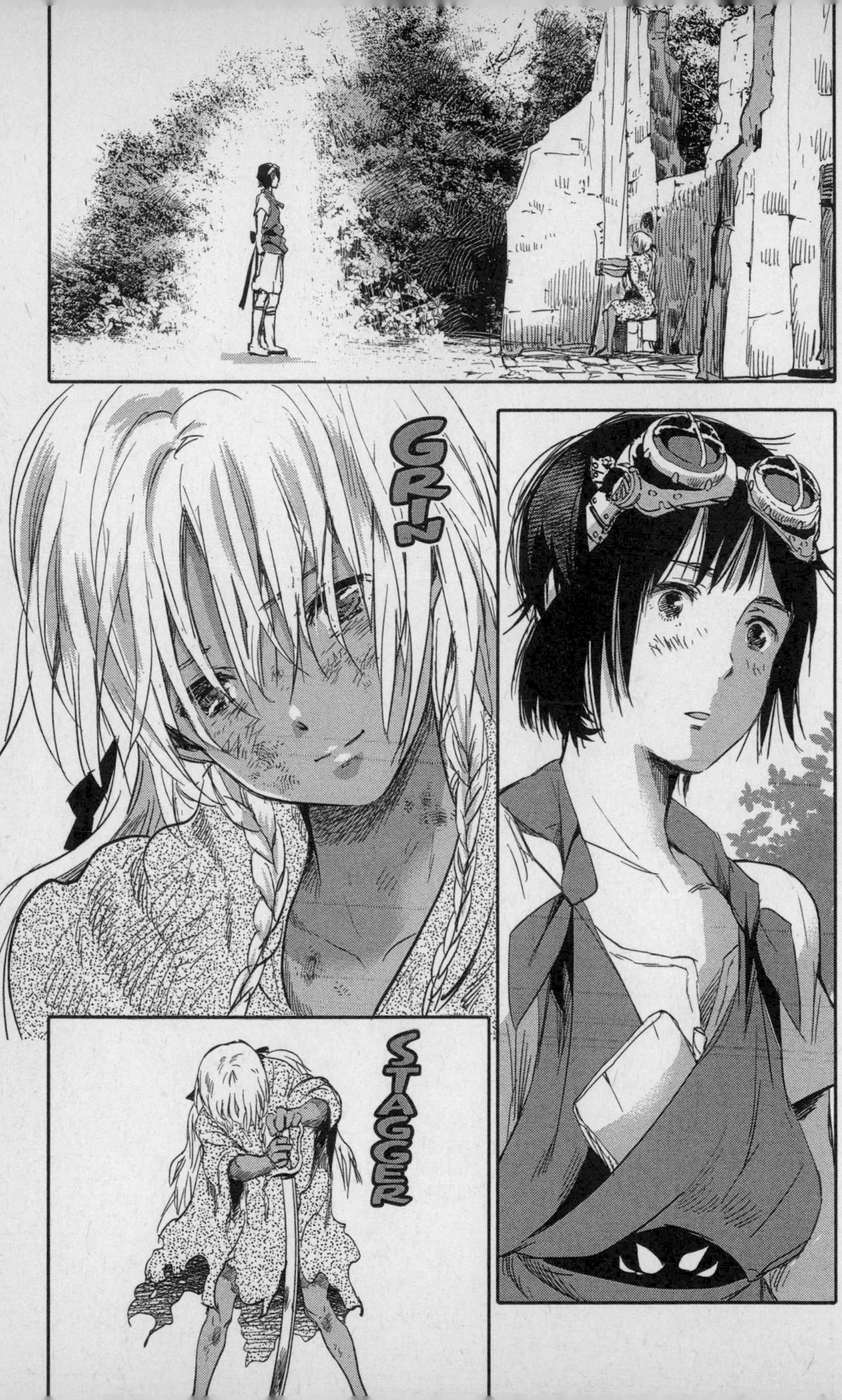
GRIN
STAGGER

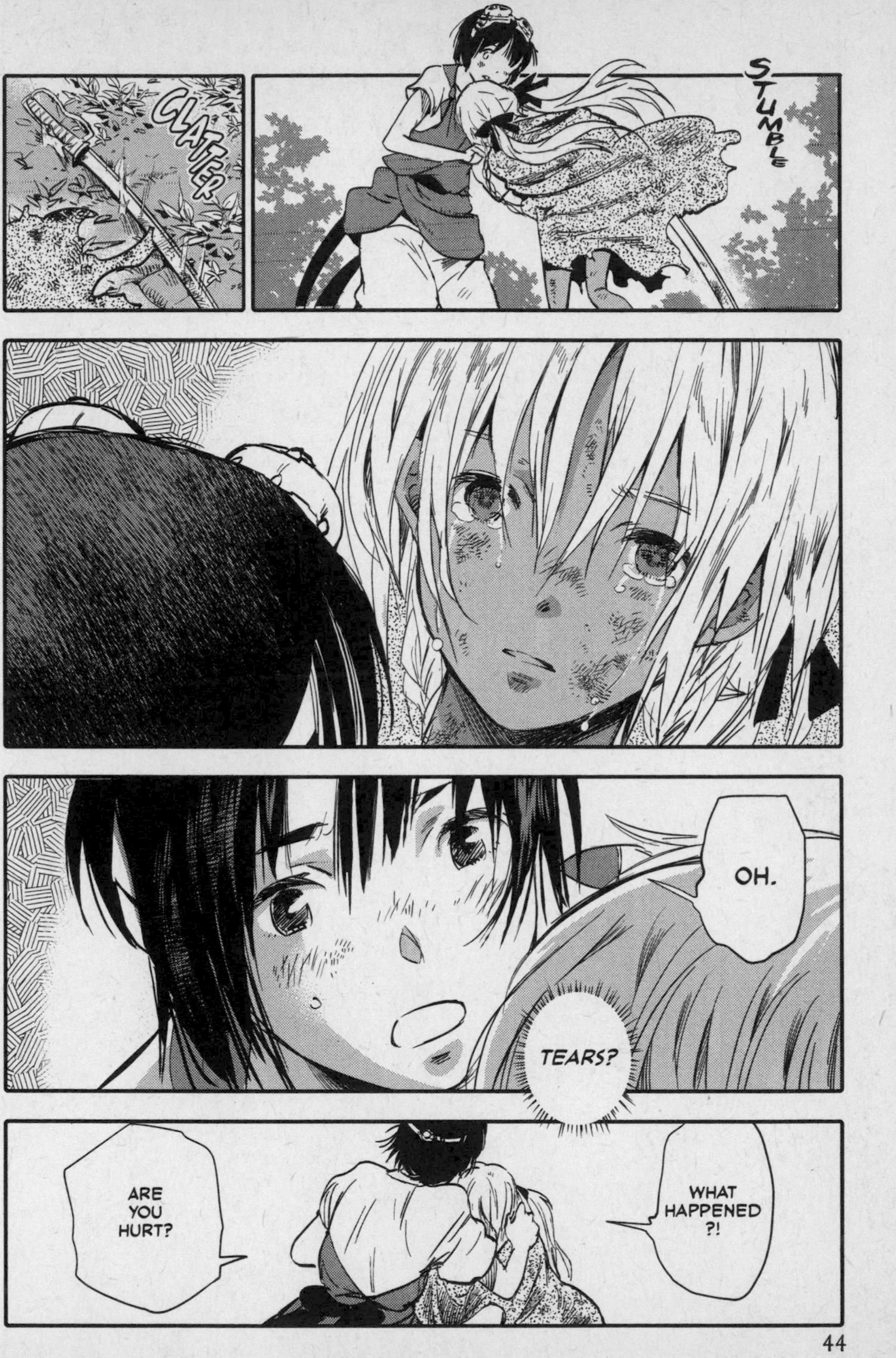
STUMBLE
CLATTER
OH.
TEARS?
WHAT HAPPENED ?!
ARE YOU HURT?

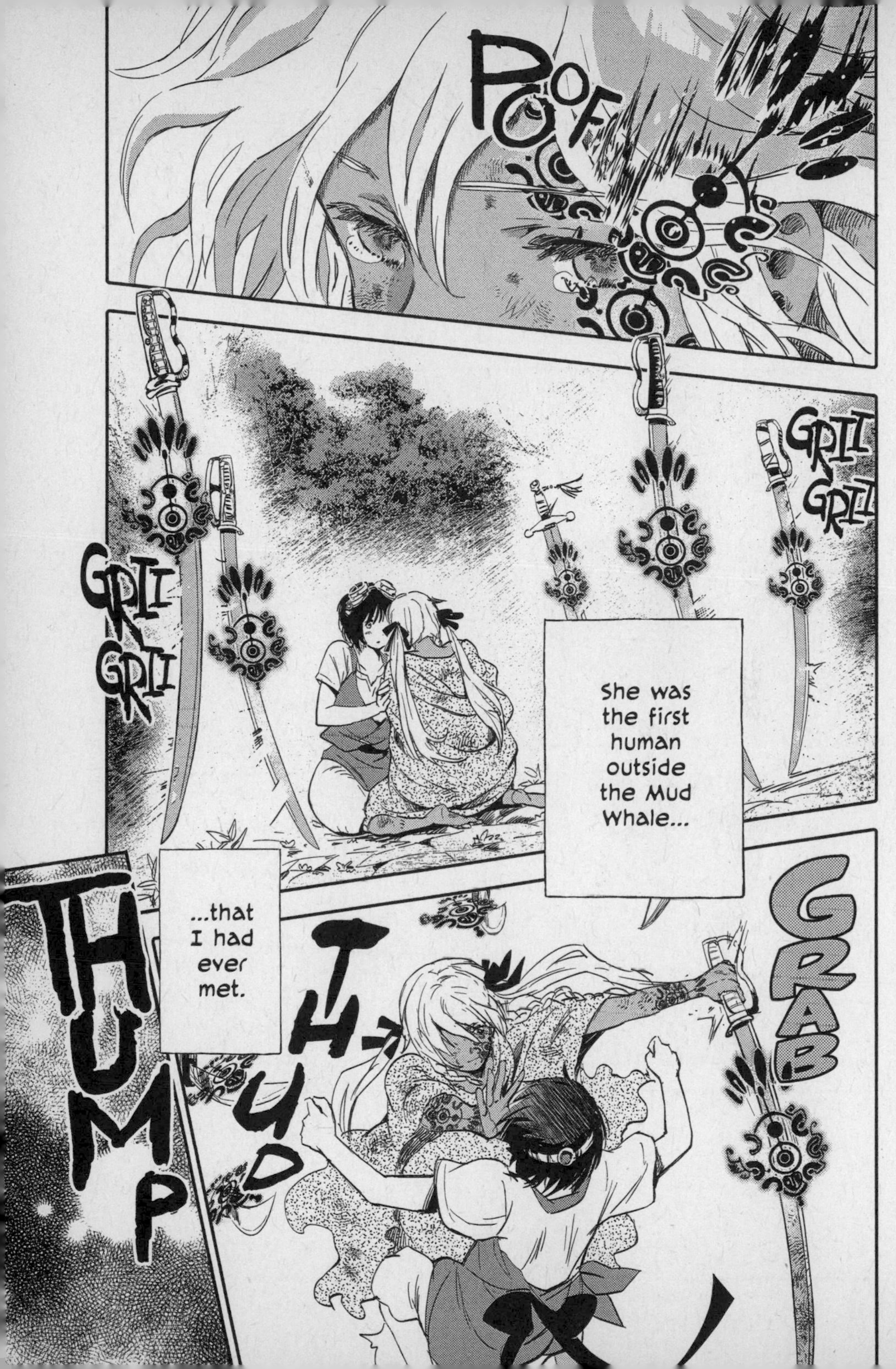
POOF
GRII GRII
She was the first human outside the Mud Whale...
GRII GRII
GRAB
...that I had ever met.
THUD
THUMP

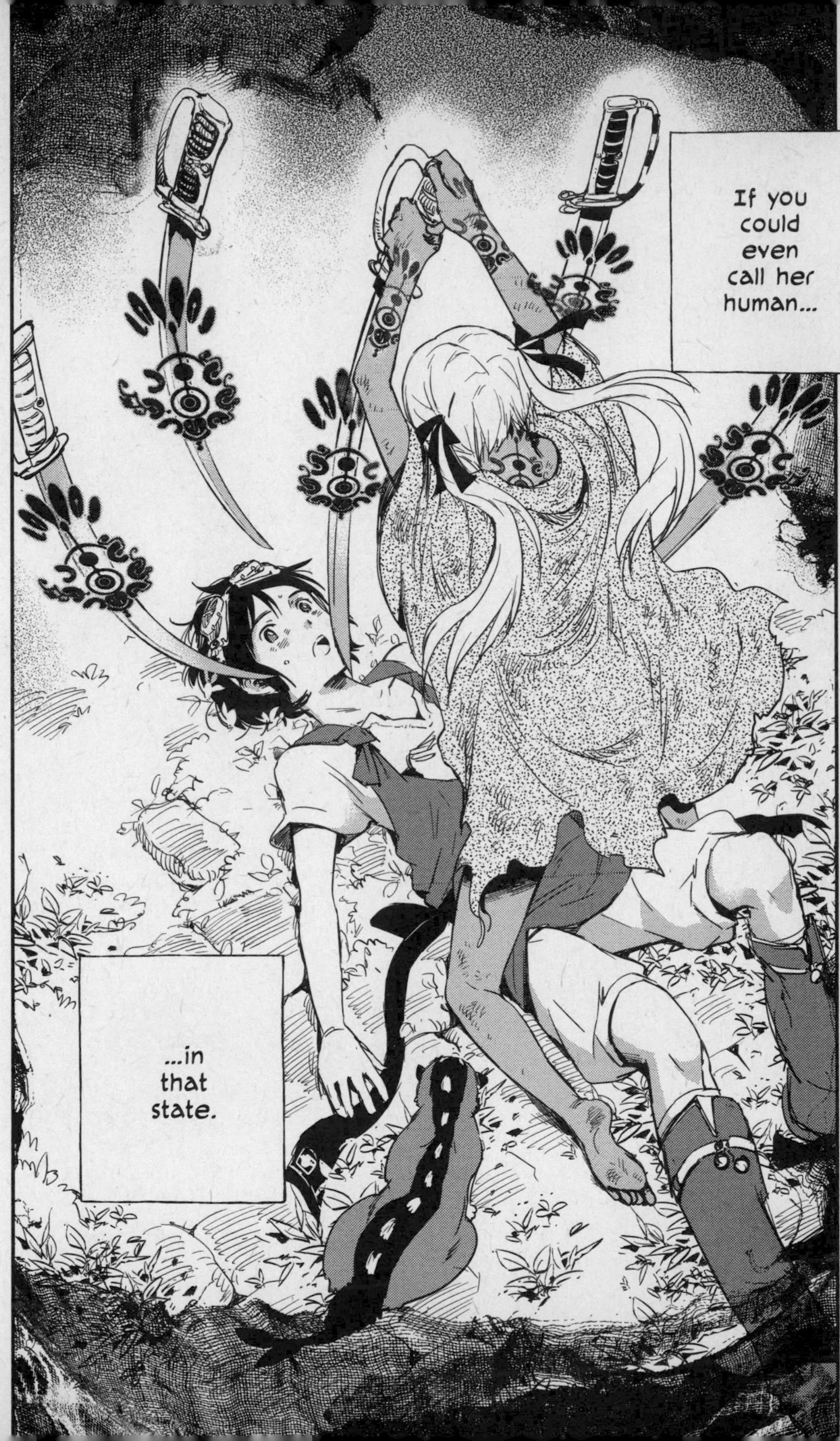
If you could even call her human...
...in that state.

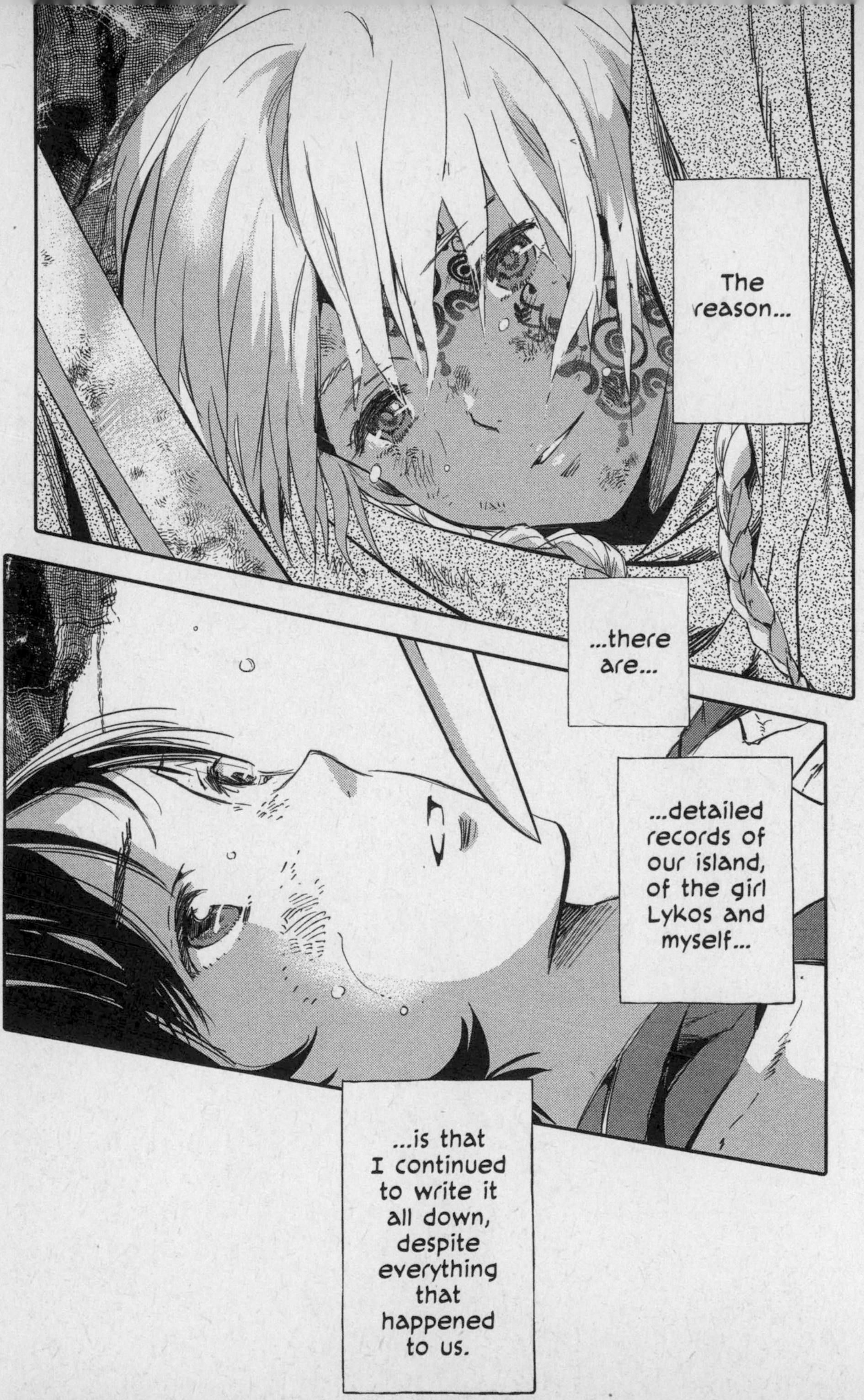
The reason...
...there are...
...detailed records of our island, of the girl Lykos and myself...
...is that I continued to write it all down, despite everything that happened to us.

Chakuro of the Sea of Sand -The End-

The Archivist's Notes

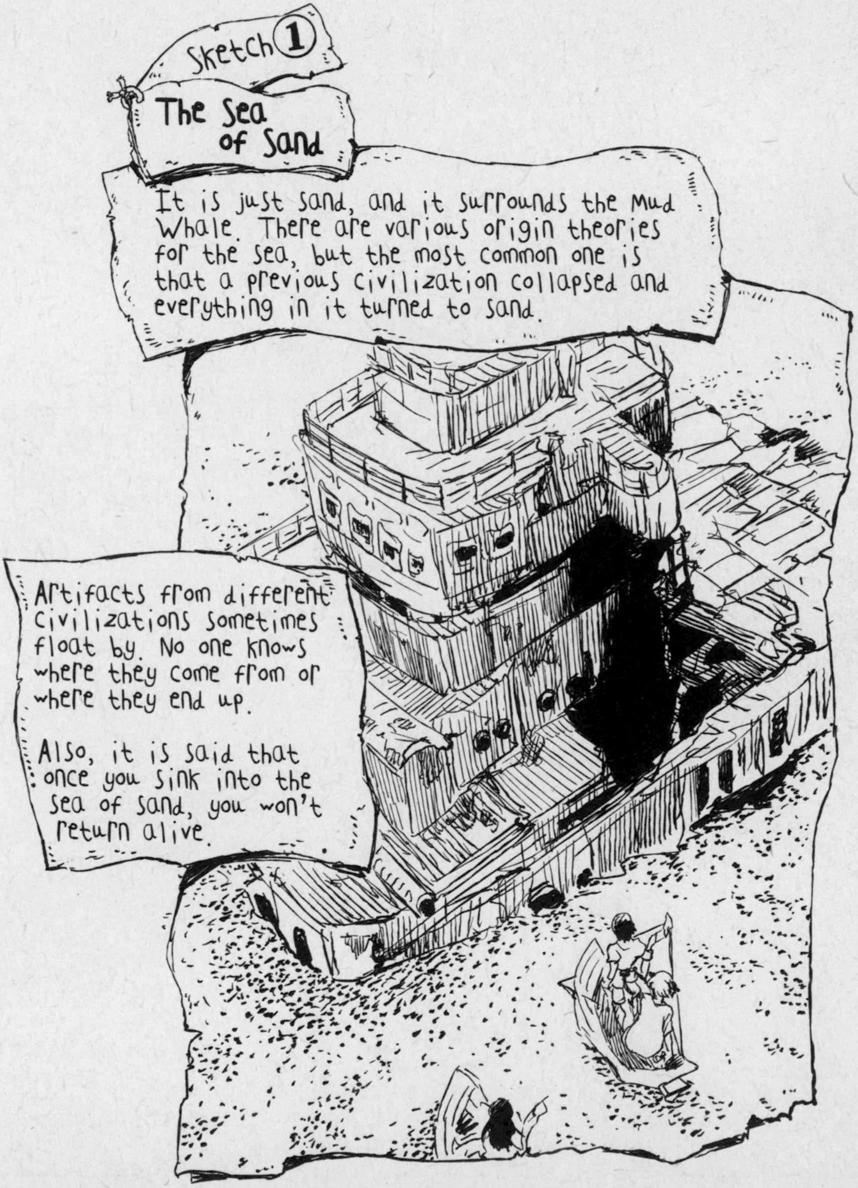
Sketch 1
The Sea of Sand
It is just sand, and it surrounds the Mud Whale. There are various origin theories for the sea, but the most common one is that a previous civilization collapsed and everything in it turned to sand.
Artifacts from different civilizations sometimes float by. No one knows where they come from or where they end up.
Also, it is said that once you sink into the sea of sand, you won't return alive.

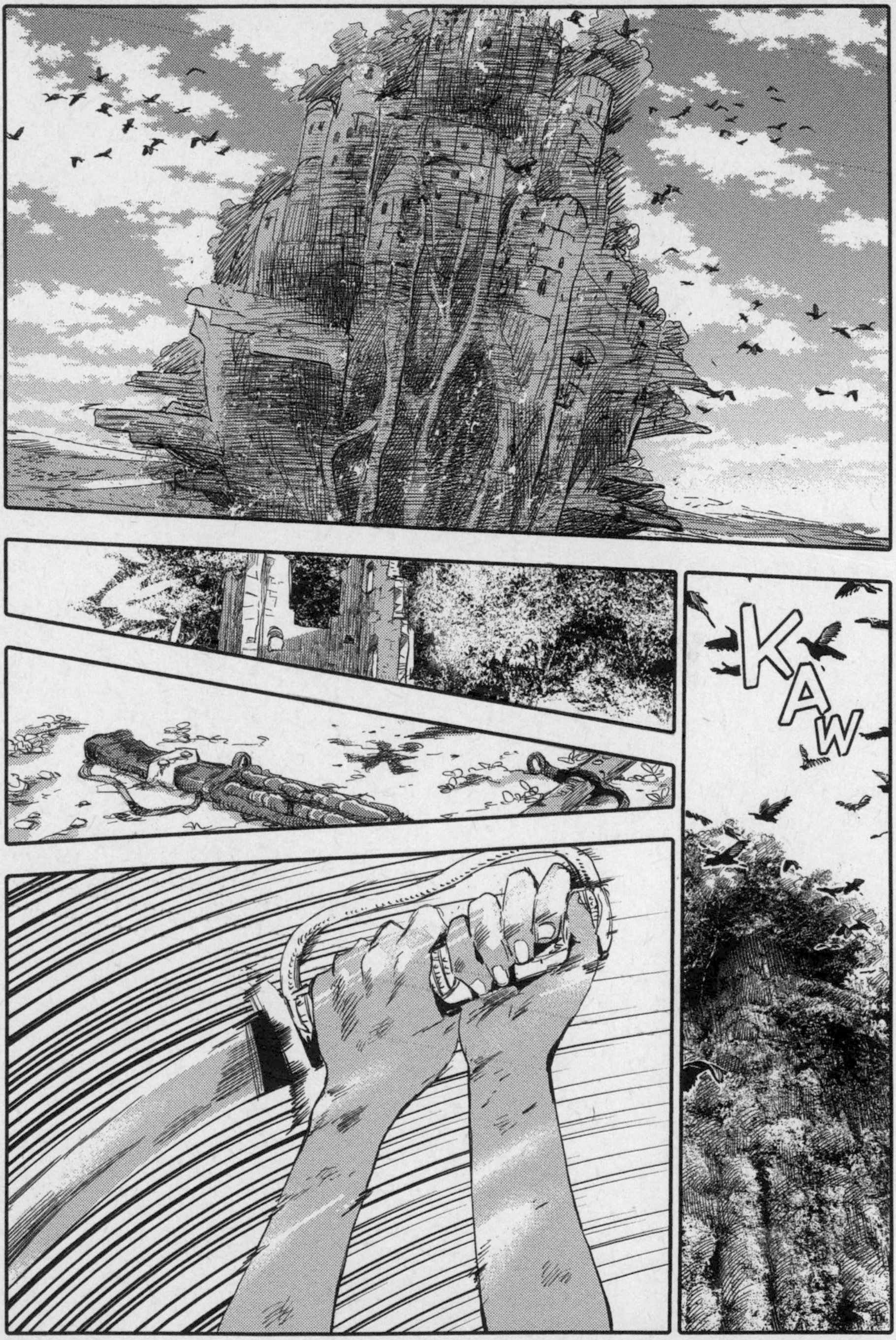
KAW

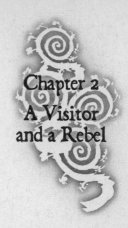

Chapter 2
A Visitor and a Rebel

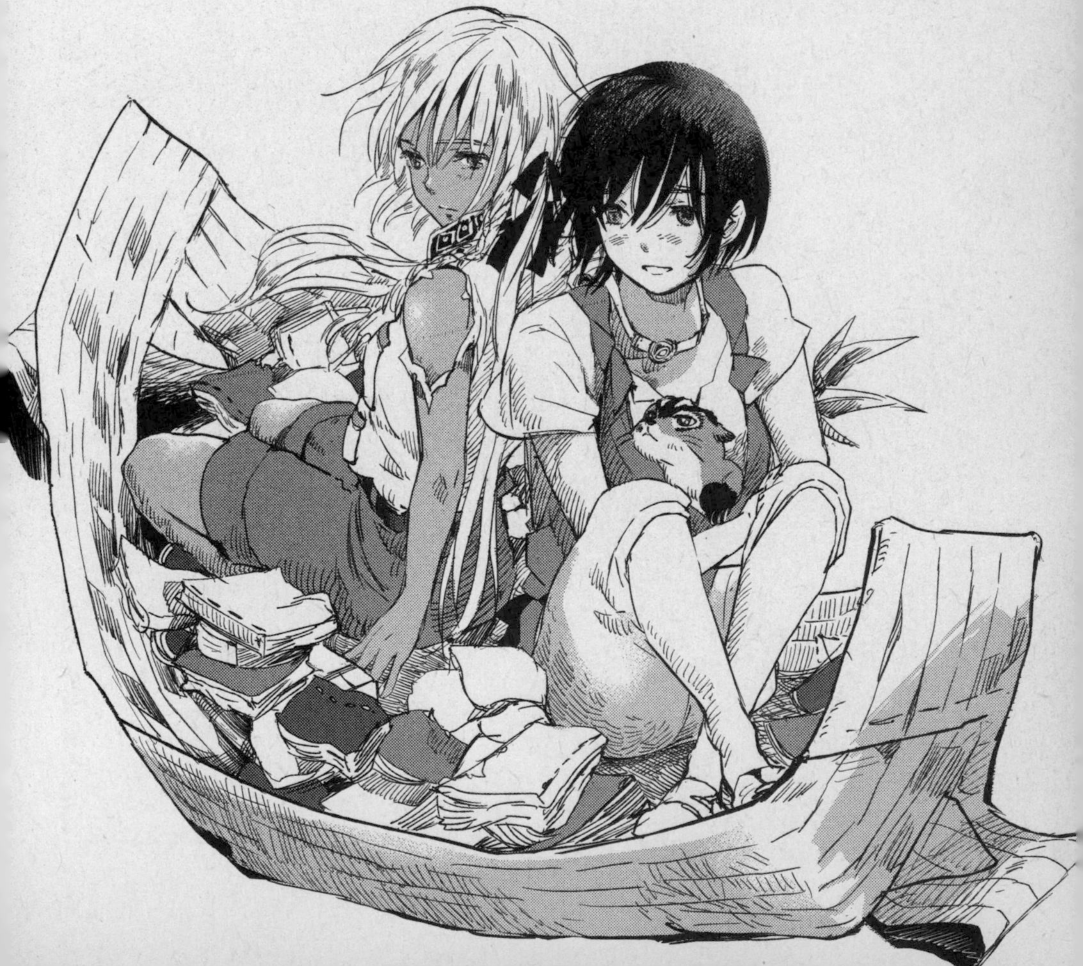

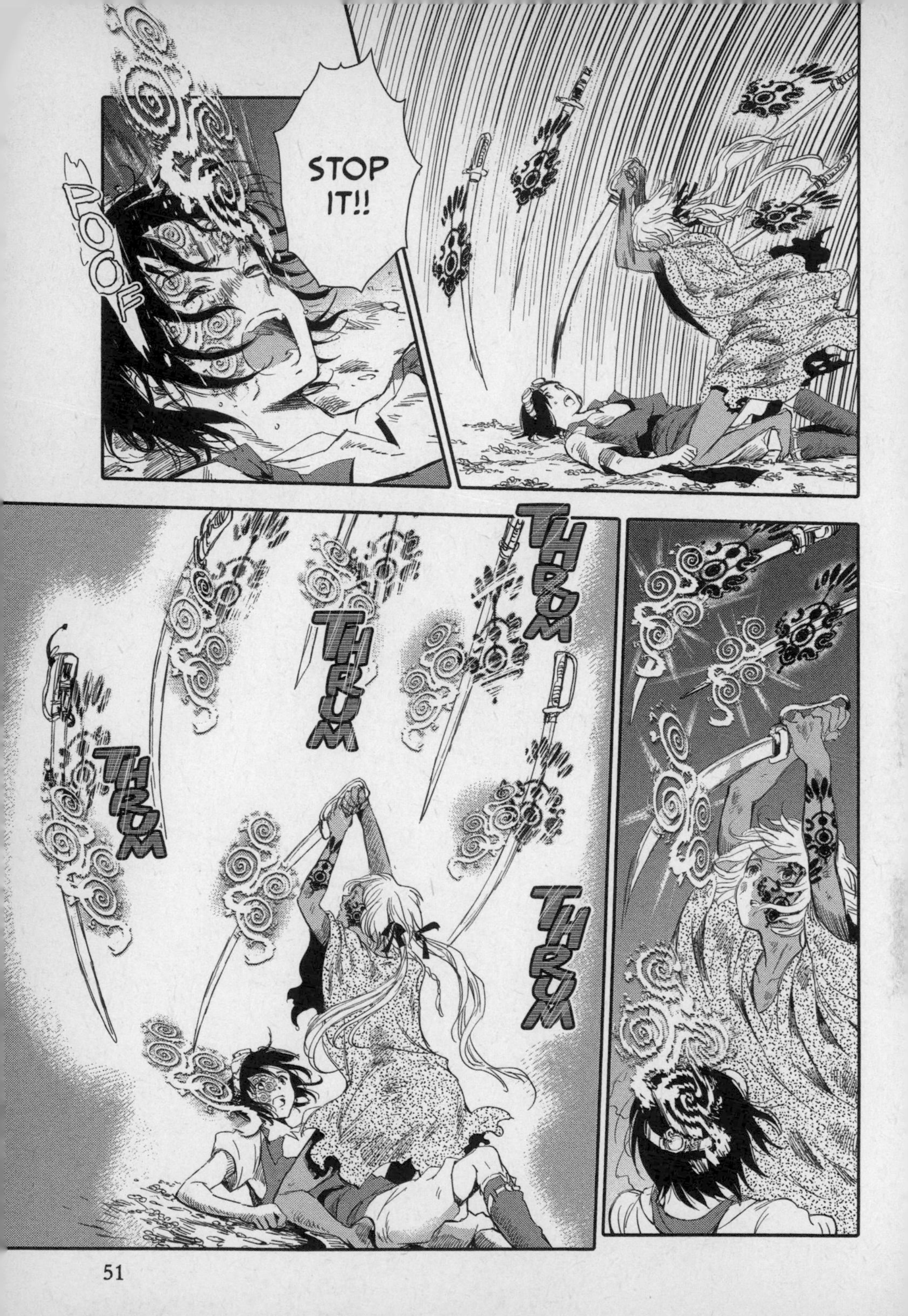
STOP IT!!
POOF
THRUM
THRUM
THRUM
THRUM

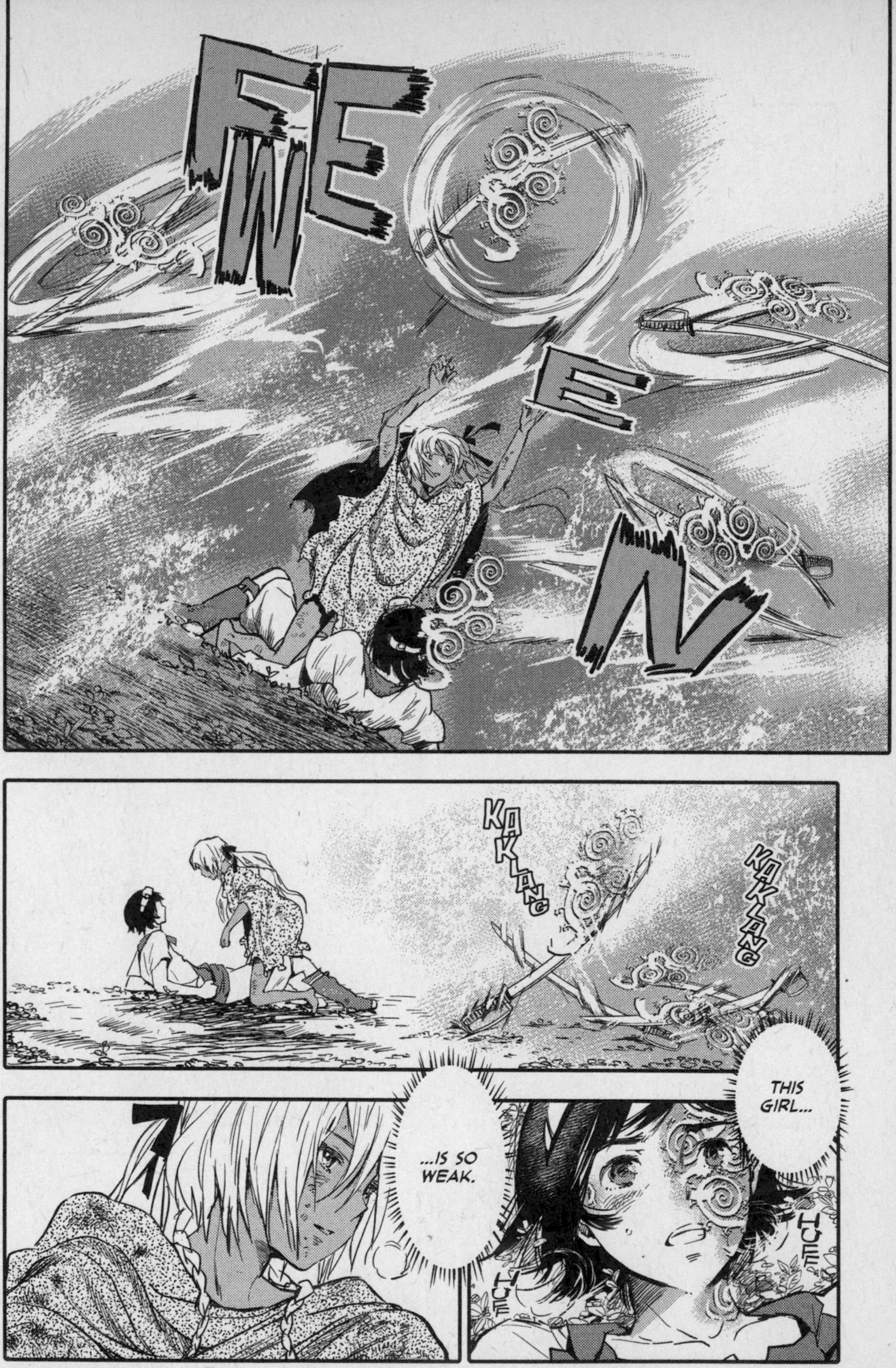
FWEEN
KAKLANG
KAKLANG
THIS GIRL...
HUE
HUE
...IS SO WEAK.

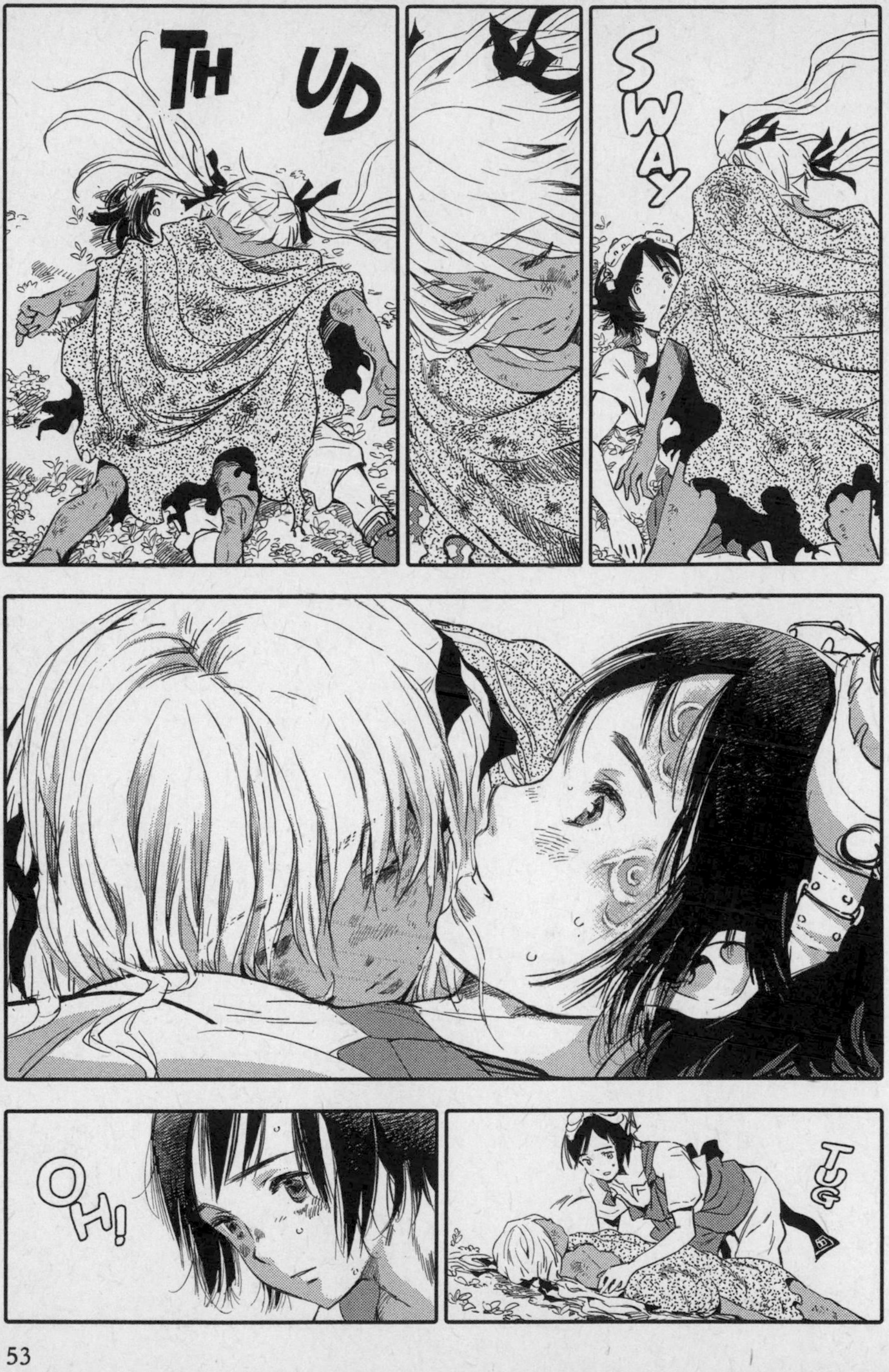
SWAY
TH UD
TUG
OH!

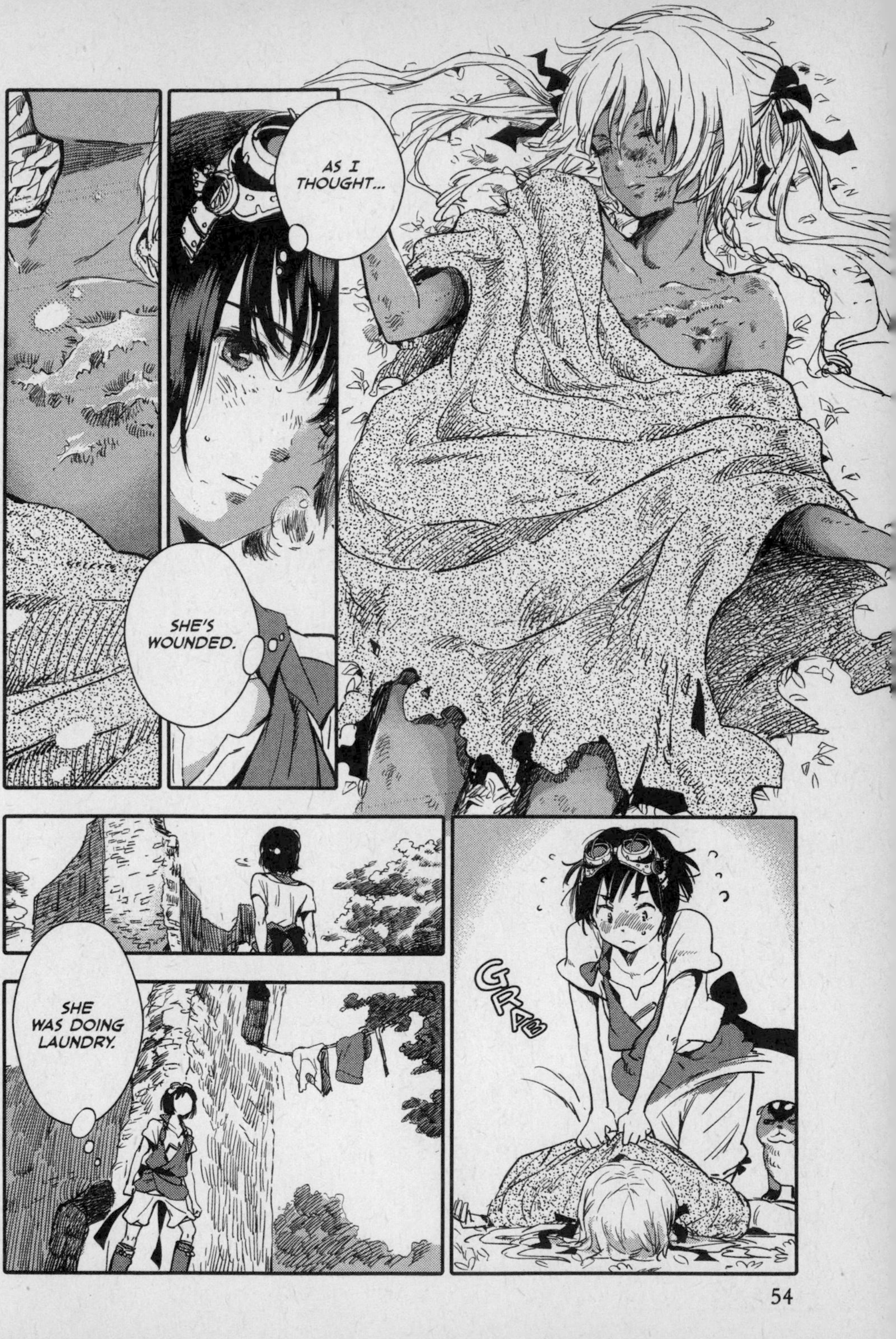
AS I THOUGHT...
SHE'S WOUNDED.
GRAB
SHE WAS DOING LAUNDRY.

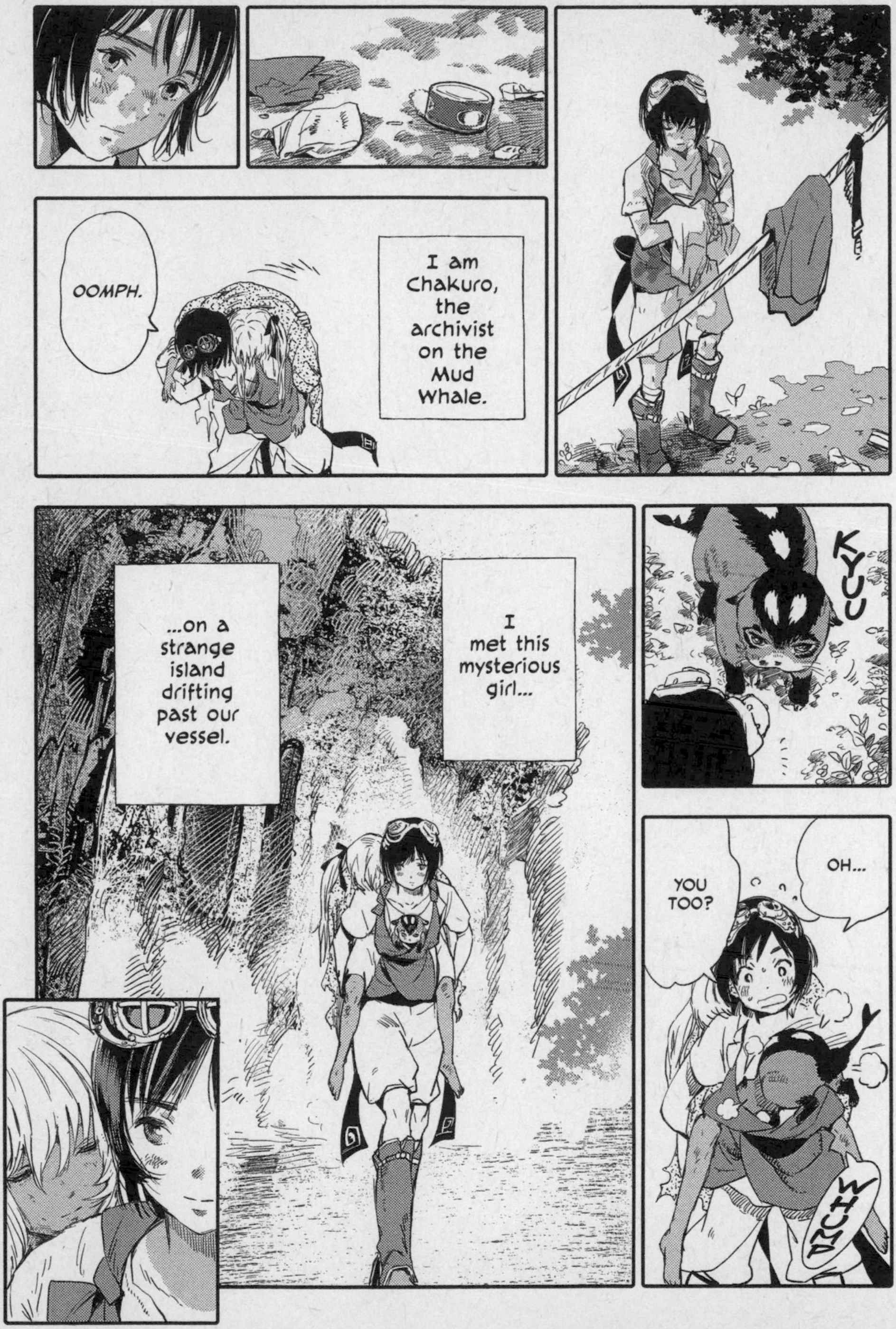
I am Chakuro, the archivist on the Mud Whale.
OOMPH.
KYUU
OH...
YOU TOO?
WHUMP
I met this mysterious girl...
...on a strange island drifting past our vessel.

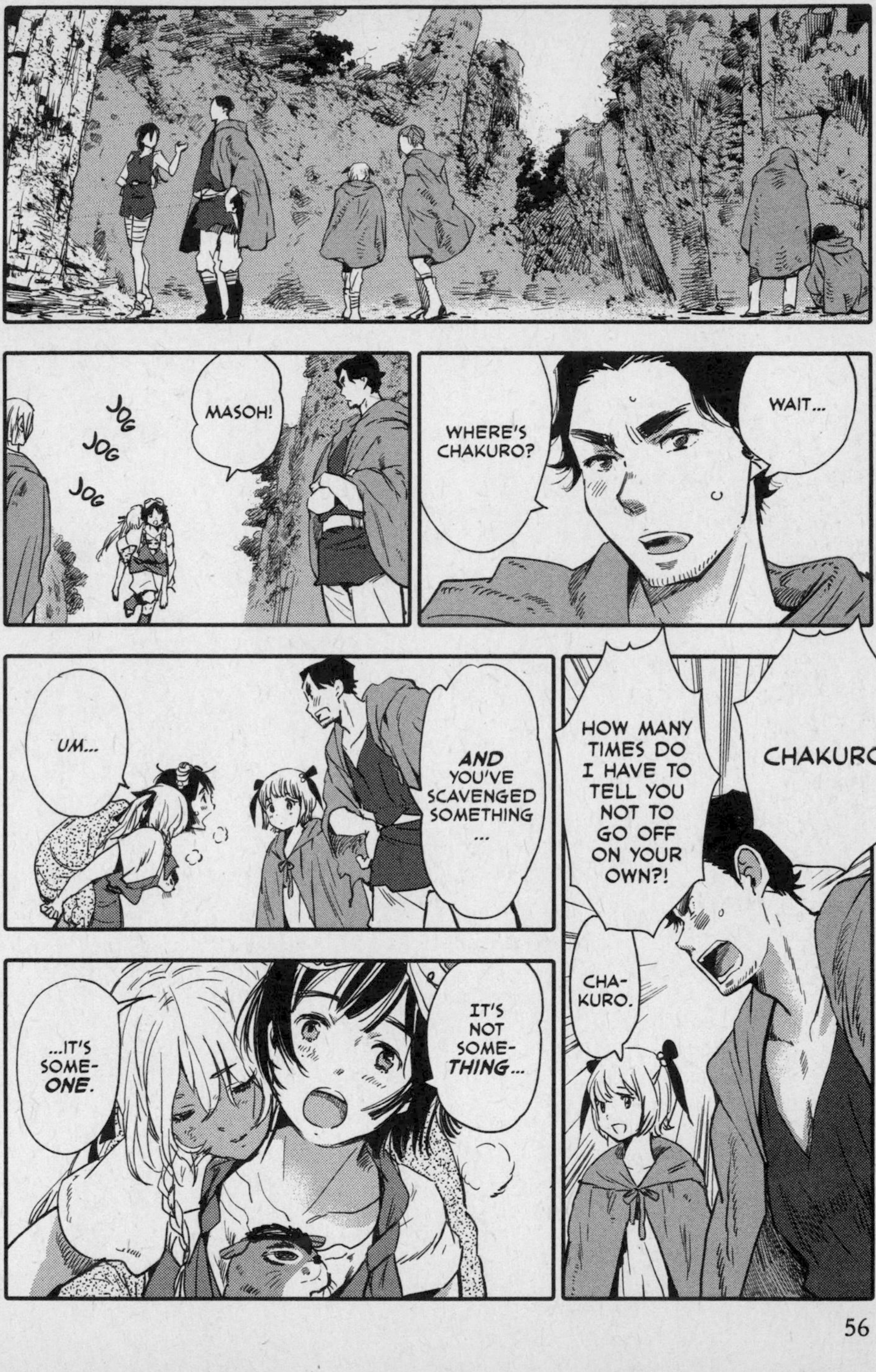
WAIT...
WHERE'S CHAKURO?
MASOH!
JOG JOG JOG
CHAKURO!
HOW MANY TIMES DO I HAVE TO TELL YOU NOT TO GO OFF ON YOUR OWN?!
CHA-KURO.
AND YOU'VE SCAVENGED SOMETHING...
UM...
IT'S NOT SOME-*THING*...
...IT'S SOME-*ONE*.

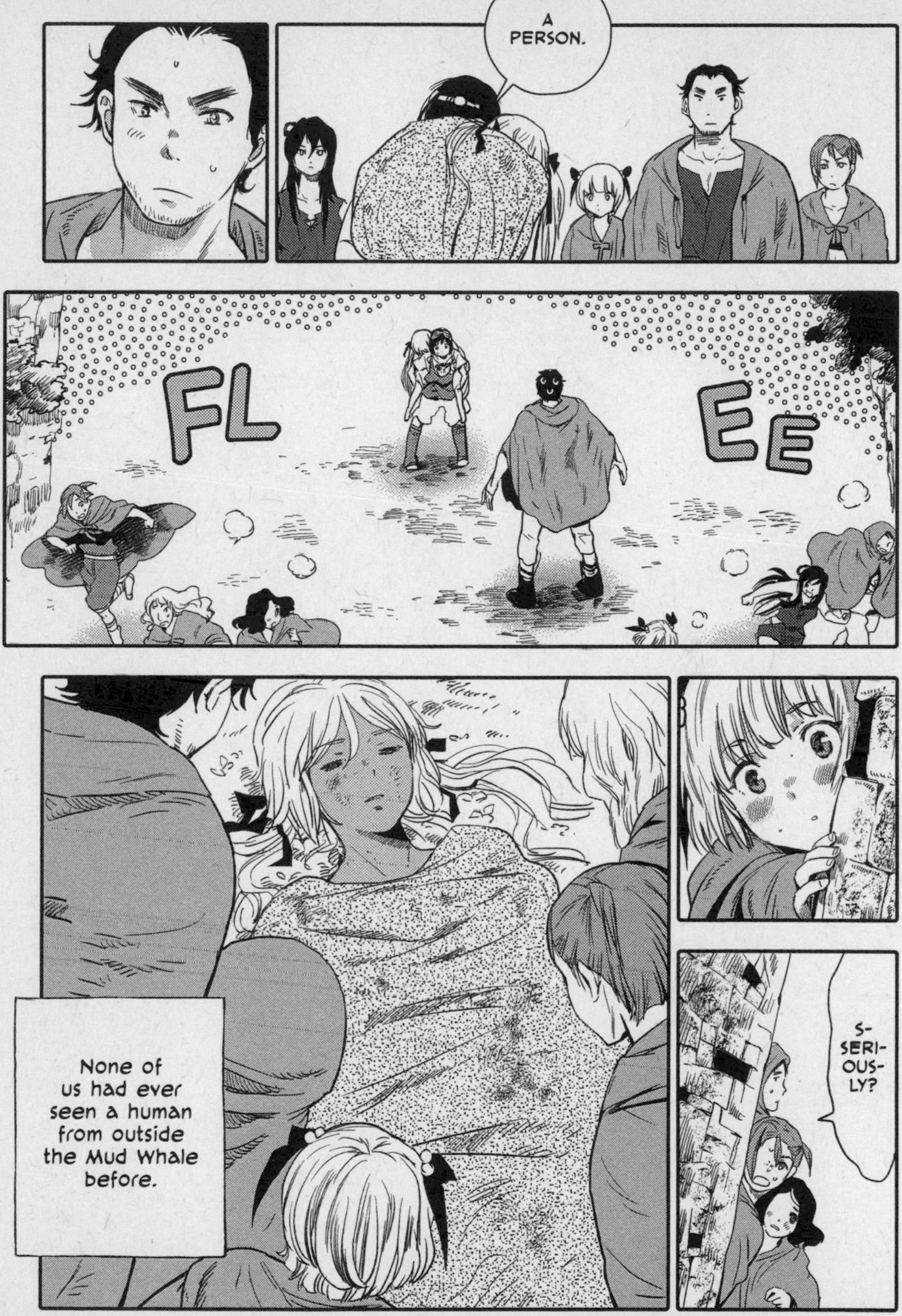
A PERSON.
FL EE
S-SERIOUSLY?
None of us had ever seen a human from outside the Mud Whale before.

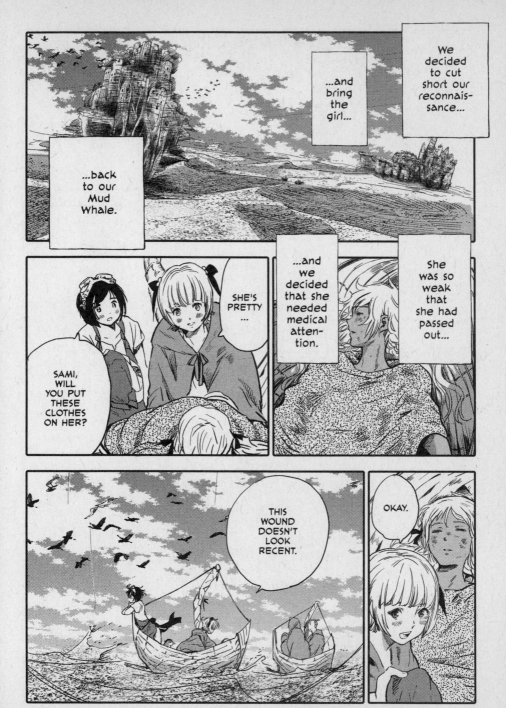

We decided to cut short our reconnaissance...
...and bring the girl...
...back to our Mud Whale.
She was so weak that she had passed out...
...and we decided that she needed medical attention.
SHE'S PRETTY ...
SAMI, WILL YOU PUT THESE CLOTHES ON HER?
OKAY.
THIS WOUND DOESN'T LOOK RECENT.

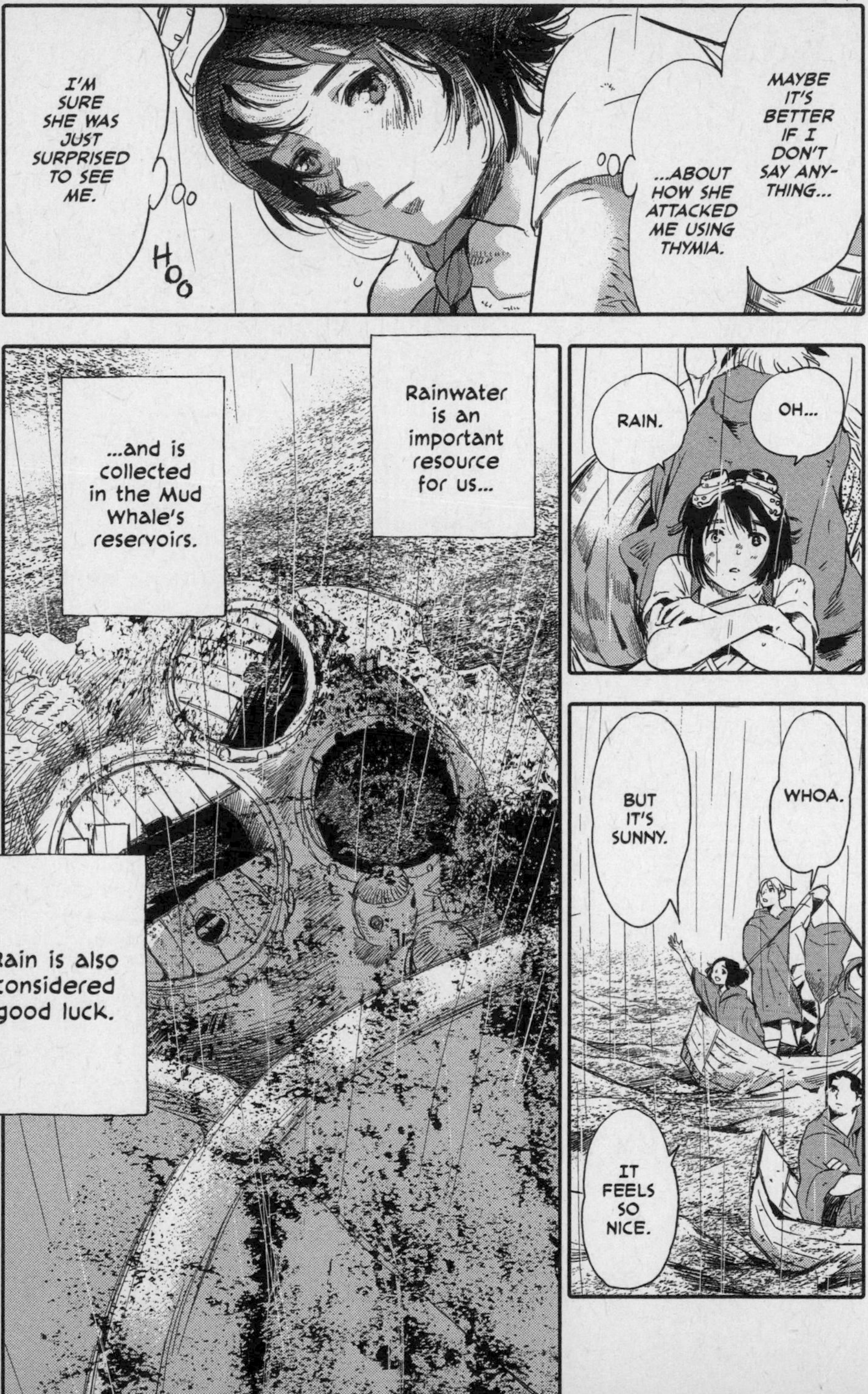
MAYBE IT'S BETTER IF I DON'T SAY ANY-THING...
...ABOUT HOW SHE ATTACKED ME USING THYMIA.
I'M SURE SHE WAS JUST SURPRISED TO SEE ME.
HOO
OH...
RAIN.
WHOA.
BUT IT'S SUNNY.
IT FEELS SO NICE.
Rainwater is an important resource for us...
...and is collected in the Mud Whale's reservoirs.
Rain is also considered good luck.

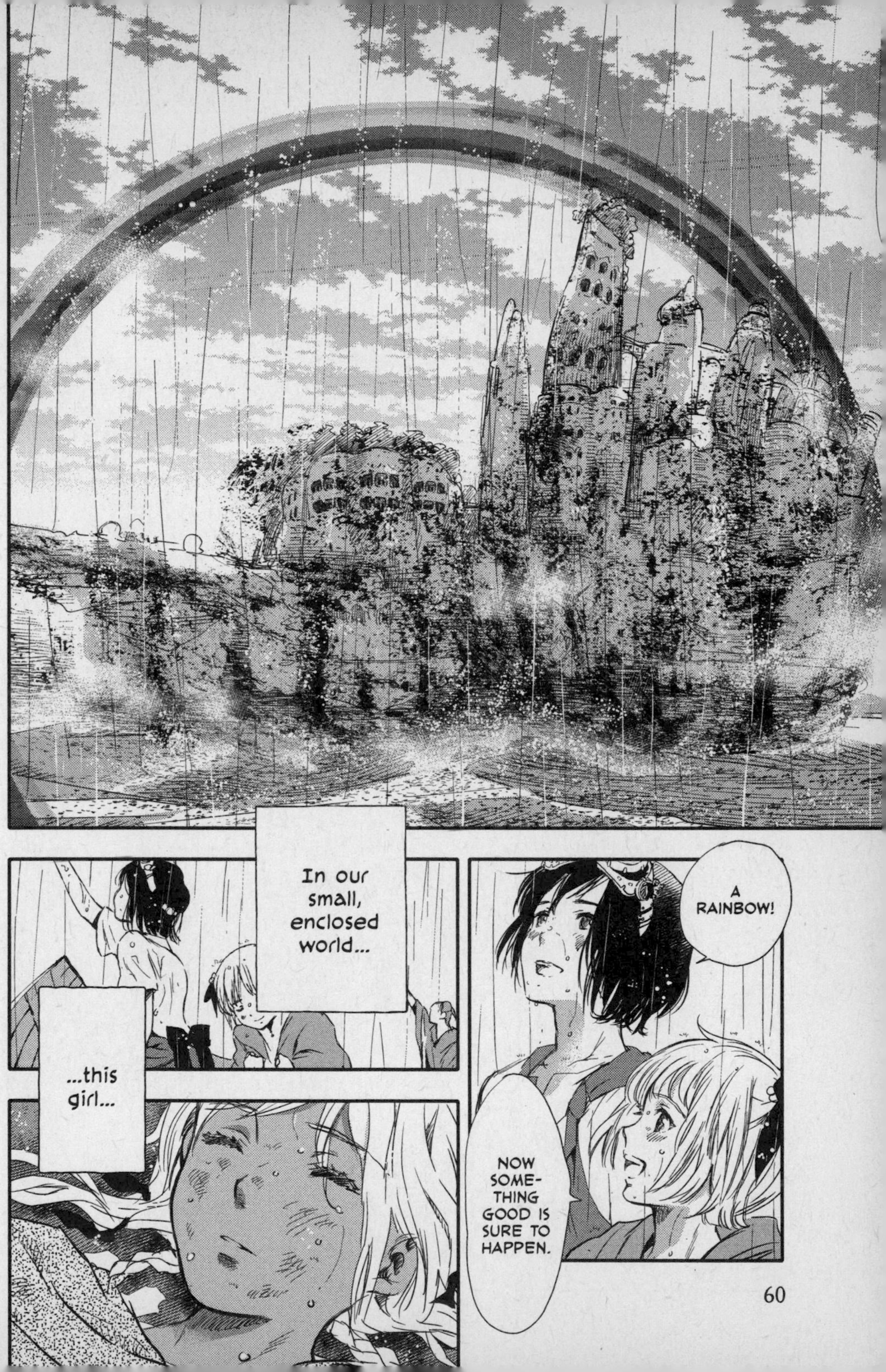
A RAINBOW!
NOW SOME-THING GOOD IS SURE TO HAPPEN.
In our small, enclosed world...
...this girl...

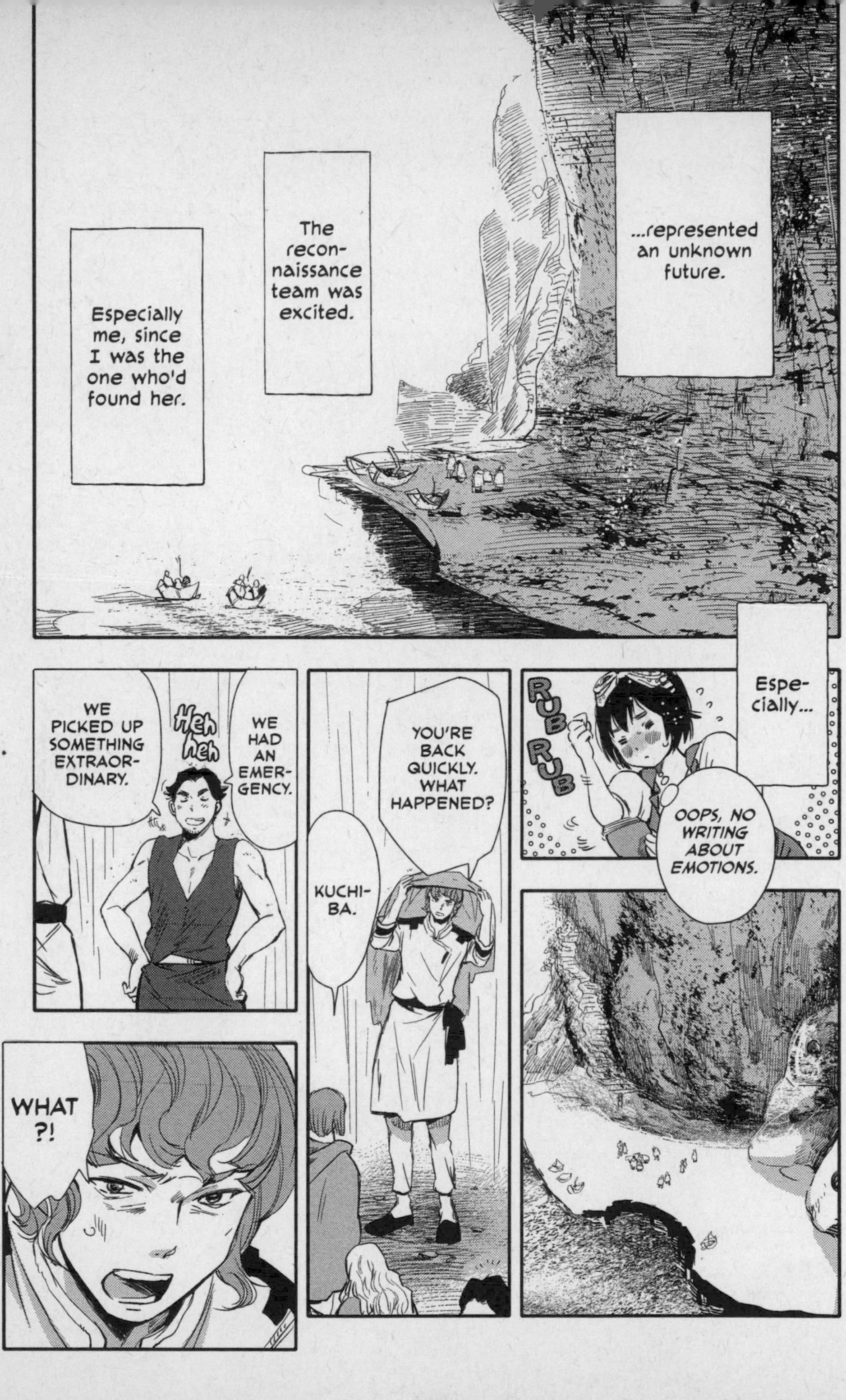
...represented an unknown future.
The reconnaissance team was excited.
Especially me, since I was the one who'd found her.
Espe-cially...
RUB RUB
OOPS, NO WRITING ABOUT EMOTIONS.
YOU'RE BACK QUICKLY. WHAT HAPPENED?
KUCHIBA.
WE HAD AN EMERGENCY.
Heh heh
WE PICKED UP SOMETHING EXTRAOR-DINARY.
WHAT?!

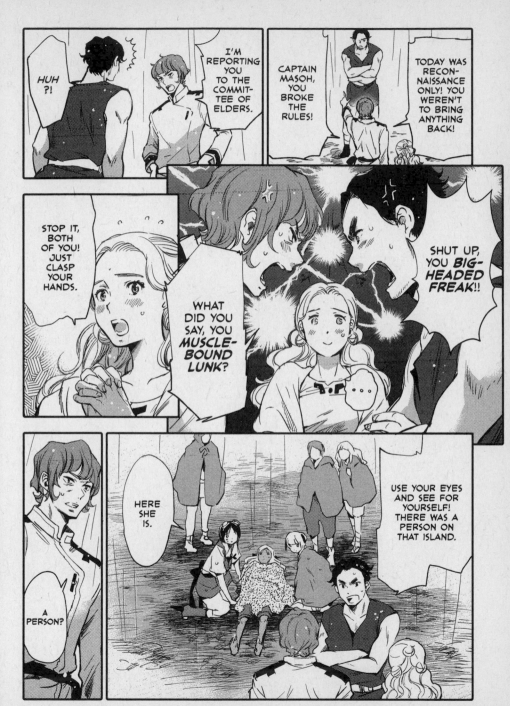

TODAY WAS RECONNAISSANCE ONLY! YOU WEREN'T TO BRING ANYTHING BACK!
CAPTAIN MASOH, YOU BROKE THE RULES!
I'M REPORTING YOU TO THE COMMITTEE OF ELDERS.
HUH?!
SHUT UP, YOU BIG-HEADED FREAK!!
WHAT DID YOU SAY, YOU MUSCLE-BOUND LUNK?
...
STOP IT, BOTH OF YOU! JUST CLASP YOUR HANDS.
USE YOUR EYES AND SEE FOR YOURSELF! THERE WAS A PERSON ON THAT ISLAND.
HERE SHE IS.
A PERSON?

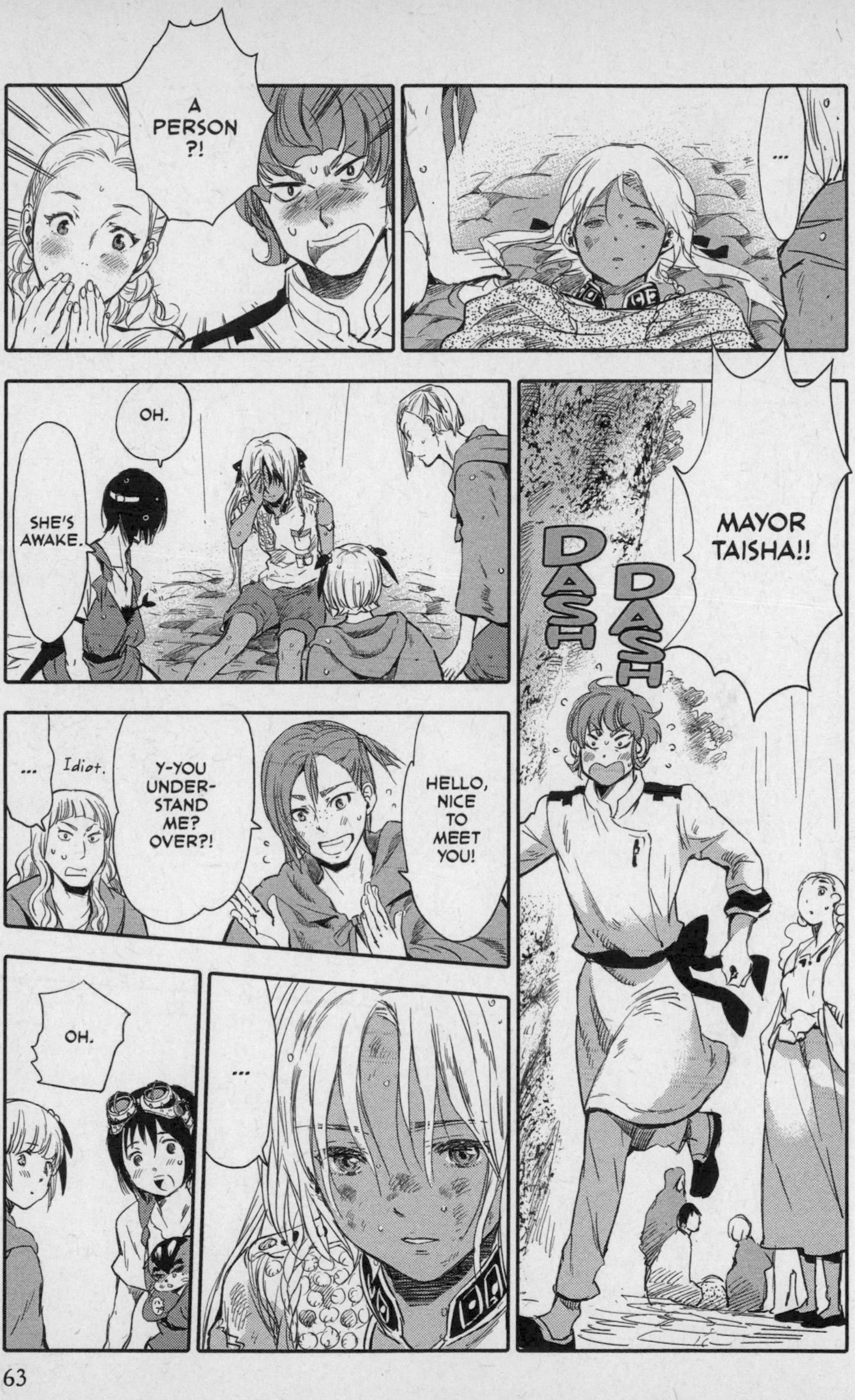
...
A PERSON ?!
MAYOR TAISHA!!
DASH DASH
OH.
SHE'S AWAKE.
HELLO, NICE TO MEET YOU!
Y-YOU UNDER-STAND ME? OVER?!
... Idiot.
...
OH.

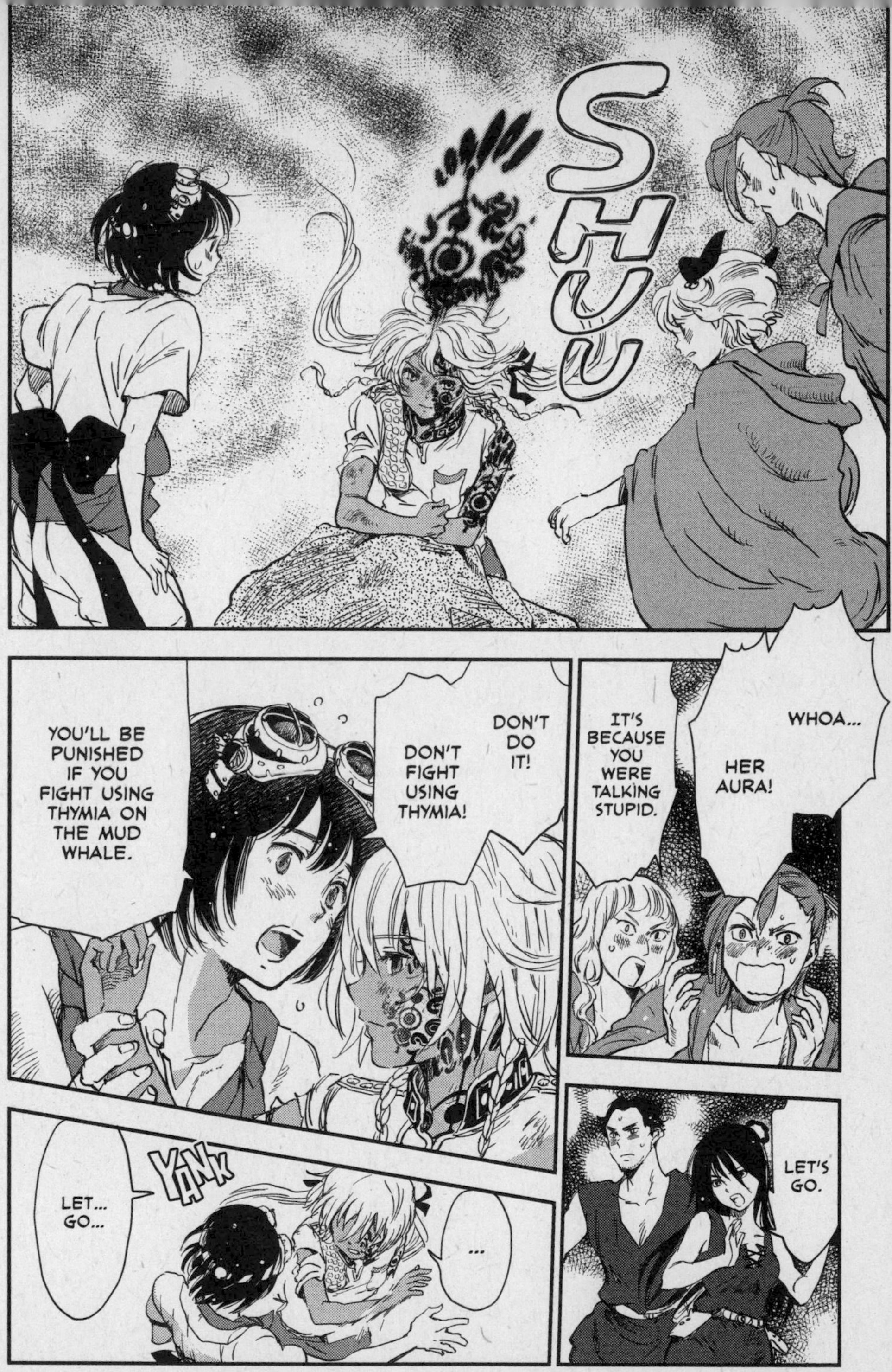
SHUU
WHOA...
HER AURA!
IT'S BECAUSE YOU WERE TALKING STUPID.
DON'T DO IT!
DON'T FIGHT USING THYMIA!
YOU'LL BE PUNISHED IF YOU FIGHT USING THYMIA ON THE MUD WHALE.
LET'S GO.
...
YANK
LET... GO...

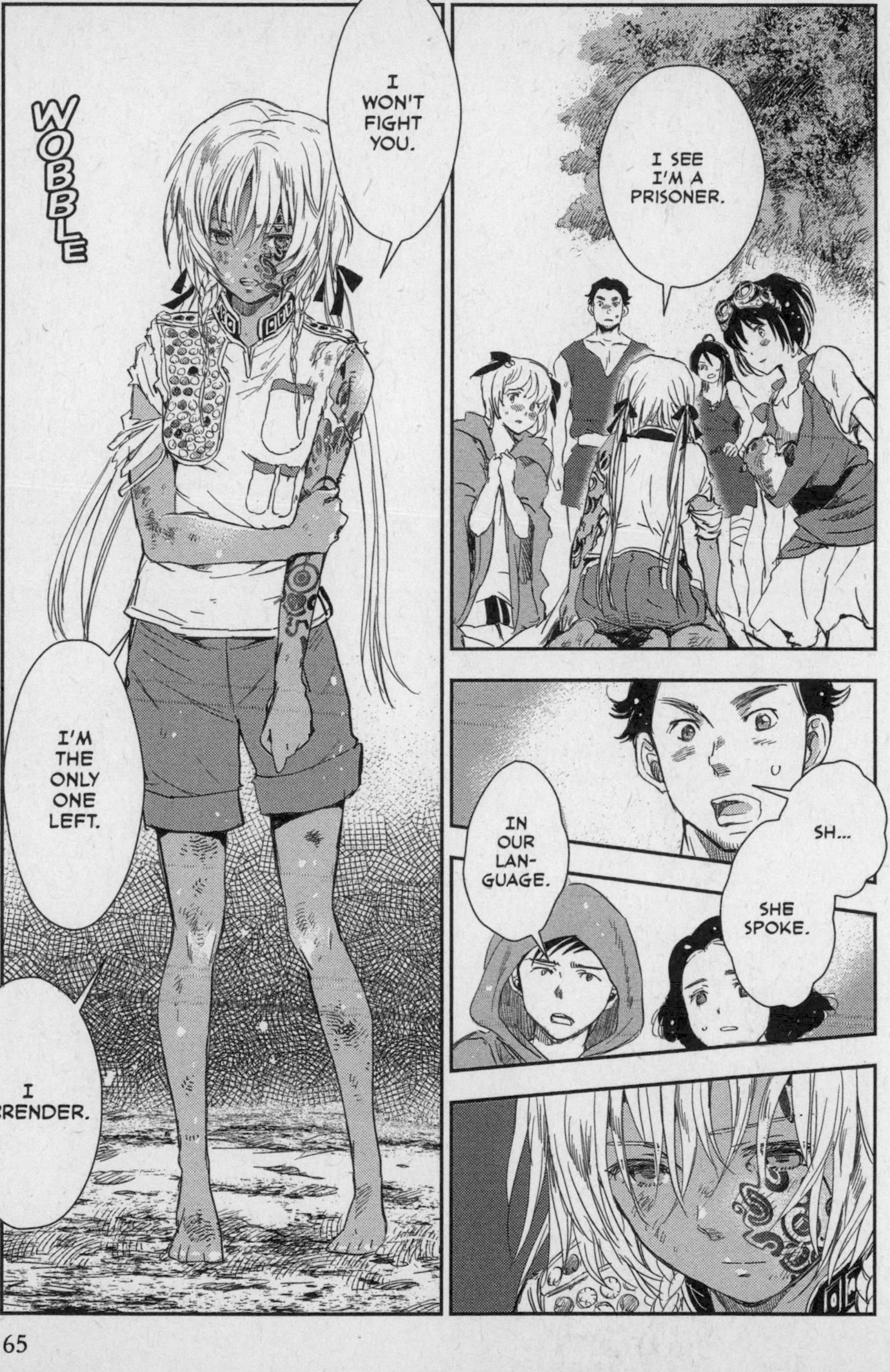
I SEE I'M A PRISONER.
SH...
SHE SPOKE.
IN OUR LANGUAGE.
WOBBLE
I WON'T FIGHT YOU.
I'M THE ONLY ONE LEFT.
I SURRENDER.

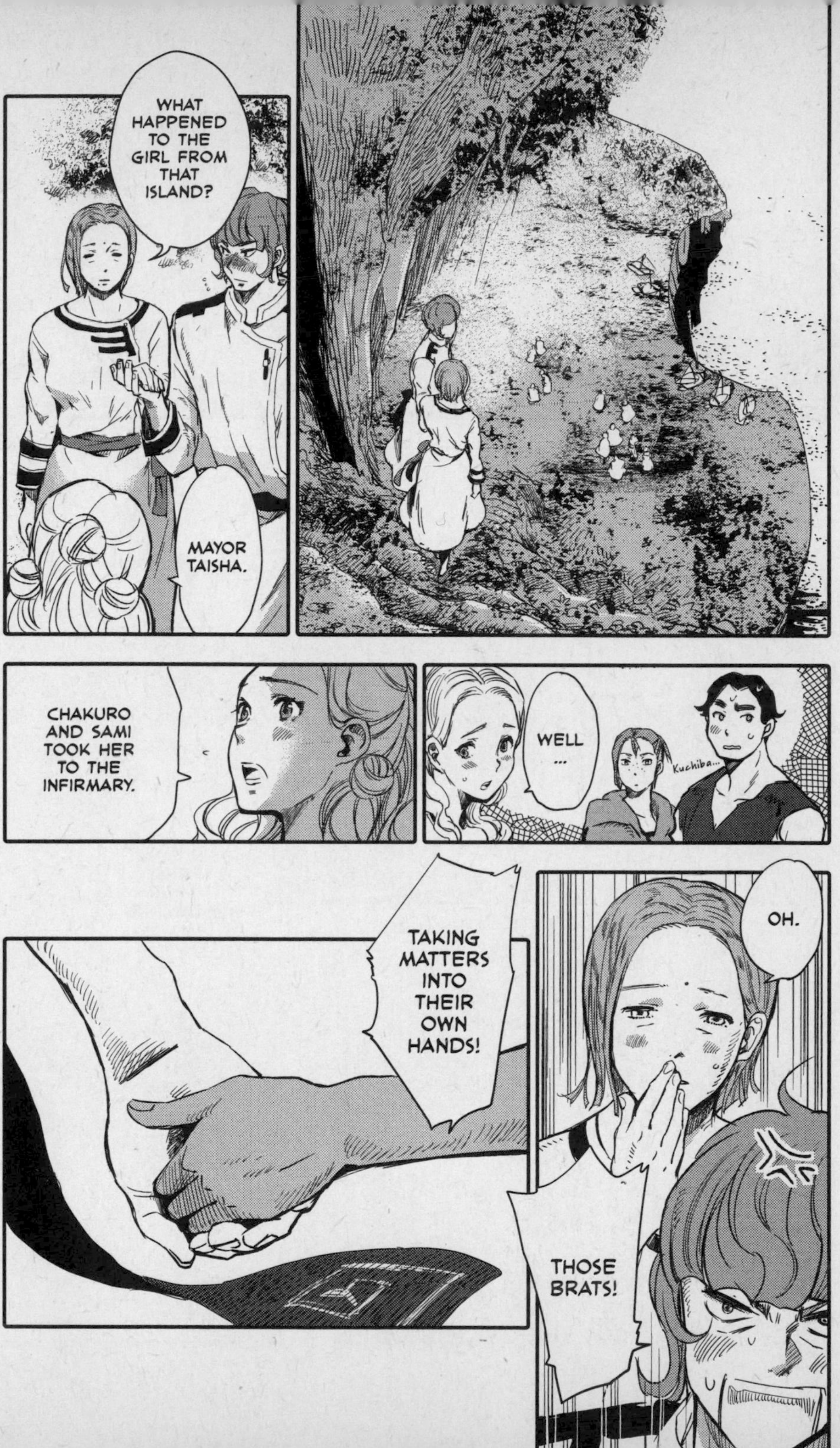
WHAT HAPPENED TO THE GIRL FROM THAT ISLAND?
MAYOR TAISHA.
WELL ...
Kuchiba...
CHAKURO AND SAMI TOOK HER TO THE INFIRMARY.
OH.
THOSE BRATS!
TAKING MATTERS INTO THEIR OWN HANDS!

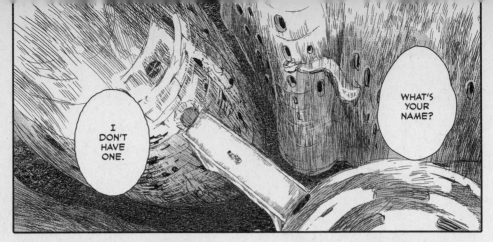

WHAT'S YOUR NAME?

I DON'T HAVE ONE.

YOUR CLOTHING HAD "LYKOS" EMBROIDERED ON IT.

YES, YOU DO!

IF IT WERE ME, I'D BE BOLTING AND MY HEART WOULD BE POUNDING OUT OF MY CHEST.

IF IT WERE ME, I'D BE SUPER CURIOUS AND EXCITED!

LYKOS, HUH...

AREN'T YOU SURPRISED TO BE SOMEWHERE UNFAMILIAR, LYKOS?

...

NOT AT ALL.

67

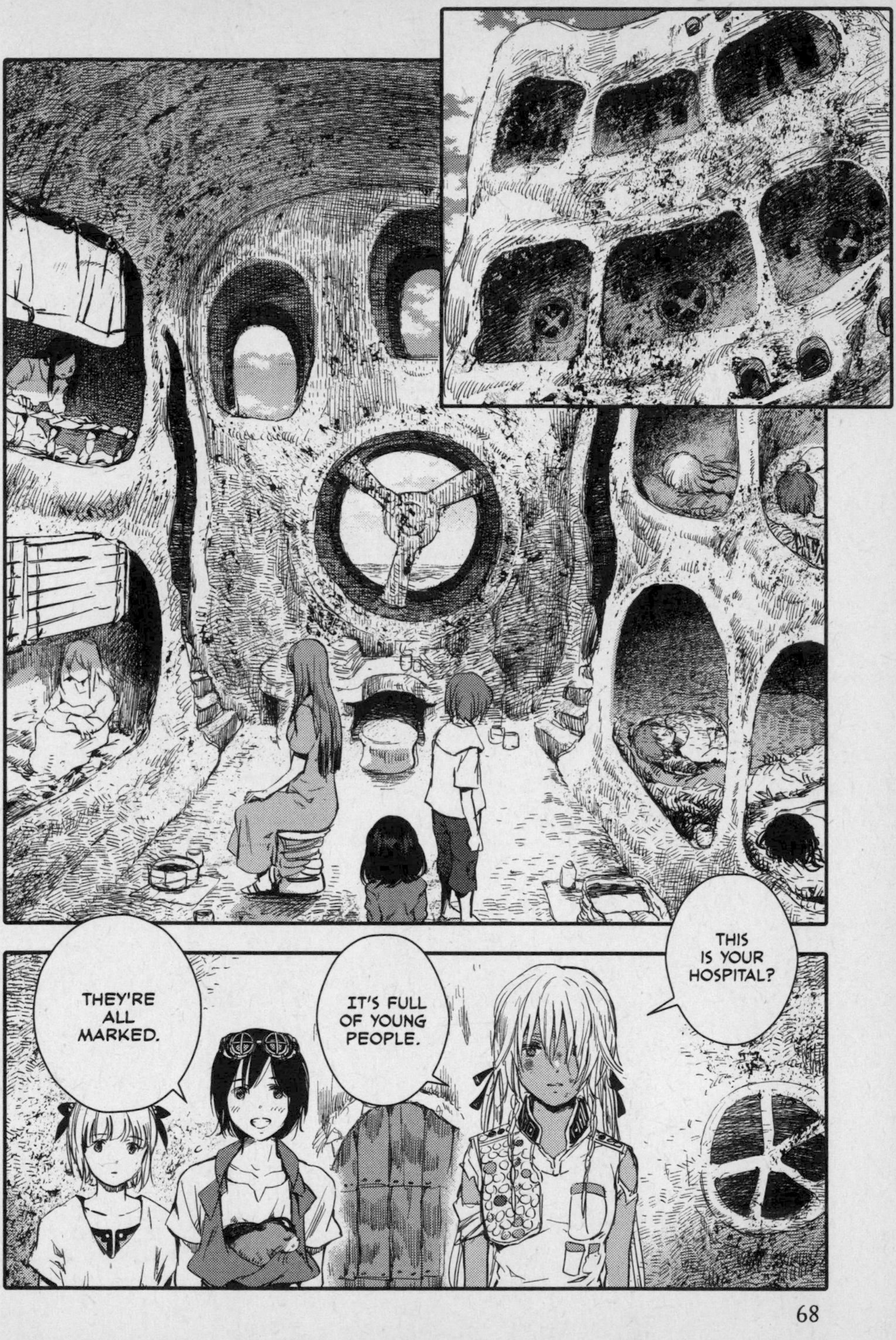
THIS IS YOUR HOSPITAL?
IT'S FULL OF YOUNG PEOPLE.
THEY'RE ALL MARKED.

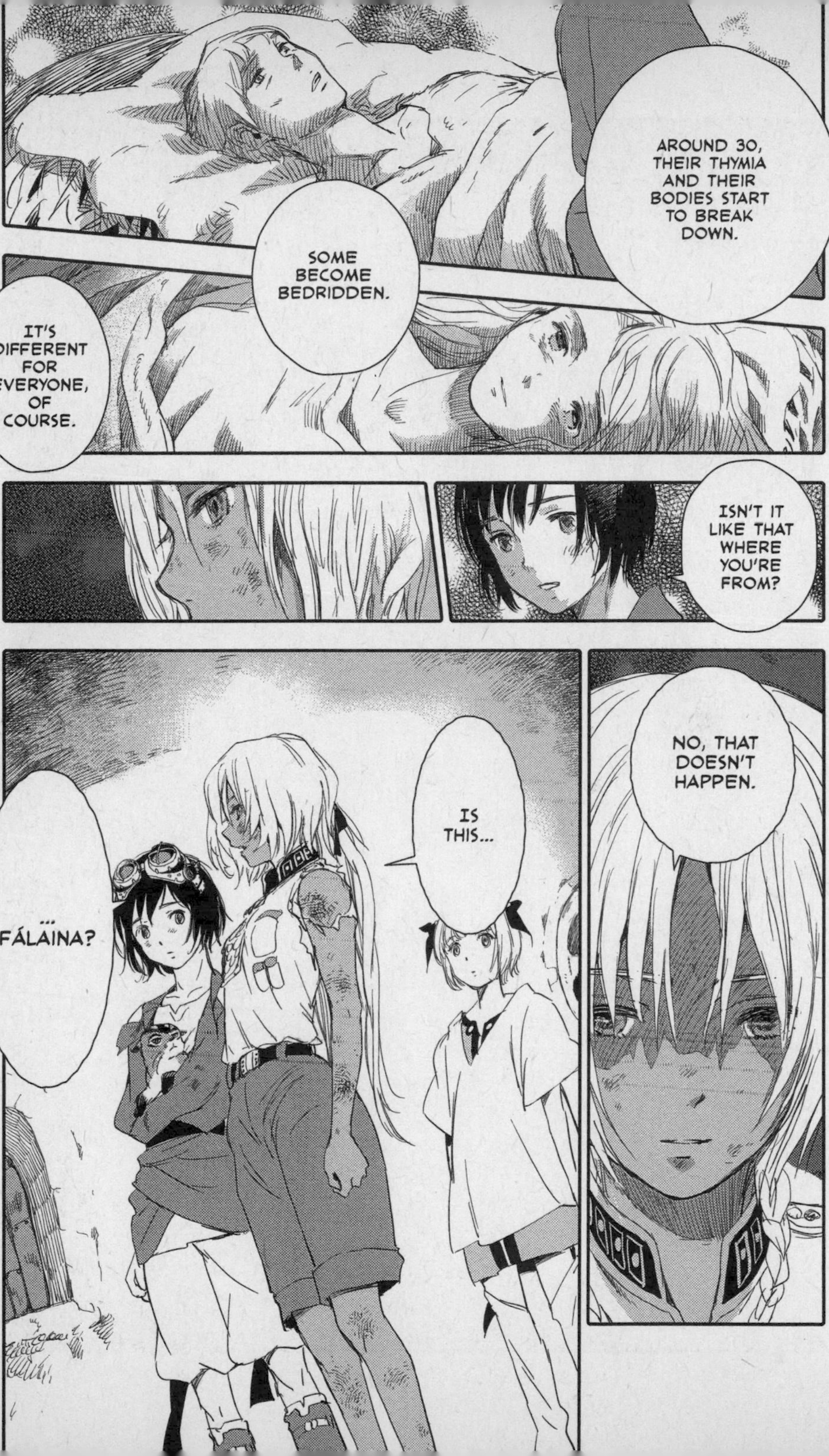
AROUND 30, THEIR THYMIA AND THEIR BODIES START TO BREAK DOWN.
SOME BECOME BEDRIDDEN.
IT'S DIFFERENT FOR EVERYONE, OF COURSE.
ISN'T IT LIKE THAT WHERE YOU'RE FROM?
NO, THAT DOESN'T HAPPEN.
IS THIS...
...FÁLAINA?

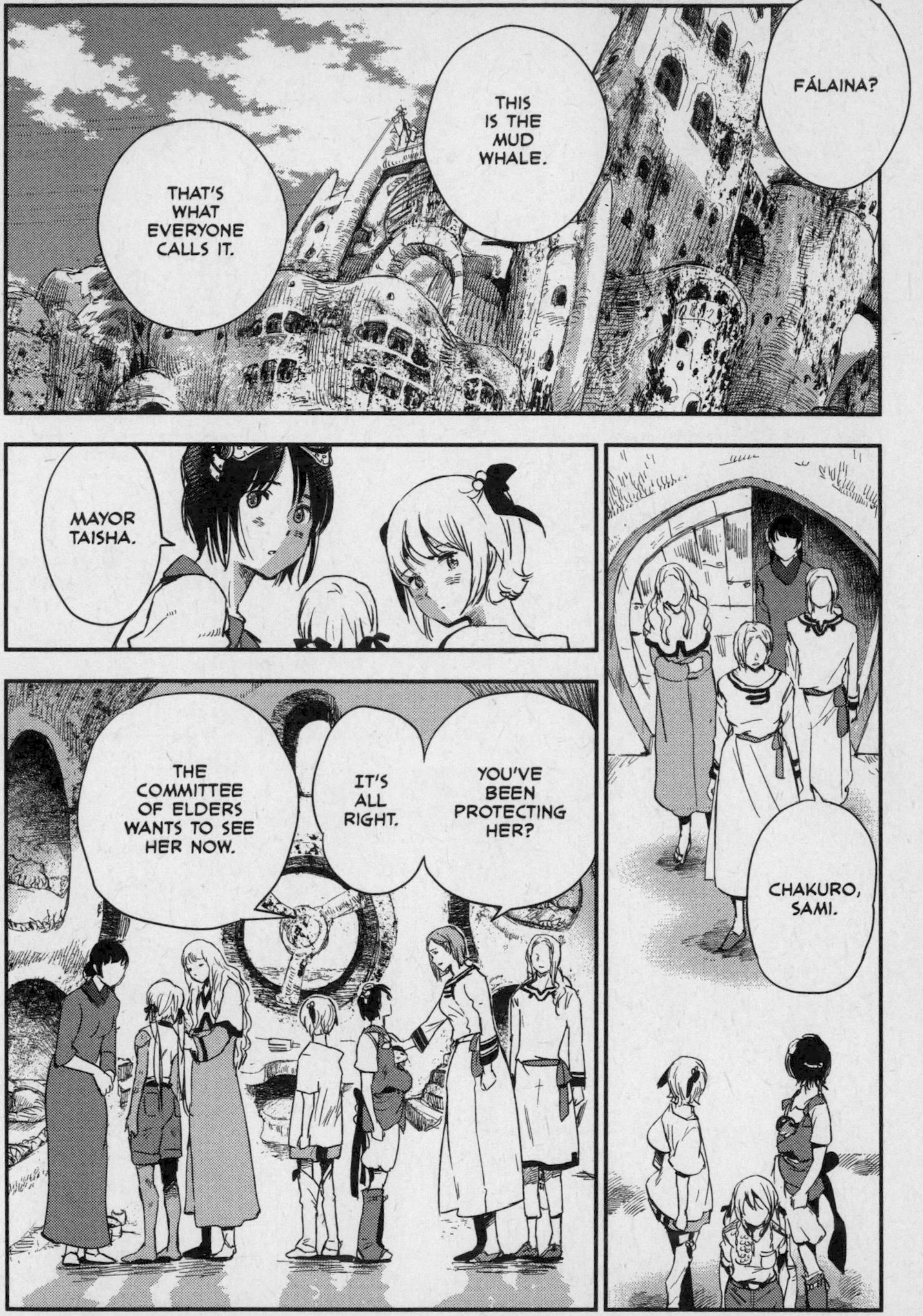
FÁLAINA?
THIS IS THE MUD WHALE.
THAT'S WHAT EVERYONE CALLS IT.
CHAKURO, SAMI.
MAYOR TAISHA.
YOU'VE BEEN PROTECTING HER?
IT'S ALL RIGHT.
THE COMMITTEE OF ELDERS WANTS TO SEE HER NOW.

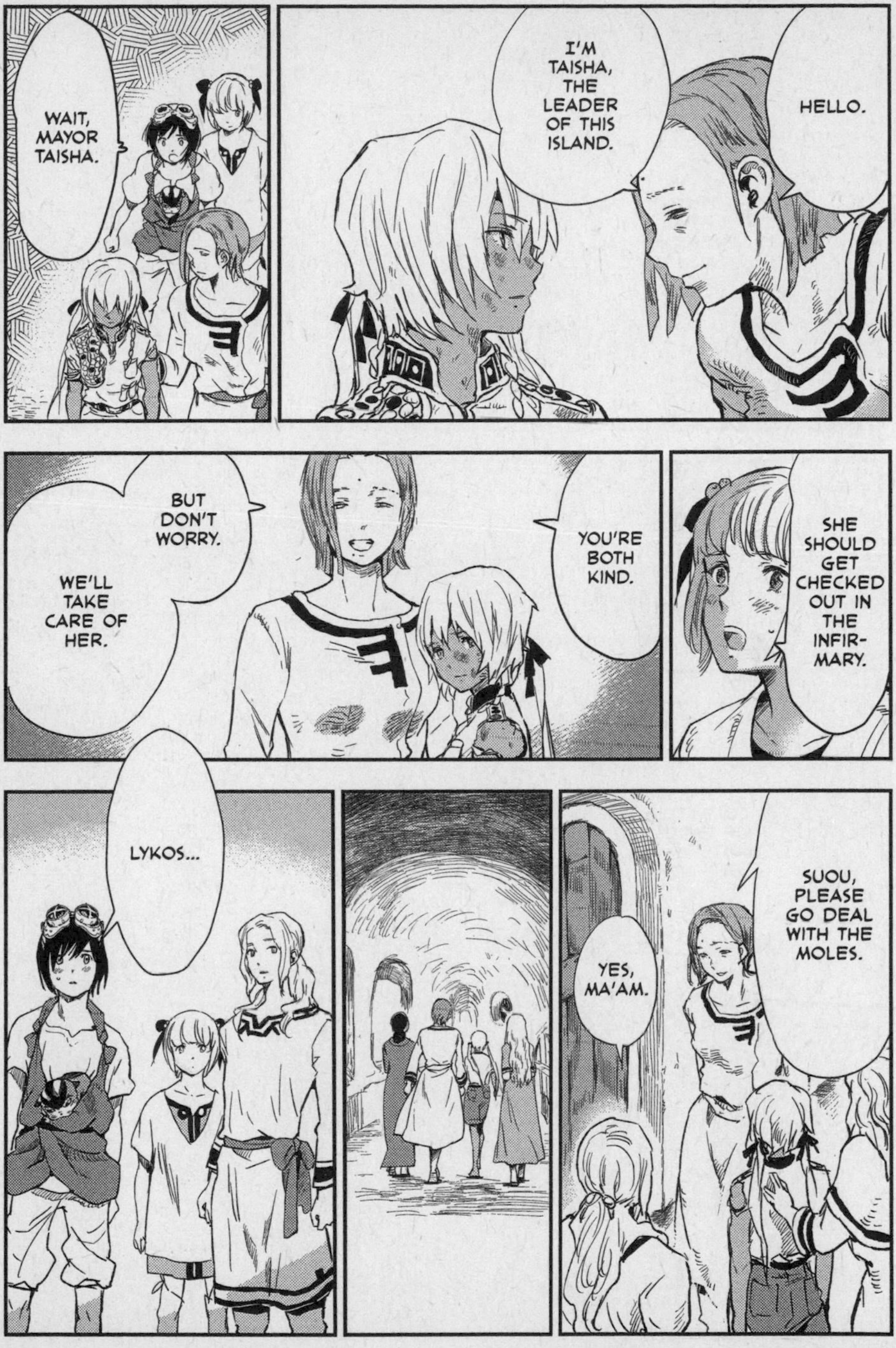
HELLO.
I'M TAISHA, THE LEADER OF THIS ISLAND.
WAIT, MAYOR TAISHA.
SHE SHOULD GET CHECKED OUT IN THE INFIRMARY.
YOU'RE BOTH KIND.
BUT DON'T WORRY.
WE'LL TAKE CARE OF HER.
SUOU, PLEASE GO DEAL WITH THE MOLES.
YES, MA'AM.
LYKOS...

SUOU!
GLOM
DID YOU SEE? THAT'S THE GIRL WHO WAS ON THE ISLAND.
ISN'T SHE CUTE? DO YOU THINK I COULD BE HER FRIEND?
YES...
THAT WOULD BE NICE.
IT'S JUST THE TIMING IS A LITTLE...
WHAT'S UP WITH THE MOLES?
BECAUSE OF THE RAINBOW...
...OUNI AND THE OTHERS BEING HELD IN THE BELLY...
...ARE BEING PARDONED.

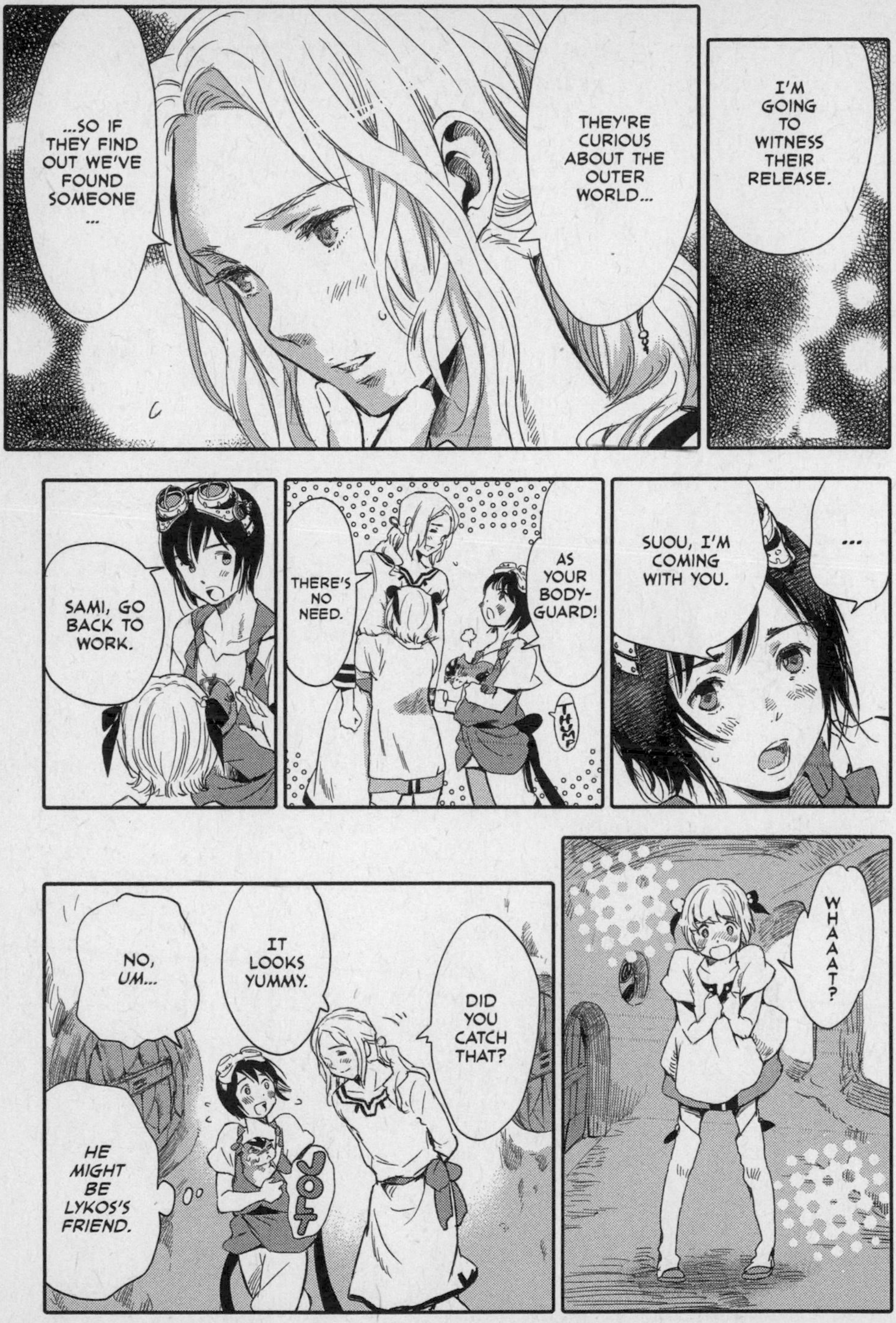
I'M GOING TO WITNESS THEIR RELEASE.
THEY'RE CURIOUS ABOUT THE OUTER WORLD...
...SO IF THEY FIND OUT WE'VE FOUND SOMEONE ...
...
SUOU, I'M COMING WITH YOU.
AS YOUR BODY-GUARD!
THUMP
THERE'S NO NEED.
SAMI, GO BACK TO WORK.
WHAAAT?
DID YOU CATCH THAT?
IT LOOKS YUMMY.
NO, UM...
VOLT
HE MIGHT BE LYKOS'S FRIEND.

On the Mud Whale, if you break the rules or commit a crime...
...you're confined to an area in the depths of the vessel called the Belly.
THE BELLY
For some reason, thymia doesn't work down there.
For the short-lived Marked...
...it's a harsh punishment to be confined, powerless, in the Belly for any length of time.
However, there is a group...
...that repeatedly flouts the rules and so is often imprisoned.

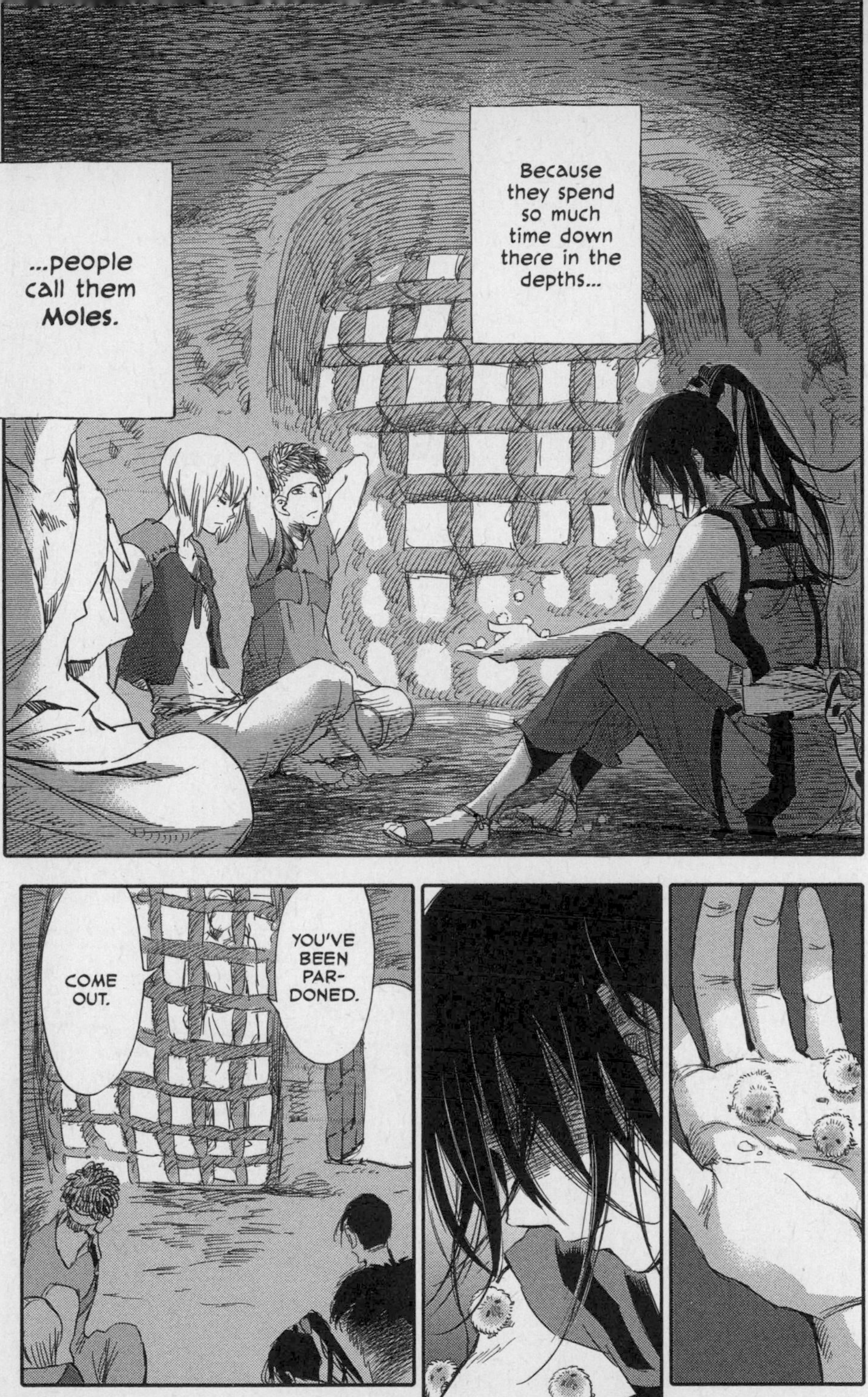
Because they spend so much time down there in the depths...
...people call them Moles.
YOU'VE BEEN PAR-DONED.
COME OUT.

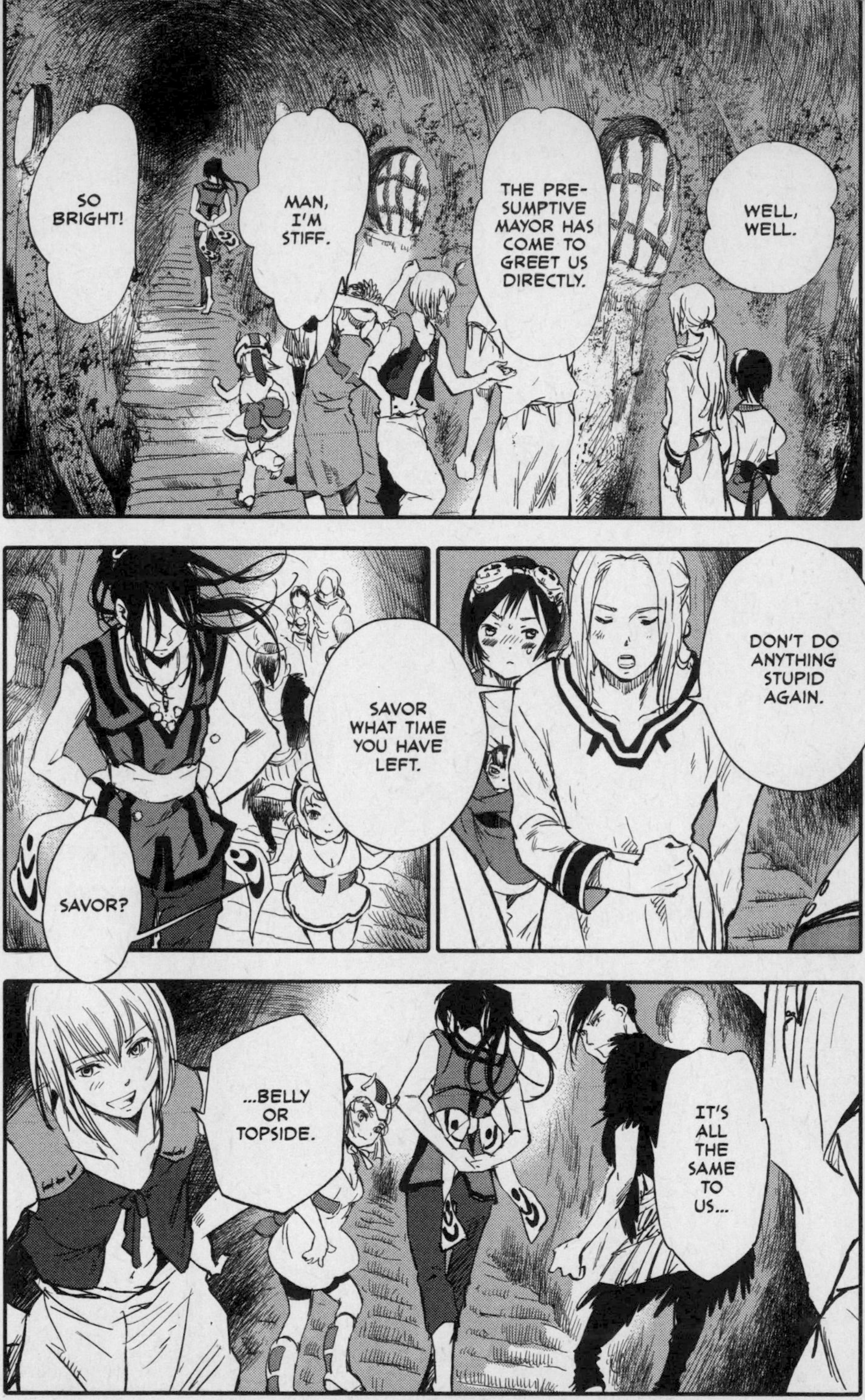
WELL, WELL.
THE PRESUMPTIVE MAYOR HAS COME TO GREET US DIRECTLY.
MAN, I'M STIFF.
SO BRIGHT!
DON'T DO ANYTHING STUPID AGAIN.
SAVOR WHAT TIME YOU HAVE LEFT.
SAVOR?
IT'S ALL THE SAME TO US...
...BELLY OR TOPSIDE.

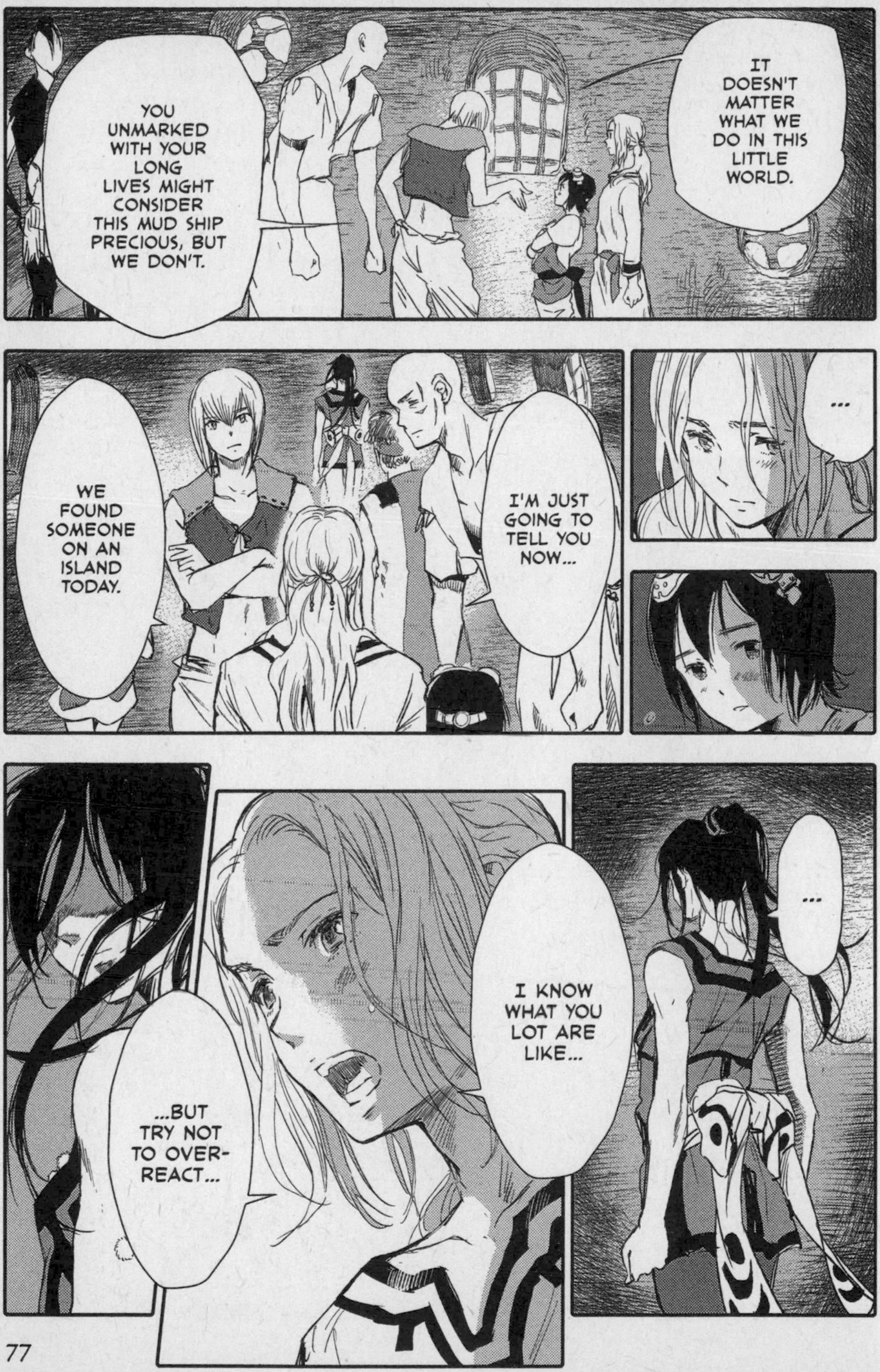
IT DOESN'T MATTER WHAT WE DO IN THIS LITTLE WORLD.
YOU UNMARKED WITH YOUR LONG LIVES MIGHT CONSIDER THIS MUD SHIP PRECIOUS, BUT WE DON'T.
...
I'M JUST GOING TO TELL YOU NOW...
WE FOUND SOMEONE ON AN ISLAND TODAY.
...
I KNOW WHAT YOU LOT ARE LIKE...
...BUT TRY NOT TO OVER-REACT...

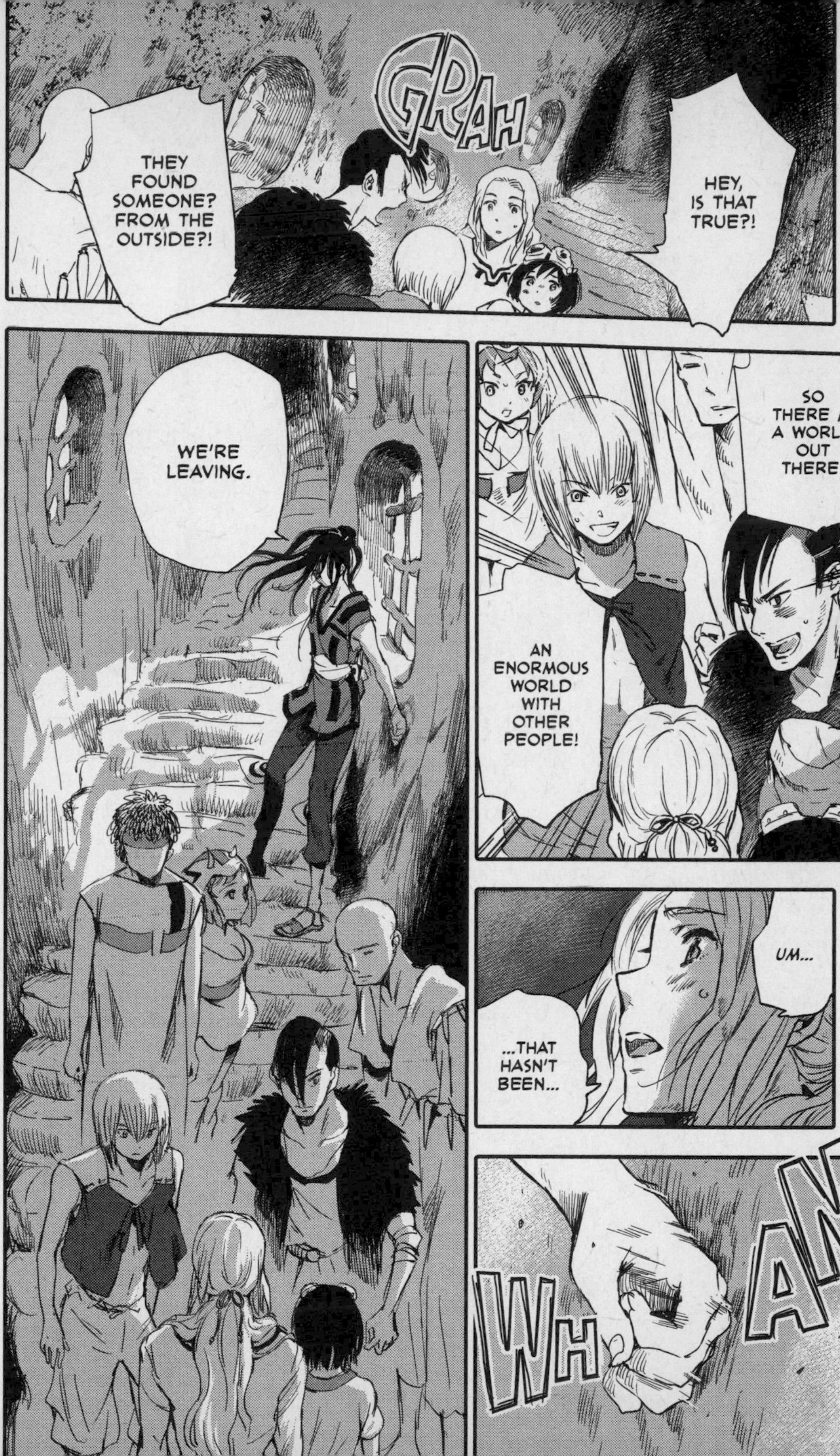
HEY, IS THAT TRUE?!
GRAH
THEY FOUND SOMEONE? FROM THE OUTSIDE?!
SO THERE *IS* A WORLD OUT THERE.
AN ENORMOUS WORLD WITH OTHER PEOPLE!
UM...
...THAT HASN'T BEEN...
WHAM
WE'RE LEAVING.

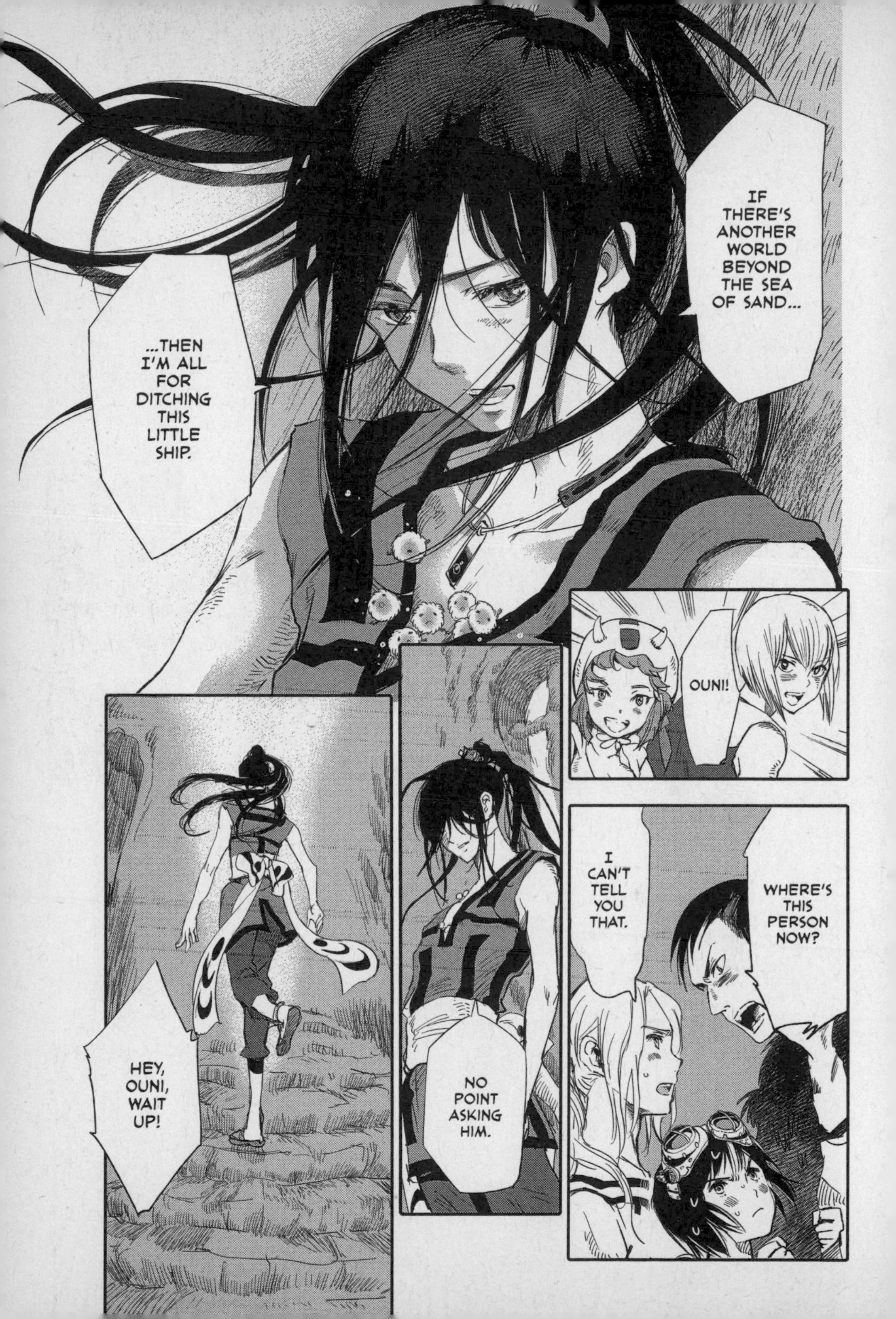
IF THERE'S ANOTHER WORLD BEYOND THE SEA OF SAND...
...THEN I'M ALL FOR DITCHING THIS LITTLE SHIP.
OUNI!
WHERE'S THIS PERSON NOW?
I CAN'T TELL YOU THAT.
NO POINT ASKING HIM.
HEY, OUNI, WAIT UP!

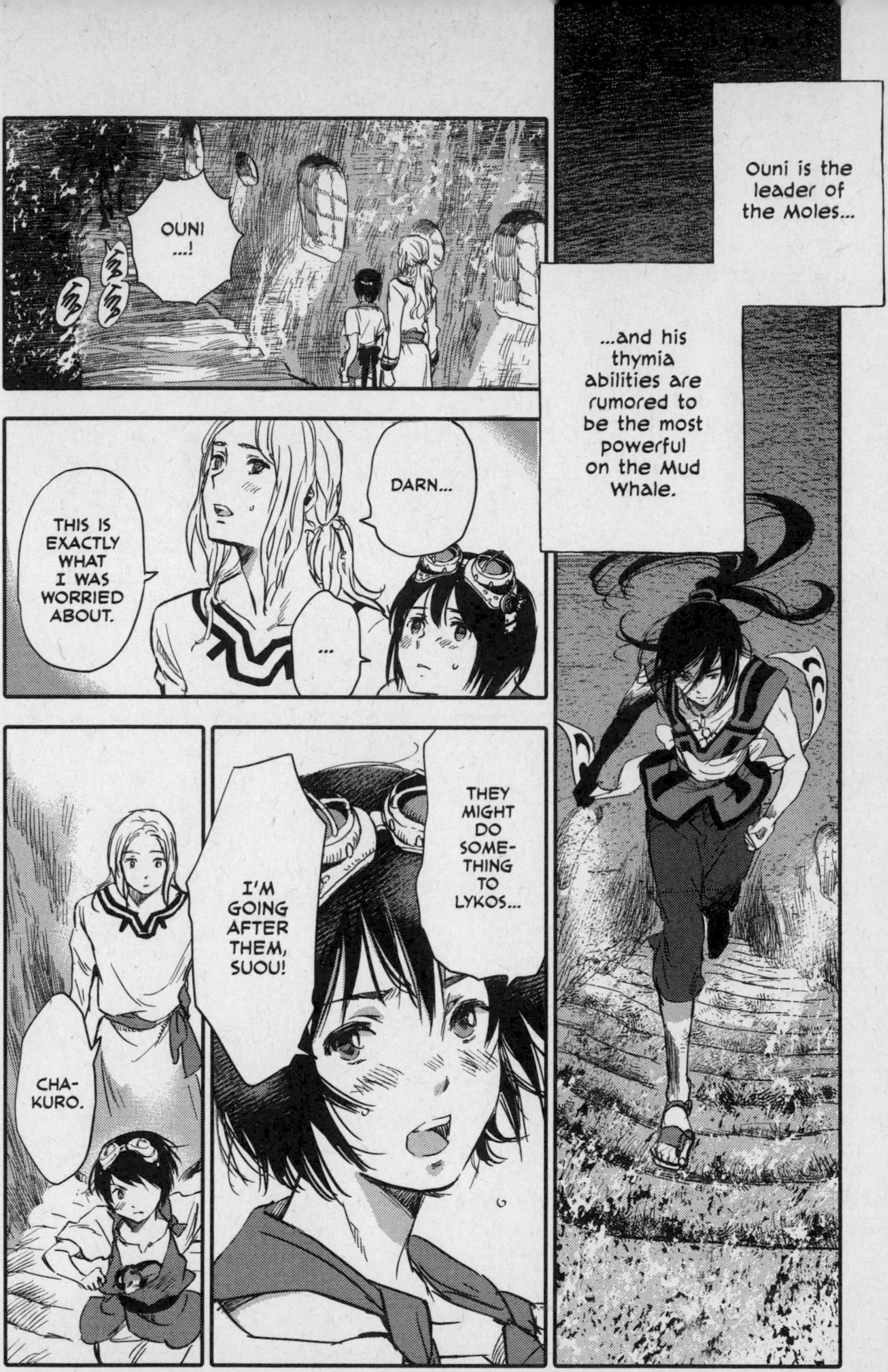
Ouni is the leader of the Moles...
...and his thymia abilities are rumored to be the most powerful on the Mud Whale.
OUNI ...!
DARN...
THIS IS EXACTLY WHAT I WAS WORRIED ABOUT.
...
THEY MIGHT DO SOME-THING TO LYKOS...
I'M GOING AFTER THEM, SUOU!
CHA-KURO.

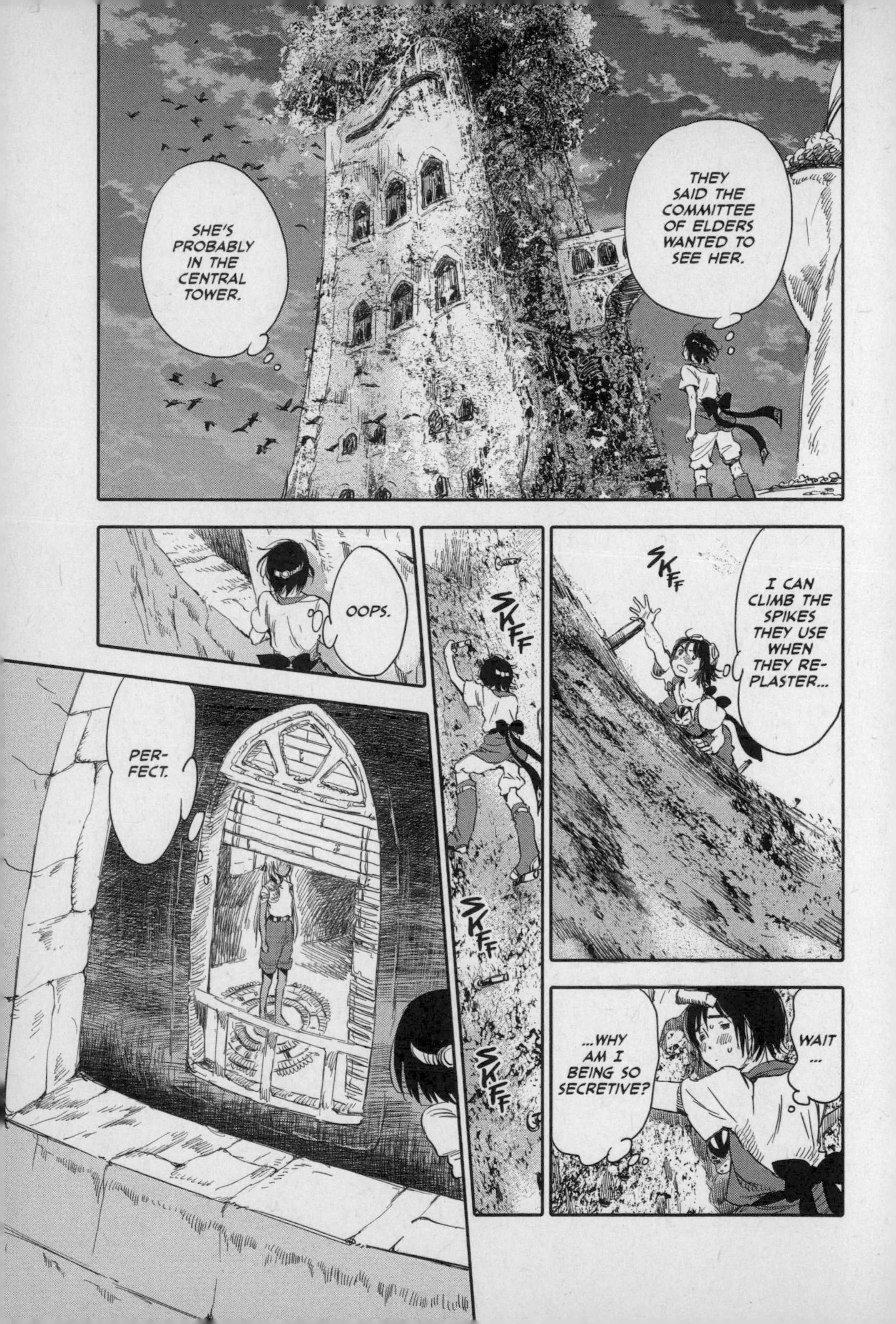
THEY SAID THE COMMITTEE OF ELDERS WANTED TO SEE HER.
SHE'S PROBABLY IN THE CENTRAL TOWER.
SKFF
I CAN CLIMB THE SPIKES THEY USE WHEN THEY RE-PLASTER...
WAIT ...
...WHY AM I BEING SO SECRETIVE?
SKFF
SKFF
SKFF
OOPS.
PER-FECT.

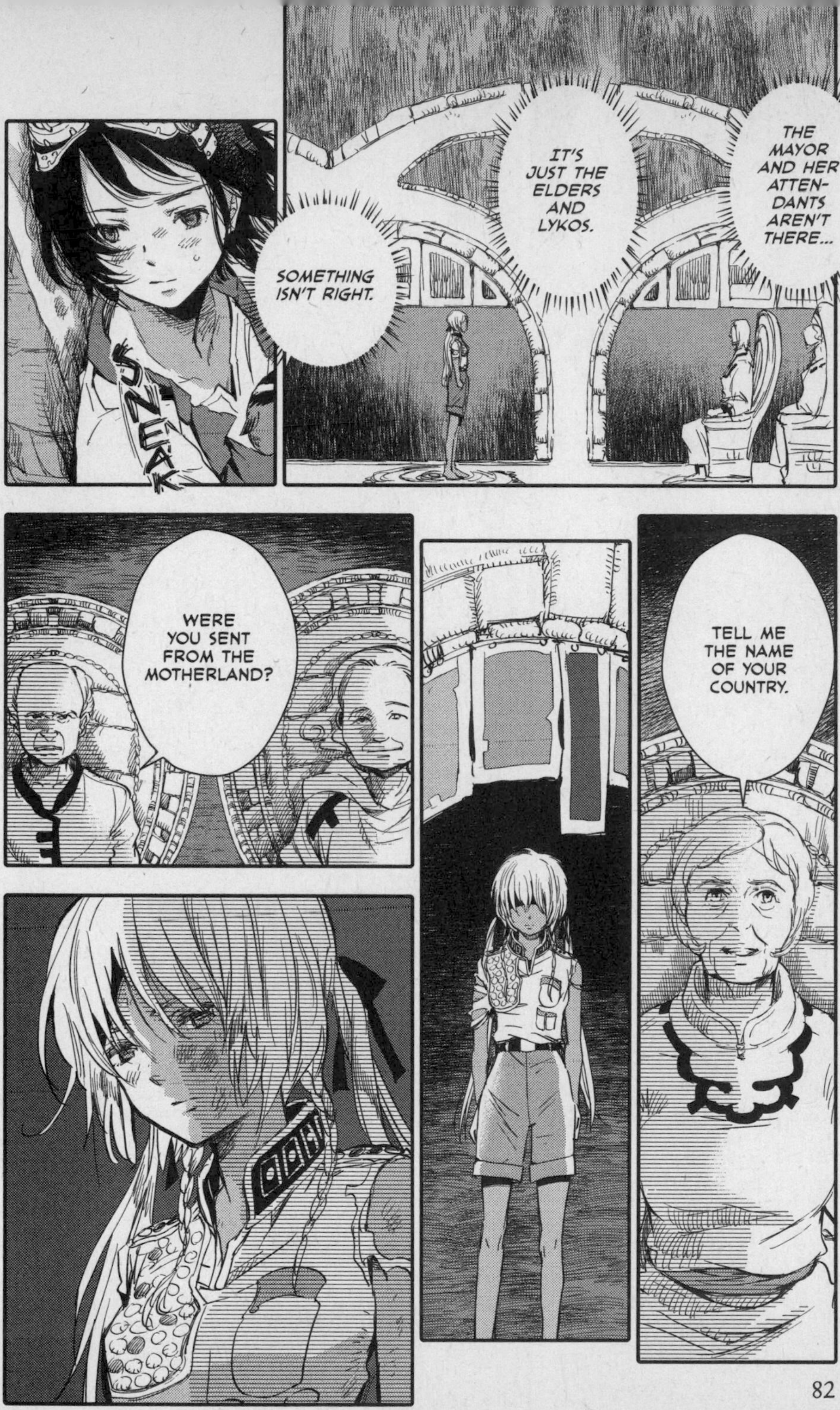
THE MAYOR AND HER ATTEN-DANTS AREN'T THERE...
IT'S JUST THE ELDERS AND LYKOS.
SOMETHING ISN'T RIGHT.
SNEAK
TELL ME THE NAME OF YOUR COUNTRY.
WERE YOU SENT FROM THE MOTHERLAND?

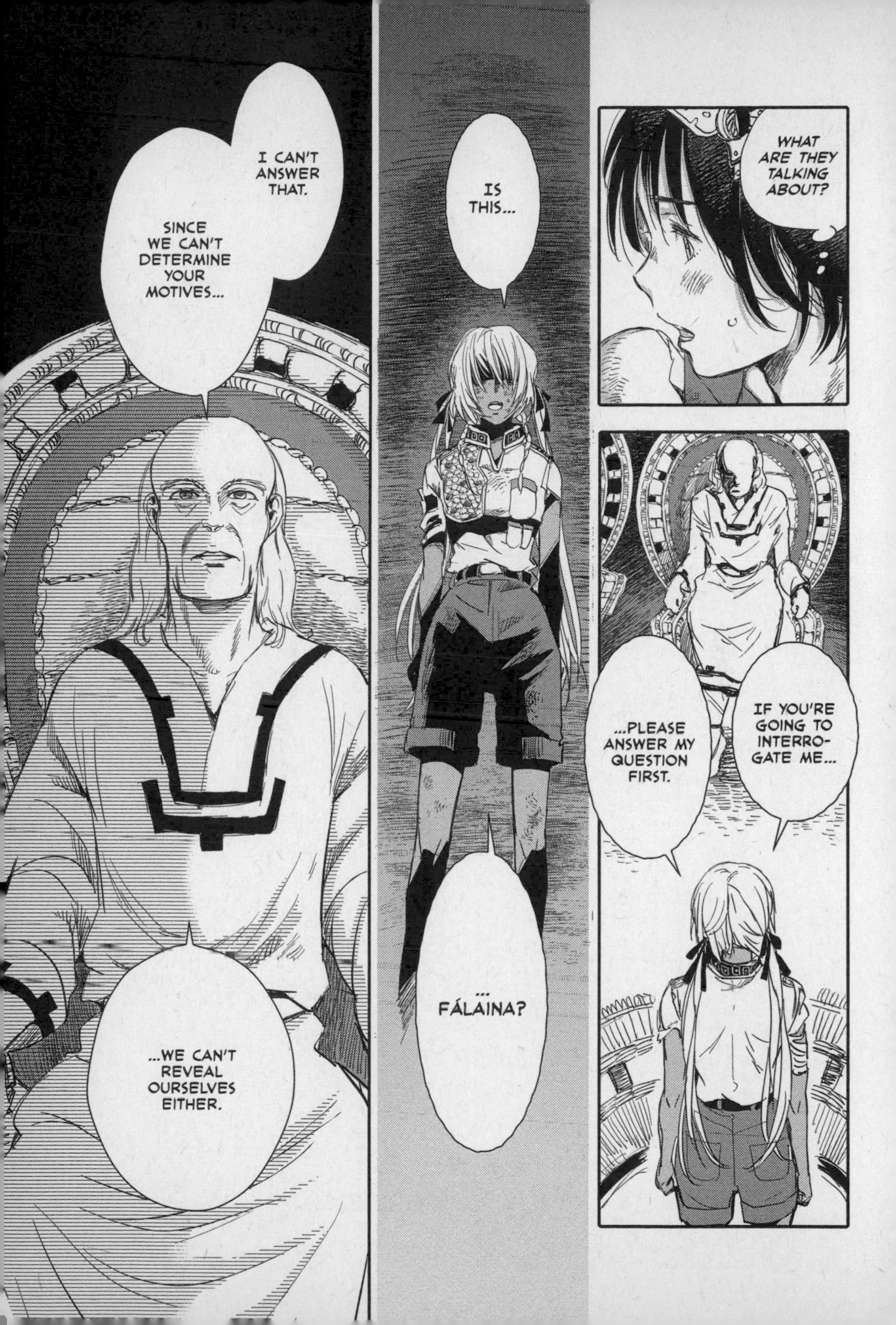
WHAT ARE THEY TALKING ABOUT?
IF YOU'RE GOING TO INTERRO-GATE ME...
...PLEASE ANSWER MY QUESTION FIRST.
IS THIS...
...FÁLAINA?
I CAN'T ANSWER THAT.
SINCE WE CAN'T DETERMINE YOUR MOTIVES...
...WE CAN'T REVEAL OURSELVES EITHER.

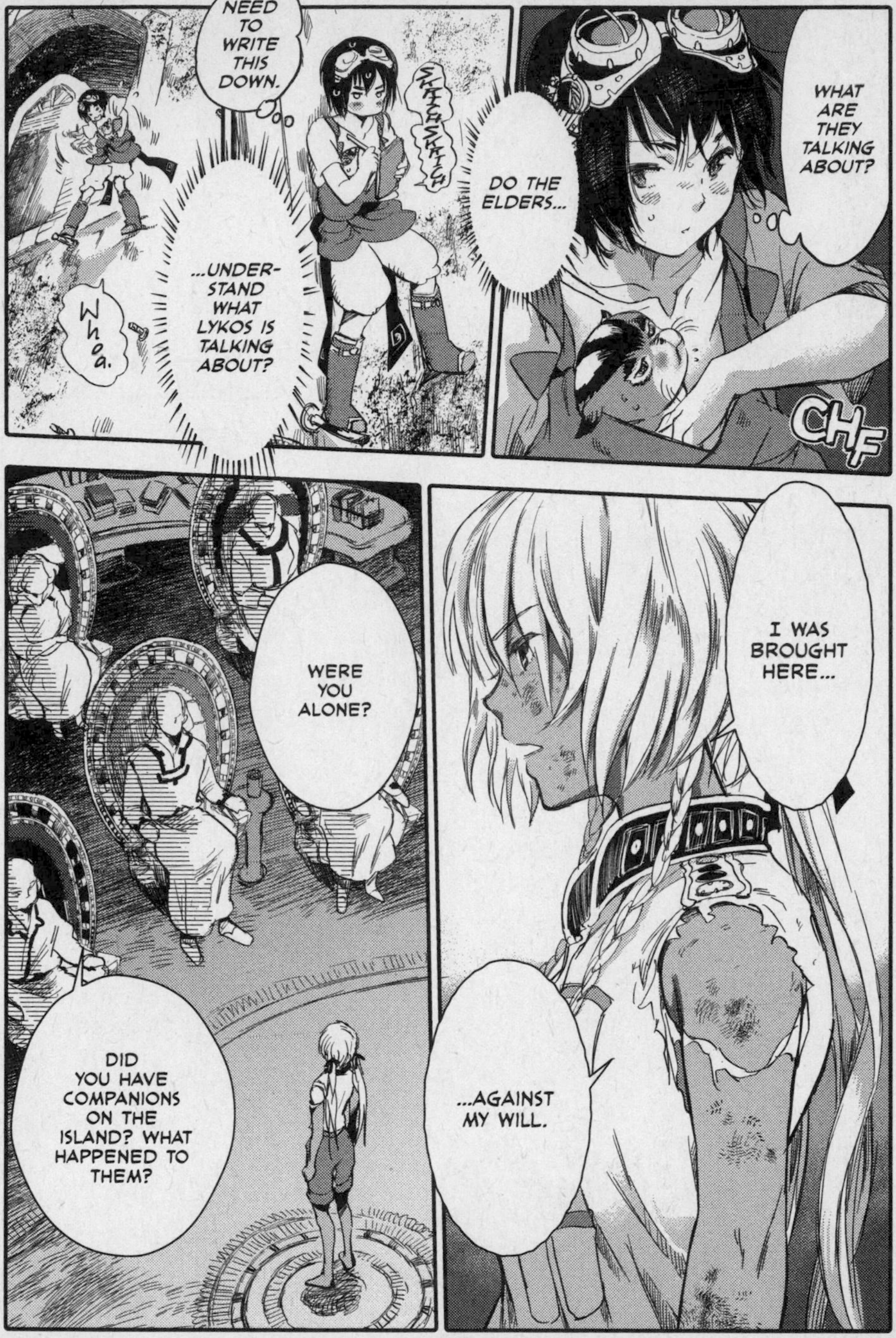
WHAT ARE THEY TALKING ABOUT?
CHF
DO THE ELDERS...
...UNDER-STAND WHAT LYKOS IS TALKING ABOUT?
NEED TO WRITE THIS DOWN.
SKRITCH SKRITCH
Whoa.
I WAS BROUGHT HERE...
...AGAINST MY WILL.
WERE YOU ALONE?
DID YOU HAVE COMPANIONS ON THE ISLAND? WHAT HAPPENED TO THEM?

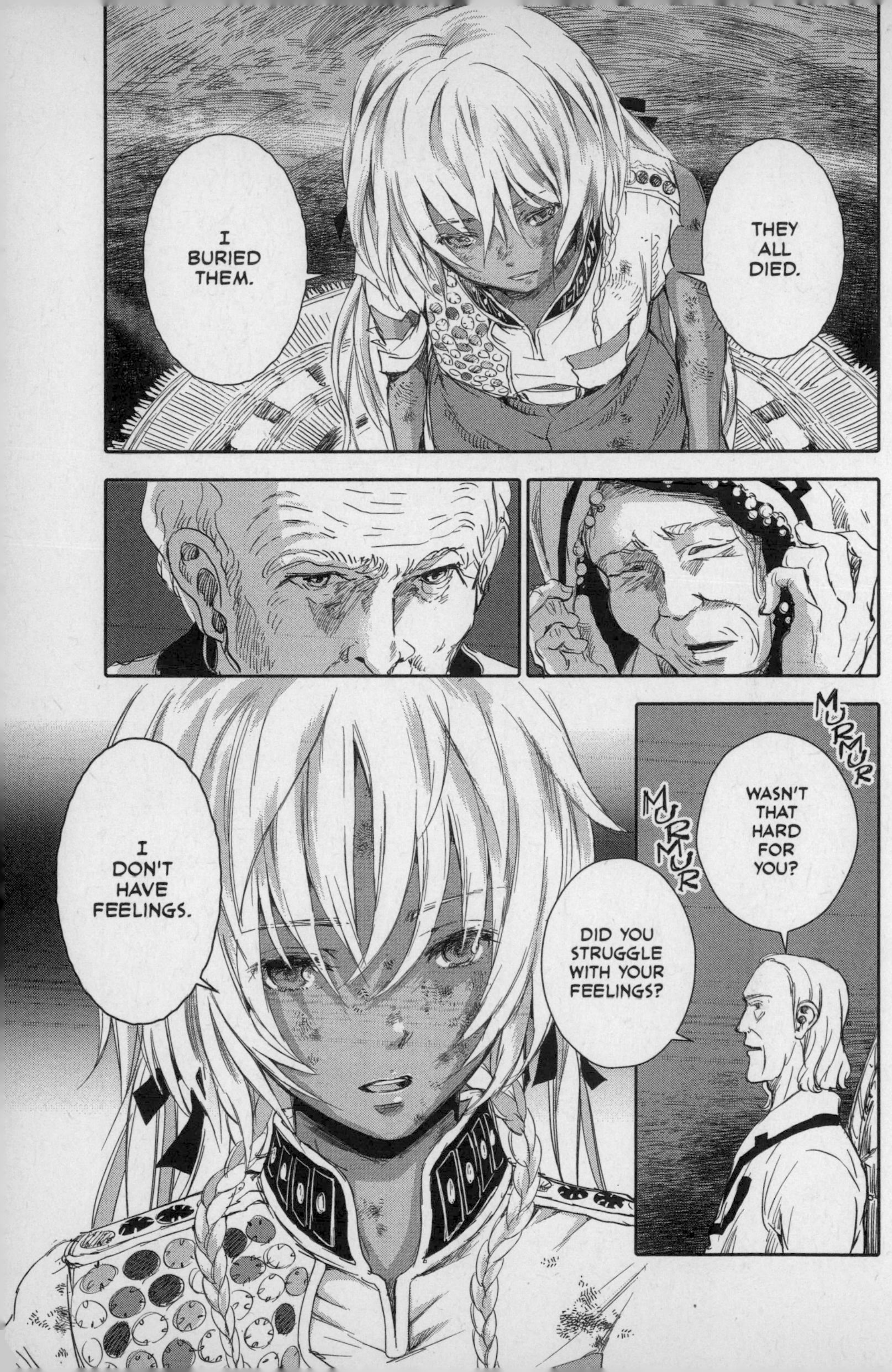
THEY ALL DIED.
I BURIED THEM.
MURMUR
MURMUR
WASN'T THAT HARD FOR YOU?
DID YOU STRUGGLE WITH YOUR FEELINGS?
I DON'T HAVE FEELINGS.

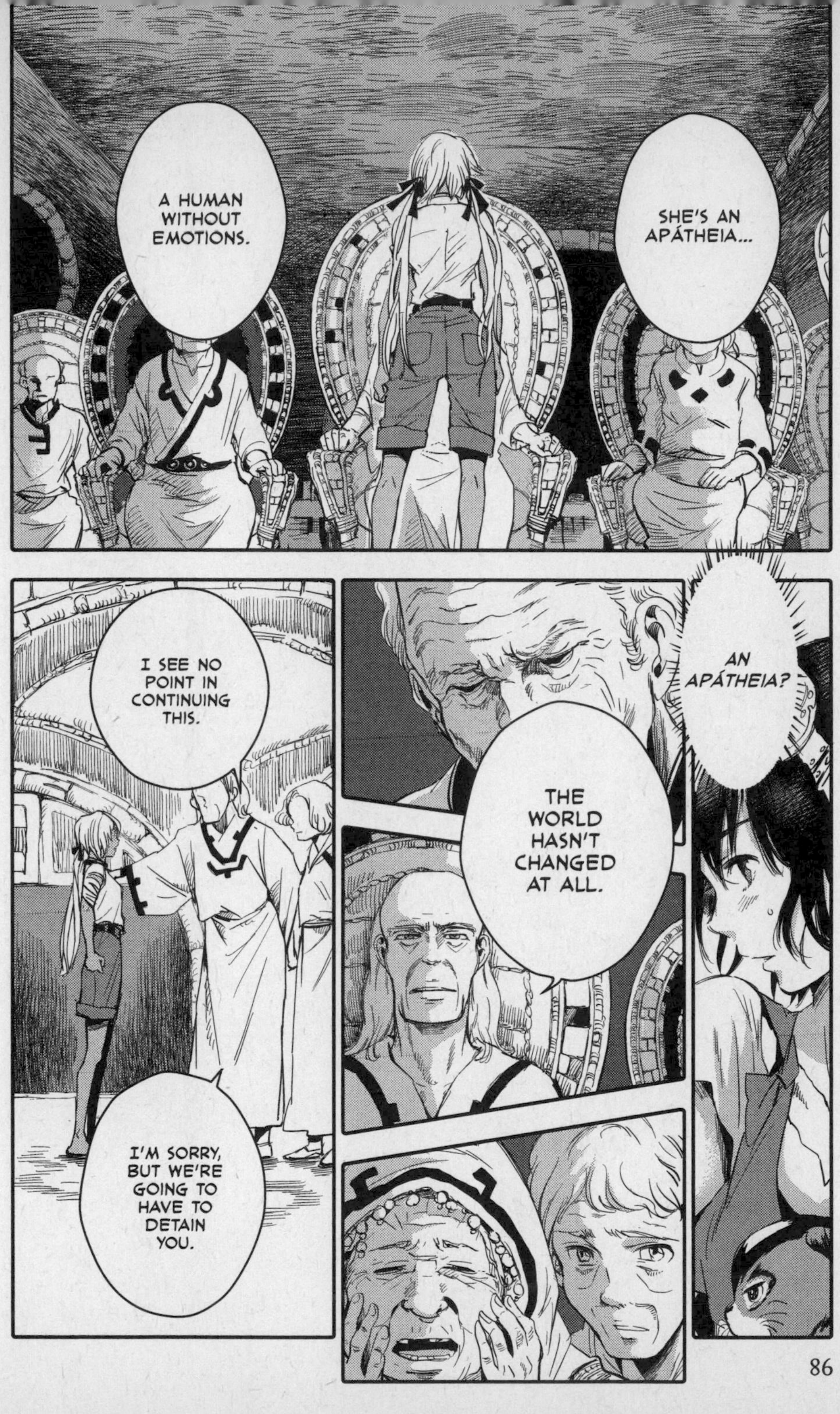

SHE'S AN APÁTHEIA...
A HUMAN WITHOUT EMOTIONS.
AN APÁTHEIA?
THE WORLD HASN'T CHANGED AT ALL.
I SEE NO POINT IN CONTINUING THIS.
I'M SORRY, BUT WE'RE GOING TO HAVE TO DETAIN YOU.

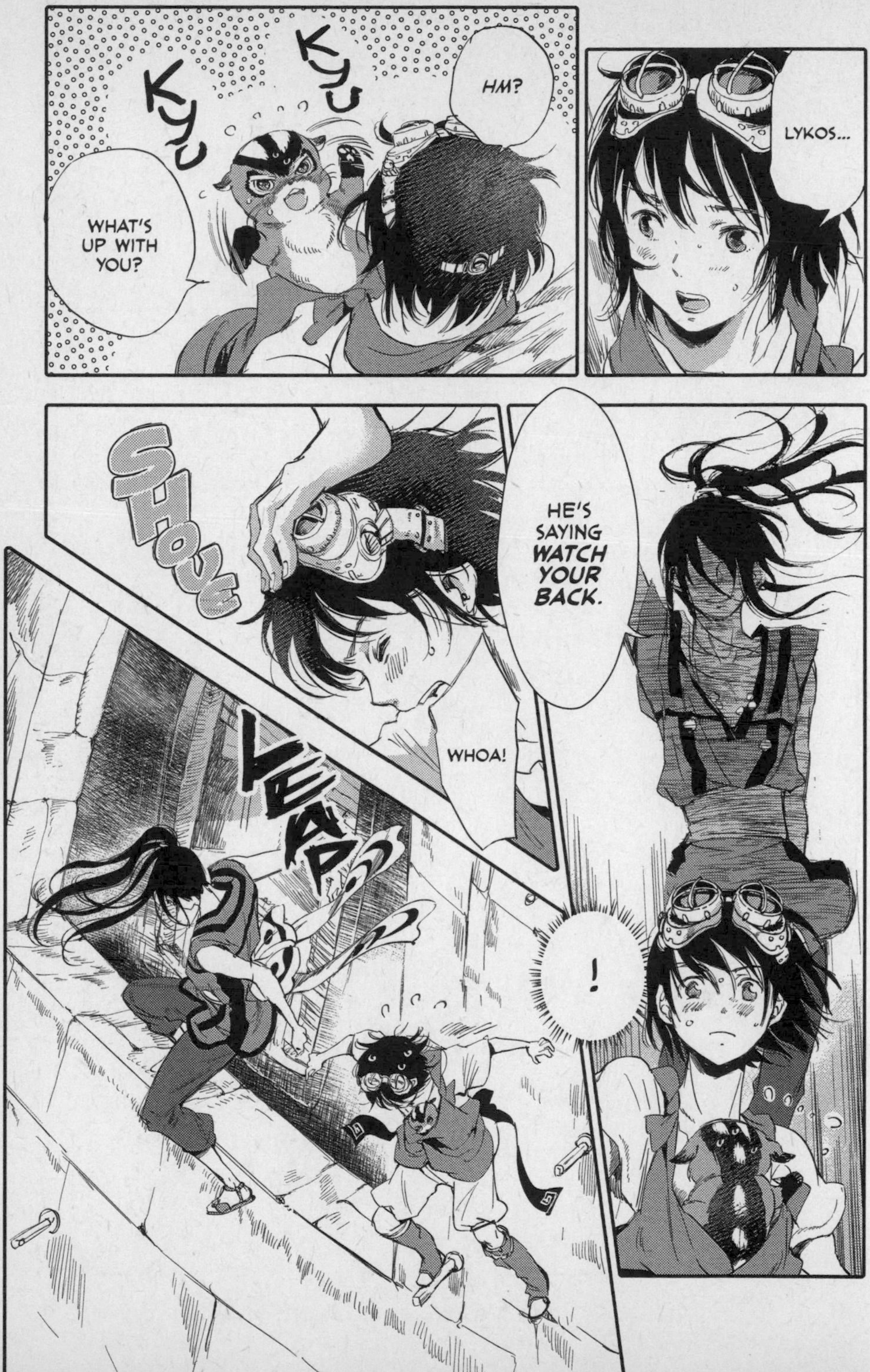
LYKOS...
HM?
KYU KYU
KYU
WHAT'S UP WITH YOU?
HE'S SAYING WATCH YOUR BACK.
!
SHOVE
WHOA!
LEAP

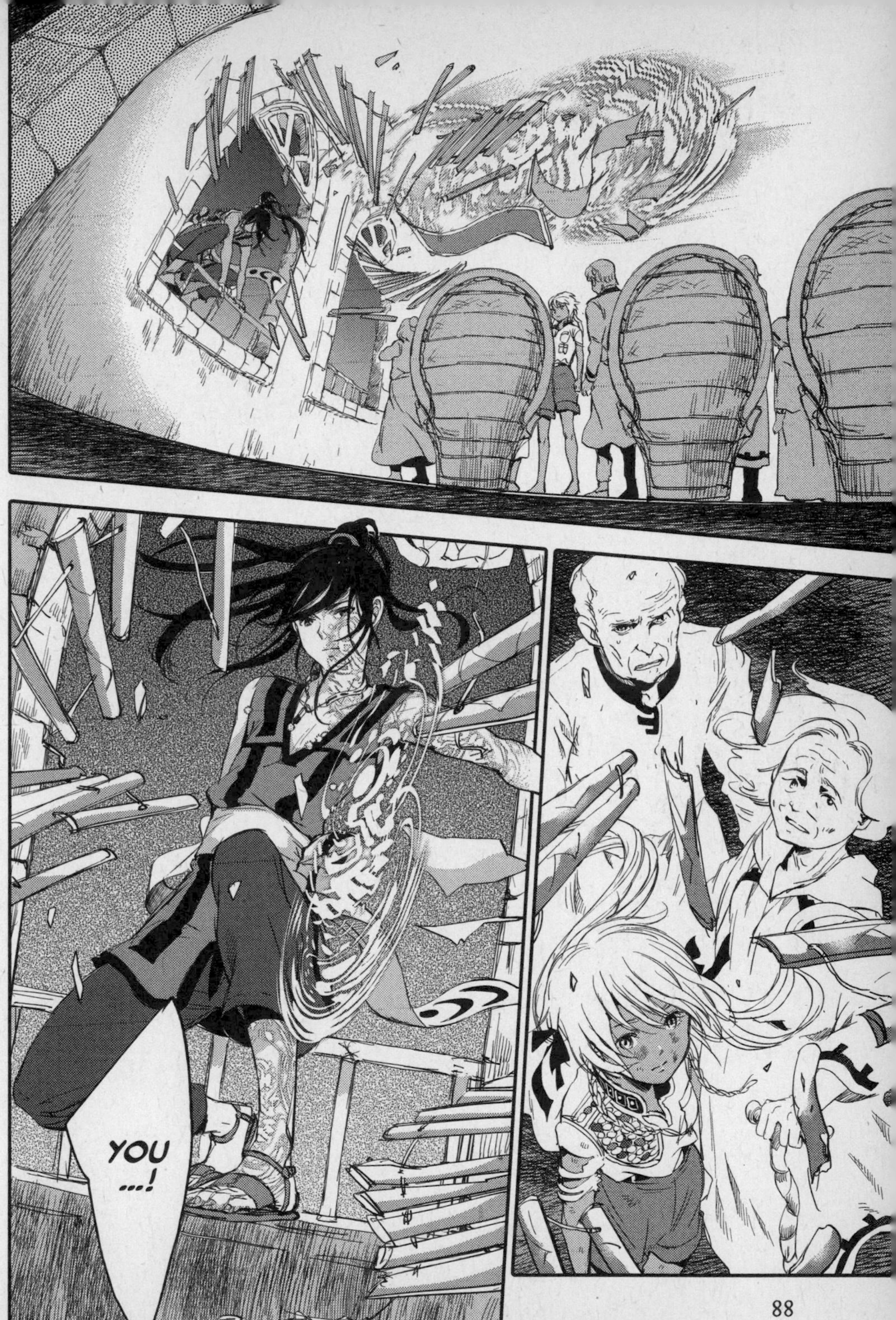
YOU ...!

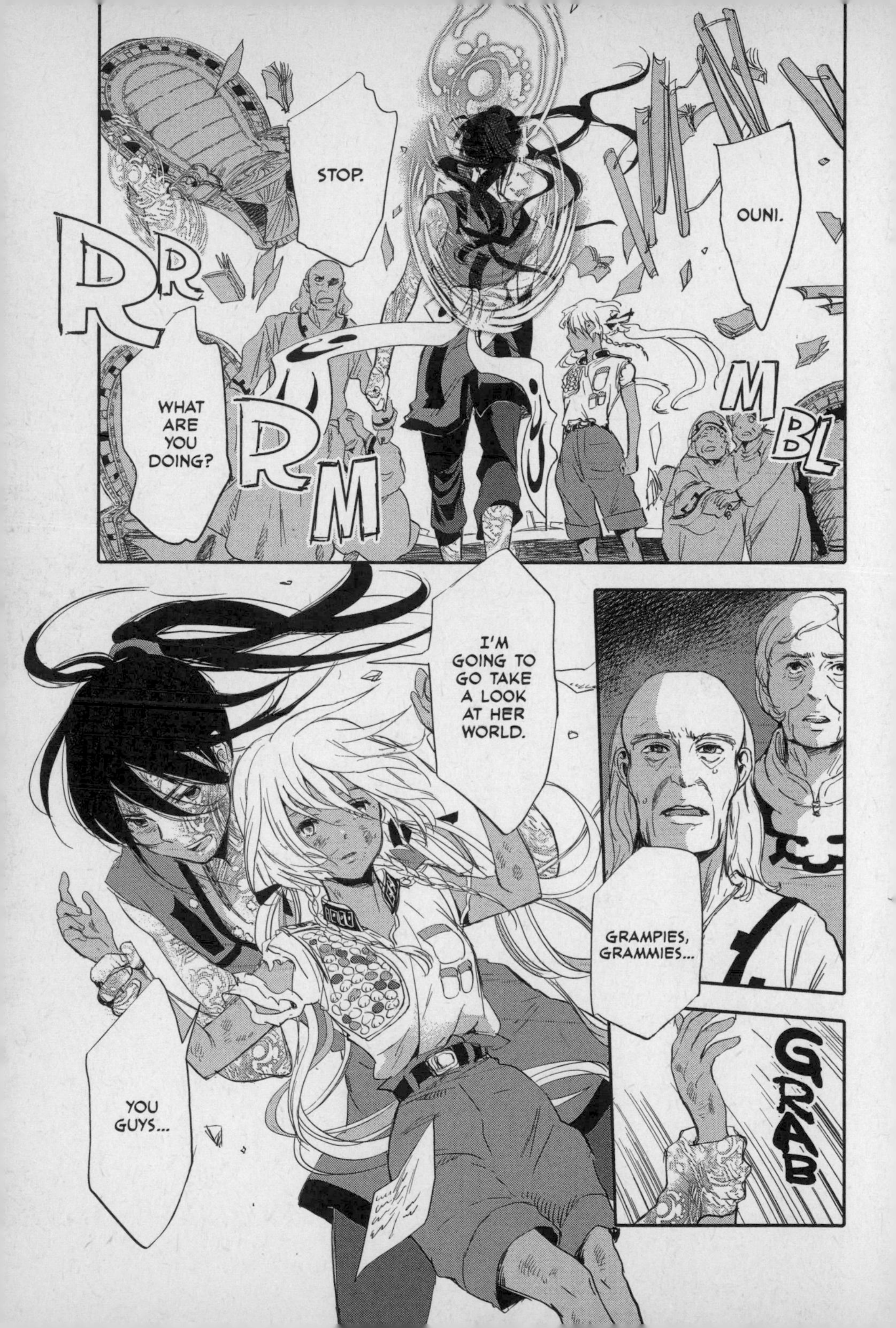
OUNI.
STOP.
MBL
DRRRM
WHAT ARE YOU DOING?
GRAMPIES, GRAMMIES...
GRAB
I'M GOING TO GO TAKE A LOOK AT HER WORLD.
YOU GUYS...

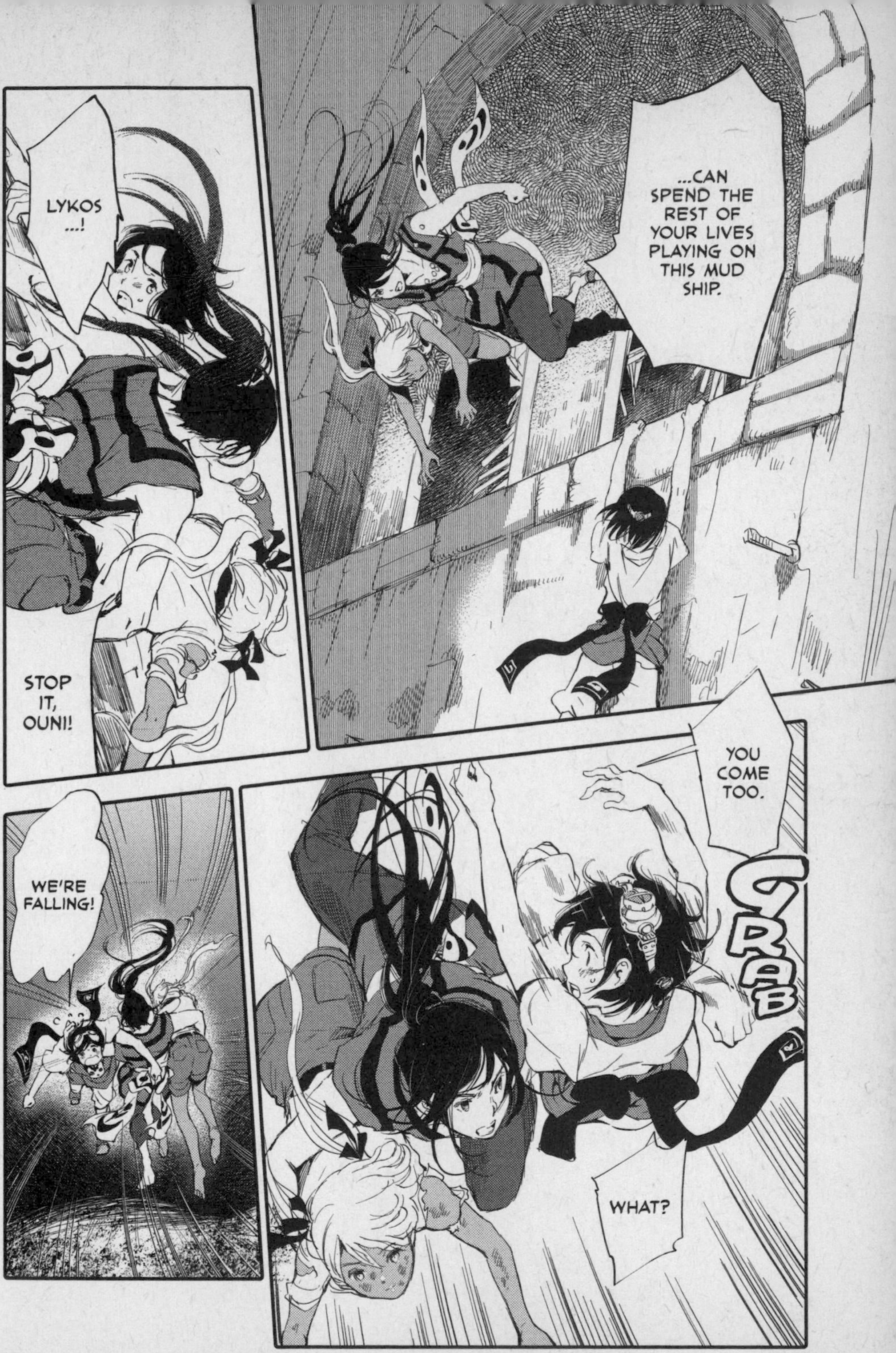
...CAN SPEND THE REST OF YOUR LIVES PLAYING ON THIS MUD SHIP.
LYKOS ...!
STOP IT, OUNI!
YOU COME TOO.
GRAB
WHAT?
WE'RE FALLING!

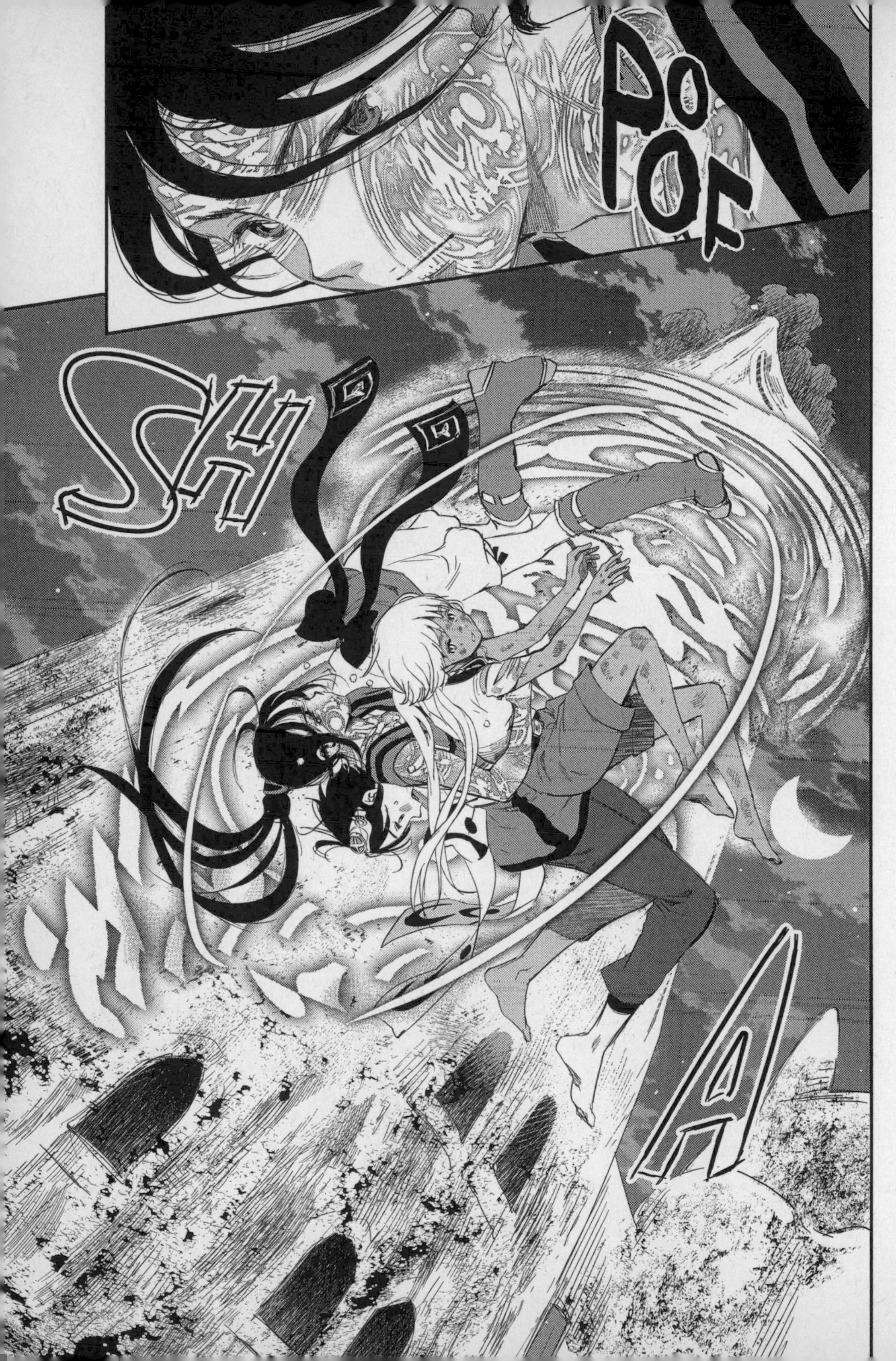
POF
SHH
AA

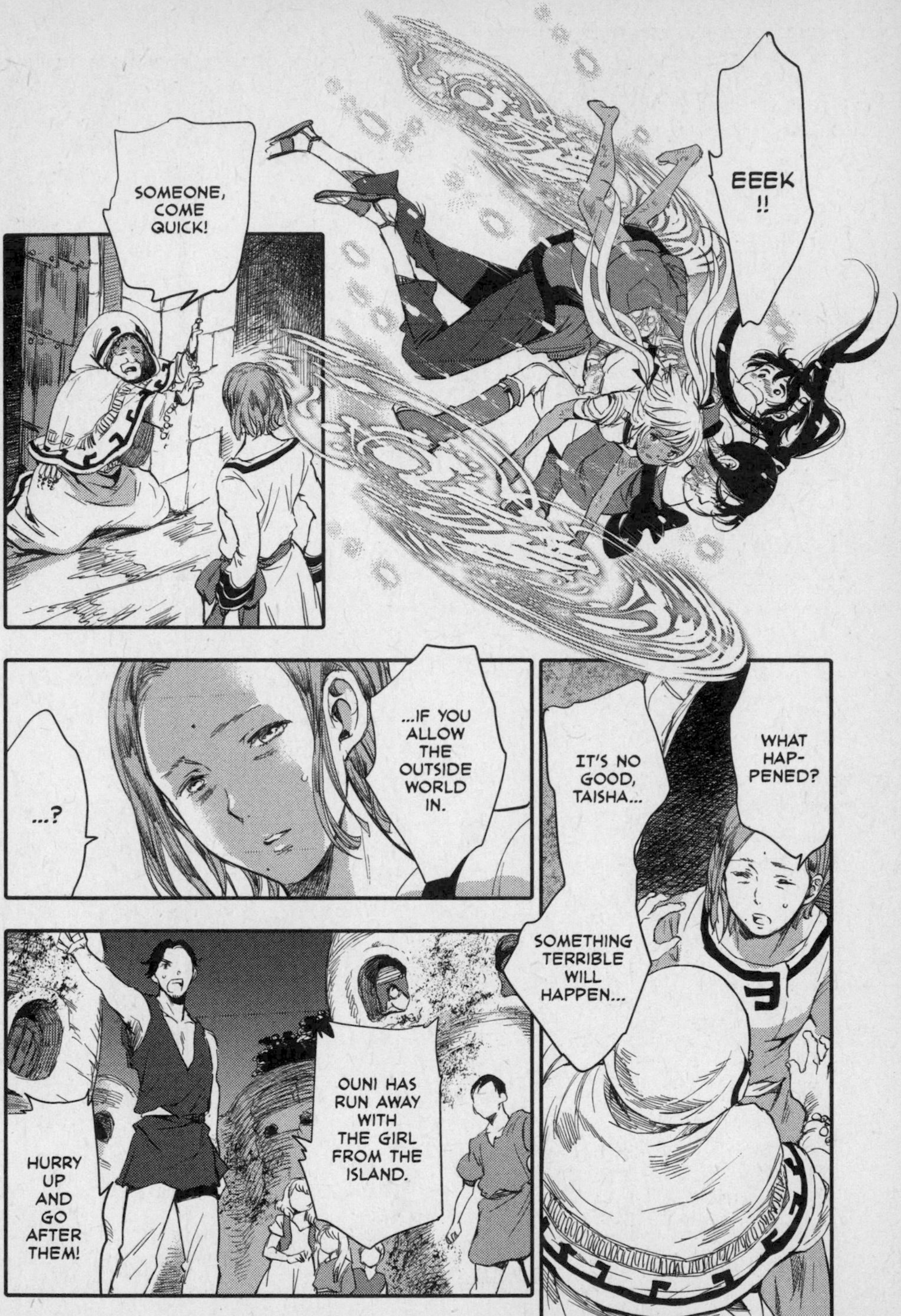
EEEK !!
SOMEONE, COME QUICK!
WHAT HAP-PENED?
IT'S NO GOOD, TAISHA...
SOMETHING TERRIBLE WILL HAPPEN...
...IF YOU ALLOW THE OUTSIDE WORLD IN.
...?
OUNI HAS RUN AWAY WITH THE GIRL FROM THE ISLAND.
HURRY UP AND GO AFTER THEM!

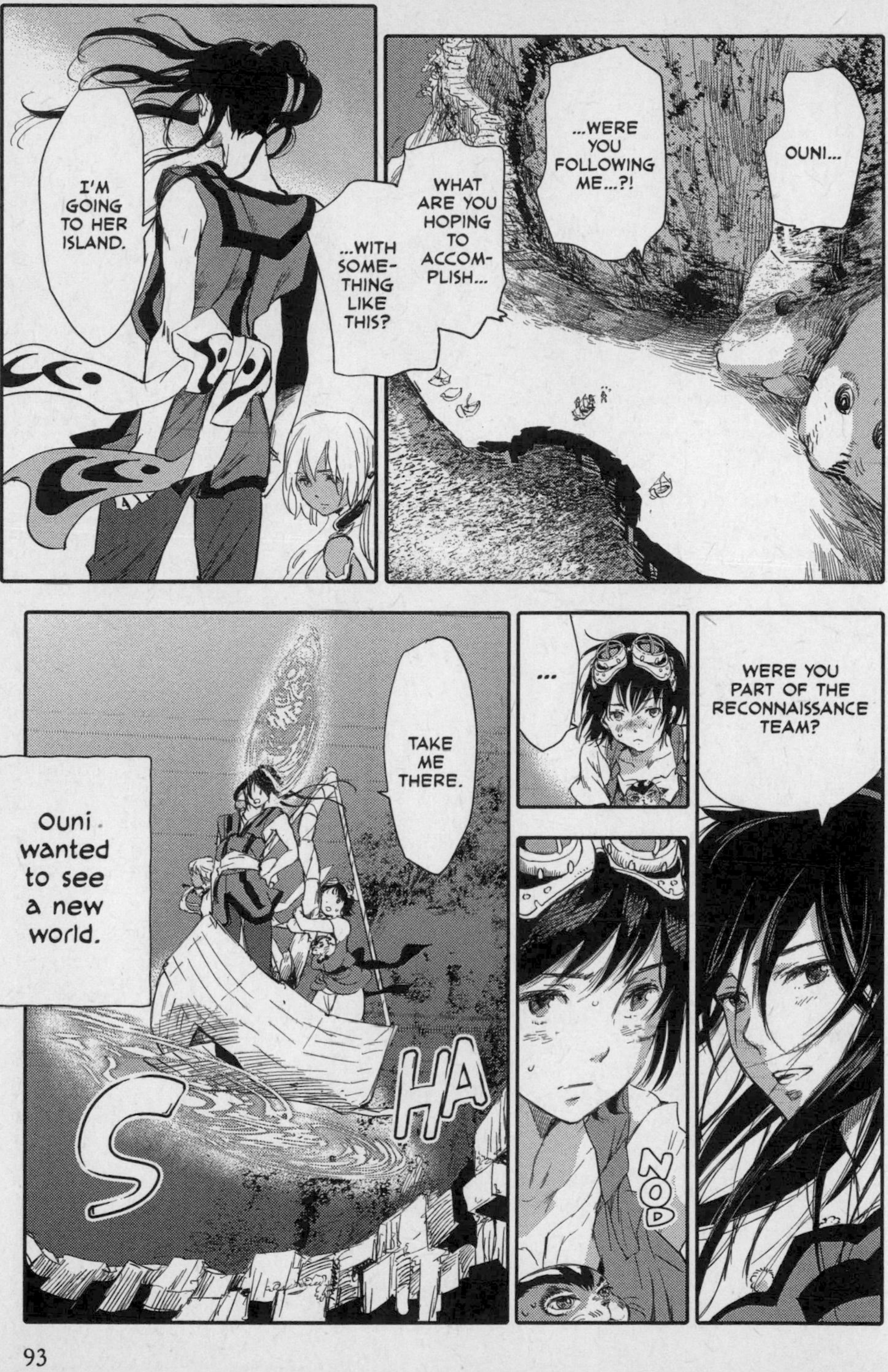
OUNI...
...WERE YOU FOLLOWING ME...?!
WHAT ARE YOU HOPING TO ACCOMPLISH...
...WITH SOMETHING LIKE THIS?
I'M GOING TO HER ISLAND.
WERE YOU PART OF THE RECONNAISSANCE TEAM?
...
NOD
TAKE ME THERE.
Ouni wanted to see a new world.
SHA

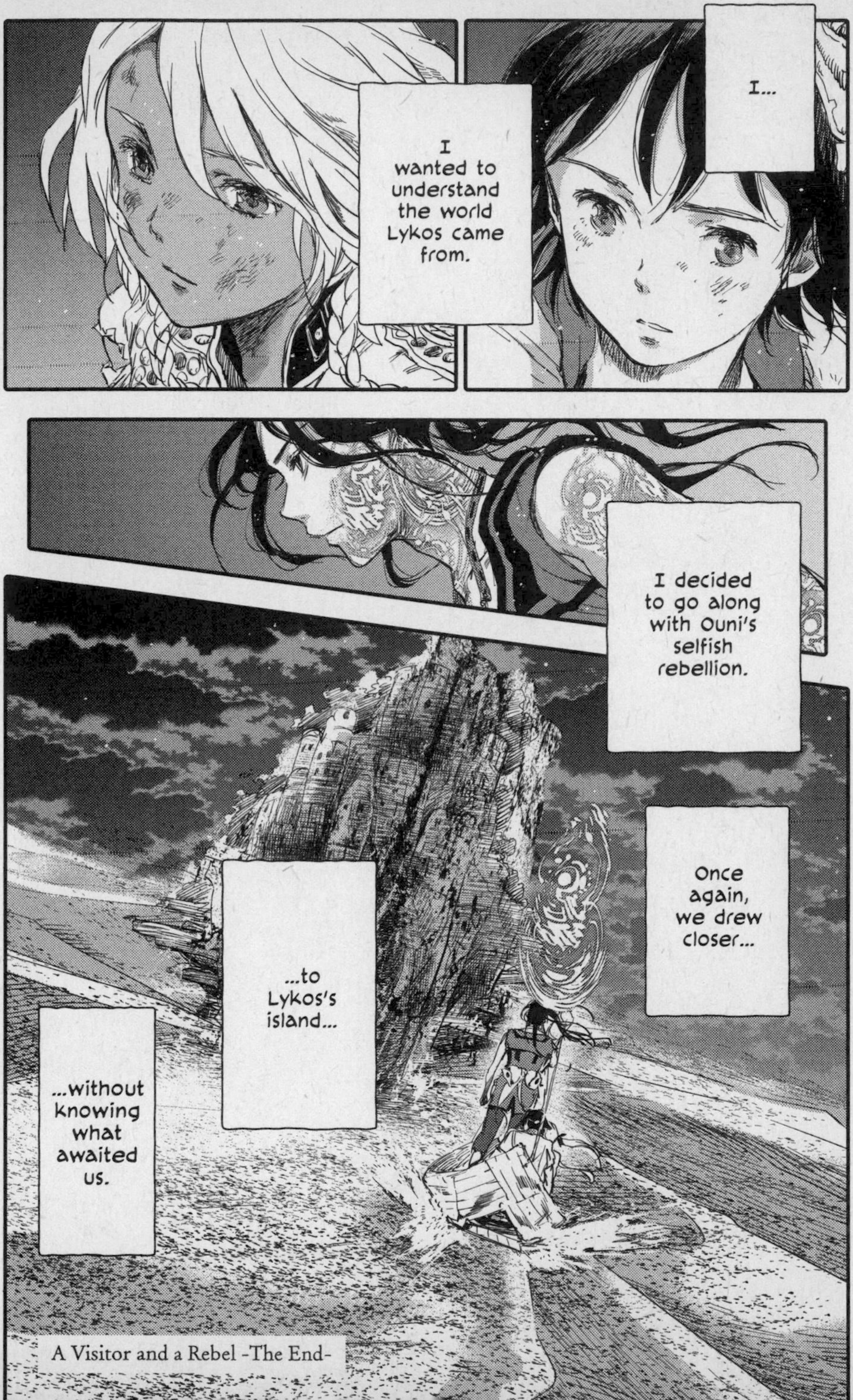
I...
I wanted to understand the world Lykos came from.
I decided to go along with Ouni's selfish rebellion.
Once again, we drew closer...
...to Lykos's island...
...without knowing what awaited us.
A Visitor and a Rebel -The End-

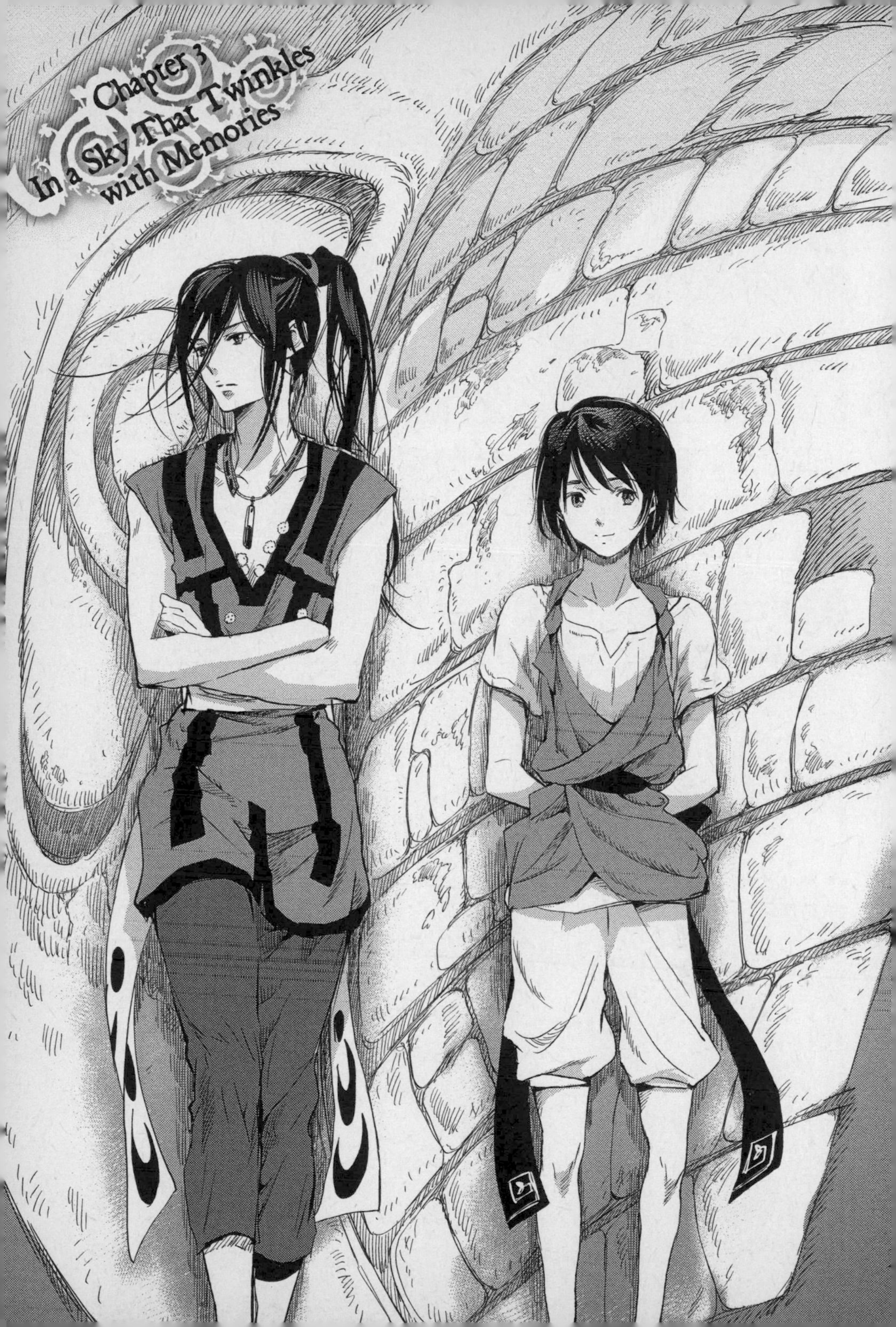
Chapter 3
In a Sky That Twinkles with Memories

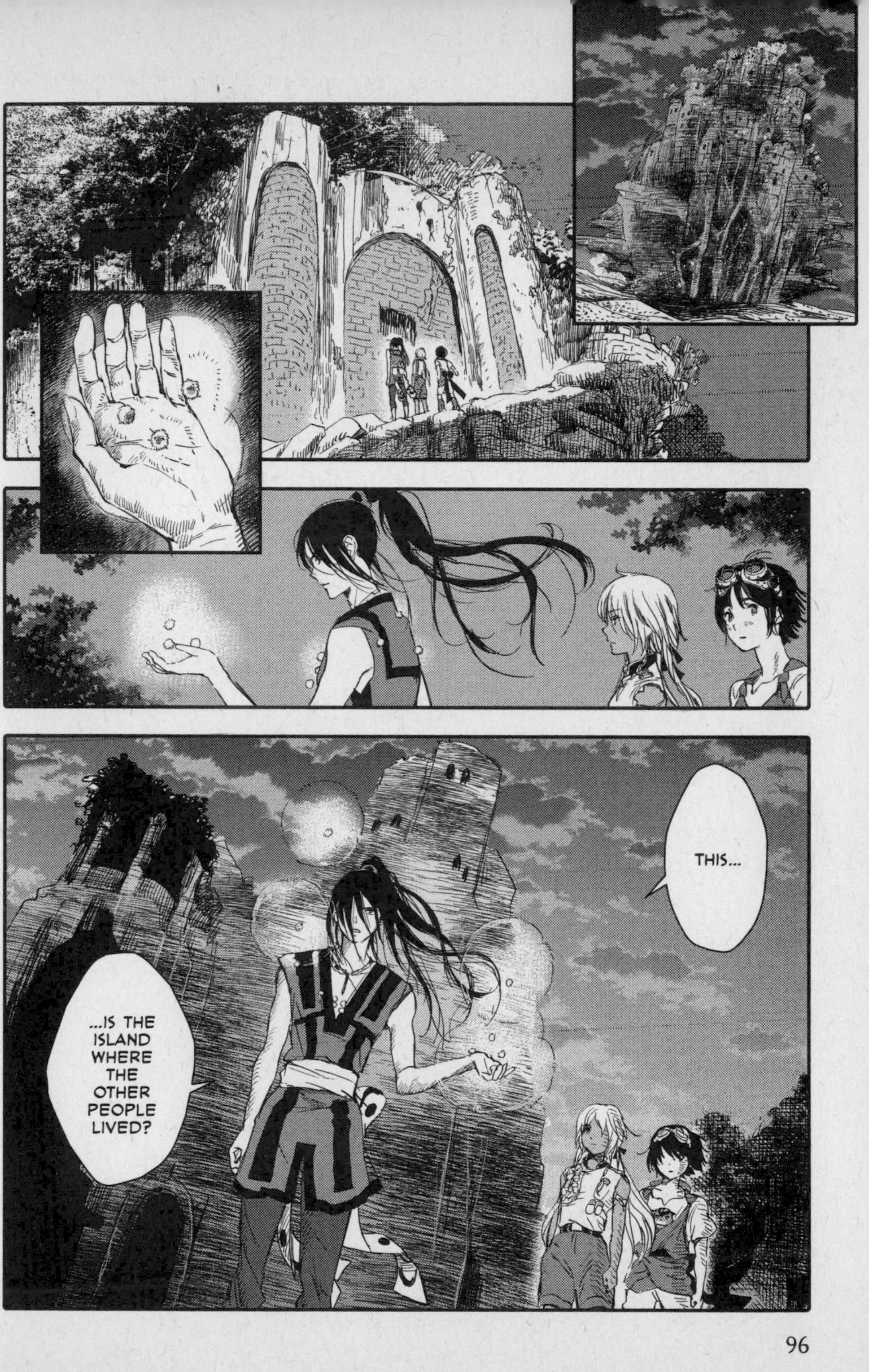
THIS...
...IS THE ISLAND WHERE THE OTHER PEOPLE LIVED?

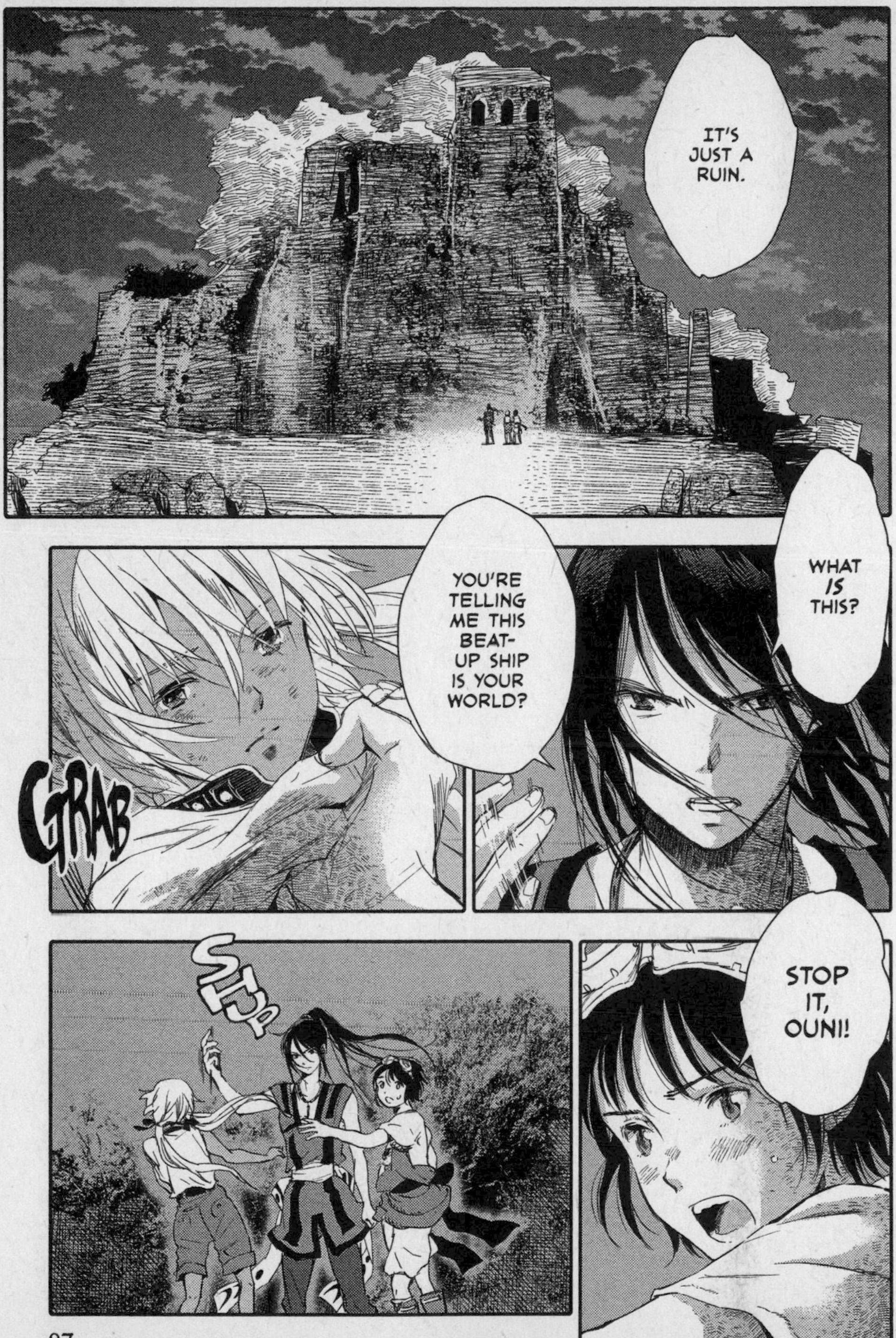
IT'S JUST A RUIN.
WHAT *IS* THIS?
YOU'RE TELLING ME THIS BEAT-UP SHIP IS YOUR WORLD?
GRAB
STOP IT, OUNI!
SHUP

YOU REALLY...

...DON'T KNOW ANYTHING, DO YOU?

We don't know any-thing...

...about the world beyond the Mud Whale.

WHAT IS THIS?

GRAVES.

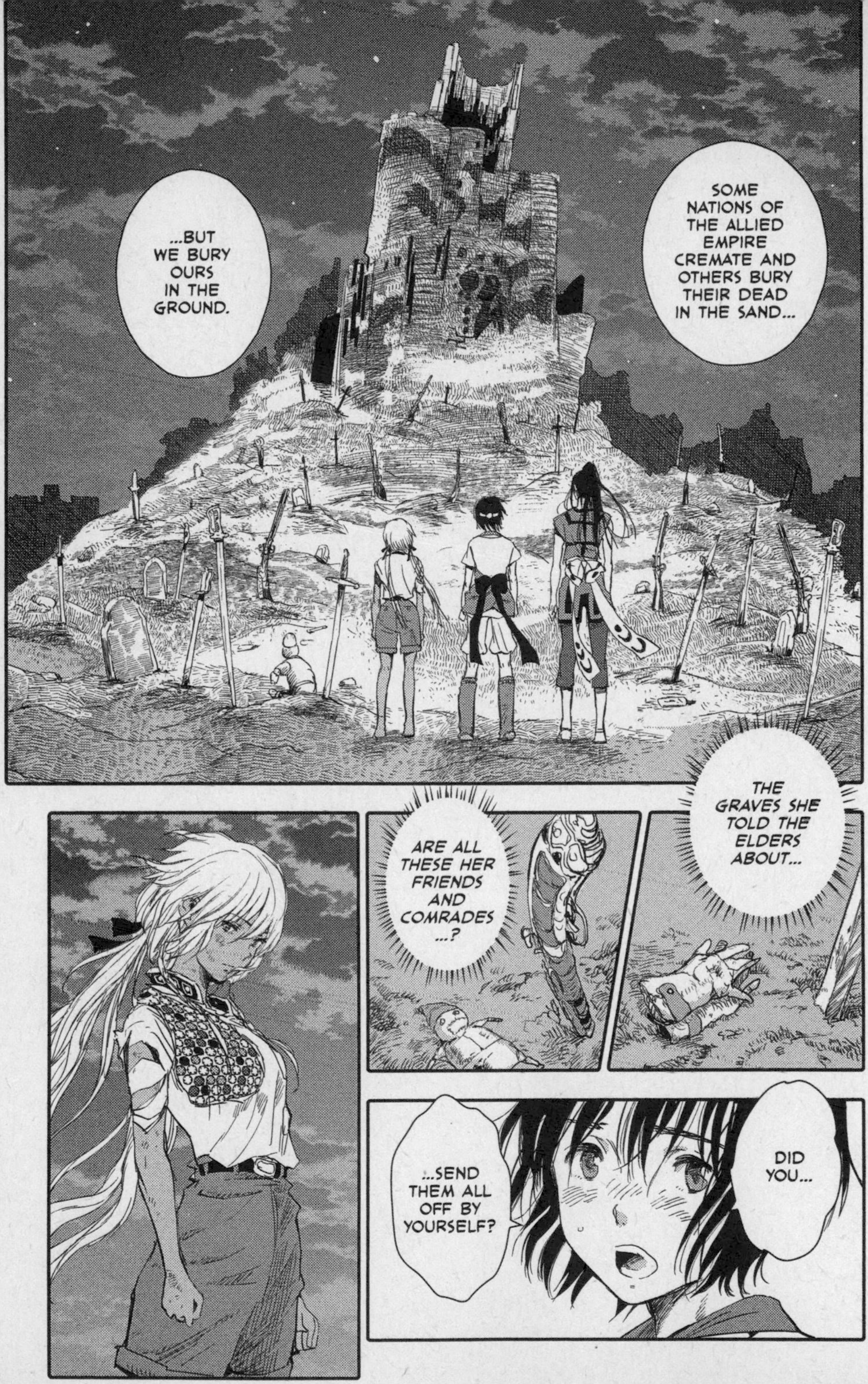
SOME NATIONS OF THE ALLIED EMPIRE CREMATE AND OTHERS BURY THEIR DEAD IN THE SAND...
...BUT WE BURY OURS IN THE GROUND.
THE GRAVES SHE TOLD THE ELDERS ABOUT...
ARE ALL THESE HER FRIENDS AND COMRADES...?
DID YOU...
...SEND THEM ALL OFF BY YOURSELF?

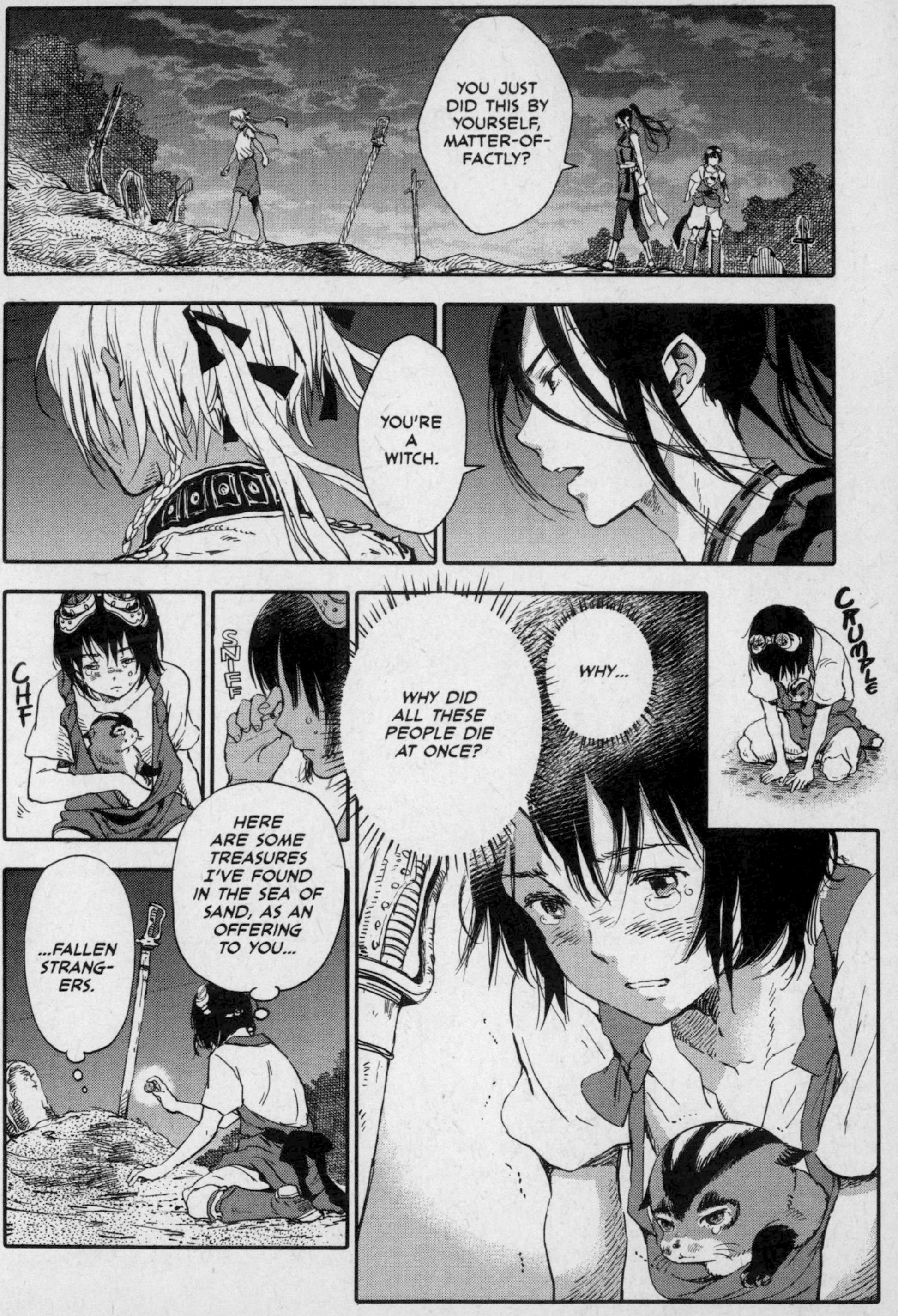
YOU JUST DID THIS BY YOURSELF, MATTER-OF-FACTLY?
YOU'RE A WITCH.
CRUMPLE
WHY...
WHY DID ALL THESE PEOPLE DIE AT ONCE?
SNIFF
CHF
HERE ARE SOME TREASURES I'VE FOUND IN THE SEA OF SAND, AS AN OFFERING TO YOU...
...FALLEN STRANGERS.

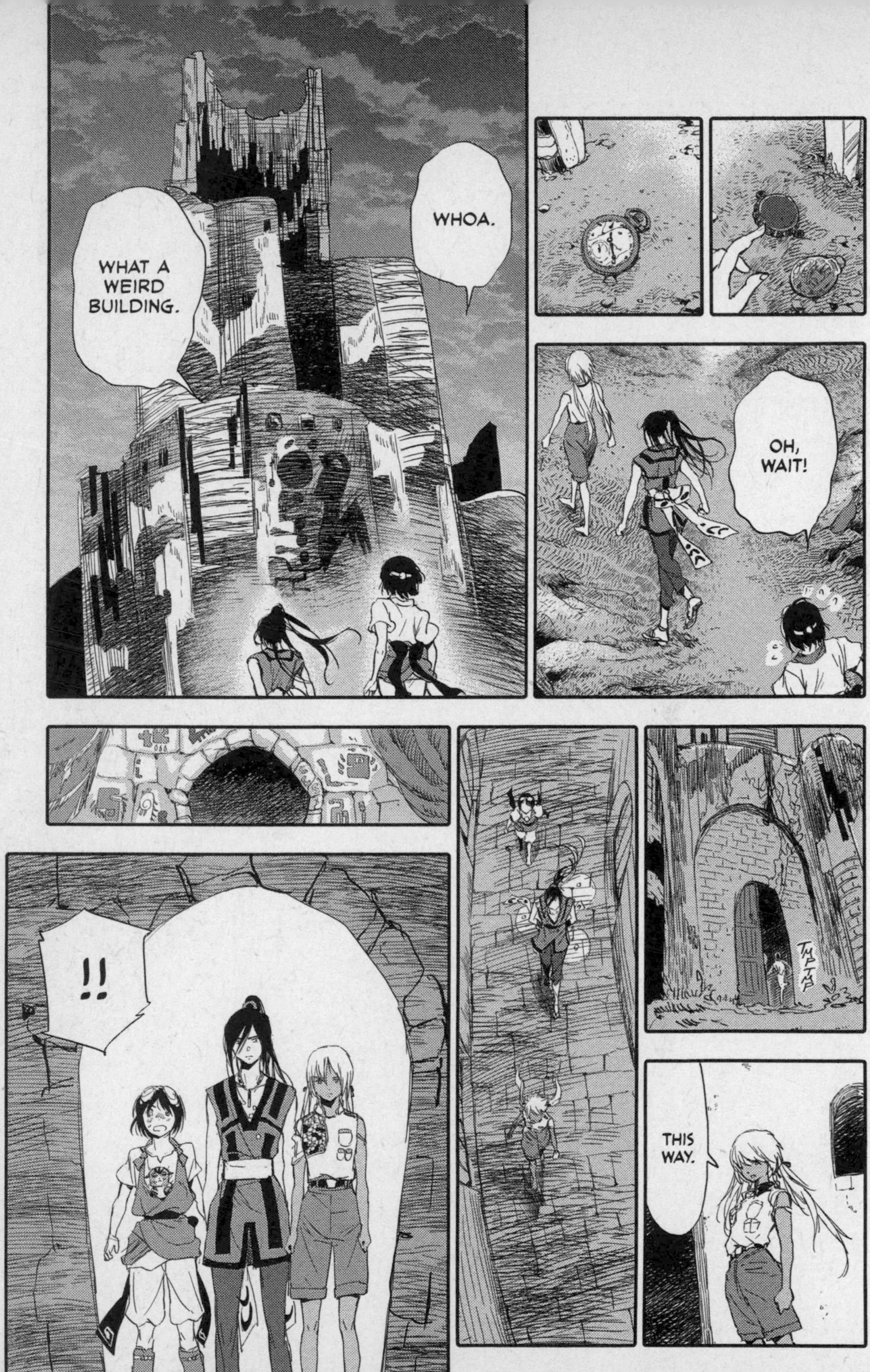
OH, WAIT!
WHOA.
WHAT A WEIRD BUILDING.
TMP TMP
THIS WAY.
!!

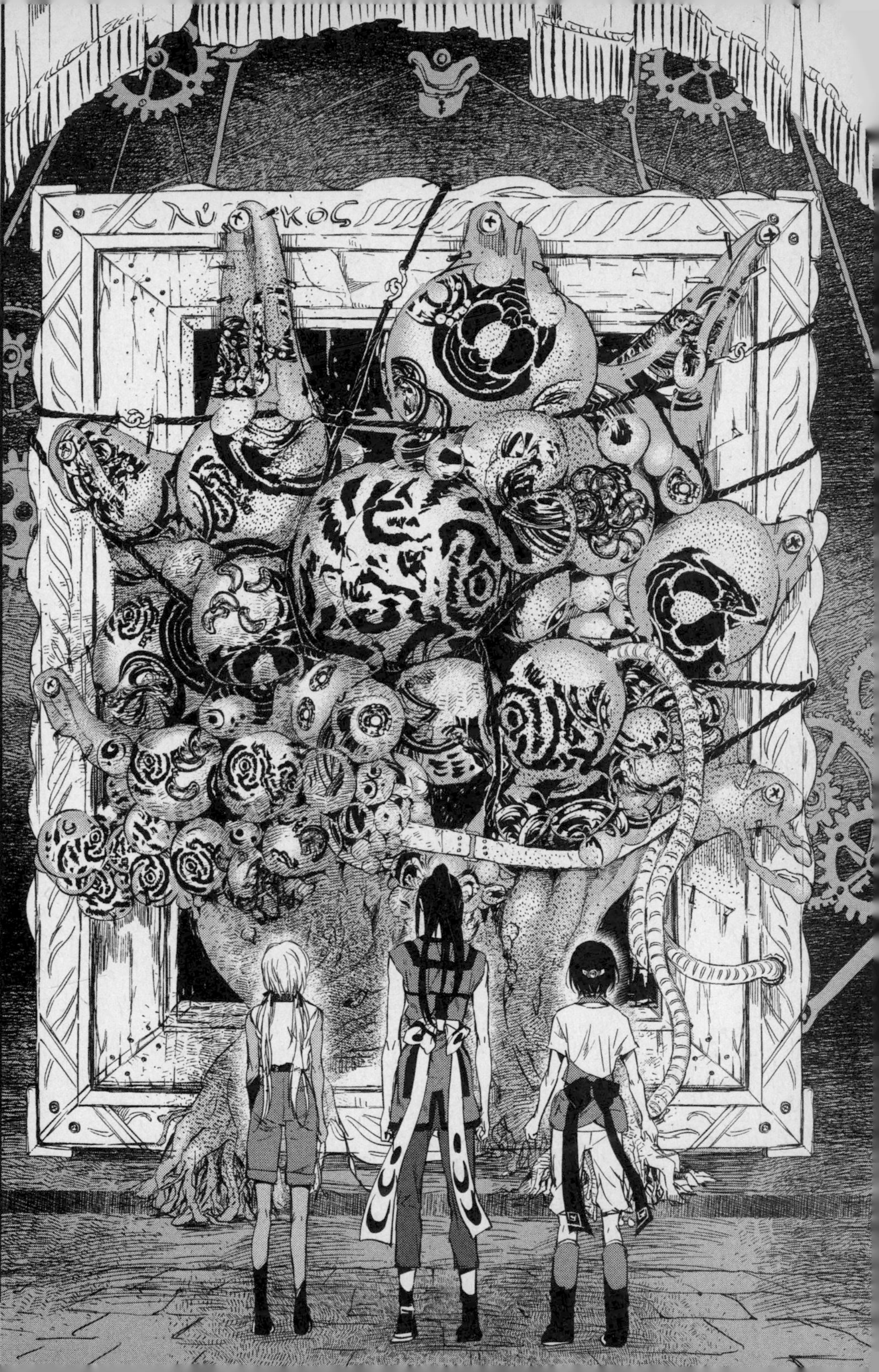

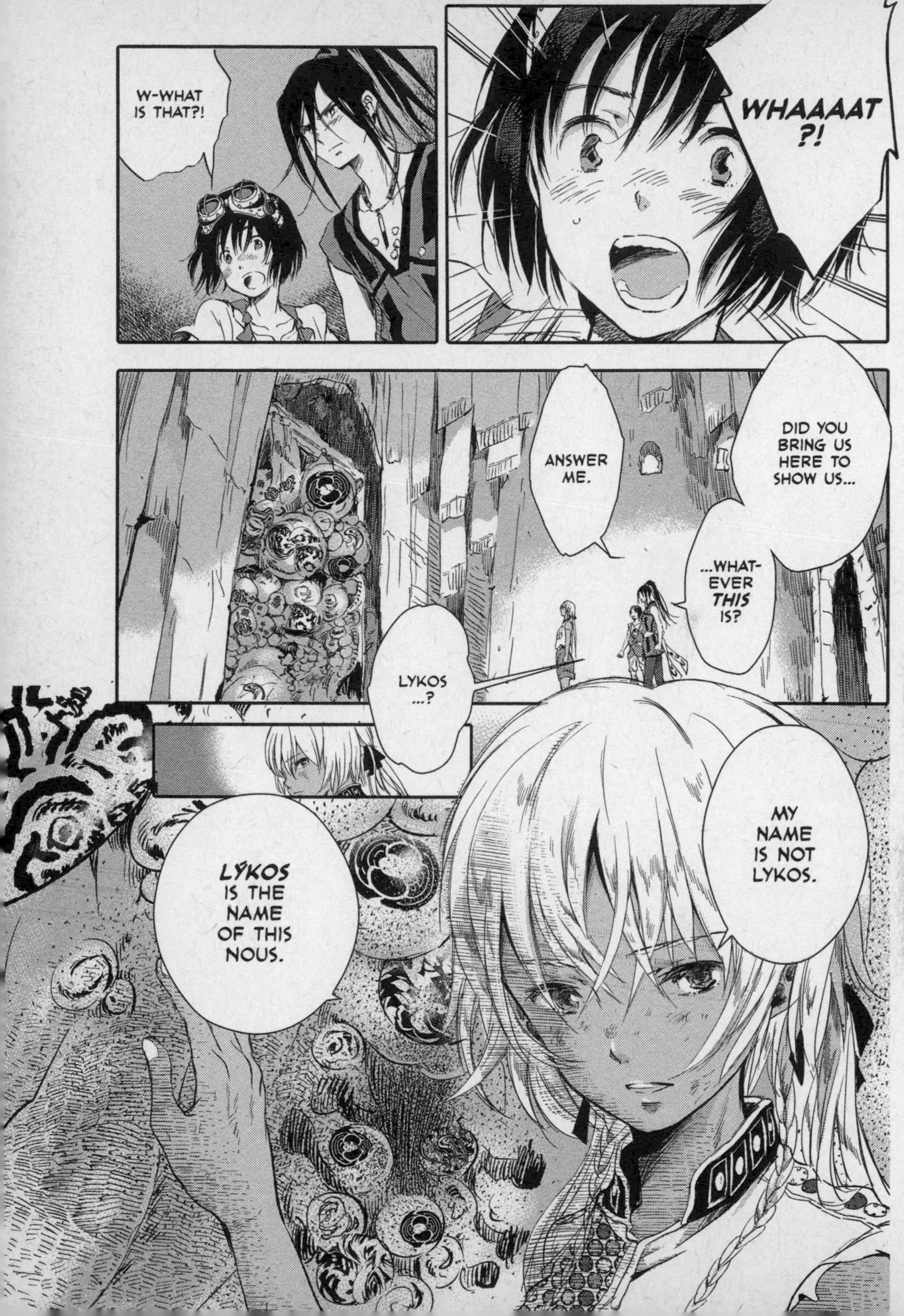
WHAAAAT ?!
W-WHAT IS THAT?!
DID YOU BRING US HERE TO SHOW US...
...WHAT-EVER *THIS* IS?
ANSWER ME.
LYKOS ...?
MY NAME IS NOT LYKOS.
LÝKOS IS THE NAME OF THIS NOUS.

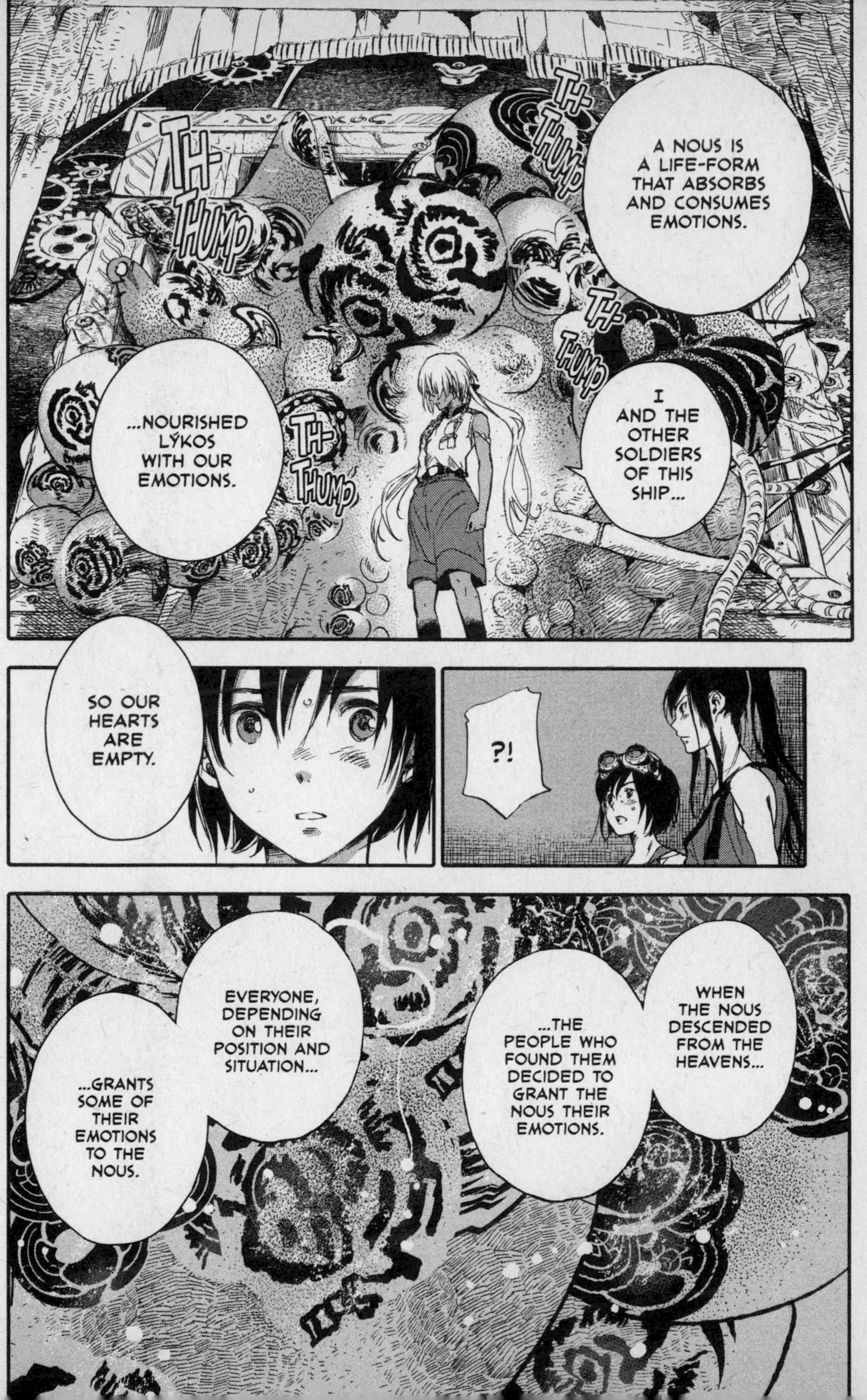
A NOUS IS A LIFE-FORM THAT ABSORBS AND CONSUMES EMOTIONS.
TH-THUMP
TH-THUMP
TH-THUMP
I AND THE OTHER SOLDIERS OF THIS SHIP...
TH-THUMP
...NOURISHED LÝKOS WITH OUR EMOTIONS.
?!
SO OUR HEARTS ARE EMPTY.
WHEN THE NOUS DESCENDED FROM THE HEAVENS...
...THE PEOPLE WHO FOUND THEM DECIDED TO GRANT THE NOUS THEIR EMOTIONS.
EVERYONE, DEPENDING ON THEIR POSITION AND SITUATION...
...GRANTS SOME OF THEIR EMOTIONS TO THE NOUS.

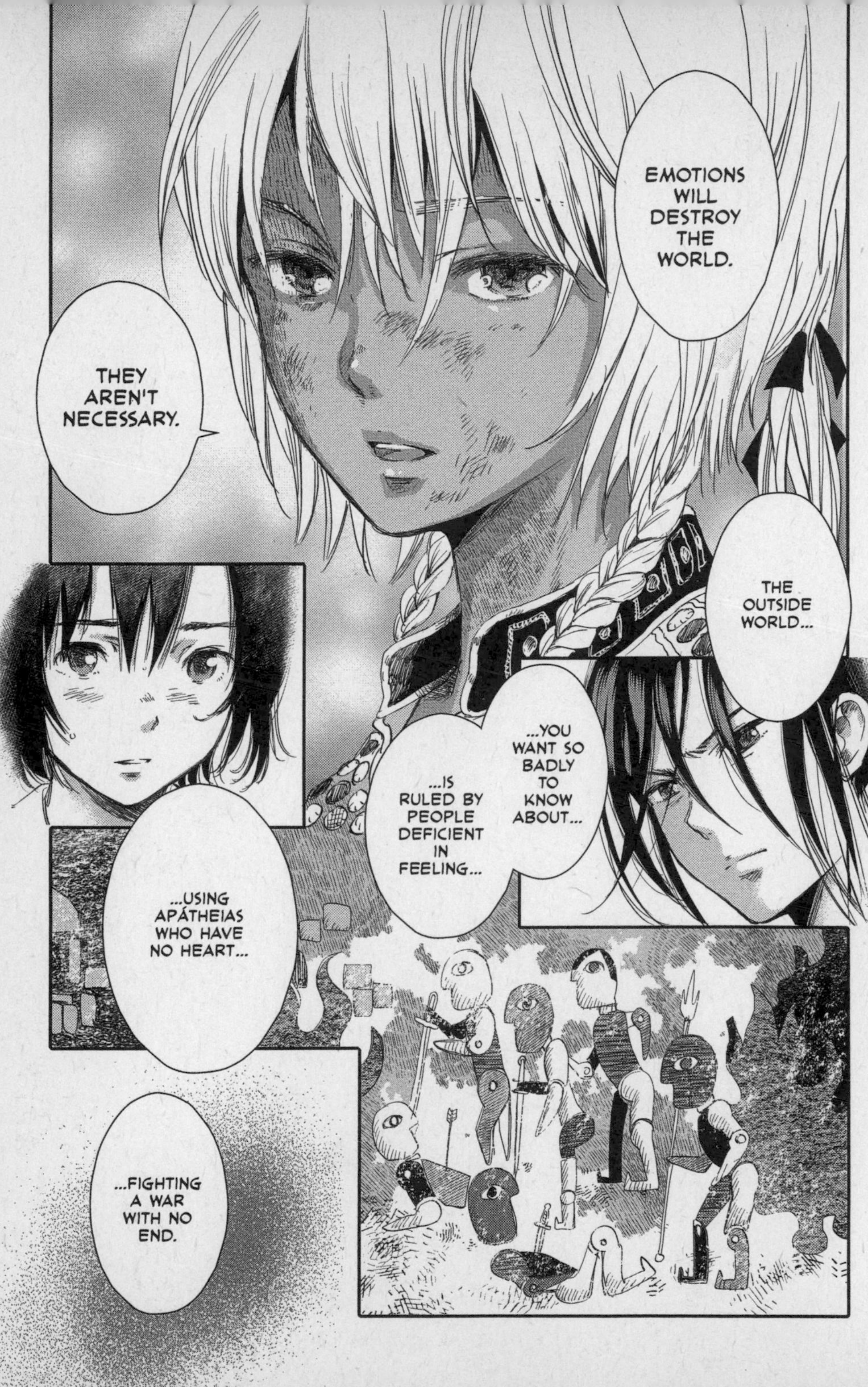
EMOTIONS WILL DESTROY THE WORLD.
THEY AREN'T NECESSARY.
THE OUTSIDE WORLD...
...YOU WANT SO BADLY TO KNOW ABOUT...
...IS RULED BY PEOPLE DEFICIENT IN FEELING...
...USING APÁTHEIAS WHO HAVE NO HEART...
...FIGHTING A WAR WITH NO END.

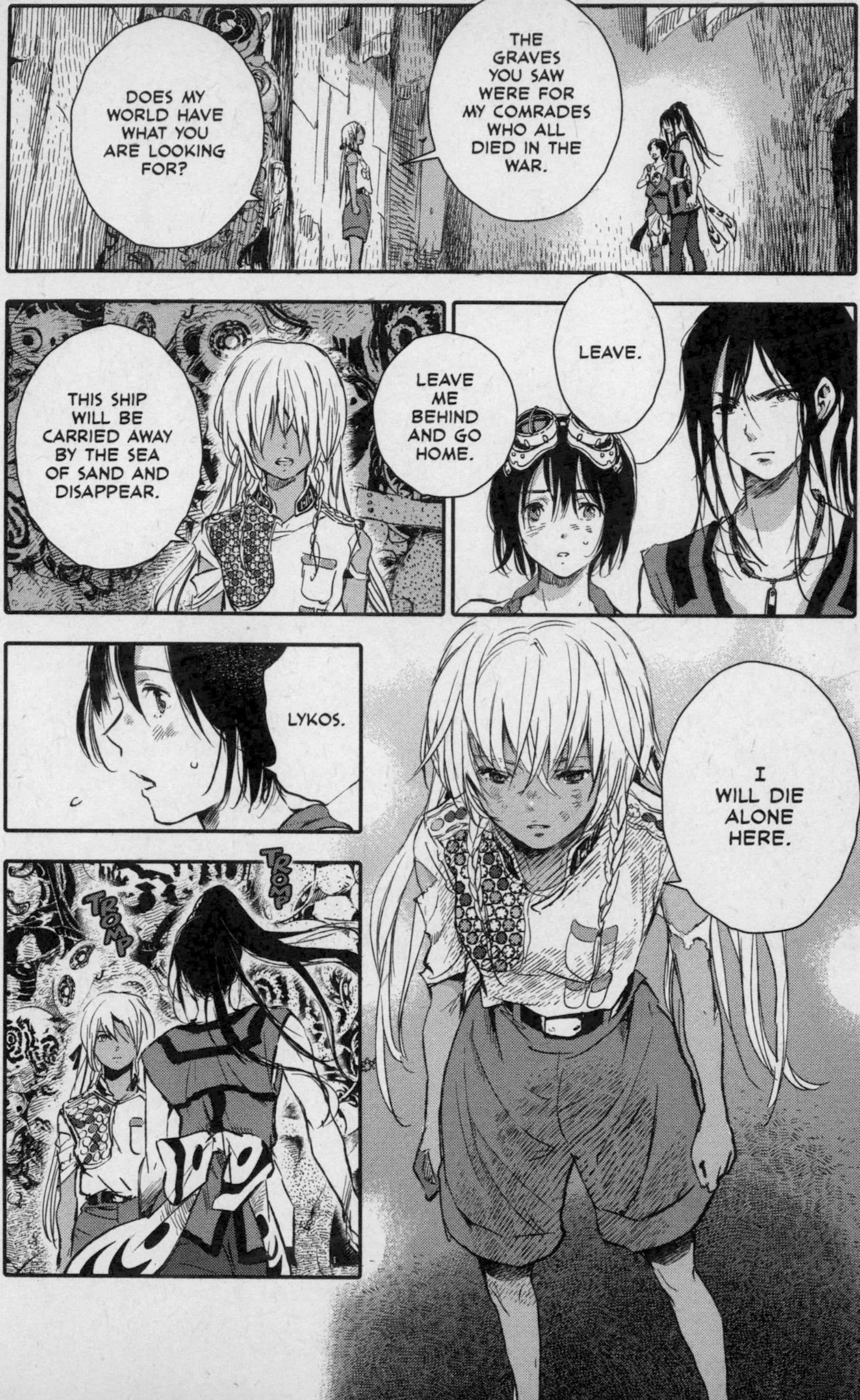
THE GRAVES YOU SAW WERE FOR MY COMRADES WHO ALL DIED IN THE WAR.
DOES MY WORLD HAVE WHAT YOU ARE LOOKING FOR?
LEAVE.
LEAVE ME BEHIND AND GO HOME.
THIS SHIP WILL BE CARRIED AWAY BY THE SEA OF SAND AND DISAPPEAR.
I WILL DIE ALONE HERE.
LYKOS.
TROMP
TROMP

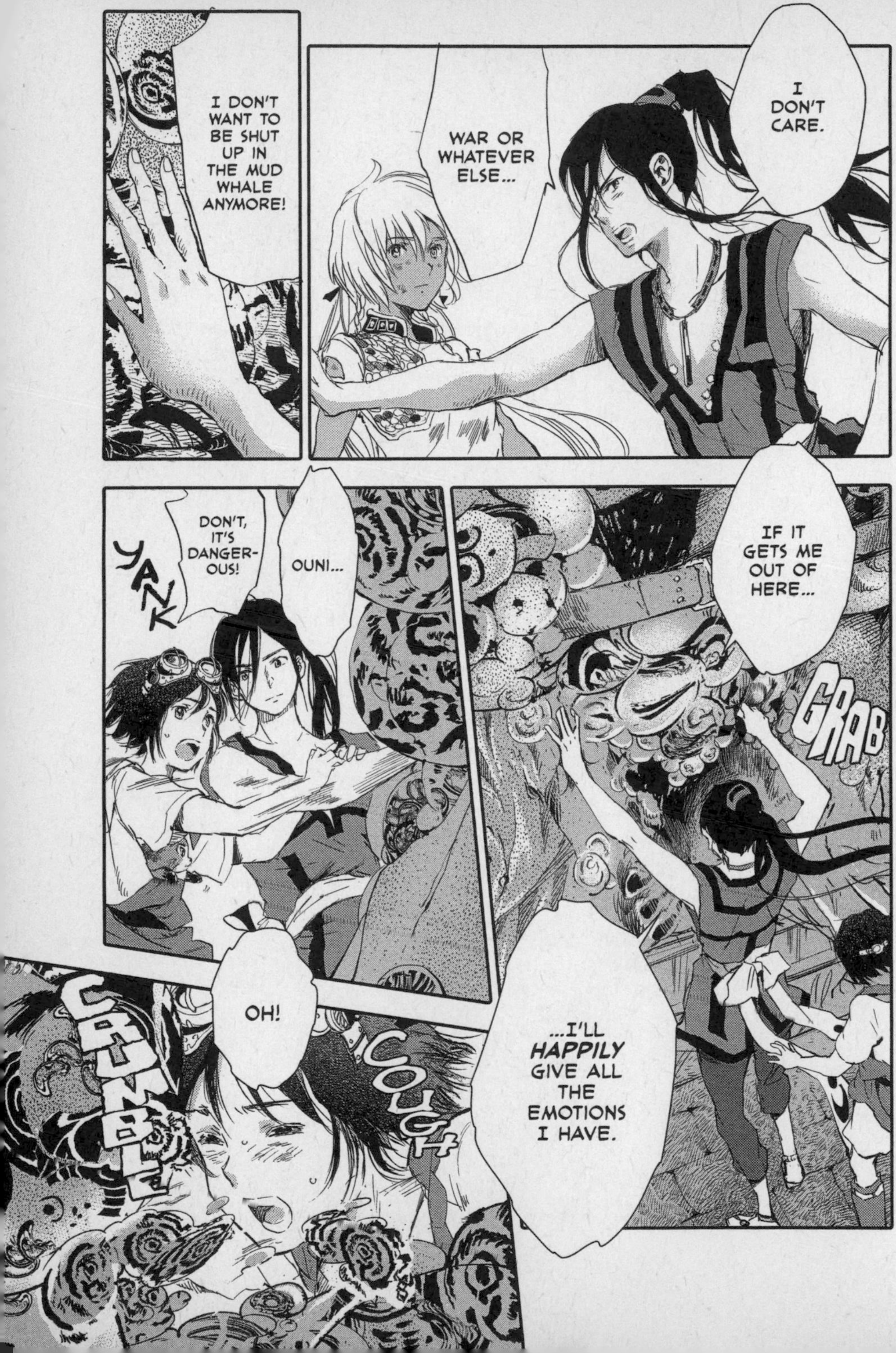
I DON'T CARE.
WAR OR WHATEVER ELSE...
I DON'T WANT TO BE SHUT UP IN THE MUD WHALE ANYMORE!
IF IT GETS ME OUT OF HERE...
GRAB
...I'LL *HAPPILY* GIVE ALL THE EMOTIONS I HAVE.
OUNI...
DON'T, IT'S DANGER-OUS!
YANK
OH!
COUGH
CRUMBLE

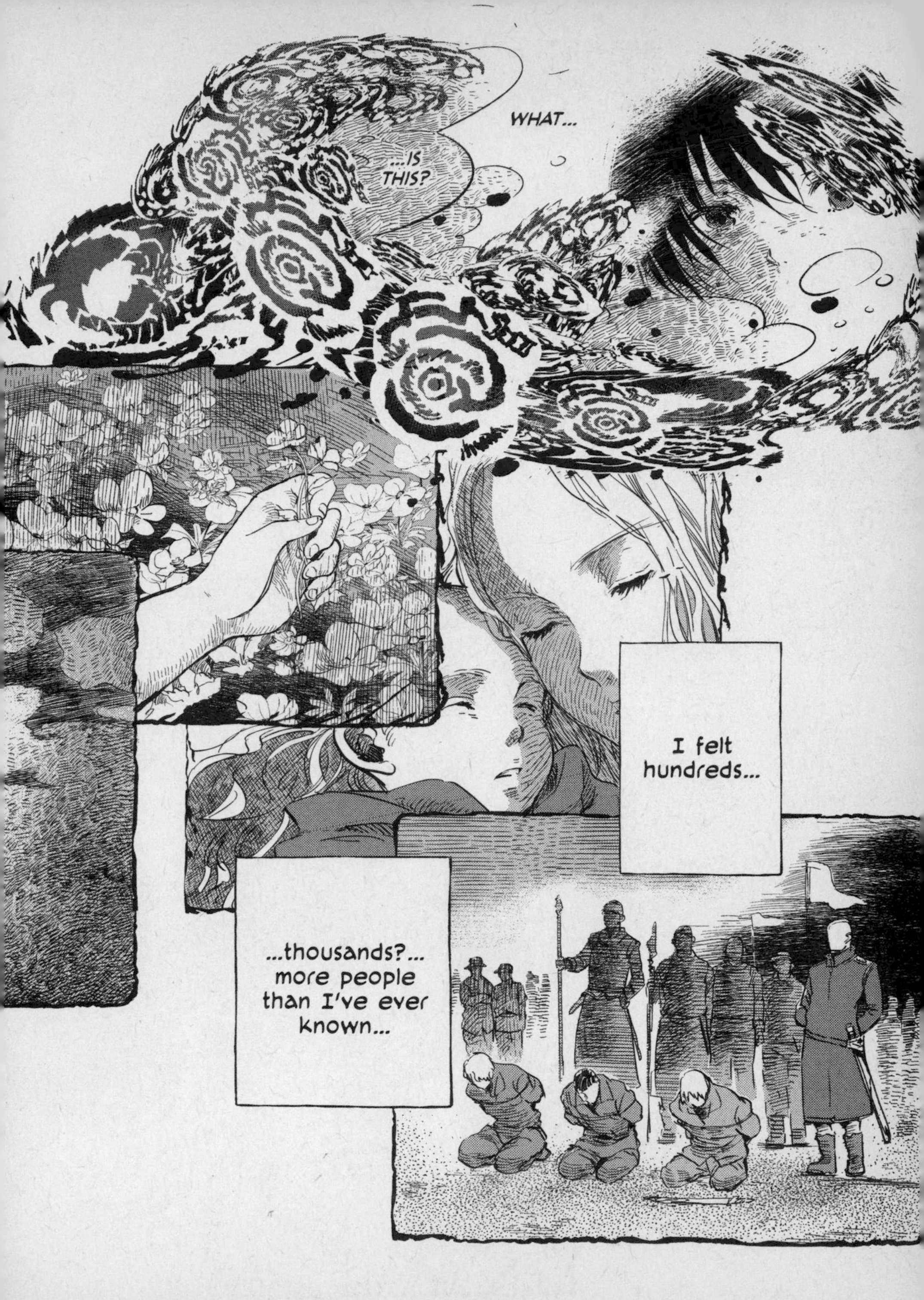
WHAT...
...IS THIS?
I felt hundreds...
...thousands?... more people than I've ever known...

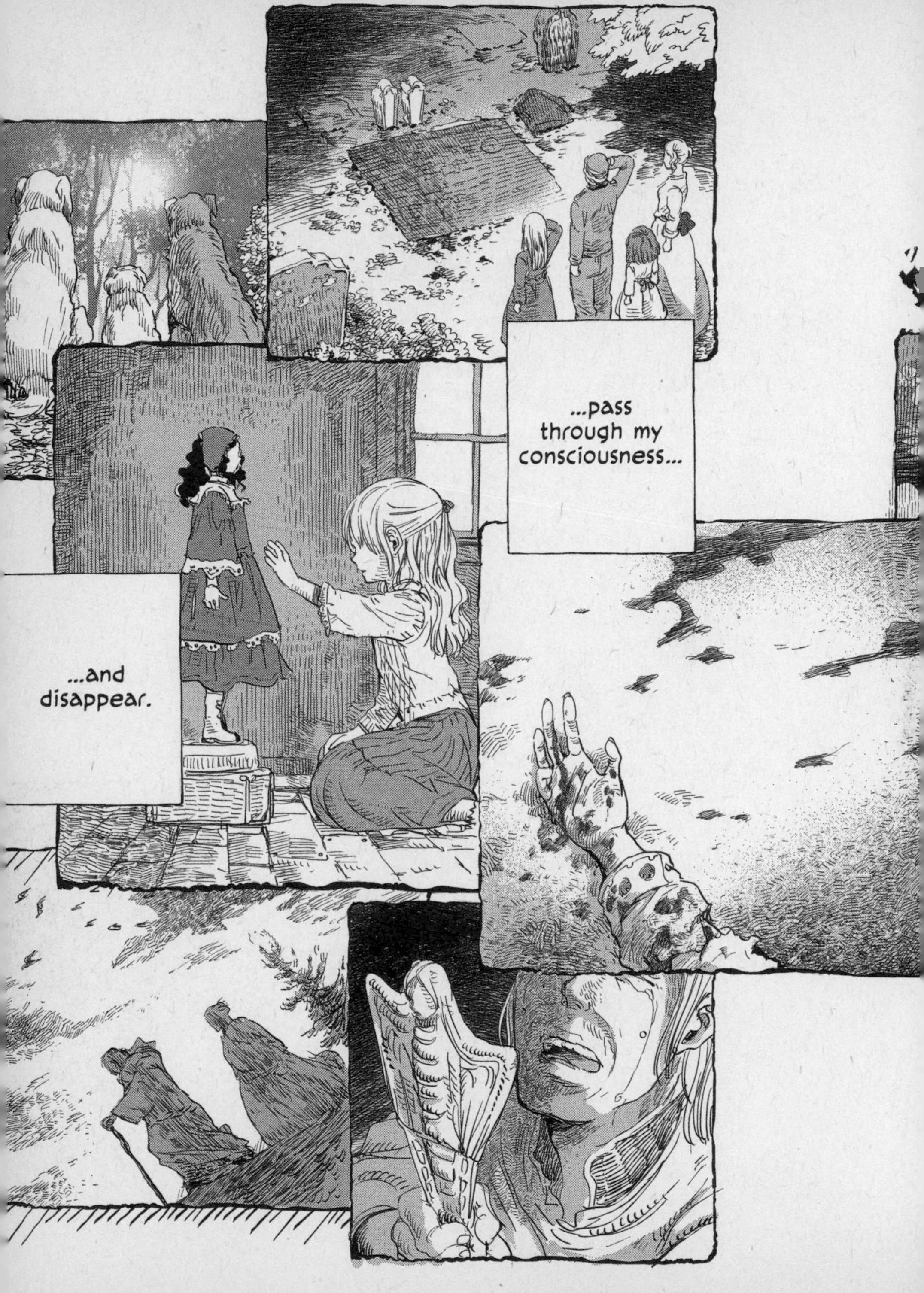
...pass through my consciousness...
...and disappear.

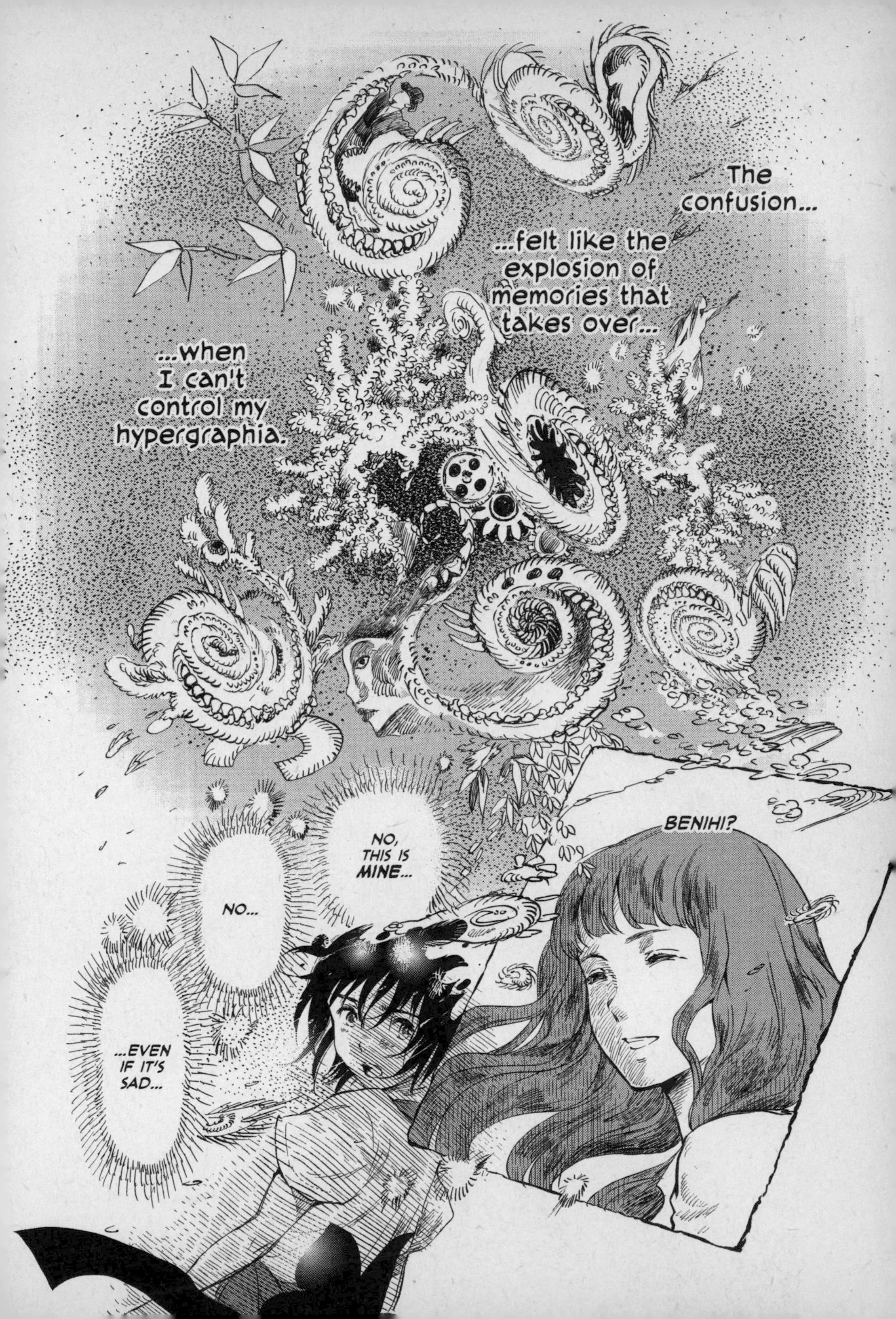
The confusion...
...felt like the explosion of memories that takes over...
...when I can't control my hypergraphia.
BENIHI?
NO, THIS IS MINE...
NO...
...EVEN IF IT'S SAD...

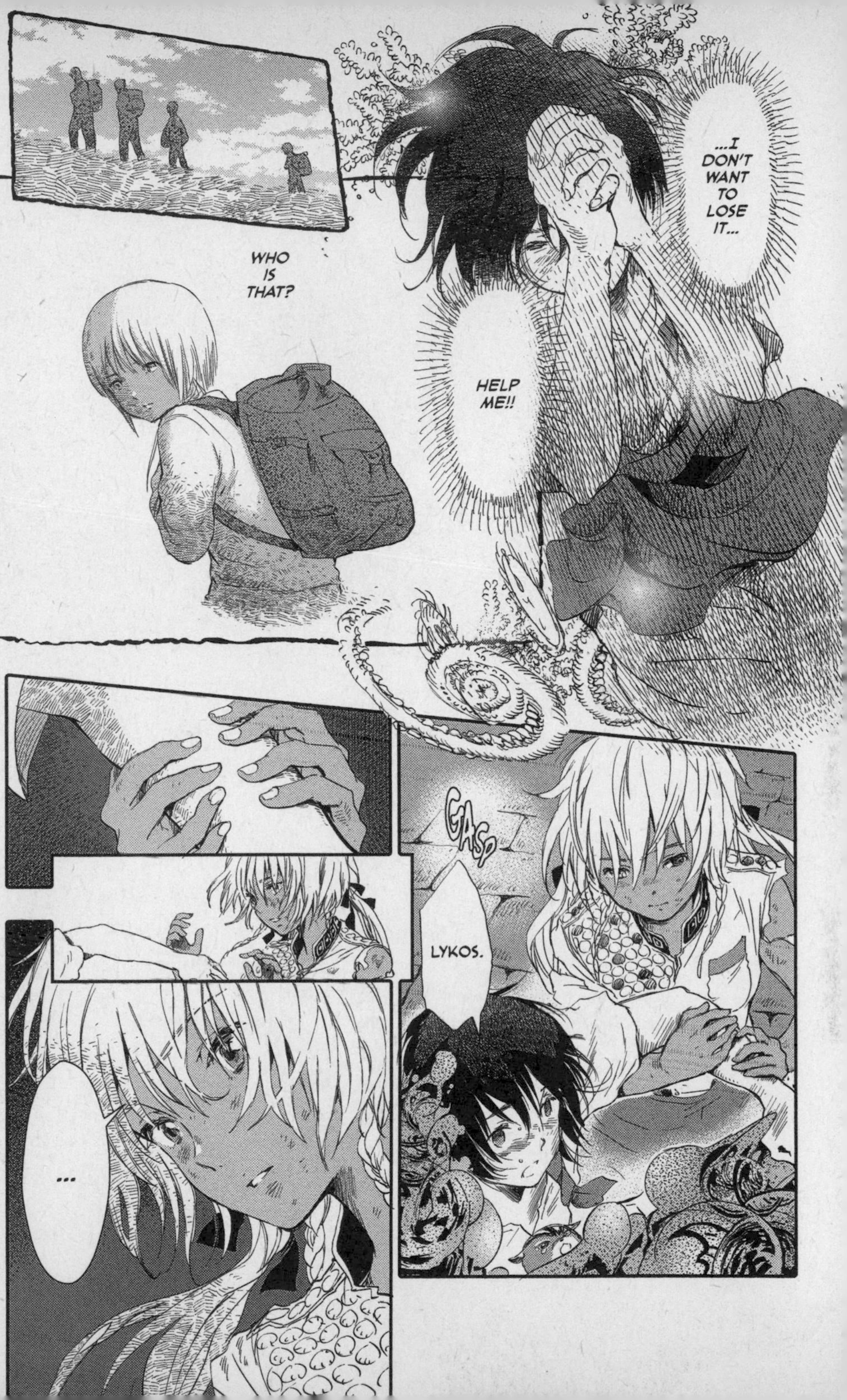
...I DON'T WANT TO LOSE IT...
HELP ME!!
WHO IS THAT?
GASP
LYKOS.
...

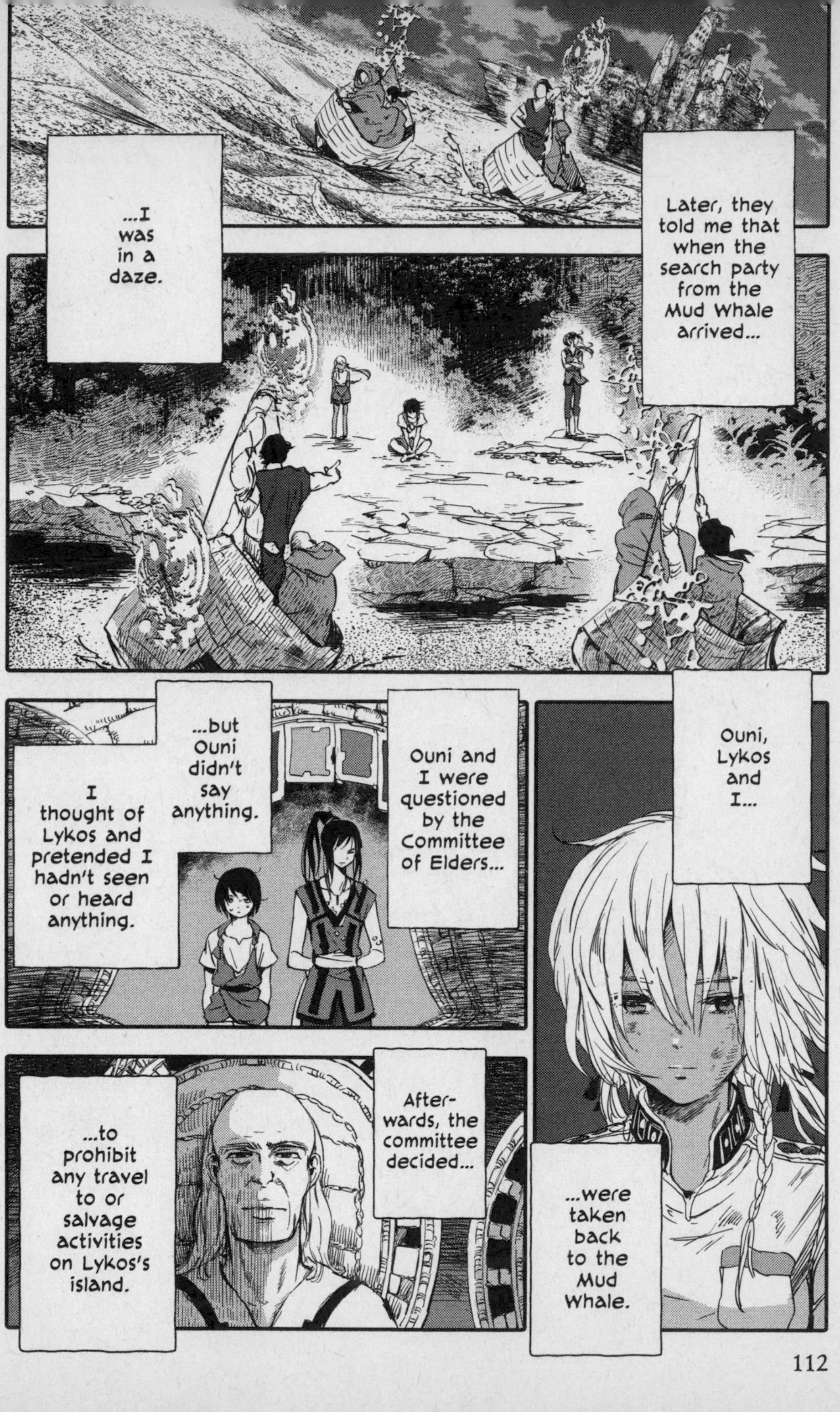
Later, they told me that when the search party from the Mud Whale arrived...
...I was in a daze.
Ouni, Lykos and I...
...were taken back to the Mud Whale.
Ouni and I were questioned by the Committee of Elders...
...but Ouni didn't say anything.
I thought of Lykos and pretended I hadn't seen or heard anything.
After-wards, the committee decided...
...to prohibit any travel to or salvage activities on Lykos's island.

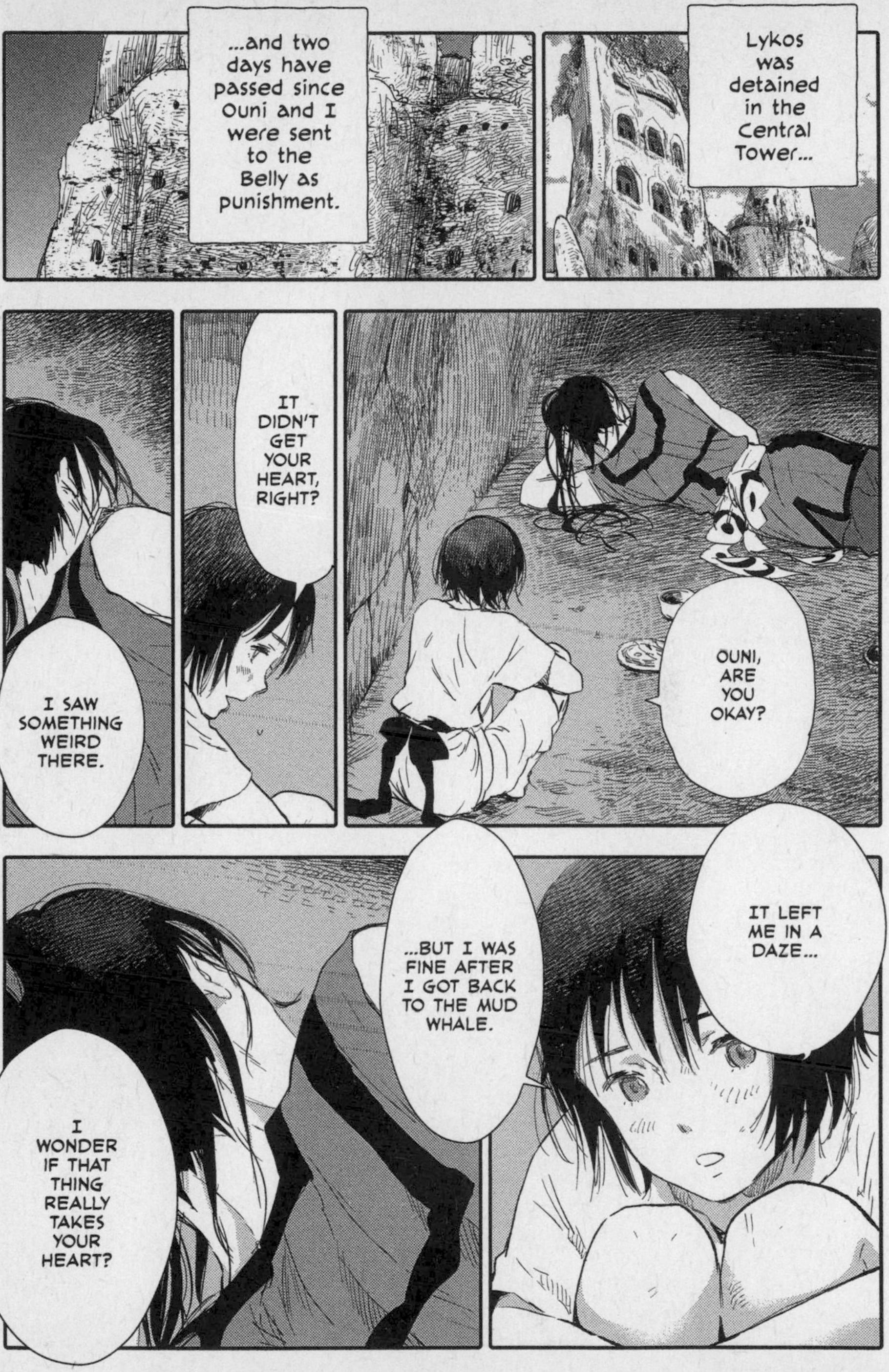
Lykos was detained in the Central Tower...
...and two days have passed since Ouni and I were sent to the Belly as punishment.
OUNI, ARE YOU OKAY?
IT DIDN'T GET YOUR HEART, RIGHT?
I SAW SOMETHING WEIRD THERE.
IT LEFT ME IN A DAZE...
...BUT I WAS FINE AFTER I GOT BACK TO THE MUD WHALE.
I WONDER IF THAT THING REALLY TAKES YOUR HEART?

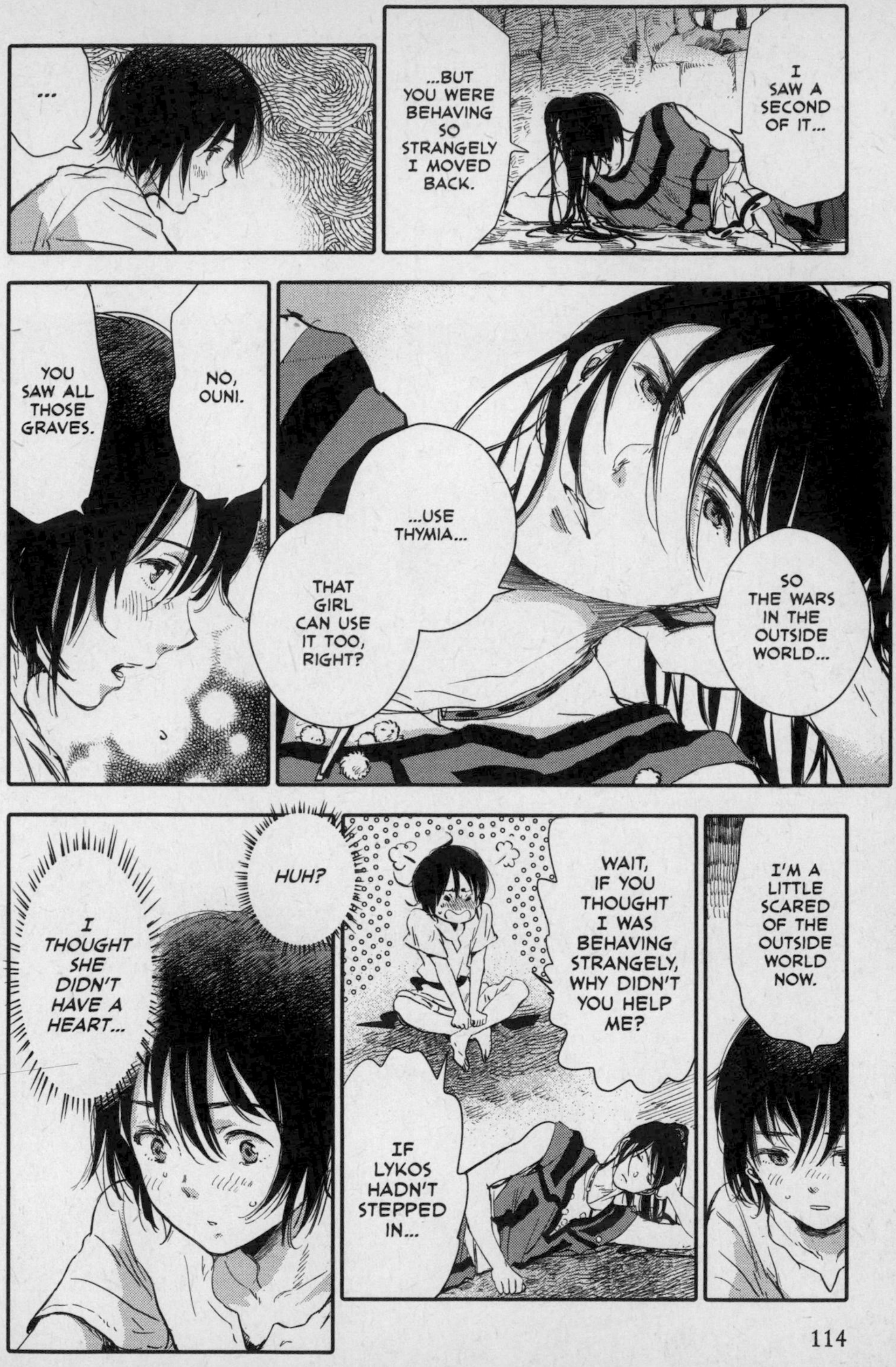
I SAW A SECOND OF IT...
...BUT YOU WERE BEHAVING SO STRANGELY I MOVED BACK.
...
SO THE WARS IN THE OUTSIDE WORLD...
...USE THYMIA...
THAT GIRL CAN USE IT TOO, RIGHT?
NO, OUNI.
YOU SAW ALL THOSE GRAVES.
I'M A LITTLE SCARED OF THE OUTSIDE WORLD NOW.
WAIT, IF YOU THOUGHT I WAS BEHAVING STRANGELY, WHY DIDN'T YOU HELP ME?
IF LYKOS HADN'T STEPPED IN...
HUH?
I THOUGHT SHE DIDN'T HAVE A HEART...

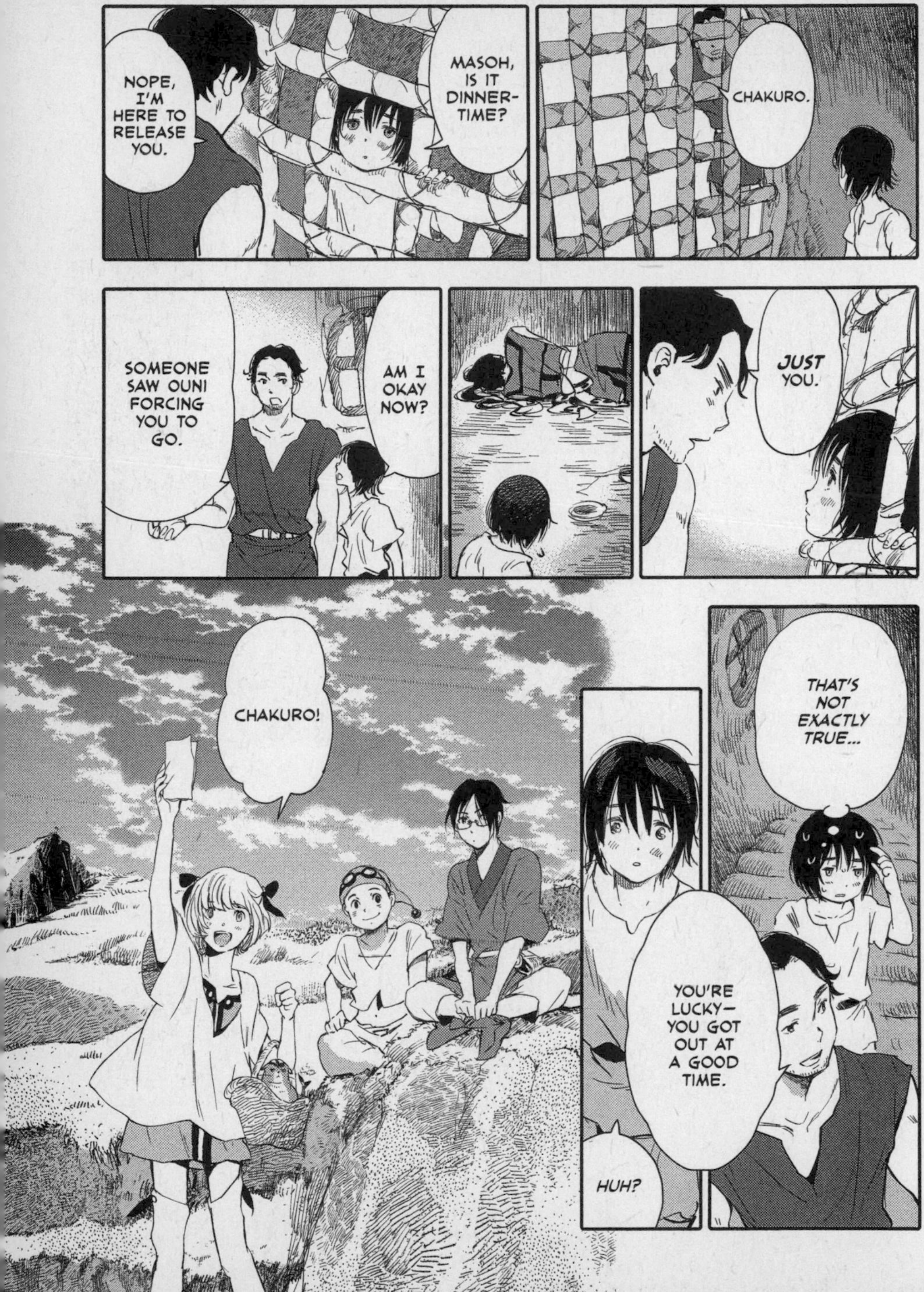
CHAKURO.
MASOH, IS IT DINNER-TIME?
NOPE, I'M HERE TO RELEASE YOU.
JUST YOU.
AM I OKAY NOW?
SOMEONE SAW OUNI FORCING YOU TO GO.
THAT'S NOT EXACTLY TRUE...
YOU'RE LUCKY— YOU GOT OUT AT A GOOD TIME.
HUH?
CHAKURO!

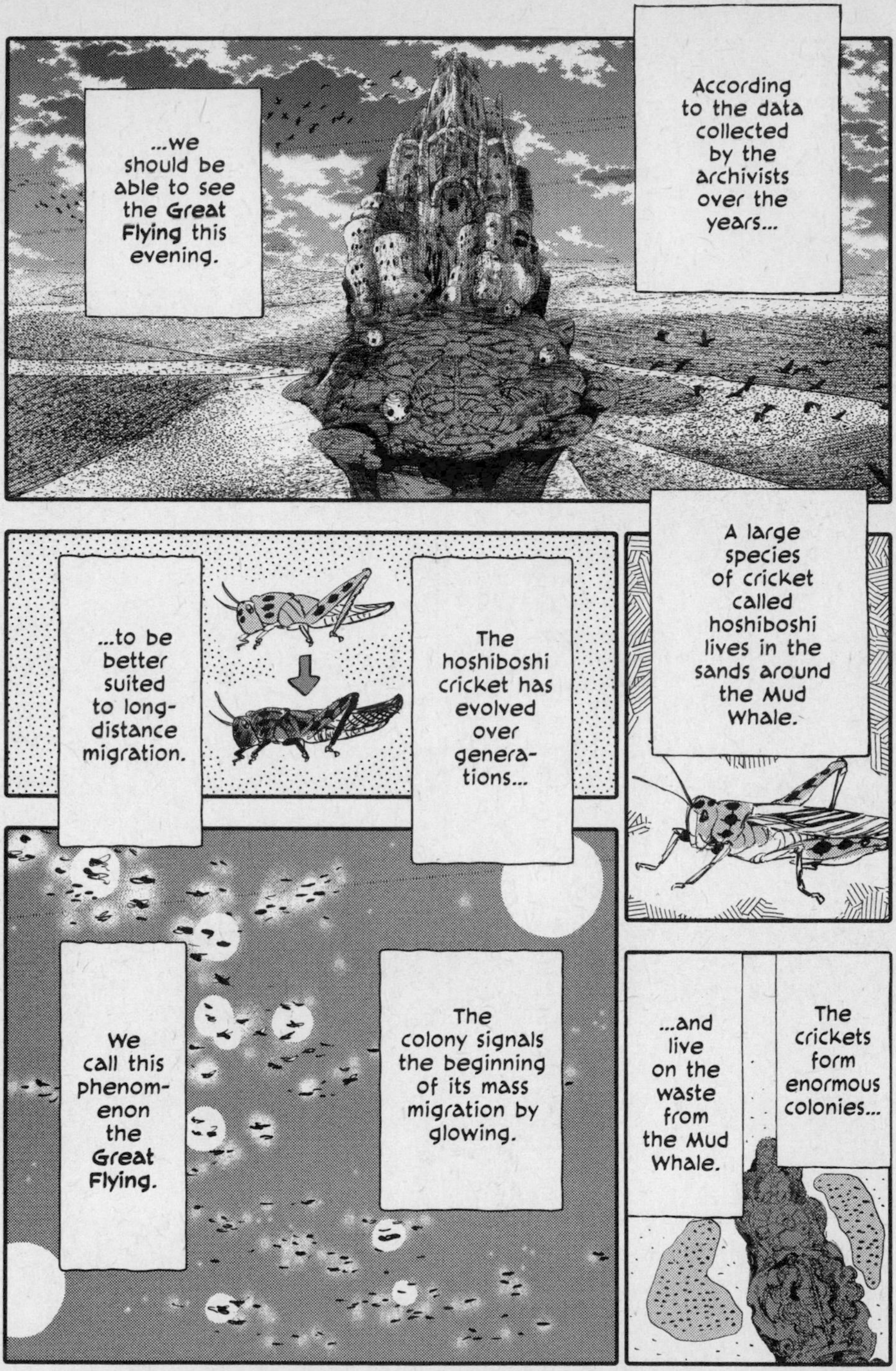
According to the data collected by the archivists over the years...
...we should be able to see the Great Flying this evening.
A large species of cricket called hoshiboshi lives in the sands around the Mud Whale.
The crickets form enormous colonies...
...and live on the waste from the Mud Whale.
The hoshiboshi cricket has evolved over generations...
...to be better suited to long-distance migration.
The colony signals the beginning of its mass migration by glowing.
We call this phenomenon the Great Flying.

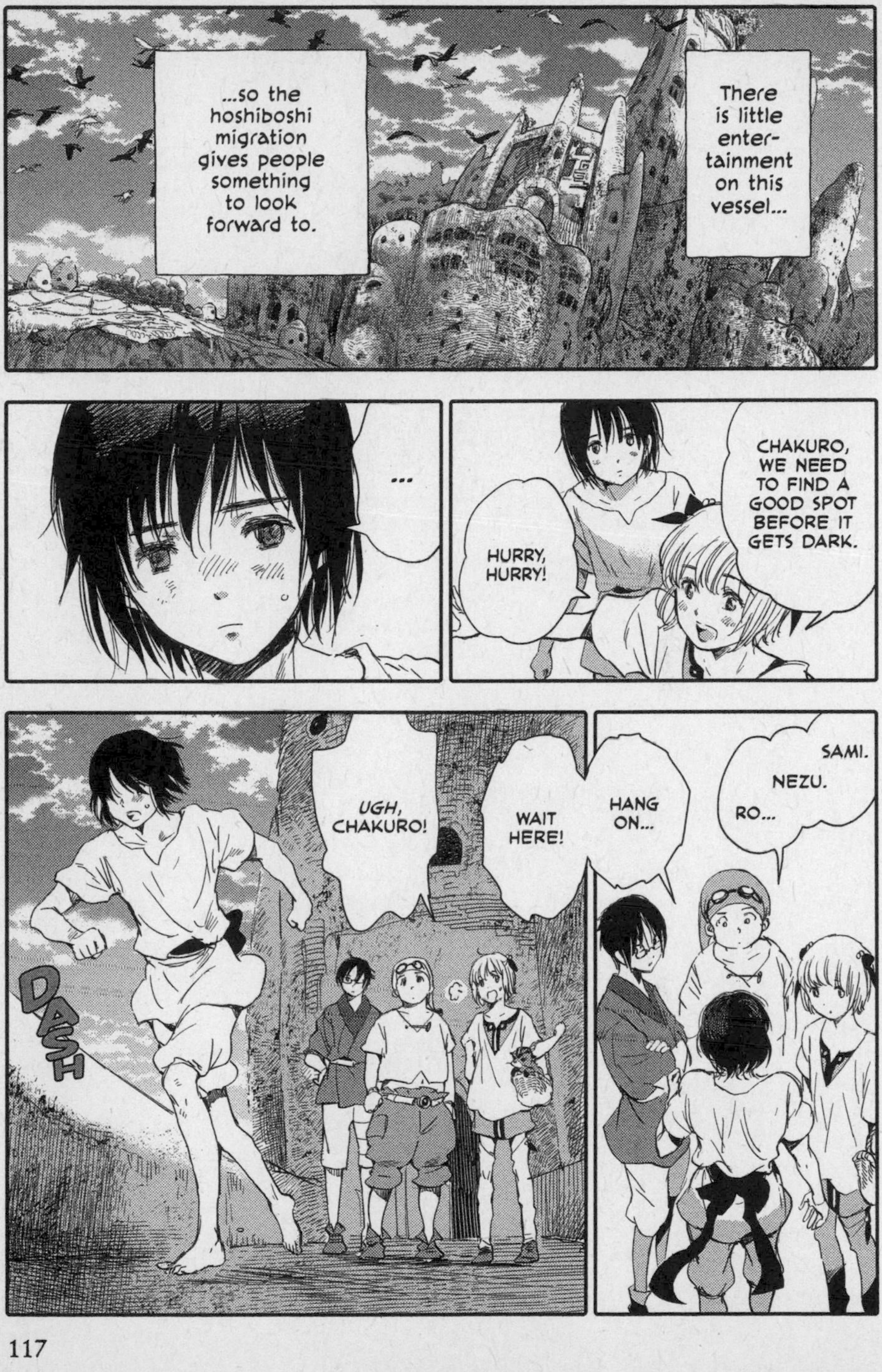
There is little enter-tainment on this vessel...
...so the hoshiboshi migration gives people something to look forward to.
CHAKURO, WE NEED TO FIND A GOOD SPOT BEFORE IT GETS DARK.
HURRY, HURRY!
...
SAMI.
NEZU.
RO...
HANG ON...
WAIT HERE!
UGH, CHAKURO!
DASH

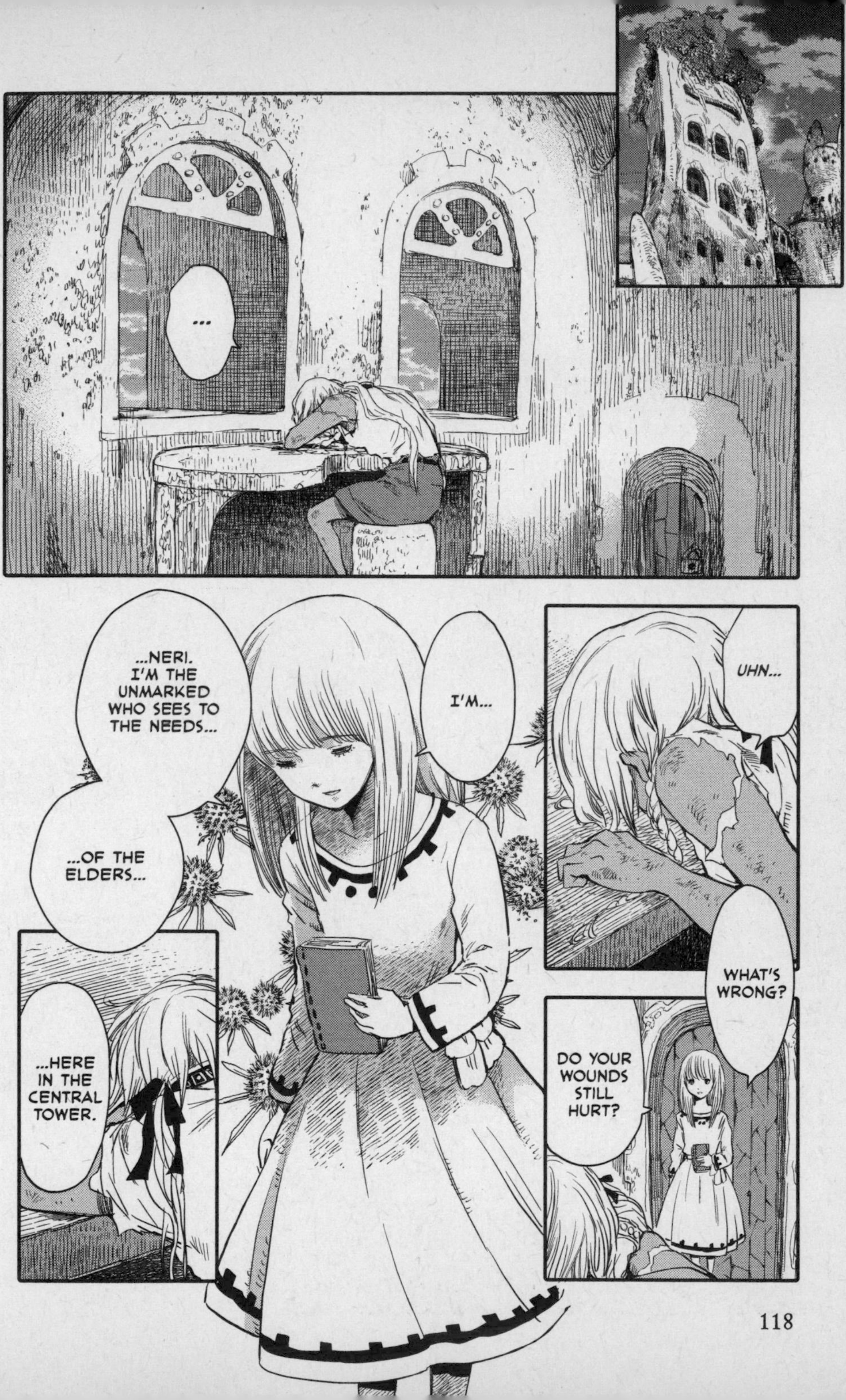
...
UHN...
WHAT'S WRONG?
DO YOUR WOUNDS STILL HURT?
I'M...
...NERI. I'M THE UNMARKED WHO SEES TO THE NEEDS...
...OF THE ELDERS...
...HERE IN THE CENTRAL TOWER.

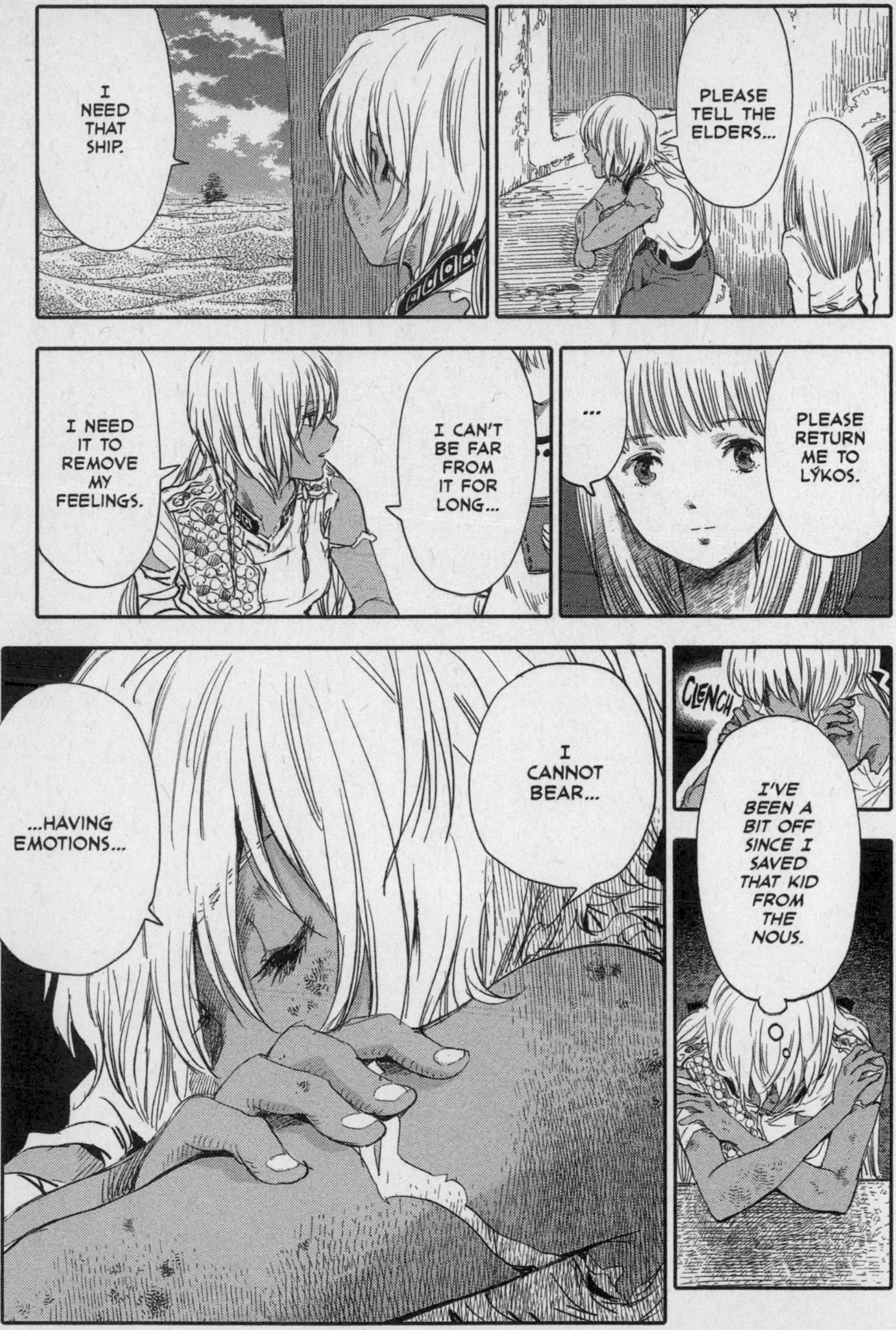
PLEASE TELL THE ELDERS...
I NEED THAT SHIP.
PLEASE RETURN ME TO LÝKOS.
...
I CAN'T BE FAR FROM IT FOR LONG...
I NEED IT TO REMOVE MY FEELINGS.
CLENCH
I'VE BEEN A BIT OFF SINCE I SAVED THAT KID FROM THE NOUS.
I CANNOT BEAR...
...HAVING EMOTIONS...

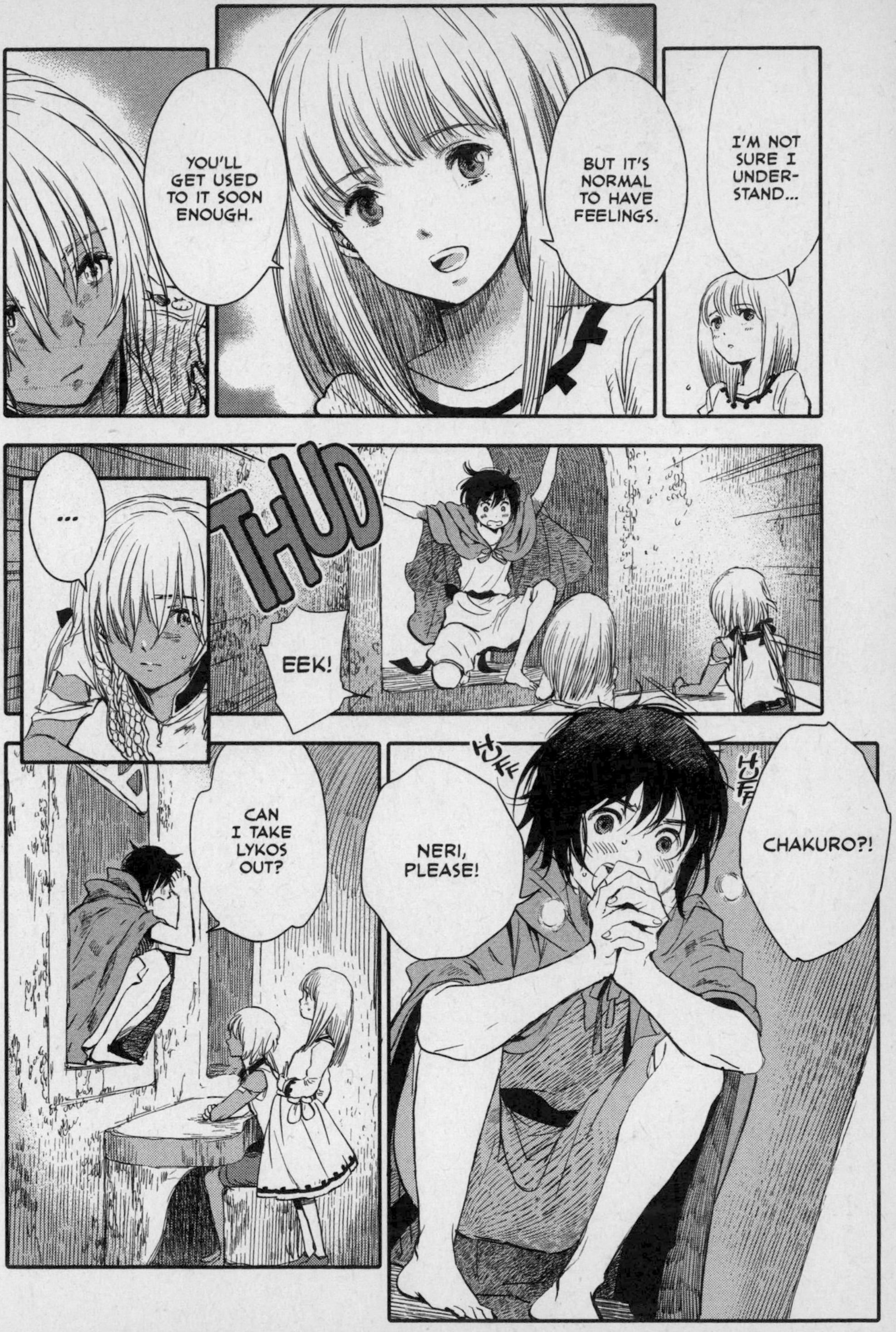
I'M NOT SURE I UNDERSTAND...
BUT IT'S NORMAL TO HAVE FEELINGS.
YOU'LL GET USED TO IT SOON ENOUGH.
THUD
EEK!
...
HUFF
HUFF
CHAKURO?!
NERI, PLEASE!
CAN I TAKE LYKOS OUT?

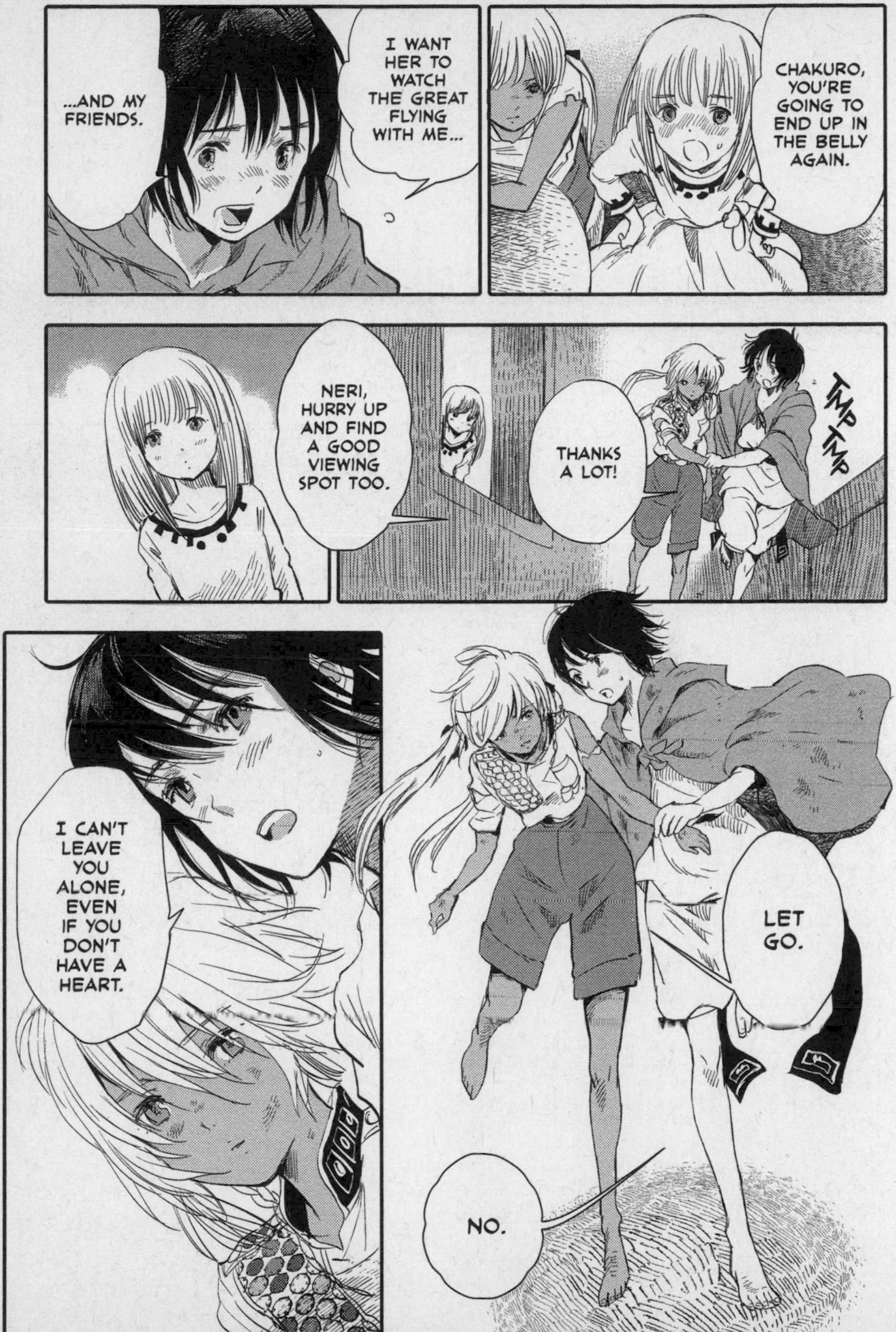
CHAKURO, YOU'RE GOING TO END UP IN THE BELLY AGAIN.
I WANT HER TO WATCH THE GREAT FLYING WITH ME...
...AND MY FRIENDS.
TMP TMP
THANKS A LOT!
NERI, HURRY UP AND FIND A GOOD VIEWING SPOT TOO.
LET GO.
NO.
I CAN'T LEAVE YOU ALONE, EVEN IF YOU DON'T HAVE A HEART.

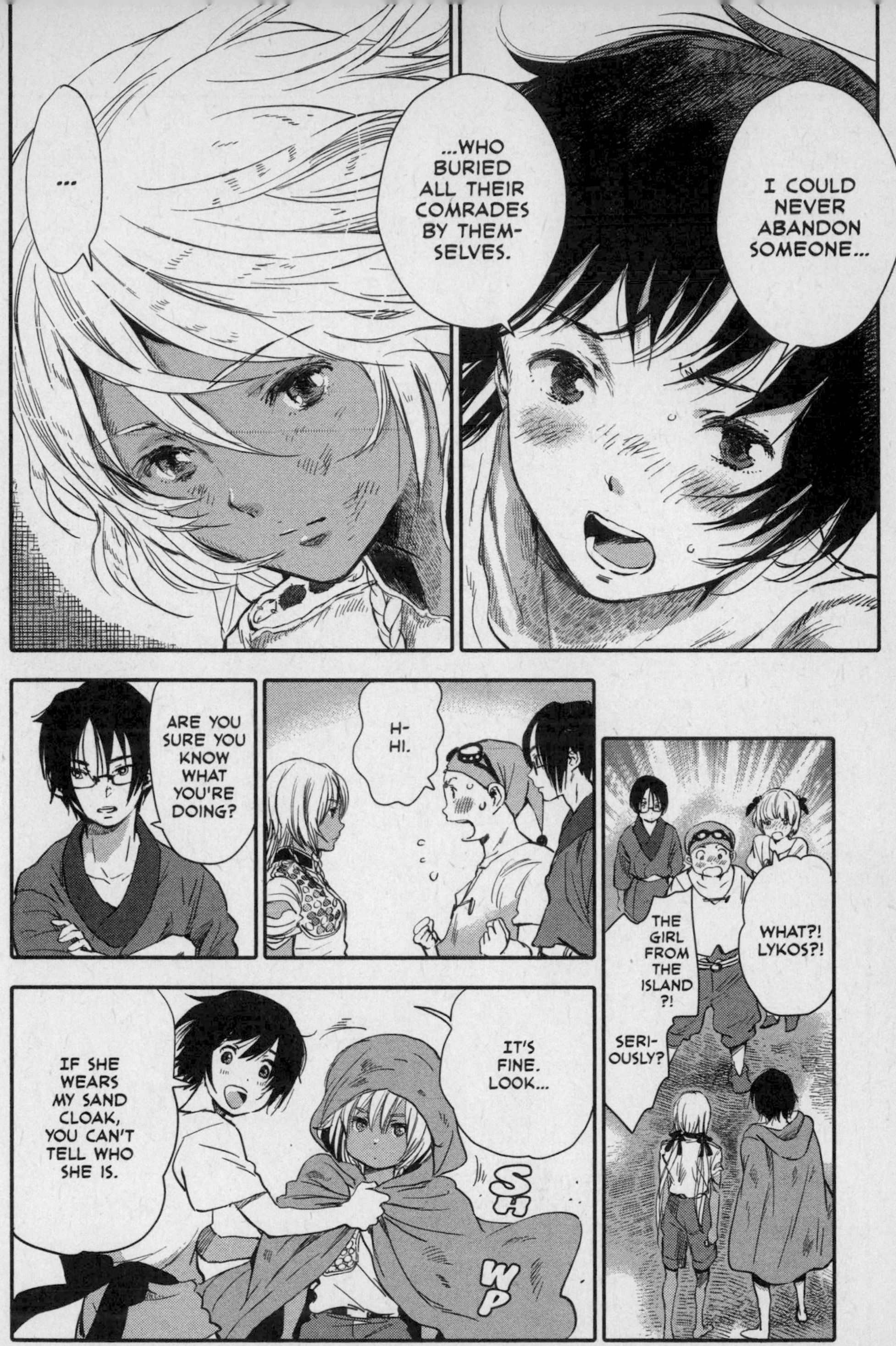
I COULD NEVER ABANDON SOMEONE...
...WHO BURIED ALL THEIR COMRADES BY THEM-SELVES.
...
WHAT?! LYKOS?!
THE GIRL FROM THE ISLAND ?!
SERI-OUSLY?
H-HI.
ARE YOU SURE YOU KNOW WHAT YOU'RE DOING?
IT'S FINE. LOOK...
IF SHE WEARS MY SAND CLOAK, YOU CAN'T TELL WHO SHE IS.
SHWP

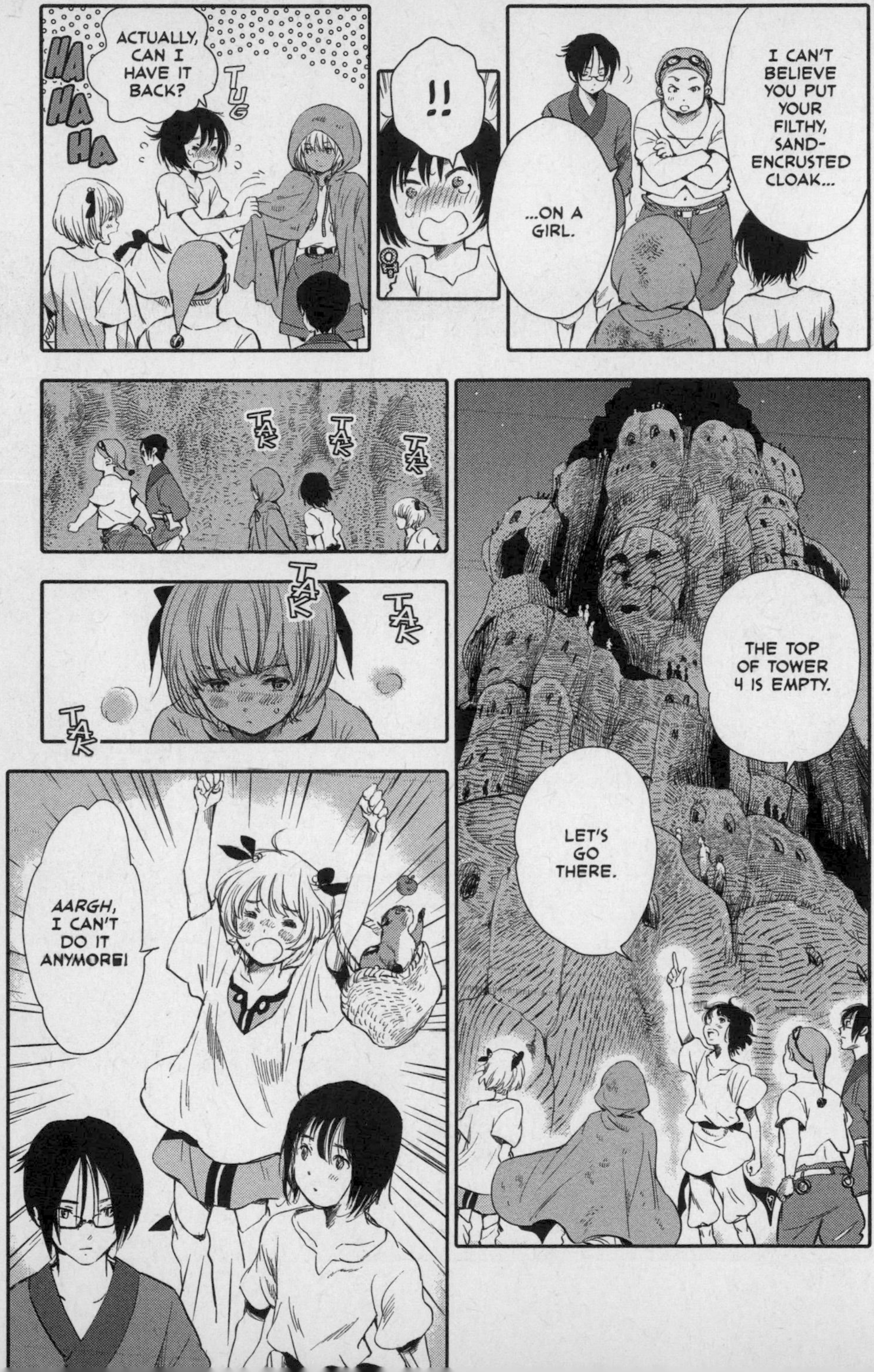
I CAN'T BELIEVE YOU PUT YOUR FILTHY, SAND-ENCRUSTED CLOAK...
...ON A GIRL.
!!
ACTUALLY, CAN I HAVE IT BACK?
TUG
HA HA HA HA
THE TOP OF TOWER 4 IS EMPTY.
LET'S GO THERE.
TAK TAK TAK
TAK TAK TAK
AARGH, I CAN'T DO IT ANYMORE!

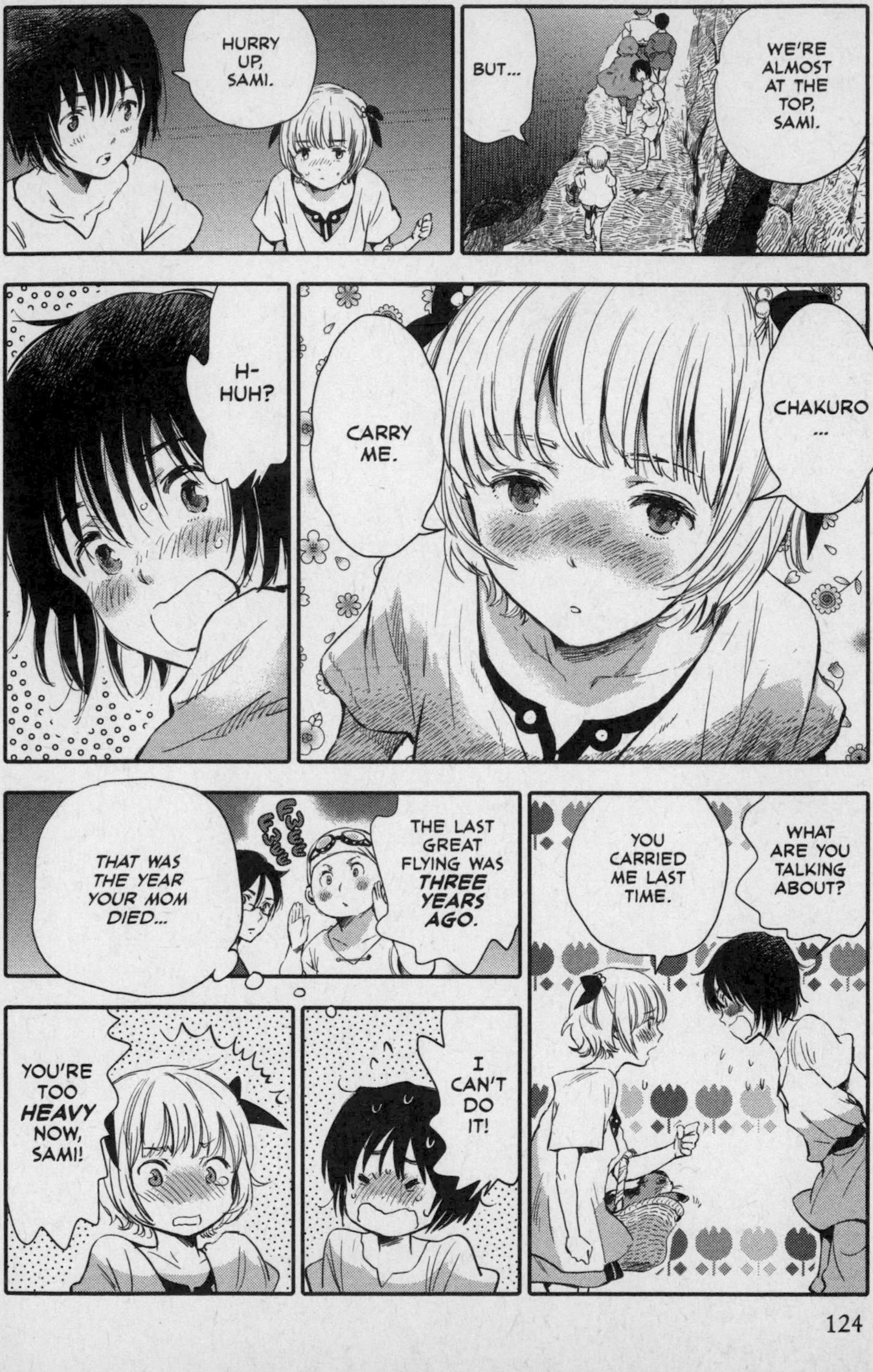
WE'RE ALMOST AT THE TOP, SAMI.
BUT...
HURRY UP, SAMI.
CHAKURO...
CARRY ME.
H-HUH?
WHAT ARE YOU TALKING ABOUT?
YOU CARRIED ME LAST TIME.
THE LAST GREAT FLYING WAS *THREE YEARS AGO*.
THAT WAS THE YEAR YOUR MOM DIED...
I CAN'T DO IT!
YOU'RE TOO *HEAVY* NOW, SAMI!

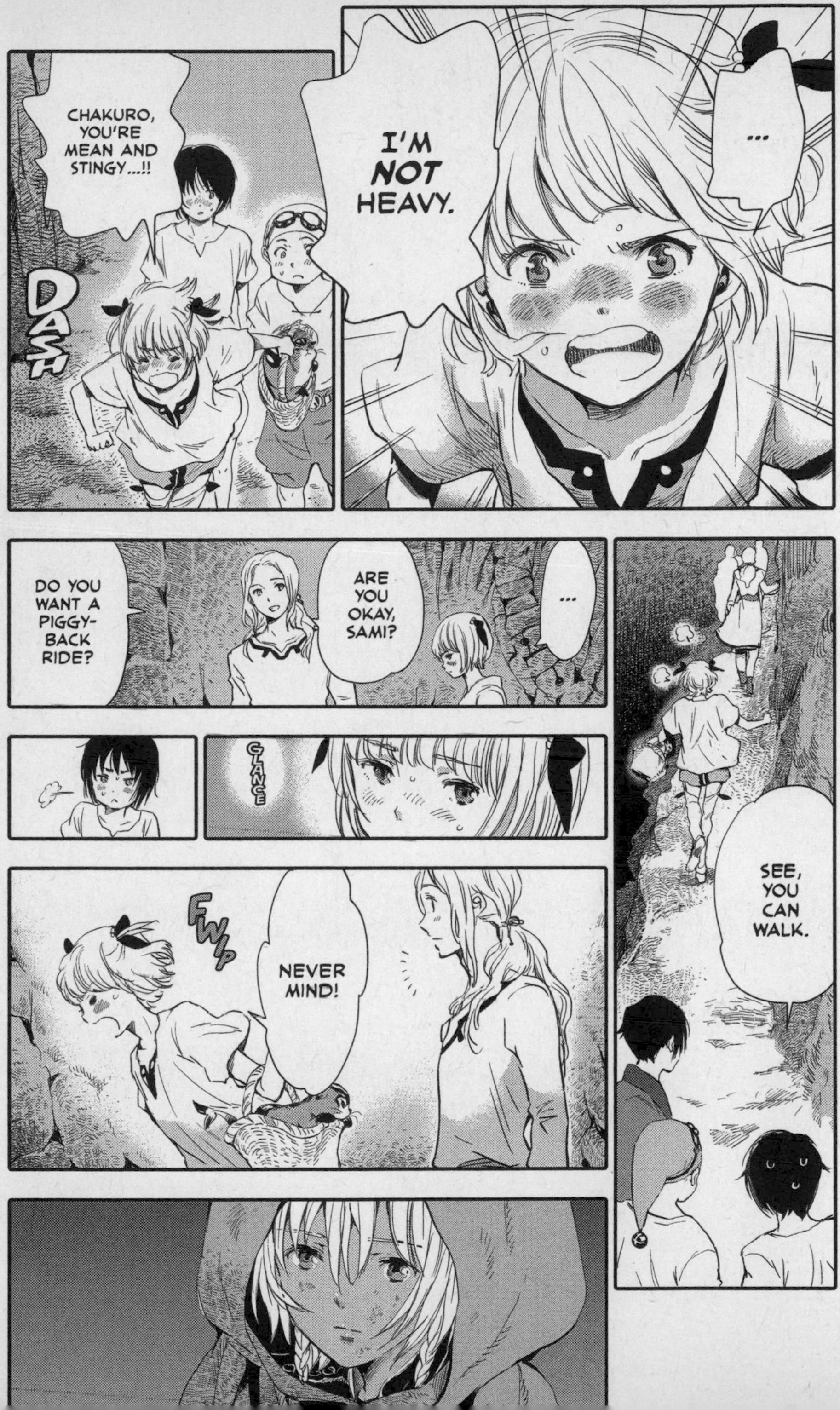
...
I'M NOT HEAVY.
CHAKURO, YOU'RE MEAN AND STINGY...!!
DASH
SEE, YOU CAN WALK.
...
ARE YOU OKAY, SAMI?
DO YOU WANT A PIGGY-BACK RIDE?
GLANCE
NEVER MIND!
FWIP

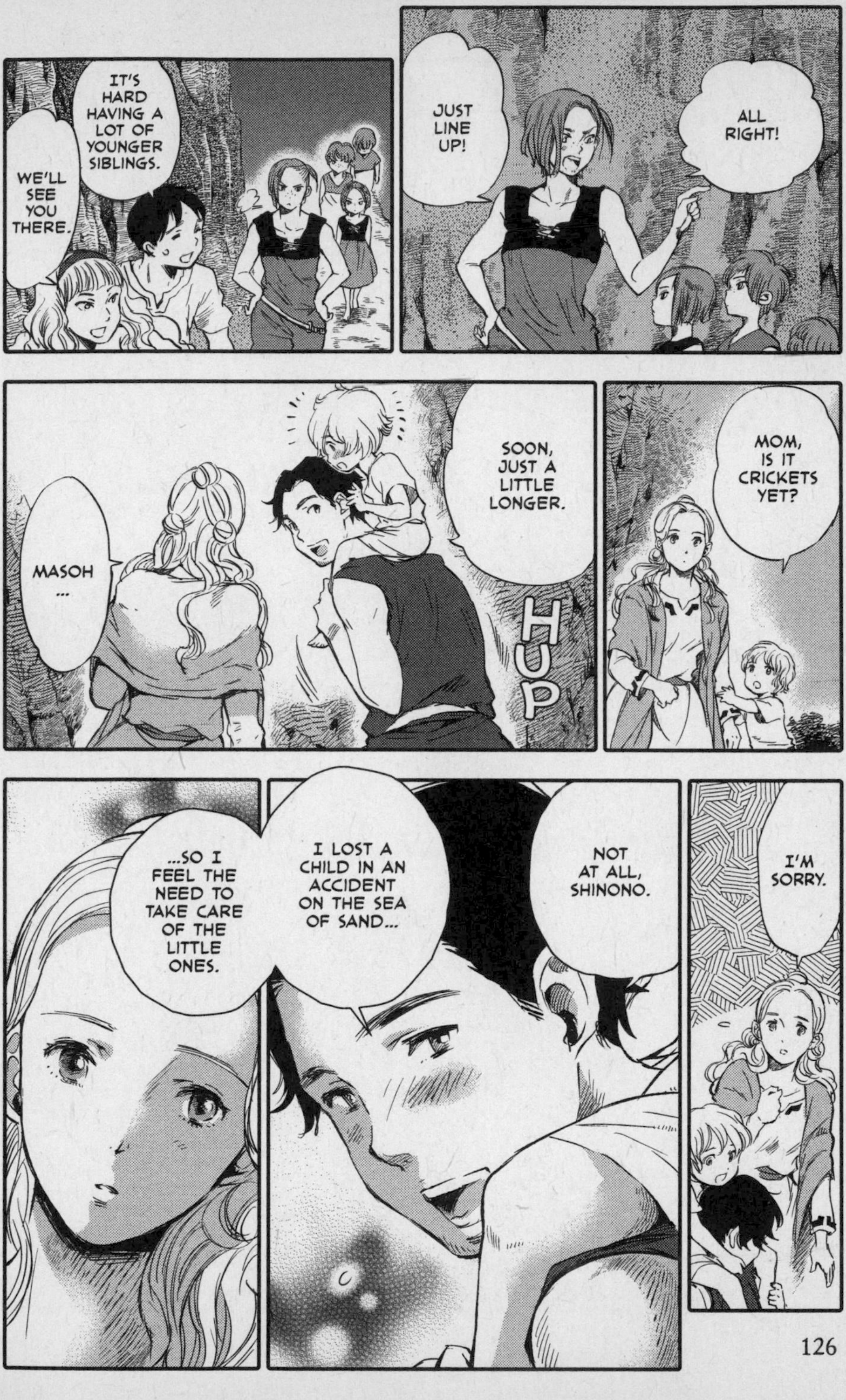
ALL RIGHT!
JUST LINE UP!
IT'S HARD HAVING A LOT OF YOUNGER SIBLINGS.
WE'LL SEE YOU THERE.
MOM, IS IT CRICKETS YET?
SOON, JUST A LITTLE LONGER.
HUP
MASOH ...
I'M SORRY.
NOT AT ALL, SHINONO.
I LOST A CHILD IN AN ACCIDENT ON THE SEA OF SAND...
...SO I FEEL THE NEED TO TAKE CARE OF THE LITTLE ONES.

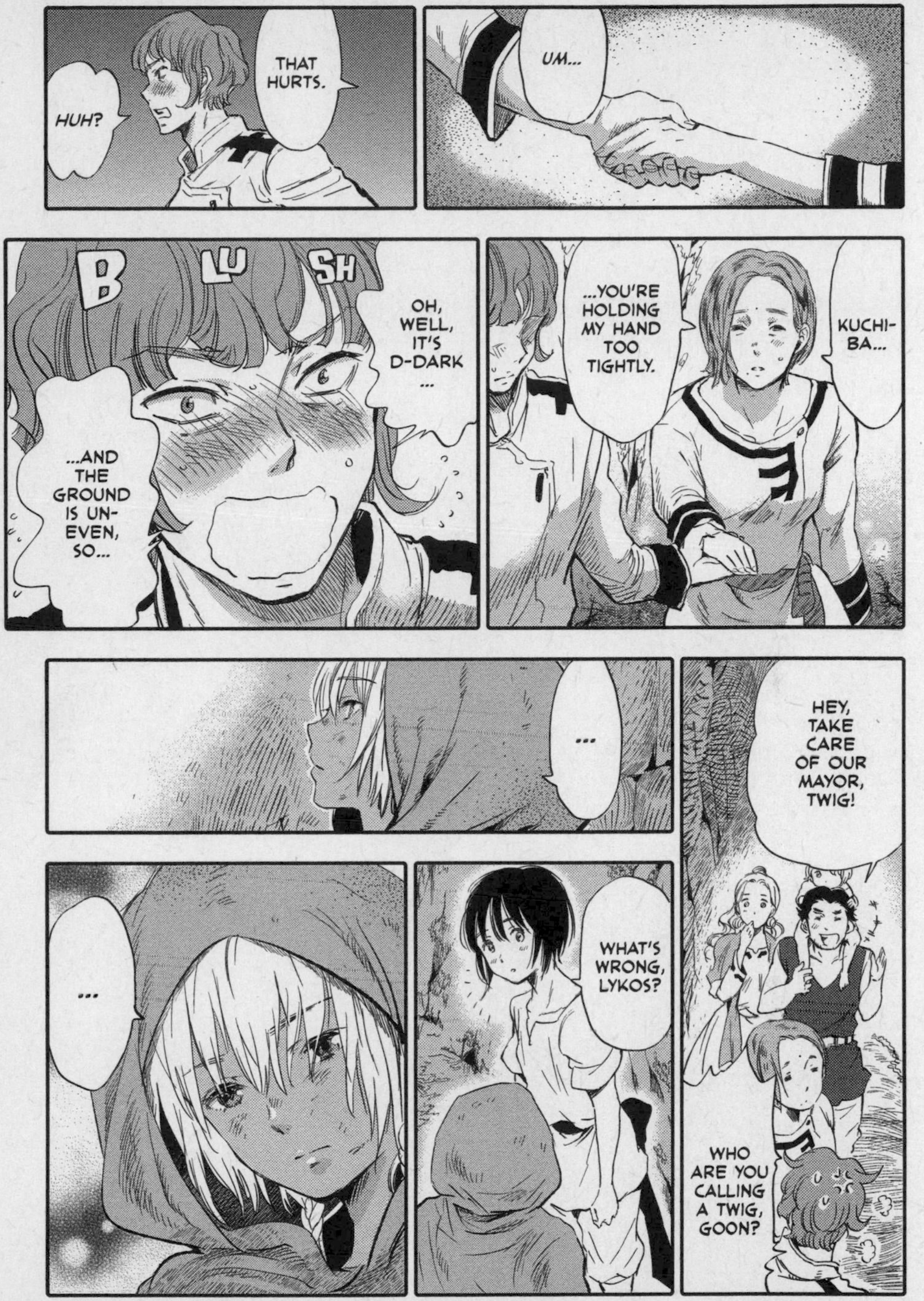
UM...
THAT HURTS.
HUH?
KUCHIBA...
...YOU'RE HOLDING MY HAND TOO TIGHTLY.
BLUSH
OH, WELL, IT'S D-DARK ...
...AND THE GROUND IS UNEVEN, SO...
HEY, TAKE CARE OF OUR MAYOR, TWIG!
WHO ARE YOU CALLING A TWIG, GOON?
...
WHAT'S WRONG, LYKOS?
...

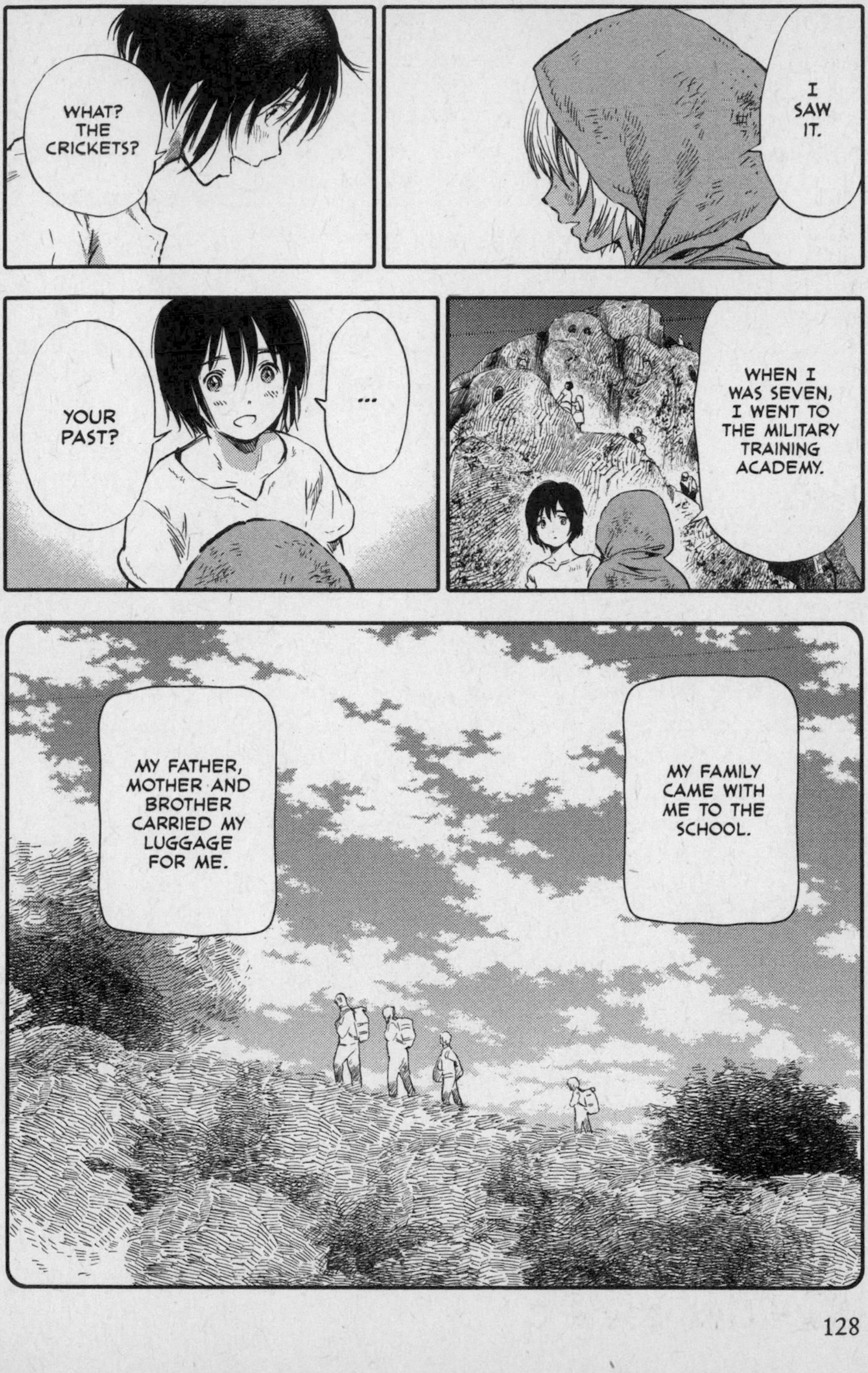
I SAW IT.
WHAT? THE CRICKETS?
WHEN I WAS SEVEN, I WENT TO THE MILITARY TRAINING ACADEMY.
...
YOUR PAST?
MY FAMILY CAME WITH ME TO THE SCHOOL.
MY FATHER, MOTHER AND BROTHER CARRIED MY LUGGAGE FOR ME.

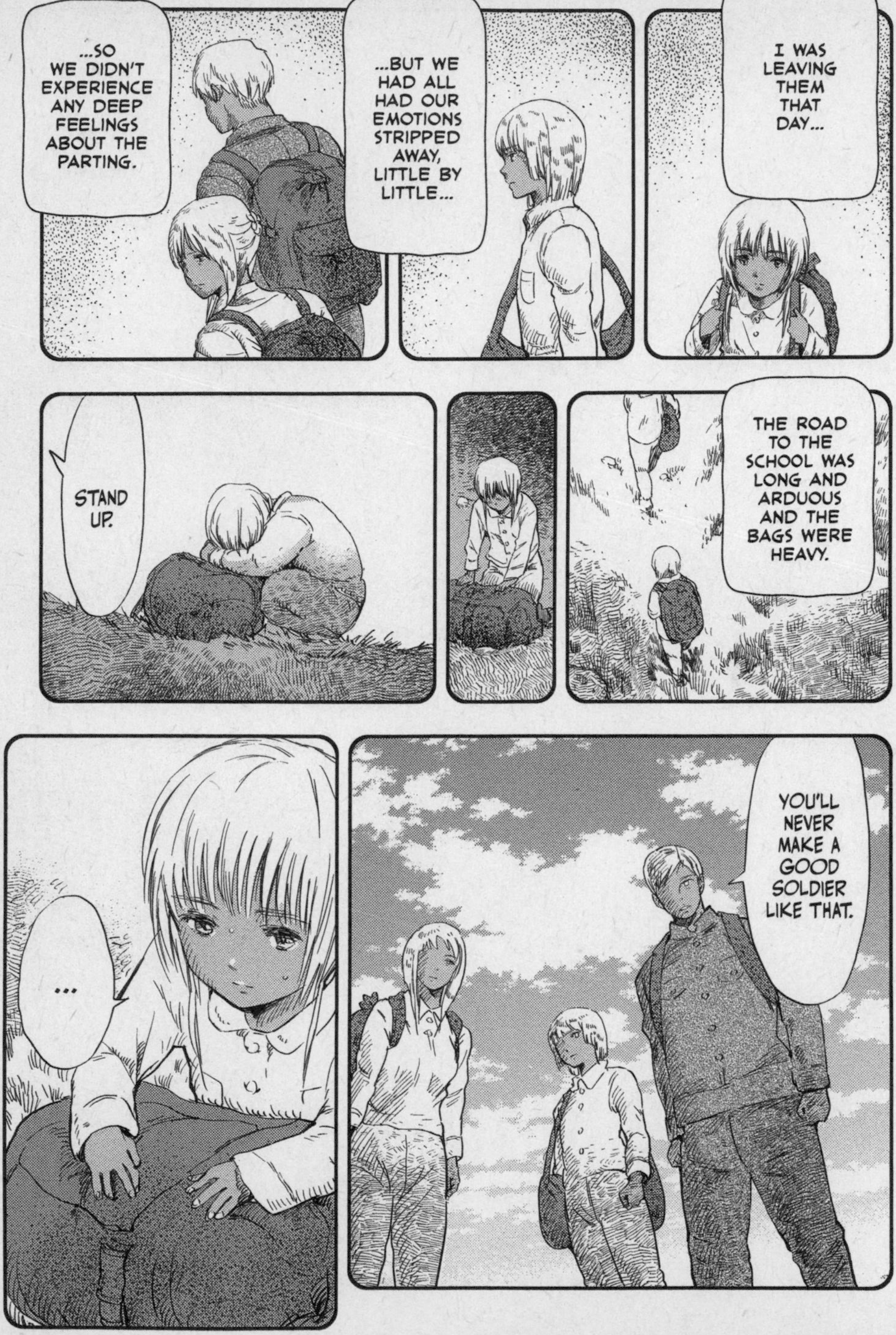
I WAS LEAVING THEM THAT DAY...
...BUT WE HAD ALL HAD OUR EMOTIONS STRIPPED AWAY, LITTLE BY LITTLE...
...SO WE DIDN'T EXPERIENCE ANY DEEP FEELINGS ABOUT THE PARTING.
THE ROAD TO THE SCHOOL WAS LONG AND ARDUOUS AND THE BAGS WERE HEAVY.
STAND UP.
YOU'LL NEVER MAKE A GOOD SOLDIER LIKE THAT.
...

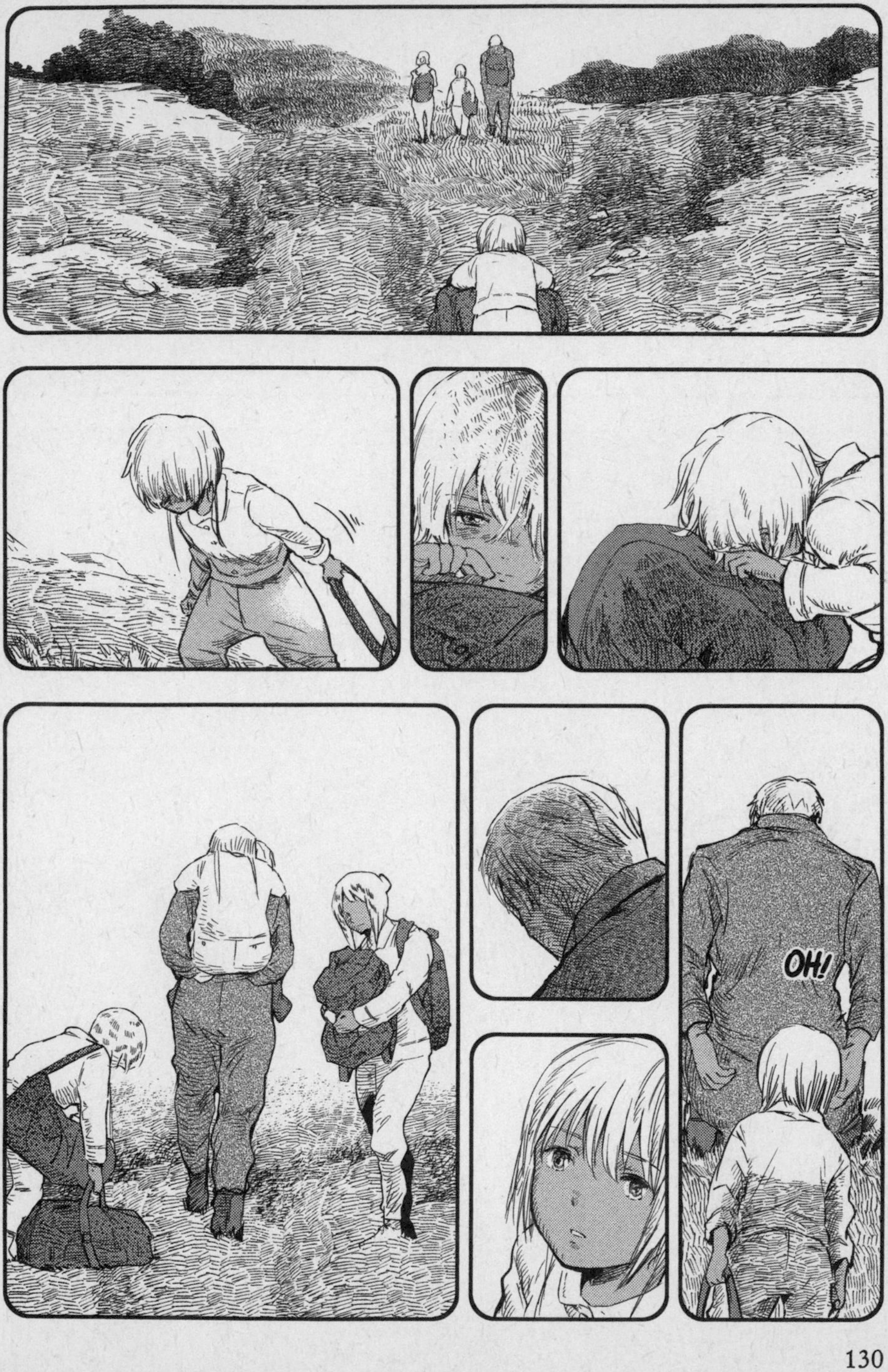
OH!

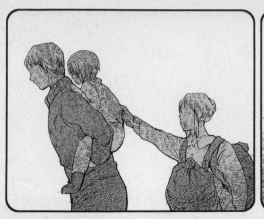

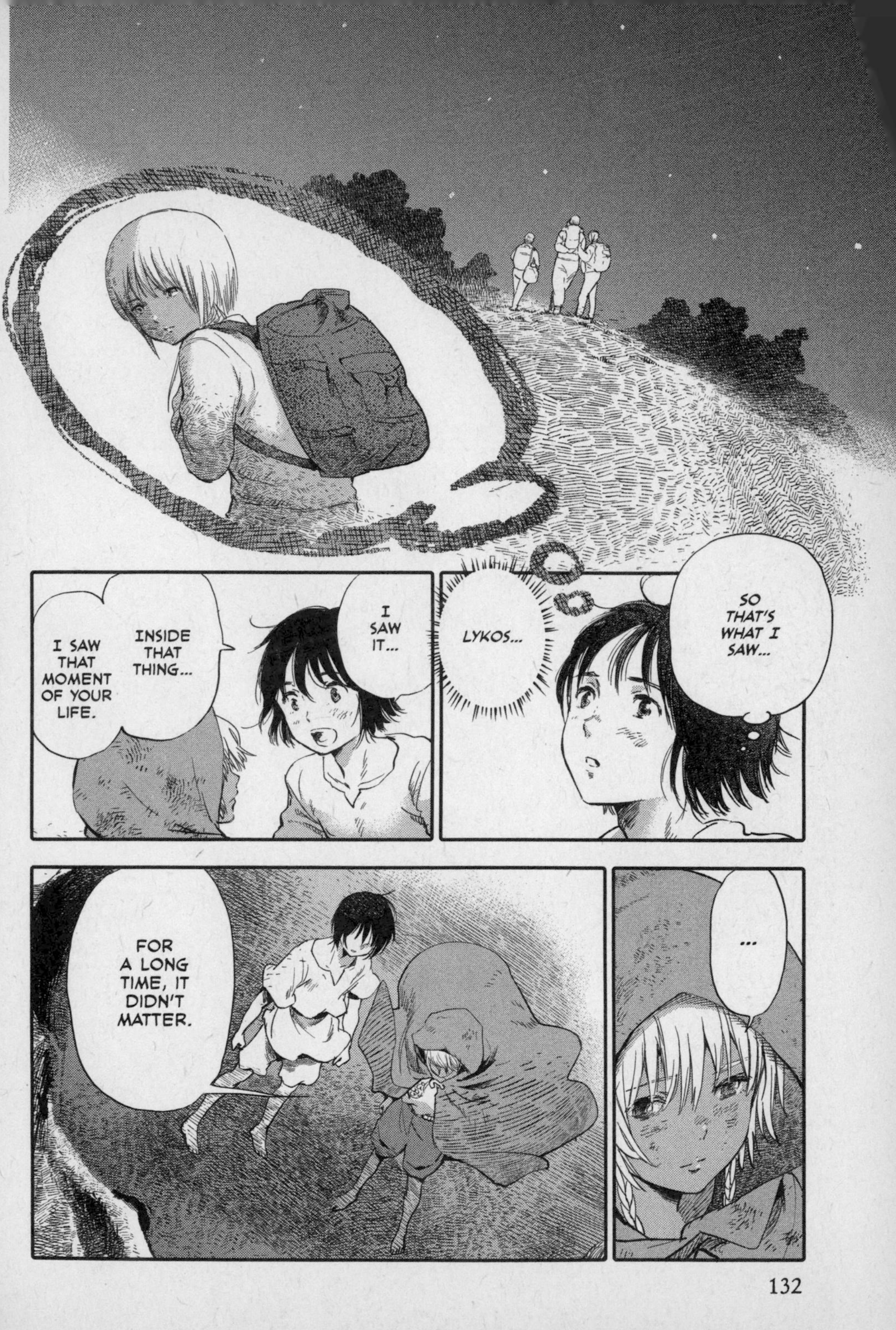
SO THAT'S WHAT I SAW...
LYKOS...
I SAW IT...
INSIDE THAT THING...
I SAW THAT MOMENT OF YOUR LIFE.
...
FOR A LONG TIME, IT DIDN'T MATTER.

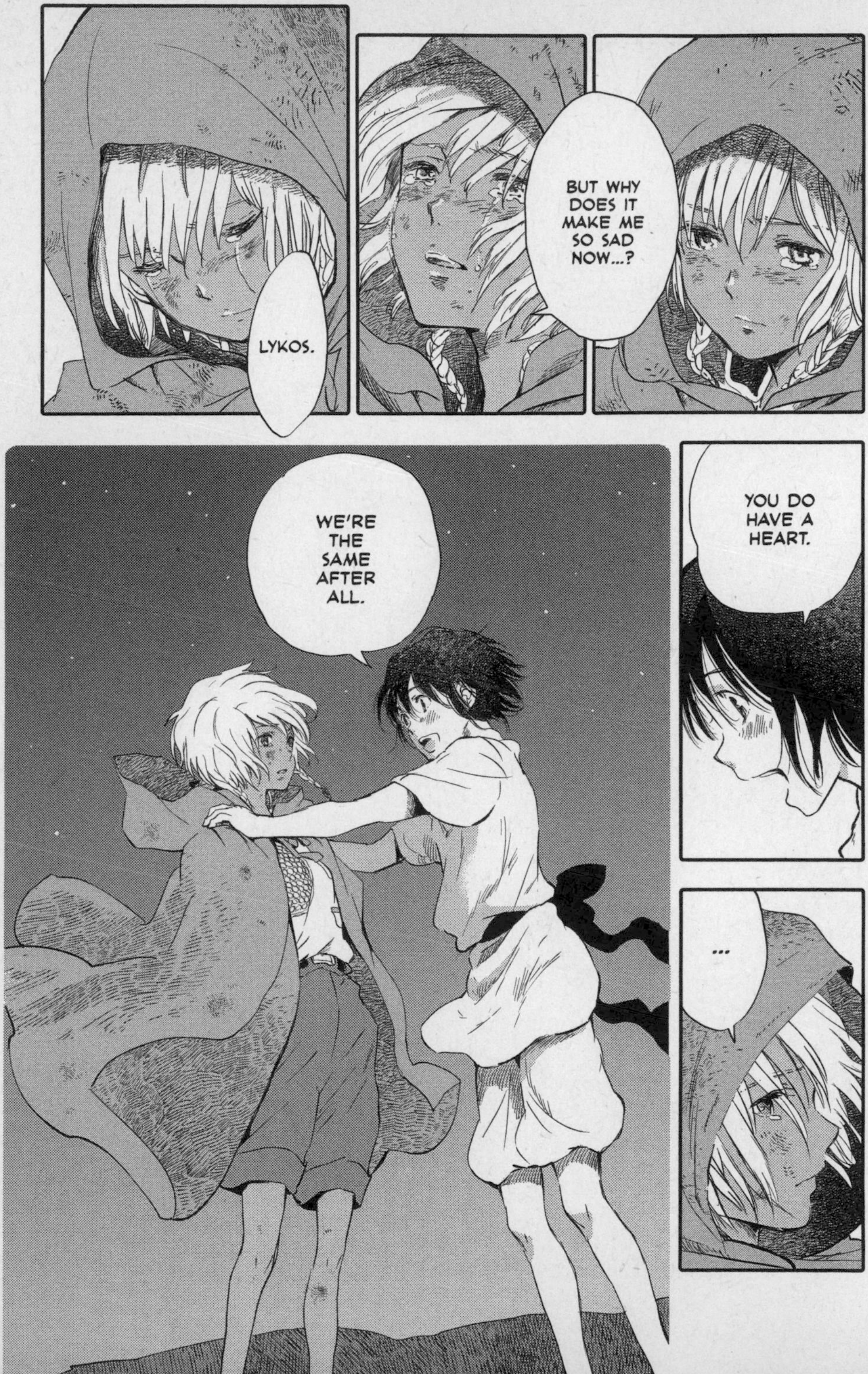
BUT WHY DOES IT MAKE ME SO SAD NOW...?
LYKOS.
YOU DO HAVE A HEART.
...
WE'RE THE SAME AFTER ALL.

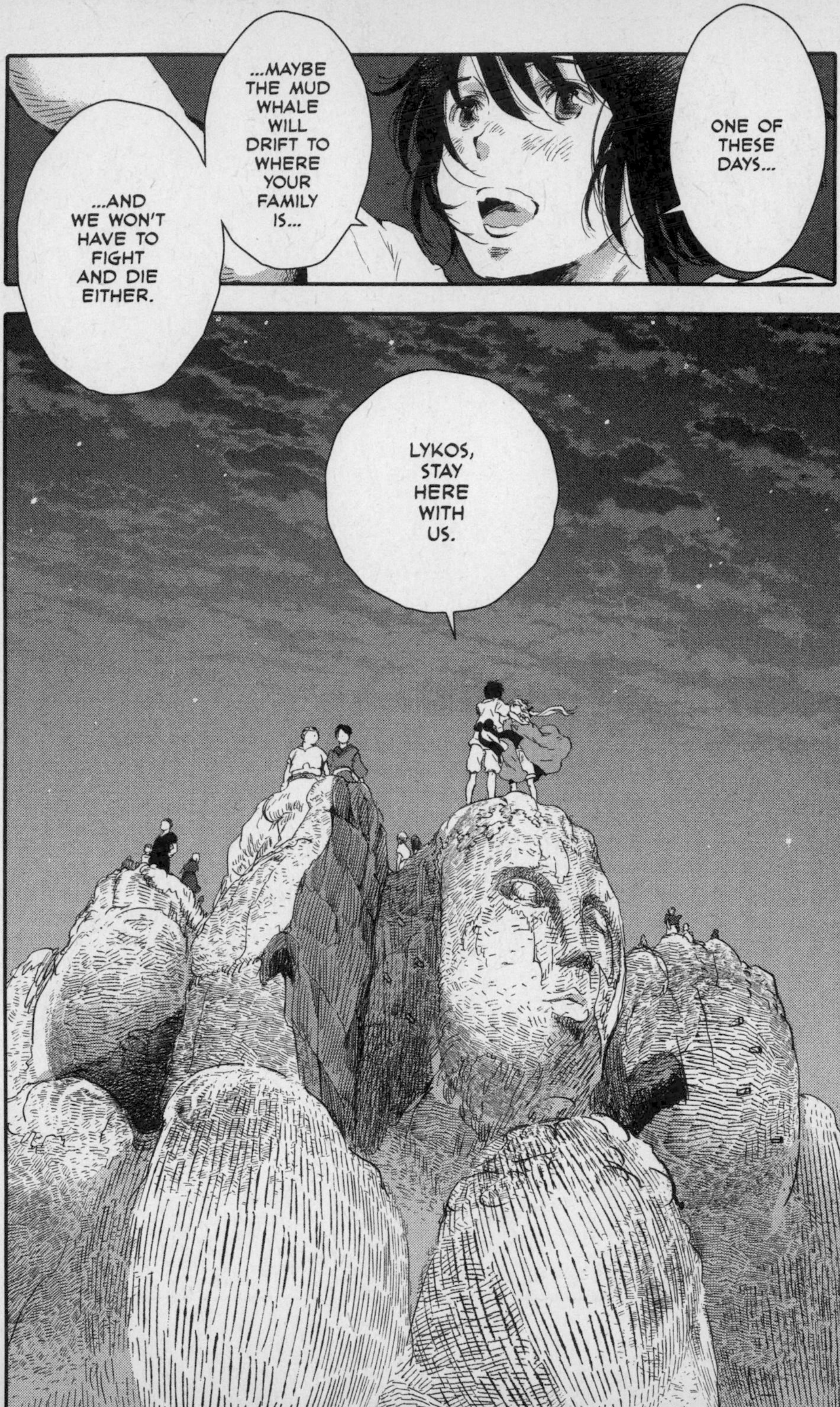
ONE OF THESE DAYS...
...MAYBE THE MUD WHALE WILL DRIFT TO WHERE YOUR FAMILY IS...
...AND WE WON'T HAVE TO FIGHT AND DIE EITHER.
LYKOS, STAY HERE WITH US.

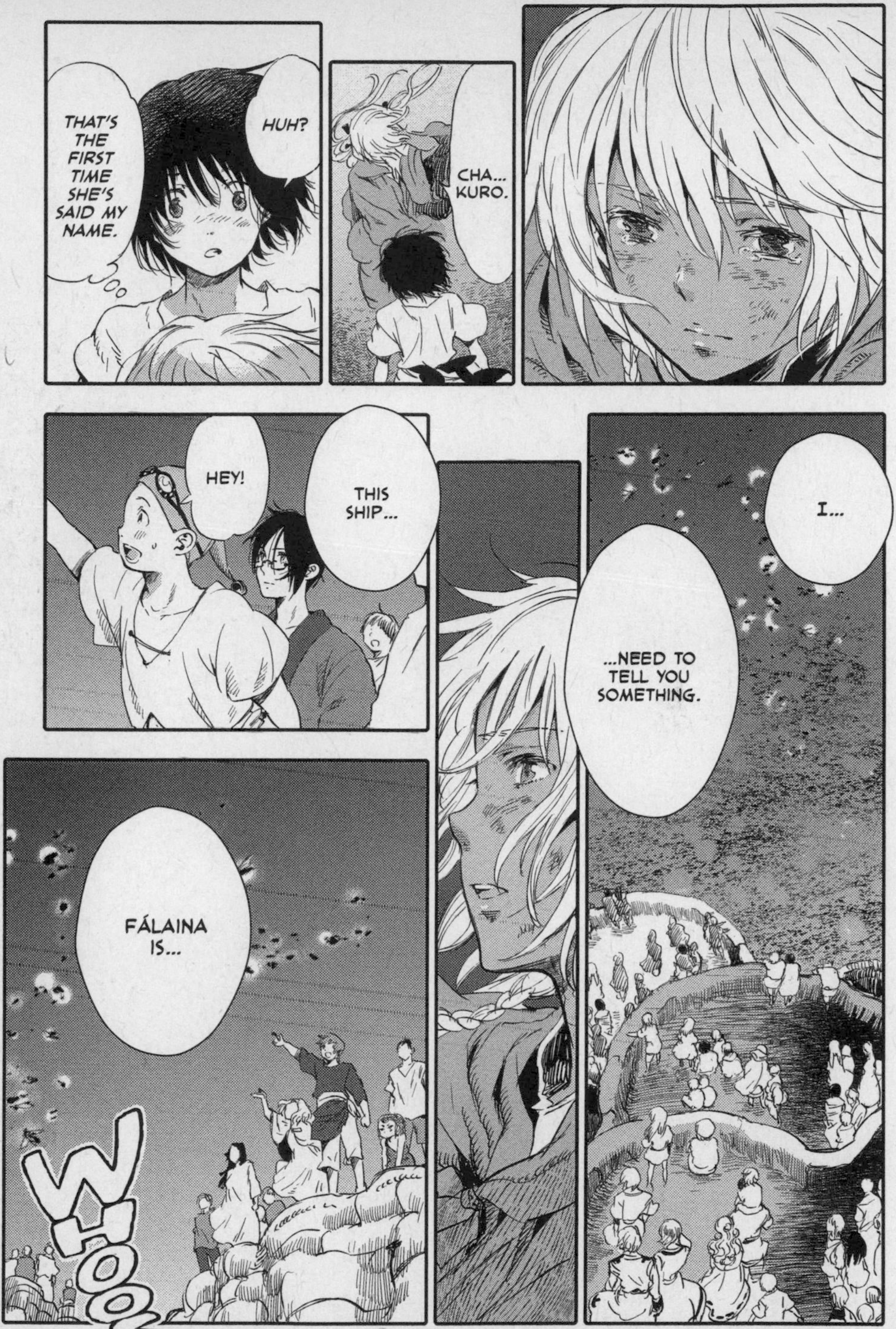
CHA... KURO.
HUH?
THAT'S THE FIRST TIME SHE'S SAID MY NAME.
I...
...NEED TO TELL YOU SOMETHING.
THIS SHIP...
HEY!
FÁLAINA IS...
WHOOMP

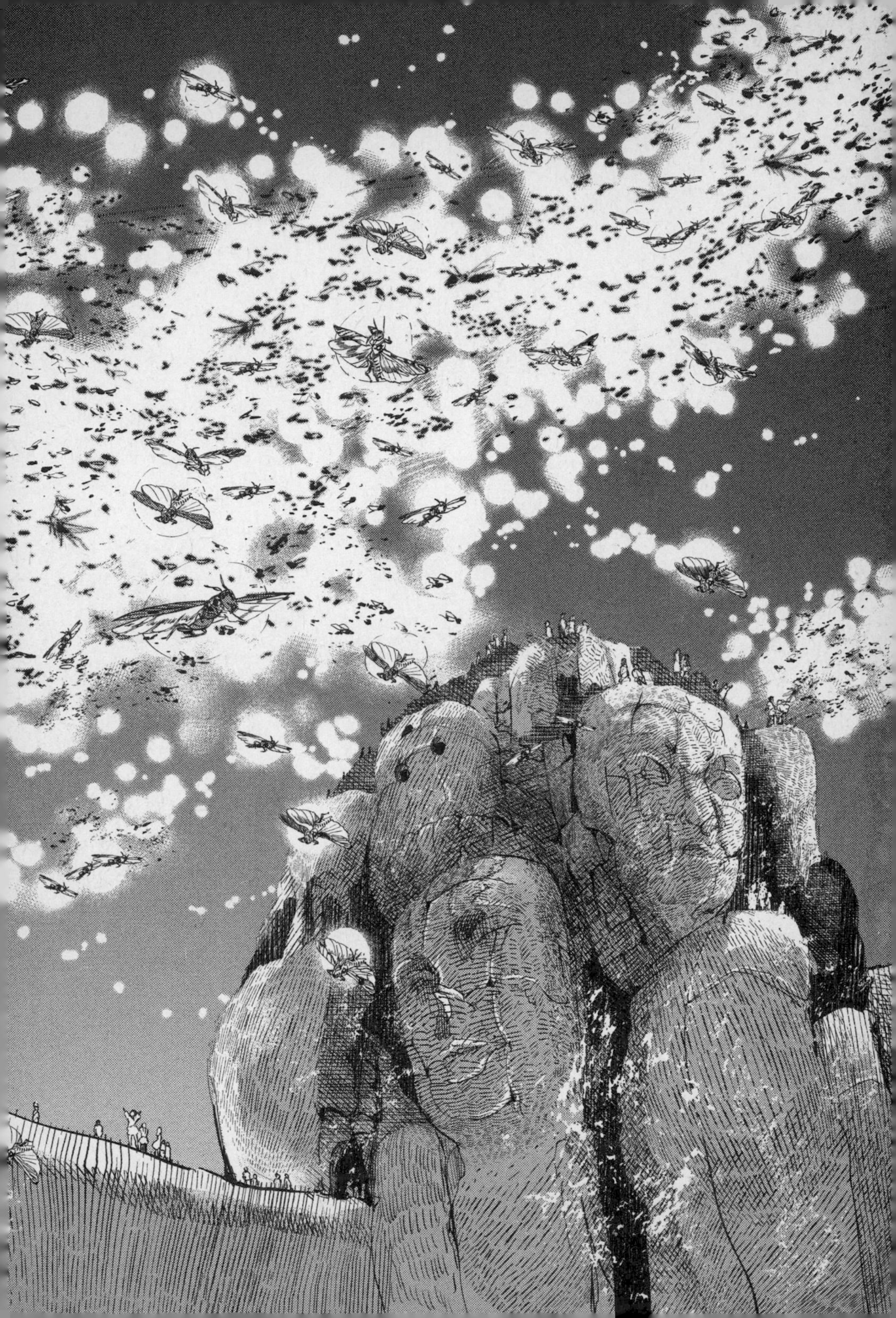

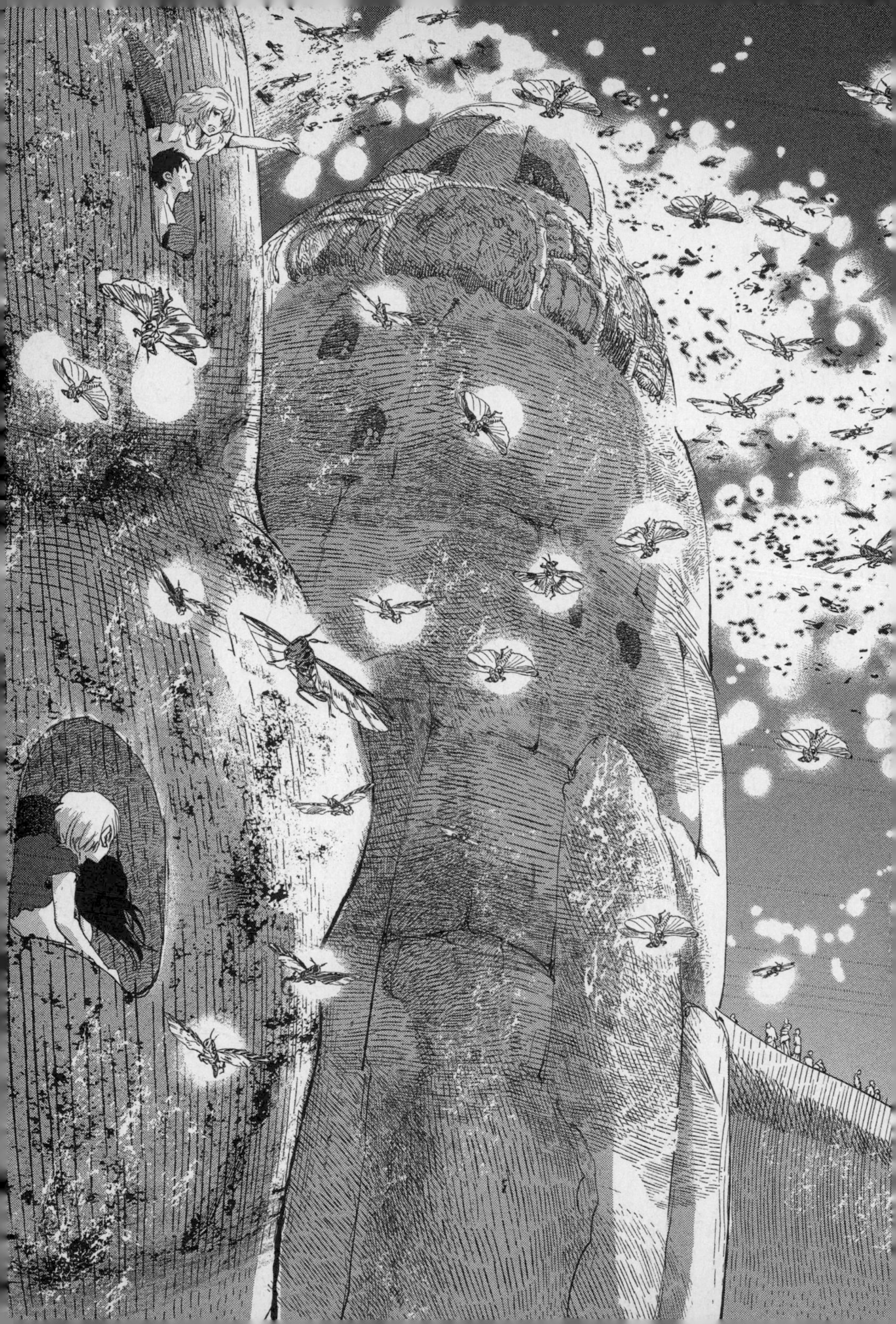

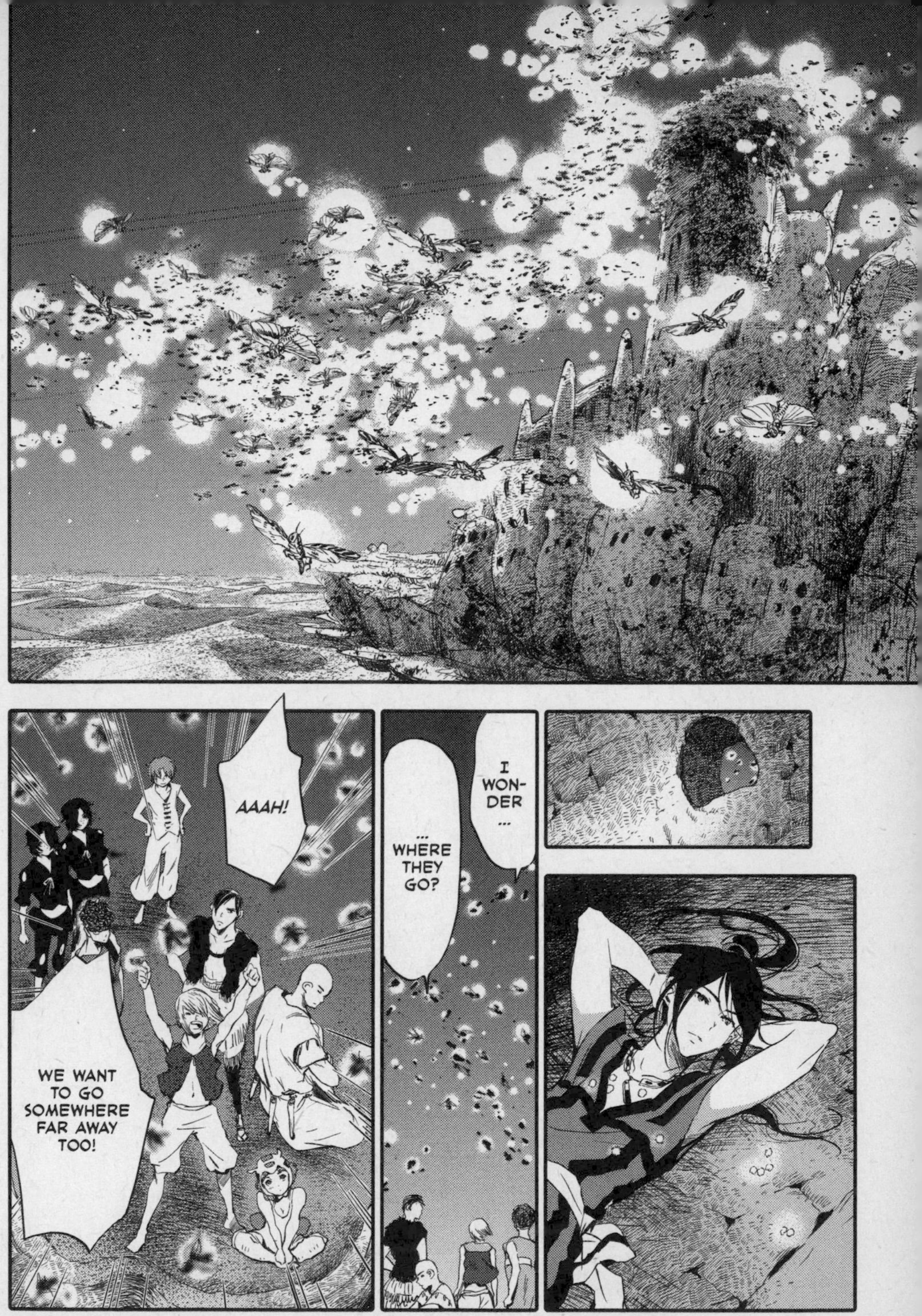
I WONDER...
...WHERE THEY GO?
AAAH!
WE WANT TO GO SOMEWHERE FAR AWAY TOO!

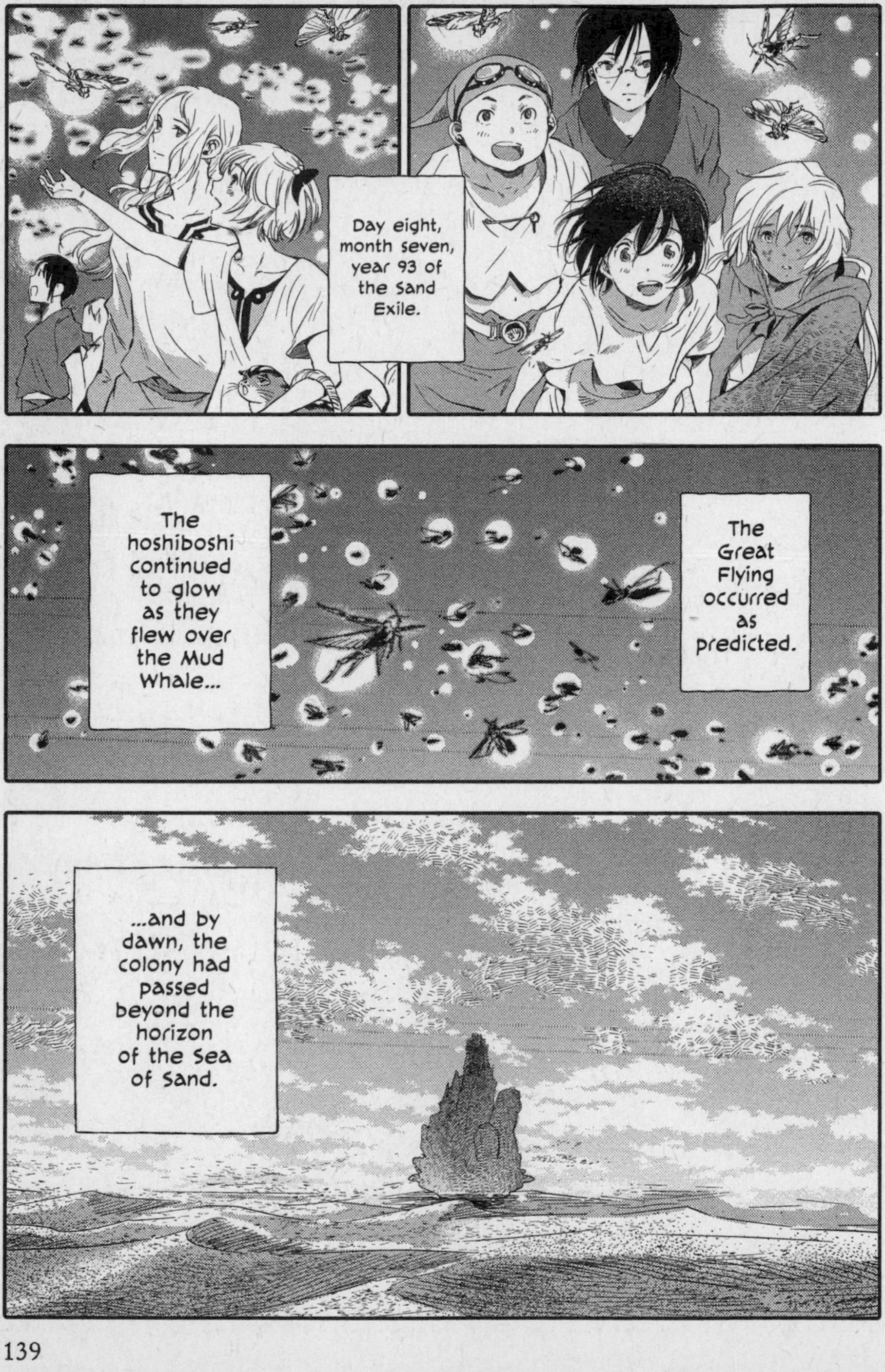
Day eight, month seven, year 93 of the Sand Exile.
The Great Flying occurred as predicted.
The hoshiboshi continued to glow as they flew over the Mud Whale...
...and by dawn, the colony had passed beyond the horizon of the Sea of Sand.

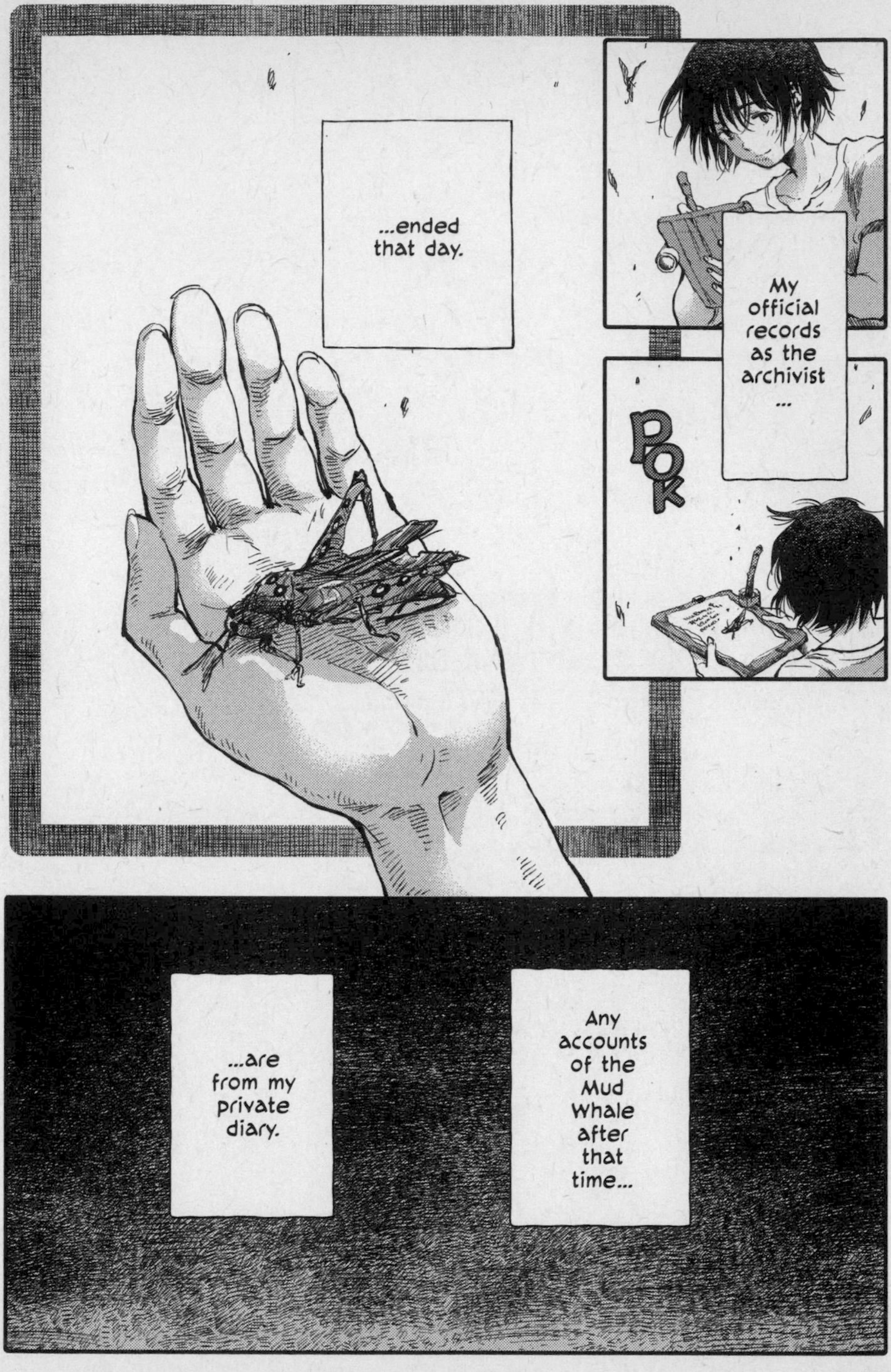
My official records as the archivist...
POK
...ended that day.
Any accounts of the Mud Whale after that time...
...are from my private diary.

In a Sky That Twinkles with Memories -The End-

The Archivist's Notes

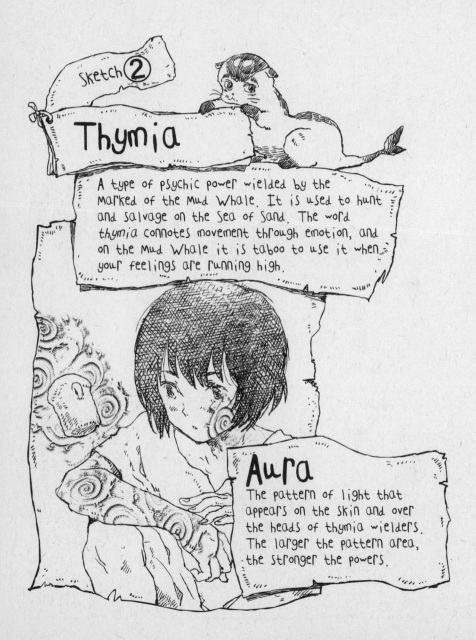

Sketch 2

Thymia

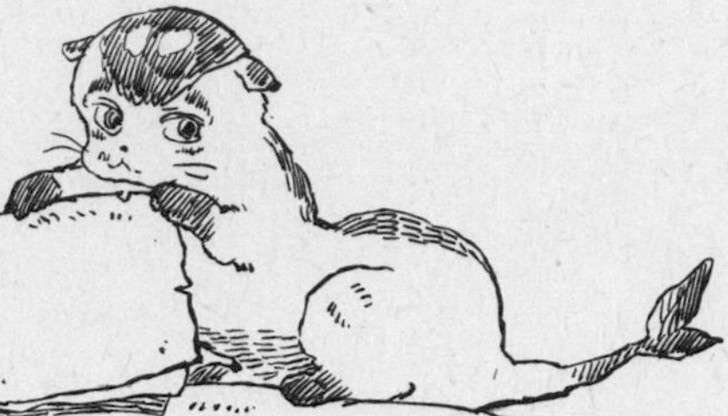

A type of psychic power wielded by the marked of the Mud Whale. It is used to hunt and salvage on the Sea of Sand. The word *thymia* connotes movement through emotion, and on the Mud Whale it is taboo to use it when your feelings are running high.

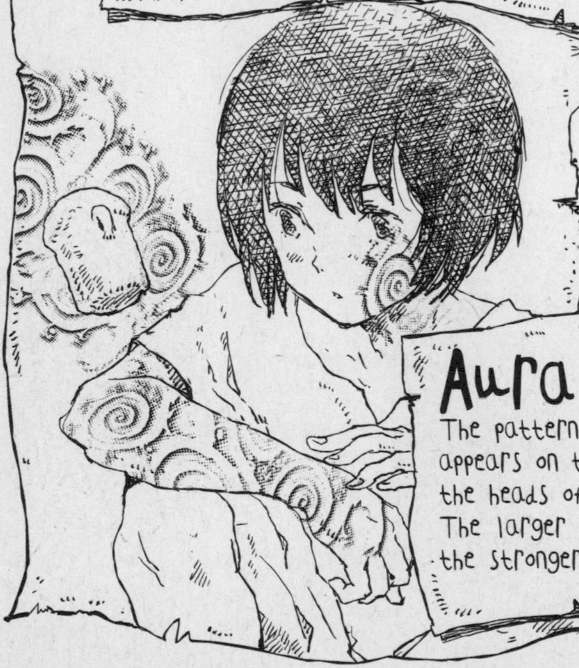

Aura

The pattern of light that appears on the skin and over the heads of thymia wielders. The larger the pattern area, the stronger the powers.

The Archivist's Notes

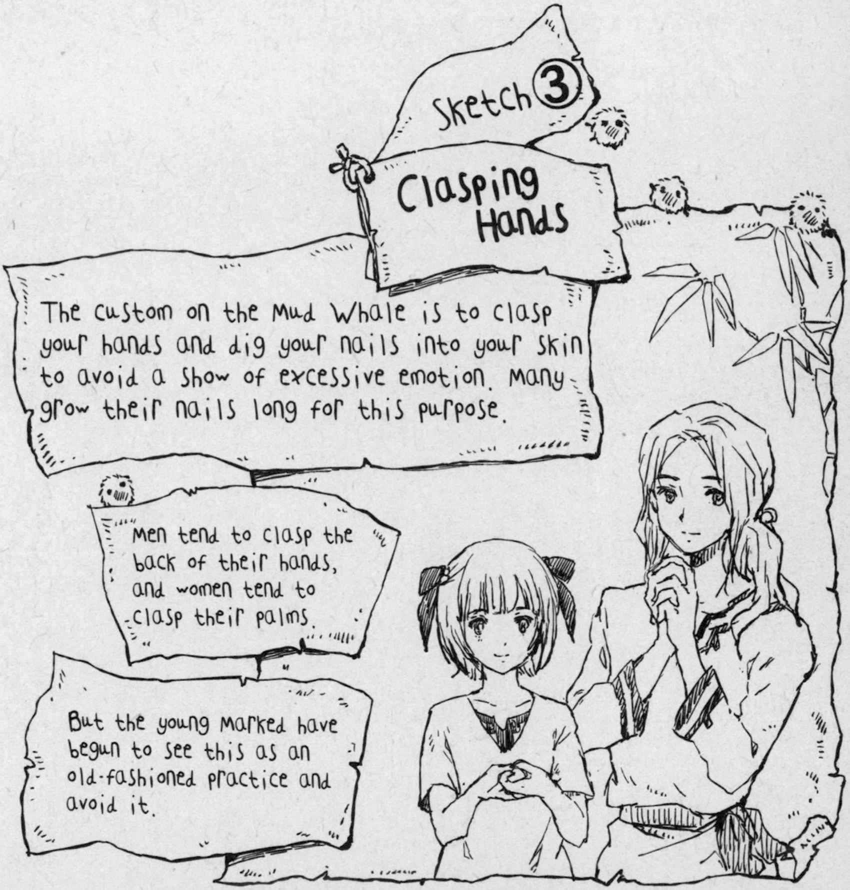
Sketch 3
Clasping Hands
The custom on the Mud Whale is to clasp your hands and dig your nails into your skin to avoid a show of excessive emotion. Many grow their nails long for this purpose.
Men tend to clasp the back of their hands, and women tend to clasp their palms.
But the young marked have begun to see this as an old-fashioned practice and avoid it.

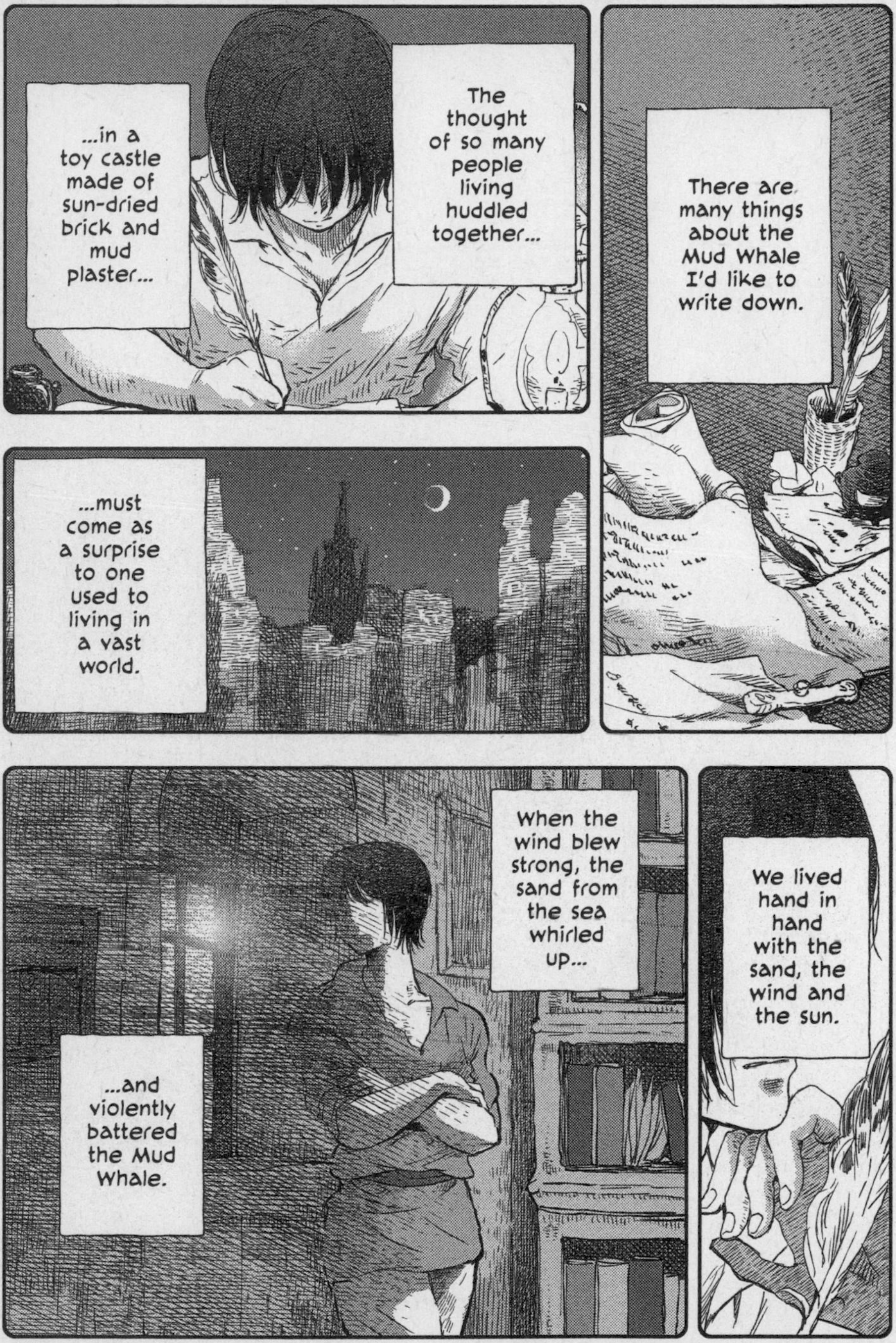
There are many things about the Mud Whale I'd like to write down.
The thought of so many people living huddled together...
...in a toy castle made of sun-dried brick and mud plaster...
...must come as a surprise to one used to living in a vast world.
We lived hand in hand with the sand, the wind and the sun.
When the wind blew strong, the sand from the sea whirled up...
...and violently battered the Mud Whale.

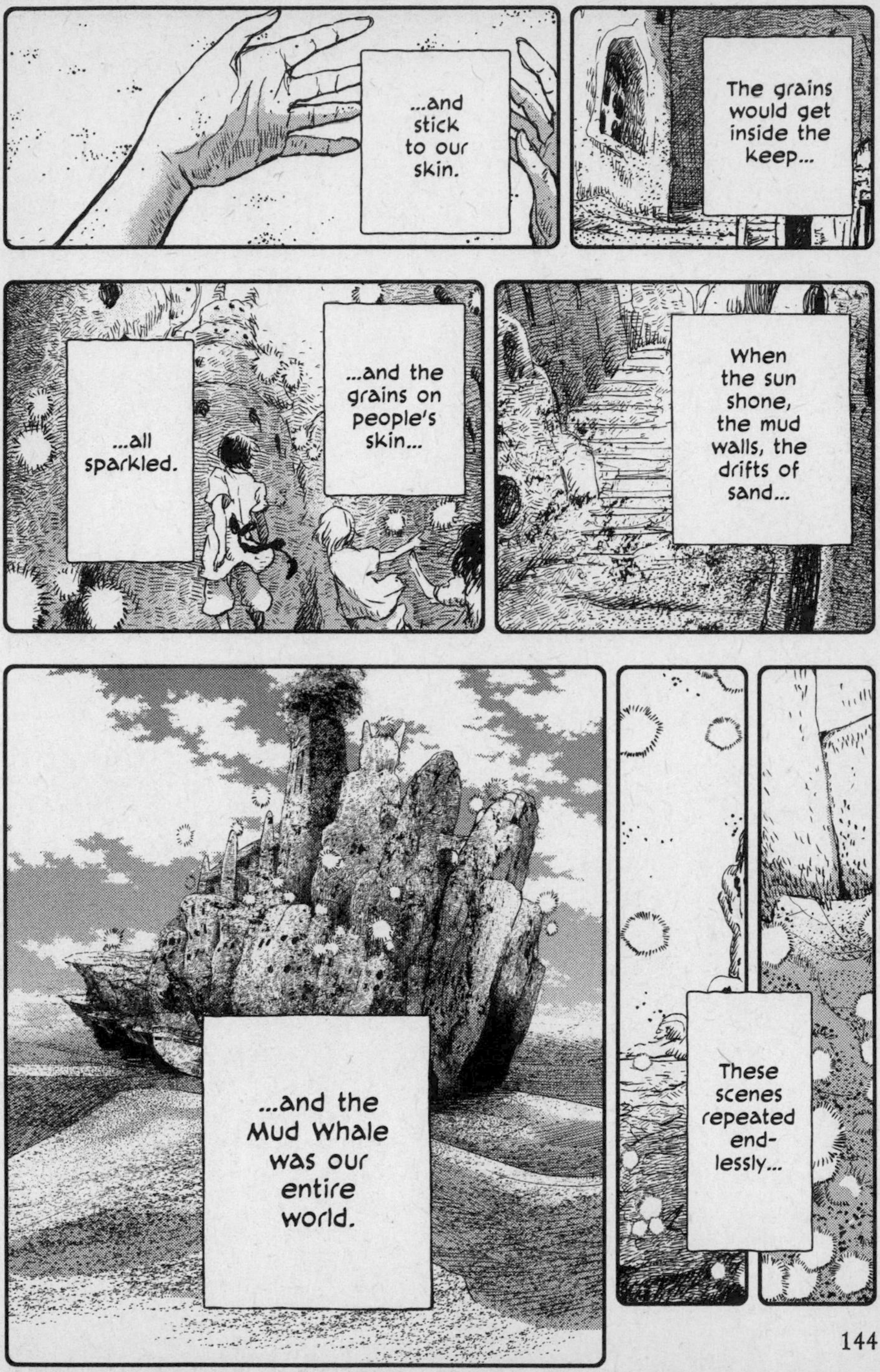
The grains would get inside the keep...
...and stick to our skin.
When the sun shone, the mud walls, the drifts of sand...
...and the grains on people's skin...
...all sparkled.
These scenes repeated end-lessly...
...and the Mud Whale was our entire world.

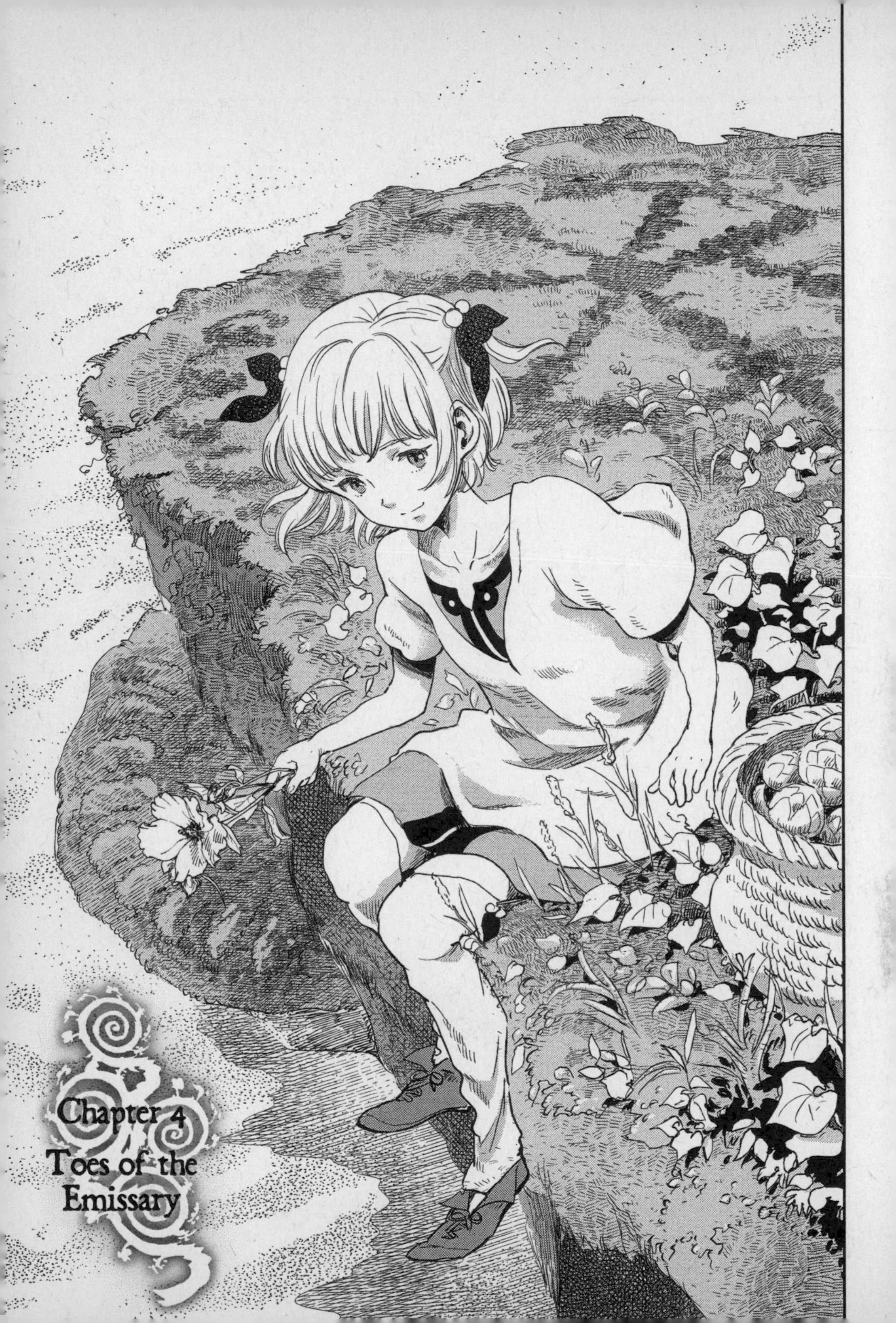
Chapter 4
Toes of the
Emissary

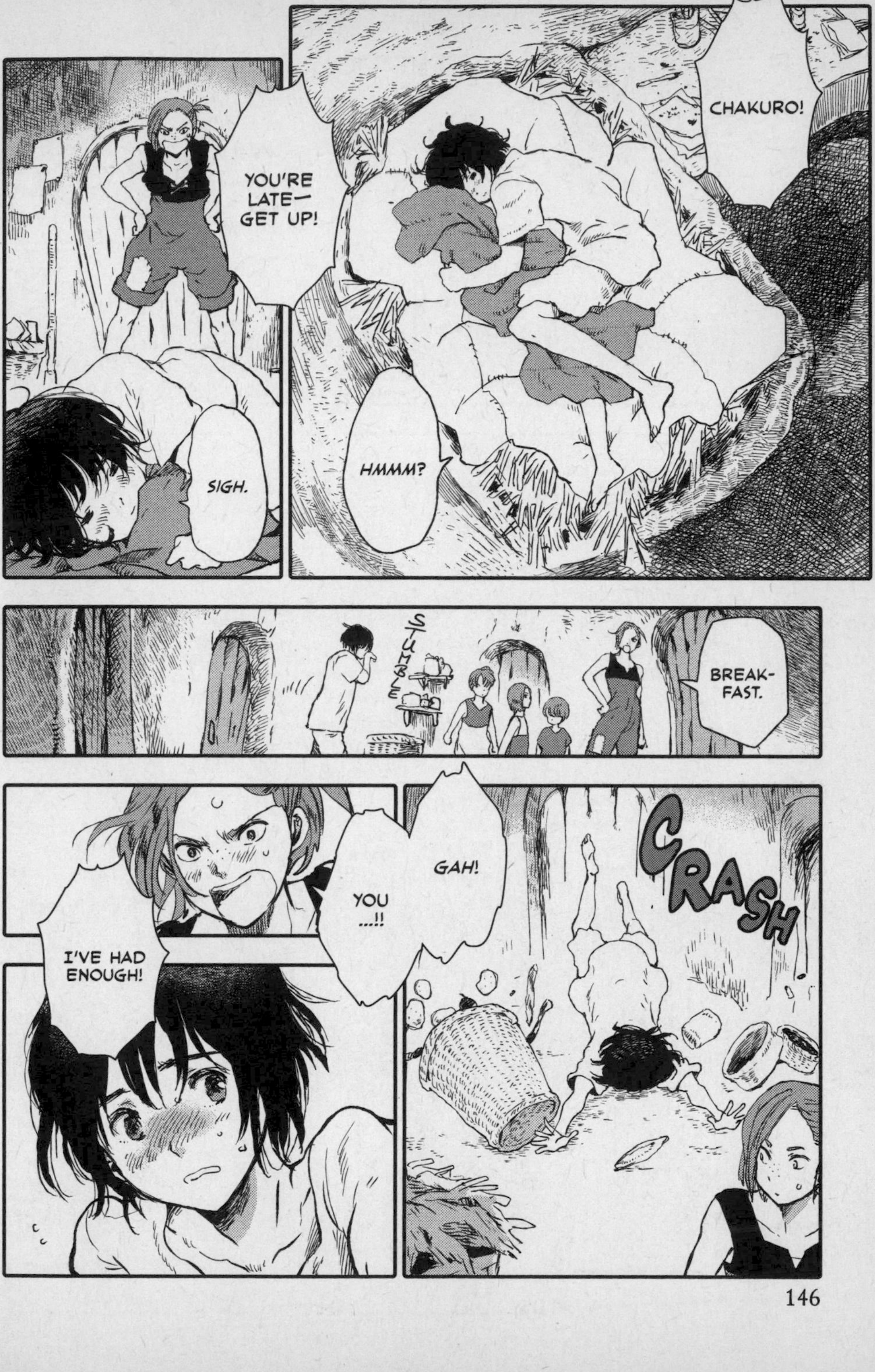
CHAKURO!
HMMM?
YOU'RE LATE— GET UP!
SIGH.
BREAK-FAST.
STUMBLE
CRASH
GAH!
YOU ...!!
I'VE HAD ENOUGH!

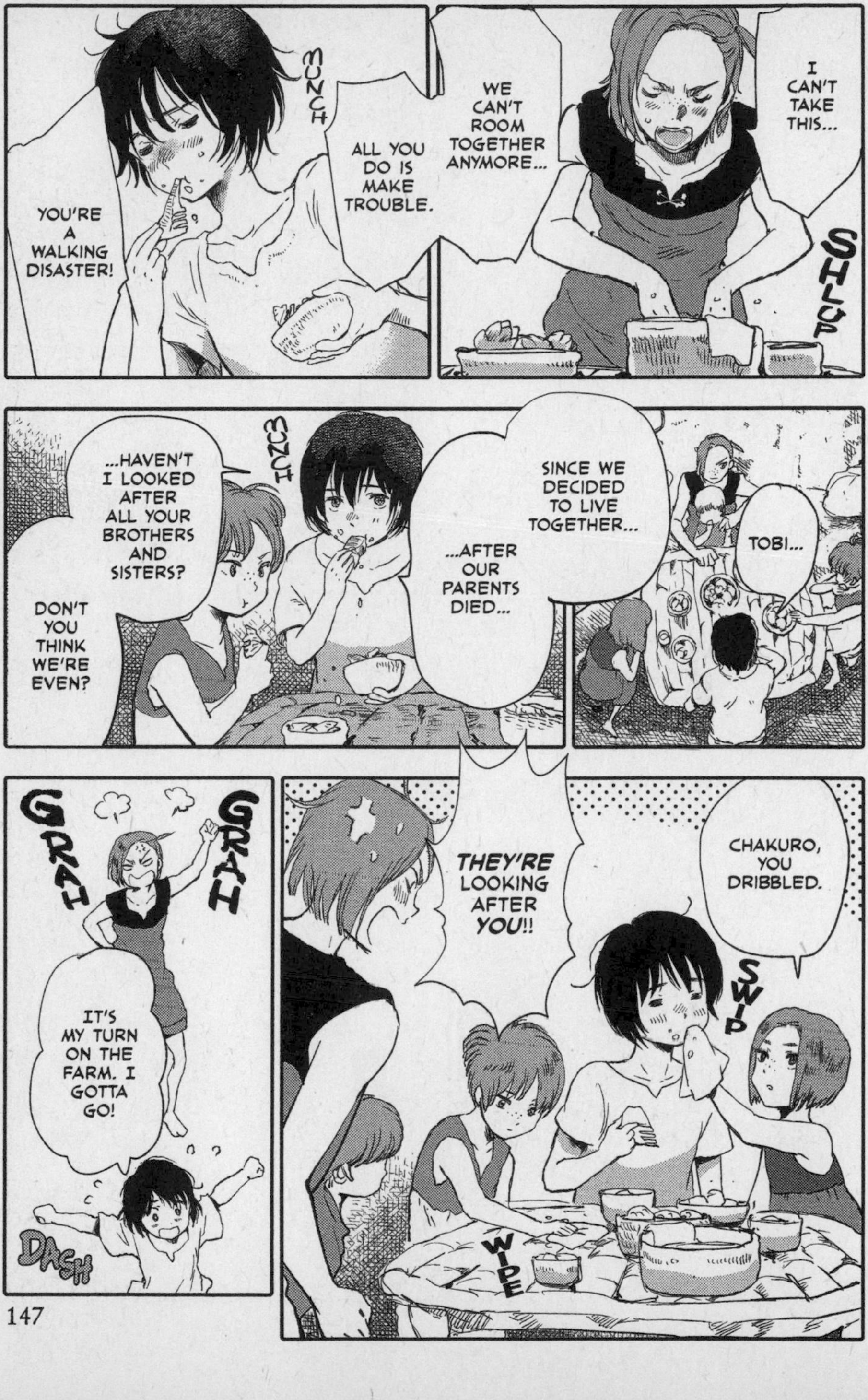
I CAN'T TAKE THIS...
SHLUP
WE CAN'T ROOM TOGETHER ANYMORE...
ALL YOU DO IS MAKE TROUBLE.
MUNCH
YOU'RE A WALKING DISASTER!
TOBI...
SINCE WE DECIDED TO LIVE TOGETHER...
...AFTER OUR PARENTS DIED...
MUNCH
...HAVEN'T I LOOKED AFTER ALL YOUR BROTHERS AND SISTERS?
DON'T YOU THINK WE'RE EVEN?
CHAKURO, YOU DRIBBLED.
SWIP
THEY'RE LOOKING AFTER YOU!!
WIPE
GRAH GRAH
IT'S MY TURN ON THE FARM. I GOTTA GO!
DASH

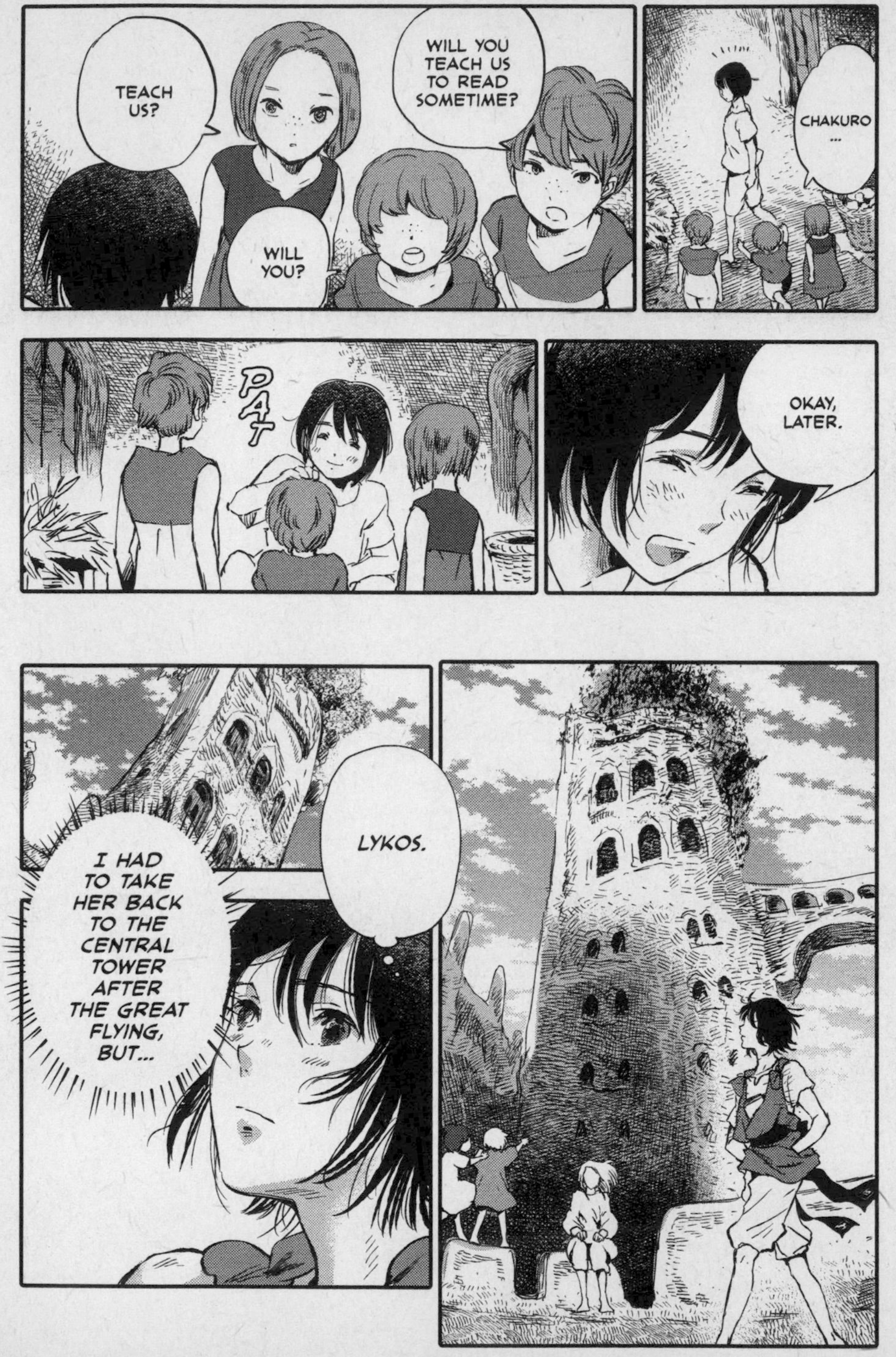
CHAKURO ...
WILL YOU TEACH US TO READ SOMETIME?
TEACH US?
WILL YOU?
OKAY, LATER.
PAT
LYKOS.
I HAD TO TAKE HER BACK TO THE CENTRAL TOWER AFTER THE GREAT FLYING, BUT...

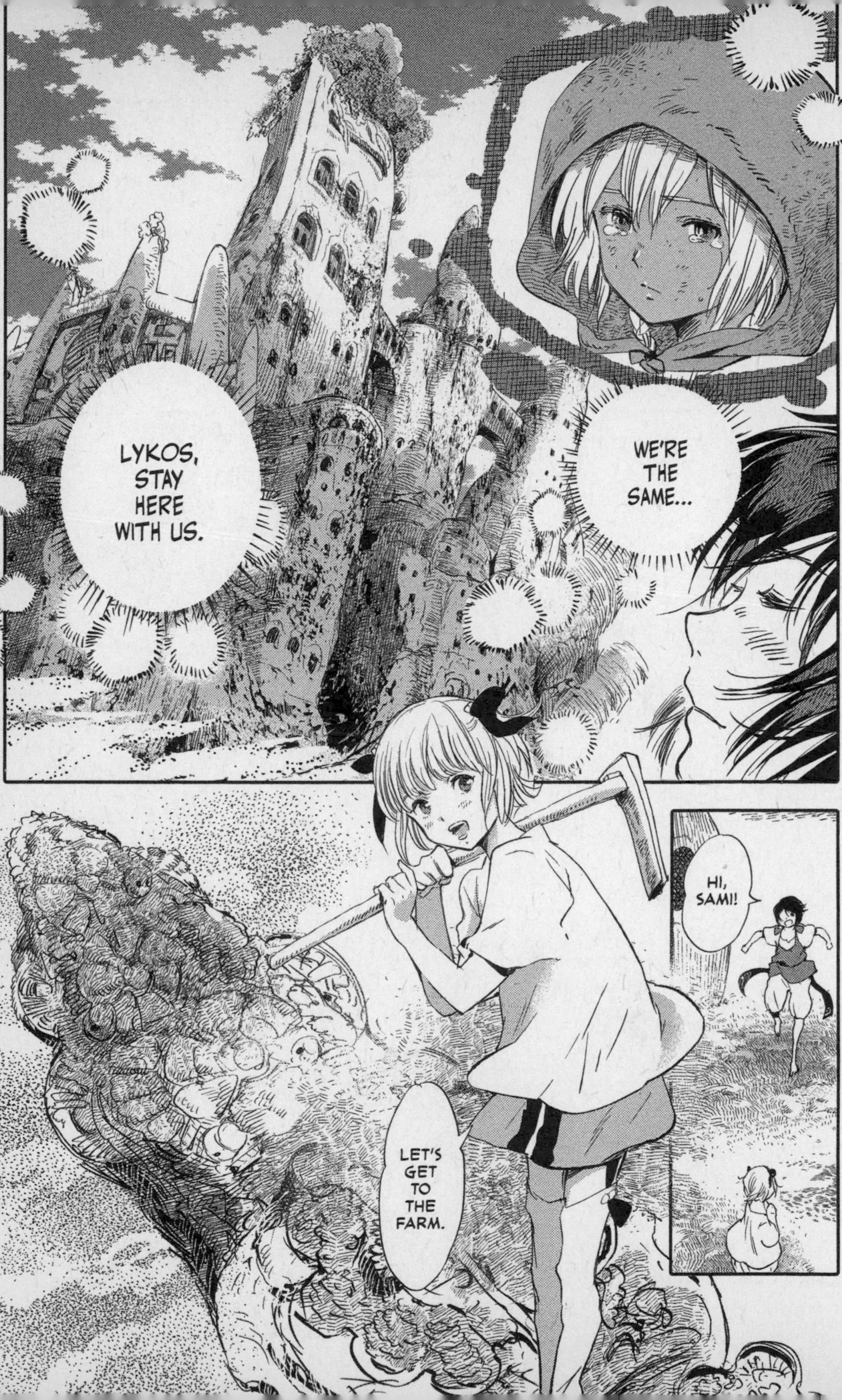
WE'RE THE SAME...
LYKOS, STAY HERE WITH US.
HI, SAMI!
LET'S GET TO THE FARM.

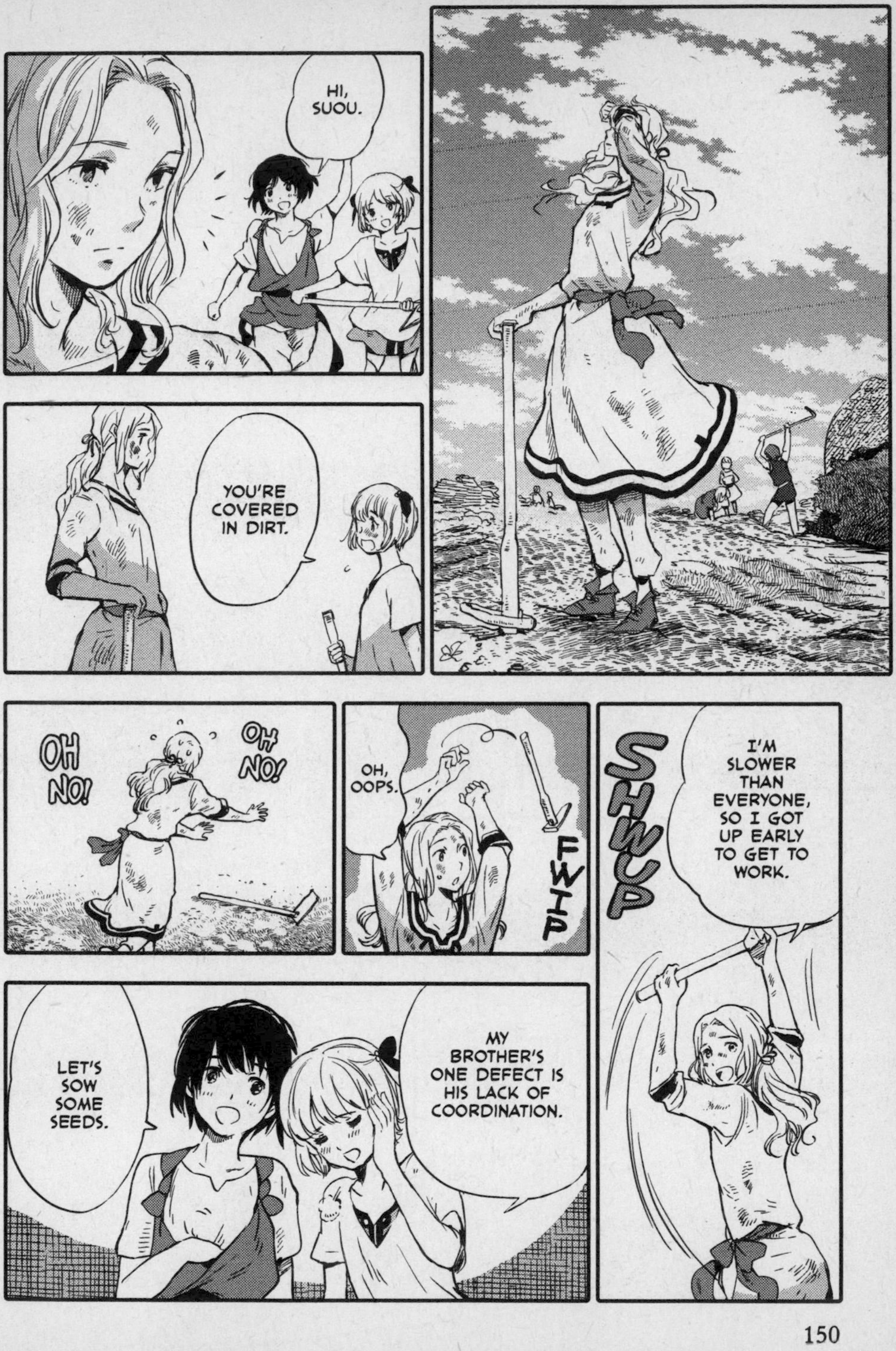
HI, SUOU.
YOU'RE COVERED IN DIRT.
SHWUP
I'M SLOWER THAN EVERYONE, SO I GOT UP EARLY TO GET TO WORK.
FWIP
OH, OOPS.
OH NO!
OH NO!
MY BROTHER'S ONE DEFECT IS HIS LACK OF COORDINATION.
LET'S SOW SOME SEEDS.

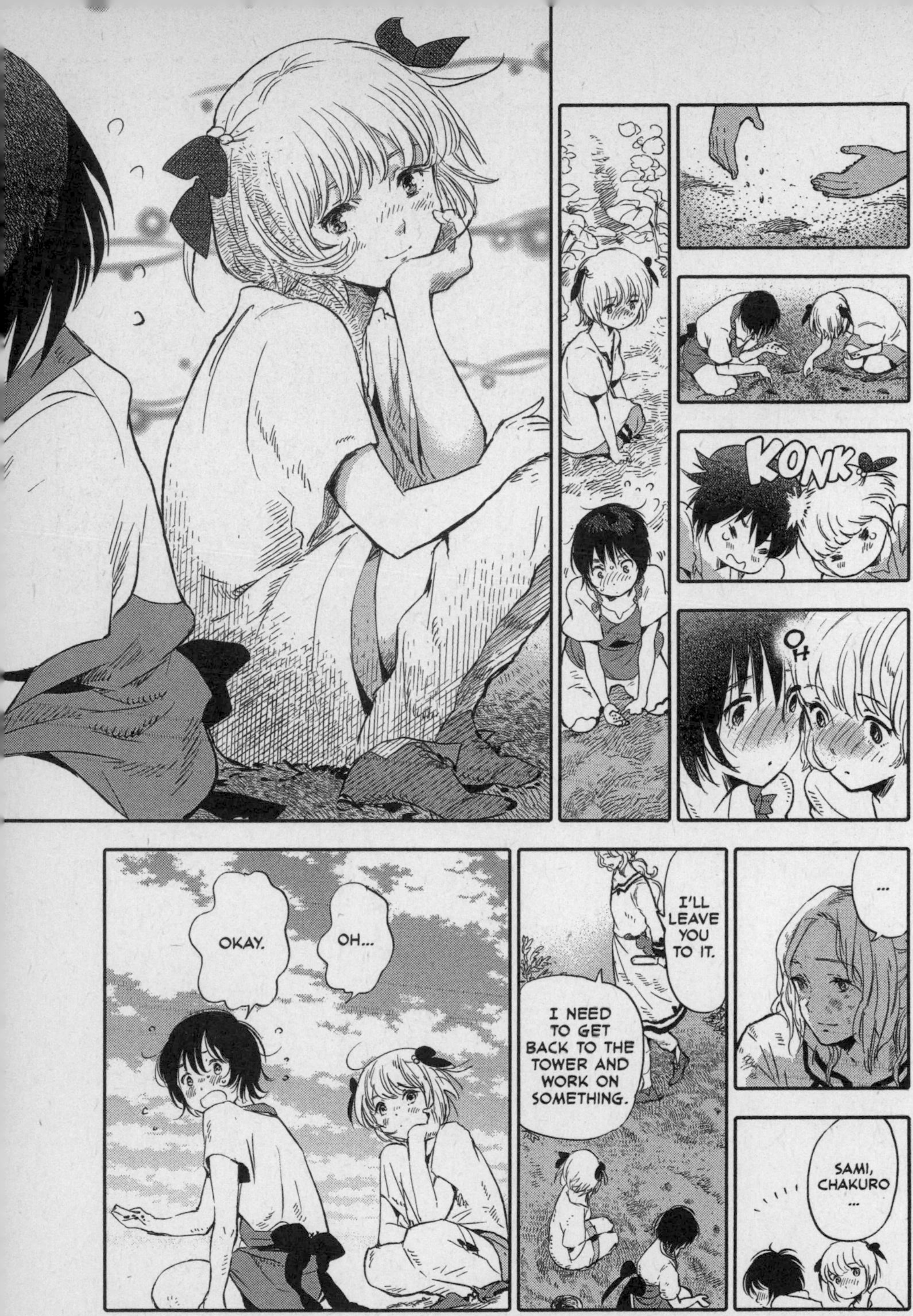
KONK
OH
...
SAMI, CHAKURO ...
I'LL LEAVE YOU TO IT.
I NEED TO GET BACK TO THE TOWER AND WORK ON SOMETHING.
OH...
OKAY.

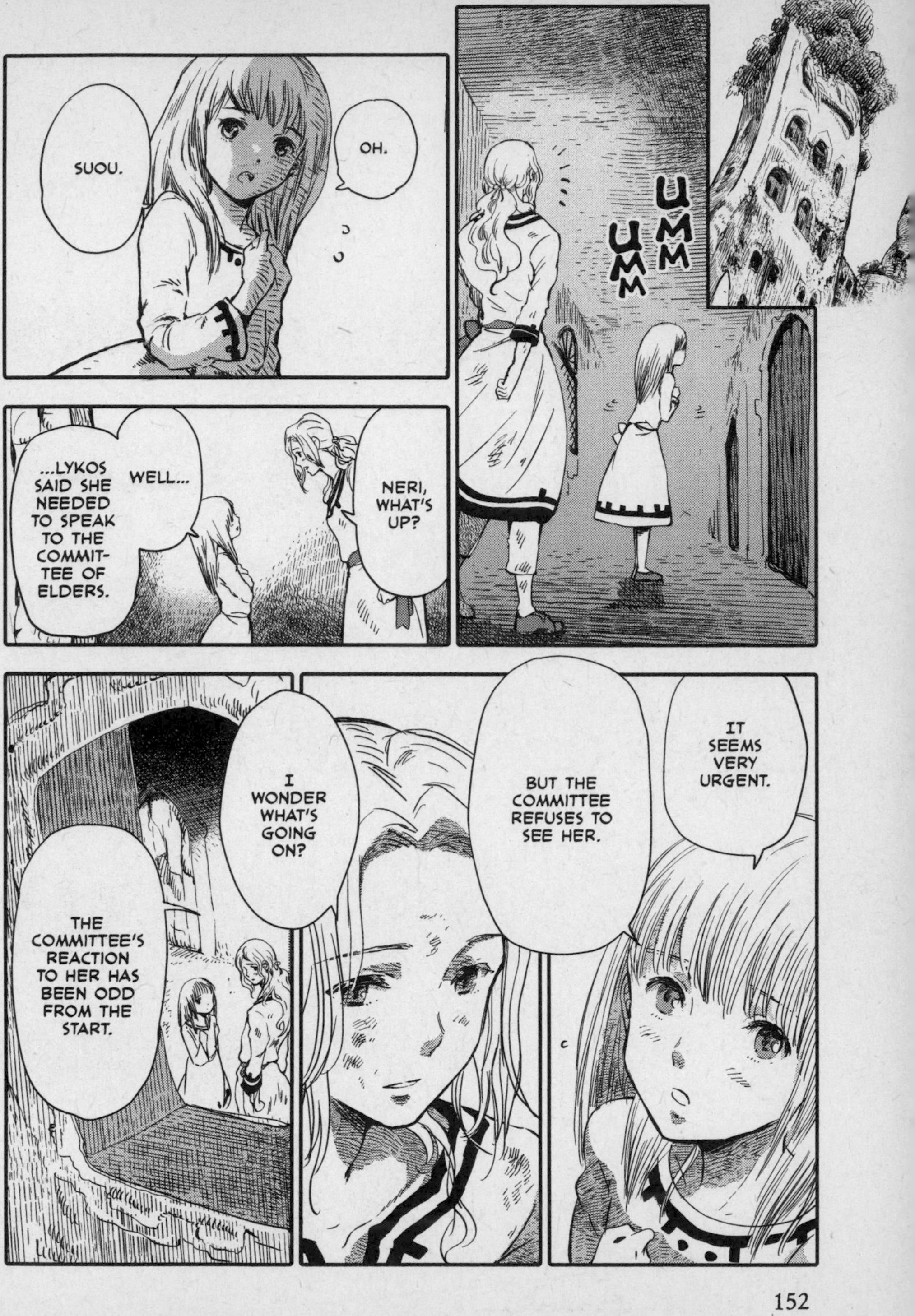
UMM UMM UMM
OH.
SUOU.
NERI, WHAT'S UP?
WELL...
...LYKOS SAID SHE NEEDED TO SPEAK TO THE COMMIT-TEE OF ELDERS.
IT SEEMS VERY URGENT.
BUT THE COMMITTEE REFUSES TO SEE HER.
I WONDER WHAT'S GOING ON?
THE COMMITTEE'S REACTION TO HER HAS BEEN ODD FROM THE START.

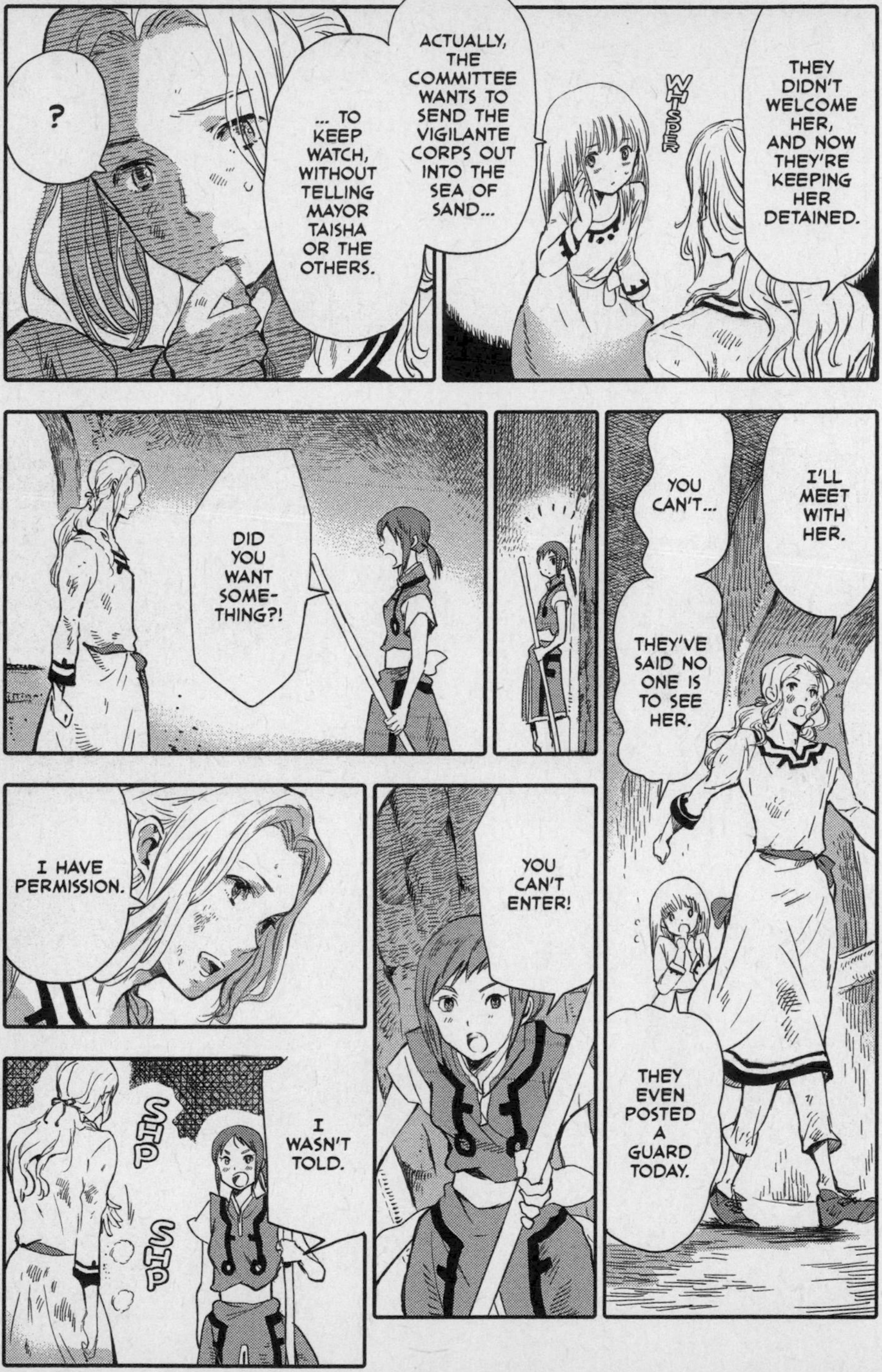
WHISPER
THEY DIDN'T WELCOME HER, AND NOW THEY'RE KEEPING HER DETAINED.
ACTUALLY, THE COMMITTEE WANTS TO SEND THE VIGILANTE CORPS OUT INTO THE SEA OF SAND...
... TO KEEP WATCH, WITHOUT TELLING MAYOR TAISHA OR THE OTHERS.
?
I'LL MEET WITH HER.
YOU CAN'T...
THEY'VE SAID NO ONE IS TO SEE HER.
THEY EVEN POSTED A GUARD TODAY.
DID YOU WANT SOME-THING?!
YOU CAN'T ENTER!
I HAVE PERMISSION.
I WASN'T TOLD.
SHP
SHP

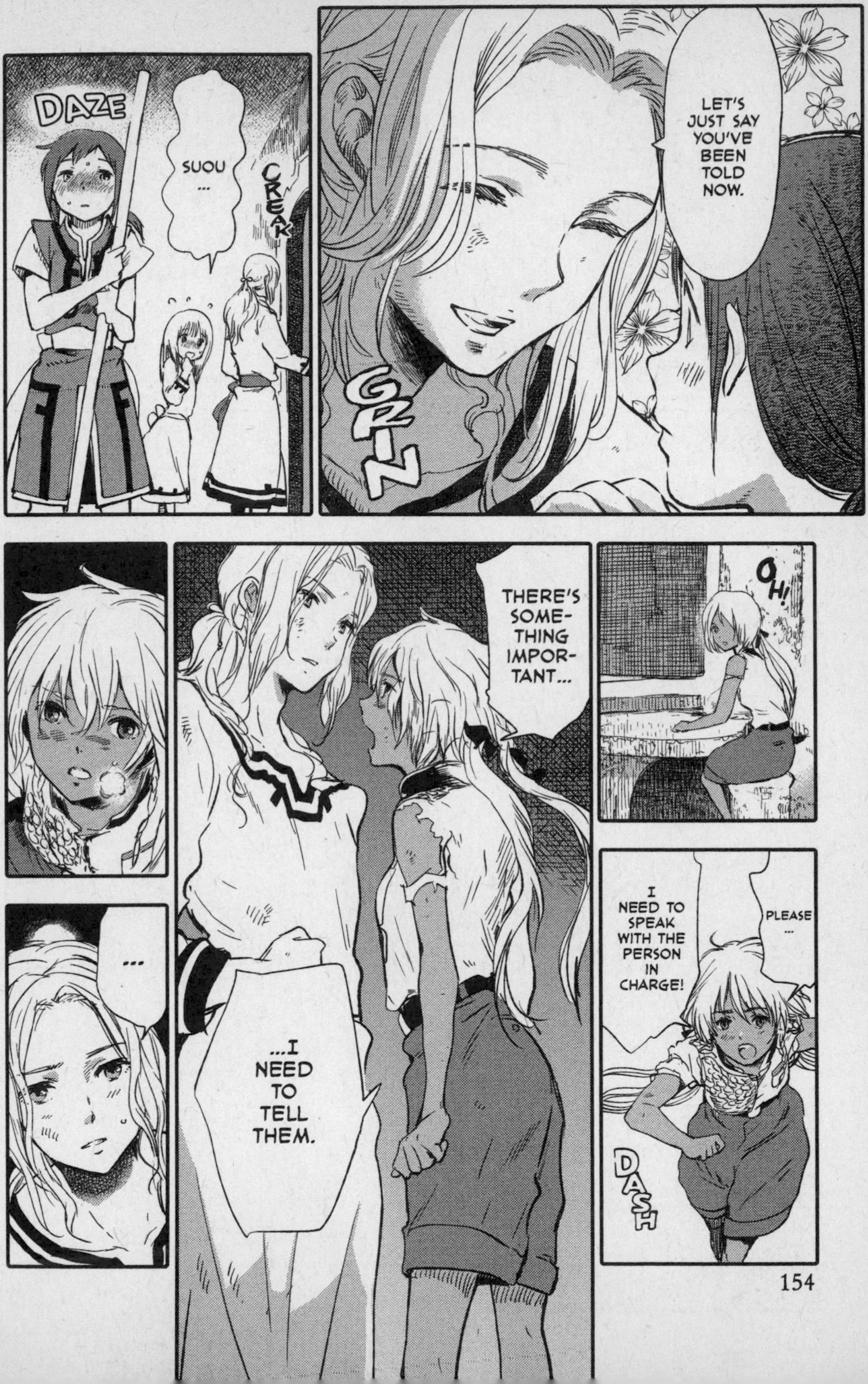
LET'S JUST SAY YOU'VE BEEN TOLD NOW.
GRIN
DAZE
SUOU ...
CREAK
OH!
PLEASE ...
I NEED TO SPEAK WITH THE PERSON IN CHARGE!
DASH
THERE'S SOME-THING IMPOR-TANT...
...I NEED TO TELL THEM.
...

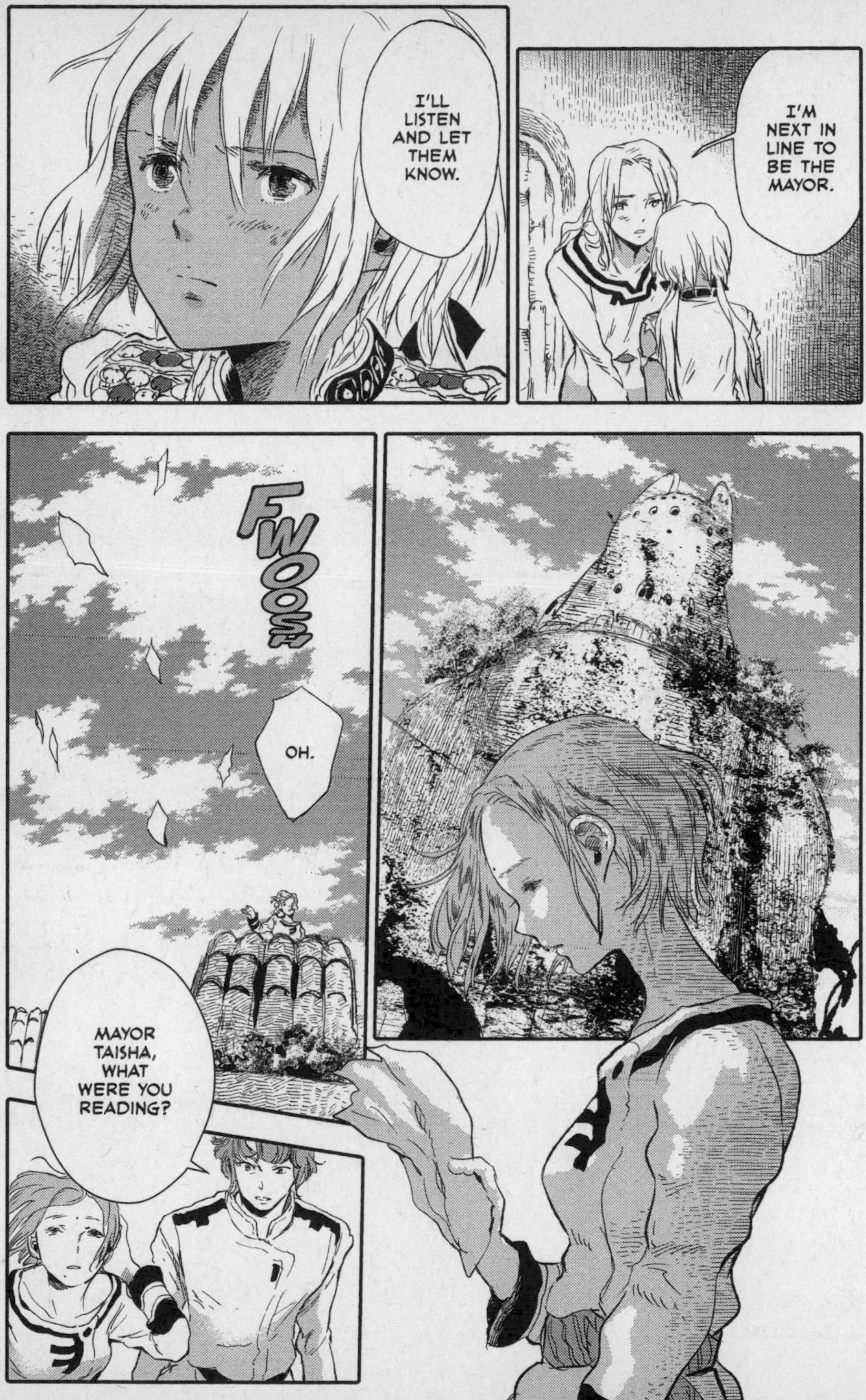
I'M NEXT IN LINE TO BE THE MAYOR.
I'LL LISTEN AND LET THEM KNOW.
FWOOSH
OH.
MAYOR TAISHA, WHAT WERE YOU READING?

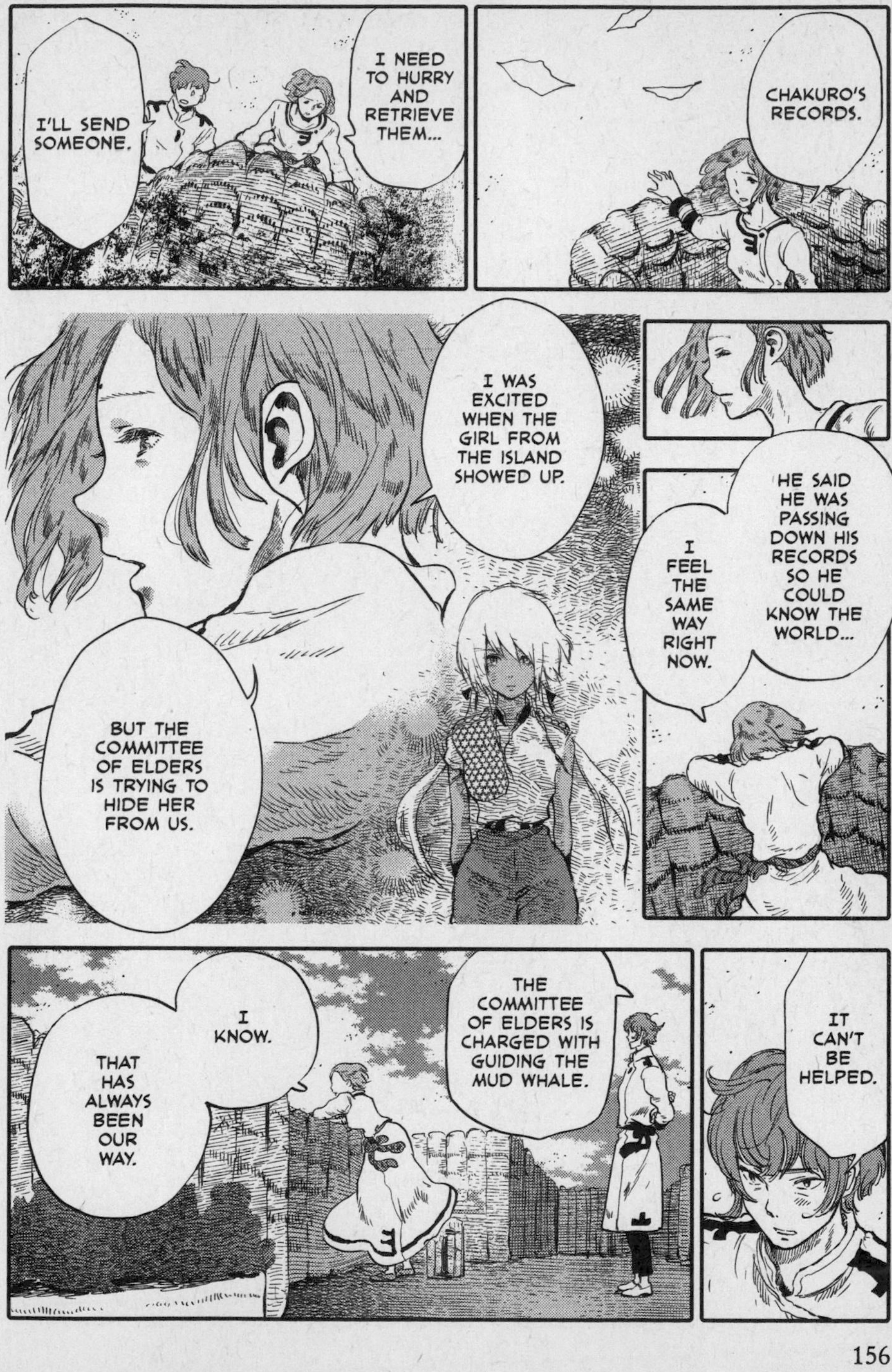
CHAKURO'S RECORDS.
I NEED TO HURRY AND RETRIEVE THEM...
I'LL SEND SOMEONE.
HE SAID HE WAS PASSING DOWN HIS RECORDS SO HE COULD KNOW THE WORLD...
I FEEL THE SAME WAY RIGHT NOW.
I WAS EXCITED WHEN THE GIRL FROM THE ISLAND SHOWED UP.
BUT THE COMMITTEE OF ELDERS IS TRYING TO HIDE HER FROM US.
IT CAN'T BE HELPED.
THE COMMITTEE OF ELDERS IS CHARGED WITH GUIDING THE MUD WHALE.
I KNOW.
THAT HAS ALWAYS BEEN OUR WAY.

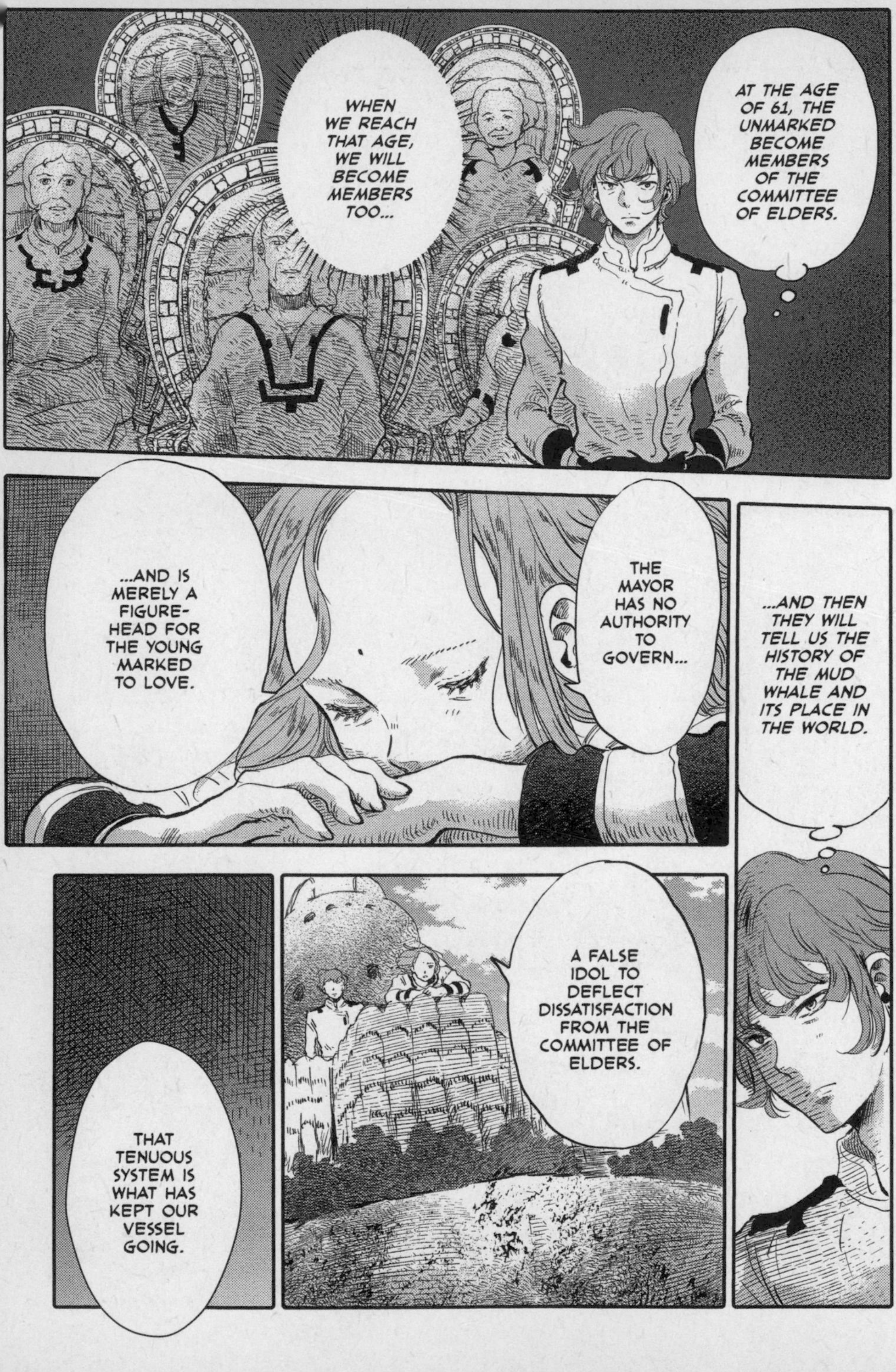
AT THE AGE OF 61, THE UNMARKED BECOME MEMBERS OF THE COMMITTEE OF ELDERS.
WHEN WE REACH THAT AGE, WE WILL BECOME MEMBERS TOO...
...AND THEN THEY WILL TELL US THE HISTORY OF THE MUD WHALE AND ITS PLACE IN THE WORLD.
THE MAYOR HAS NO AUTHORITY TO GOVERN...
...AND IS MERELY A FIGURE-HEAD FOR THE YOUNG MARKED TO LOVE.
A FALSE IDOL TO DEFLECT DISSATISFACTION FROM THE COMMITTEE OF ELDERS.
THAT TENUOUS SYSTEM IS WHAT HAS KEPT OUR VESSEL GOING.

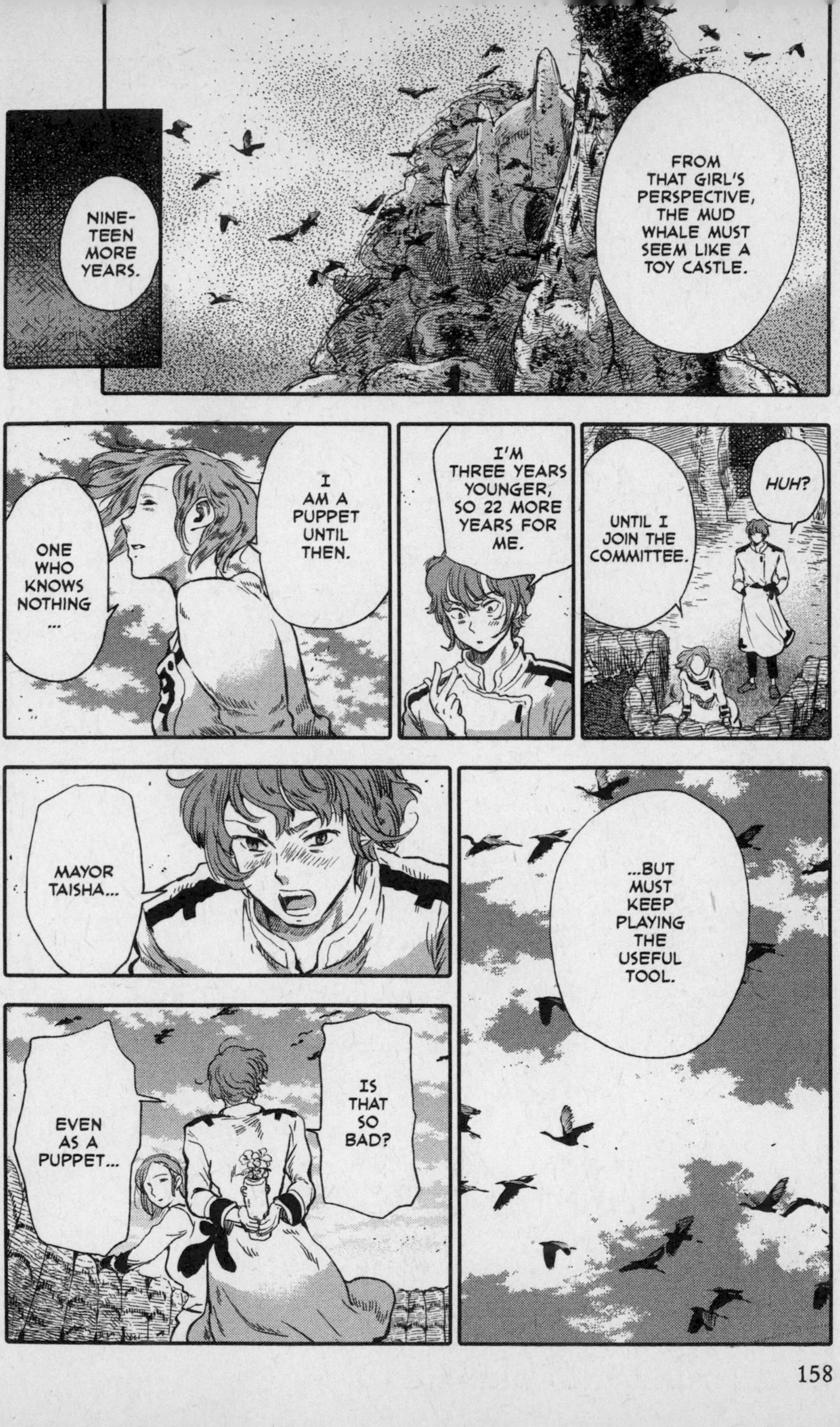
FROM THAT GIRL'S PERSPECTIVE, THE MUD WHALE MUST SEEM LIKE A TOY CASTLE.
NINE-TEEN MORE YEARS.
UNTIL I JOIN THE COMMITTEE.
HUH?
I'M THREE YEARS YOUNGER, SO 22 MORE YEARS FOR ME.
I AM A PUPPET UNTIL THEN.
ONE WHO KNOWS NOTHING...
...BUT MUST KEEP PLAYING THE USEFUL TOOL.
MAYOR TAISHA...
IS THAT SO BAD?
EVEN AS A PUPPET...

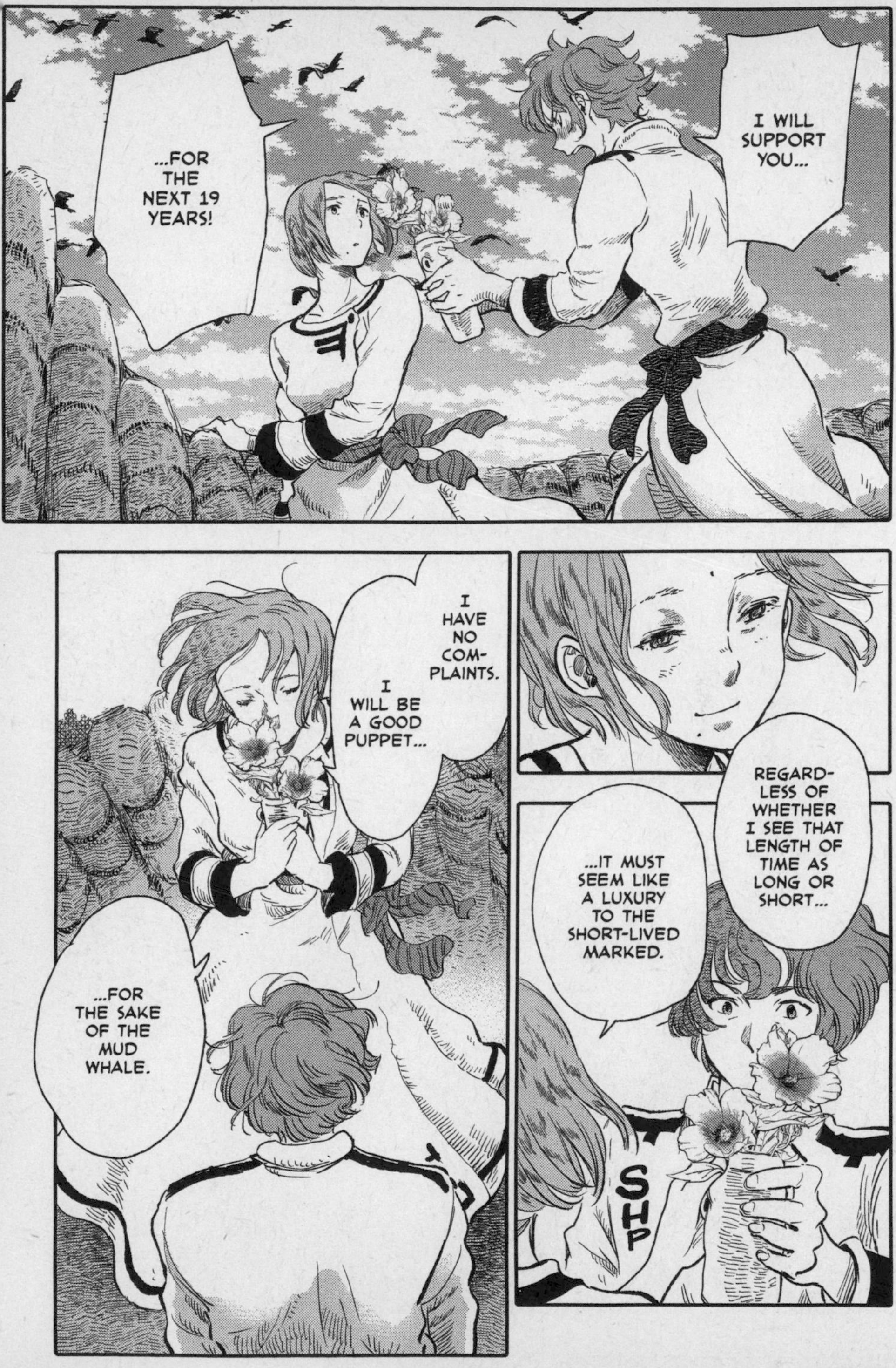
I WILL SUPPORT YOU...
...FOR THE NEXT 19 YEARS!
REGARDLESS OF WHETHER I SEE THAT LENGTH OF TIME AS LONG OR SHORT...
...IT MUST SEEM LIKE A LUXURY TO THE SHORT-LIVED MARKED.
SHP
I HAVE NO COMPLAINTS.
I WILL BE A GOOD PUPPET...
...FOR THE SAKE OF THE MUD WHALE.

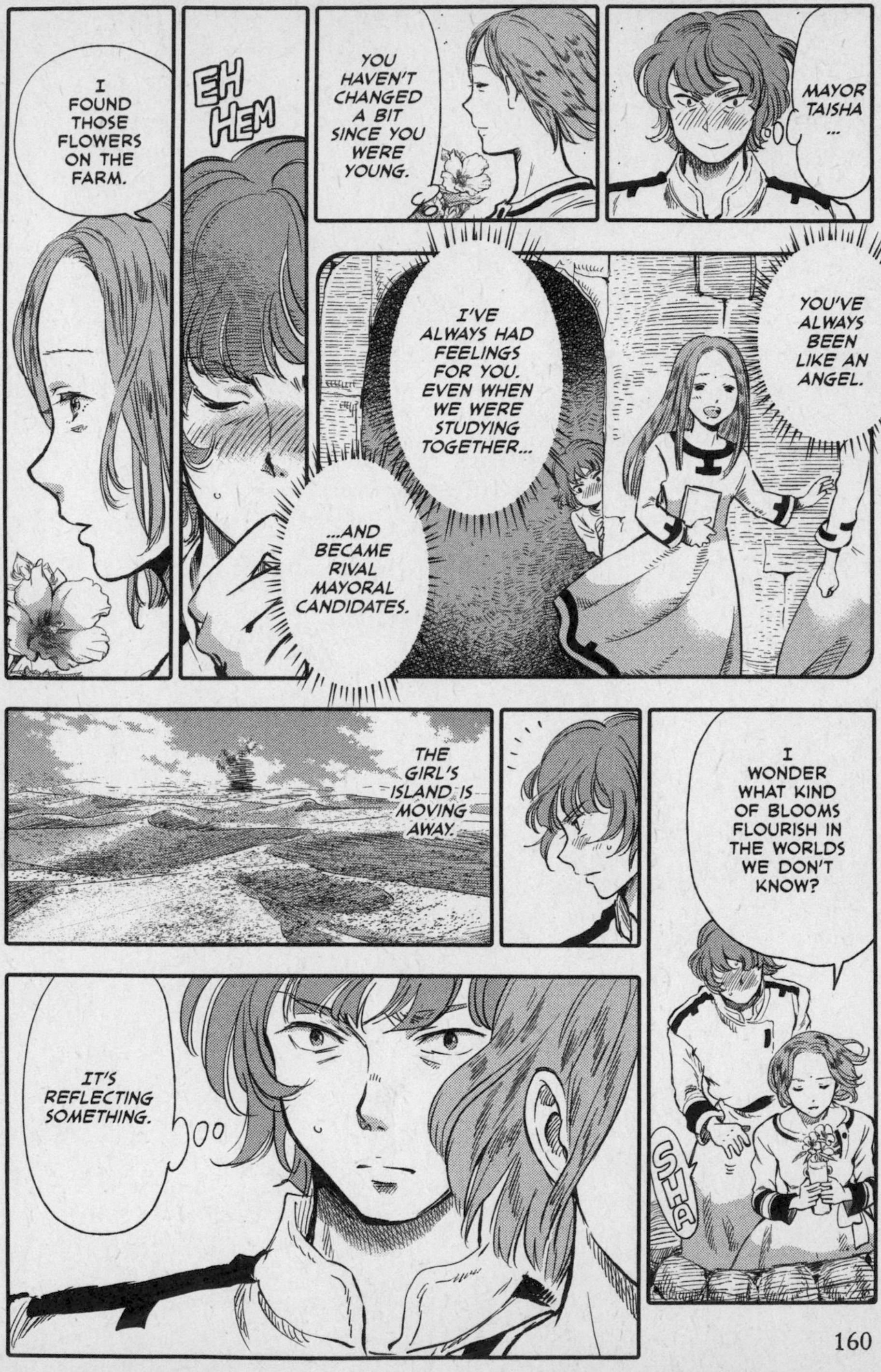
MAYOR TAISHA ...
YOU HAVEN'T CHANGED A BIT SINCE YOU WERE YOUNG.
YOU'VE ALWAYS BEEN LIKE AN ANGEL.
I'VE ALWAYS HAD FEELINGS FOR YOU. EVEN WHEN WE WERE STUDYING TOGETHER...
...AND BECAME RIVAL MAYORAL CANDIDATES.
EH HEM
I FOUND THOSE FLOWERS ON THE FARM.
I WONDER WHAT KIND OF BLOOMS FLOURISH IN THE WORLDS WE DON'T KNOW?
SUHA
THE GIRL'S ISLAND IS MOVING AWAY.
IT'S REFLECTING SOMETHING.

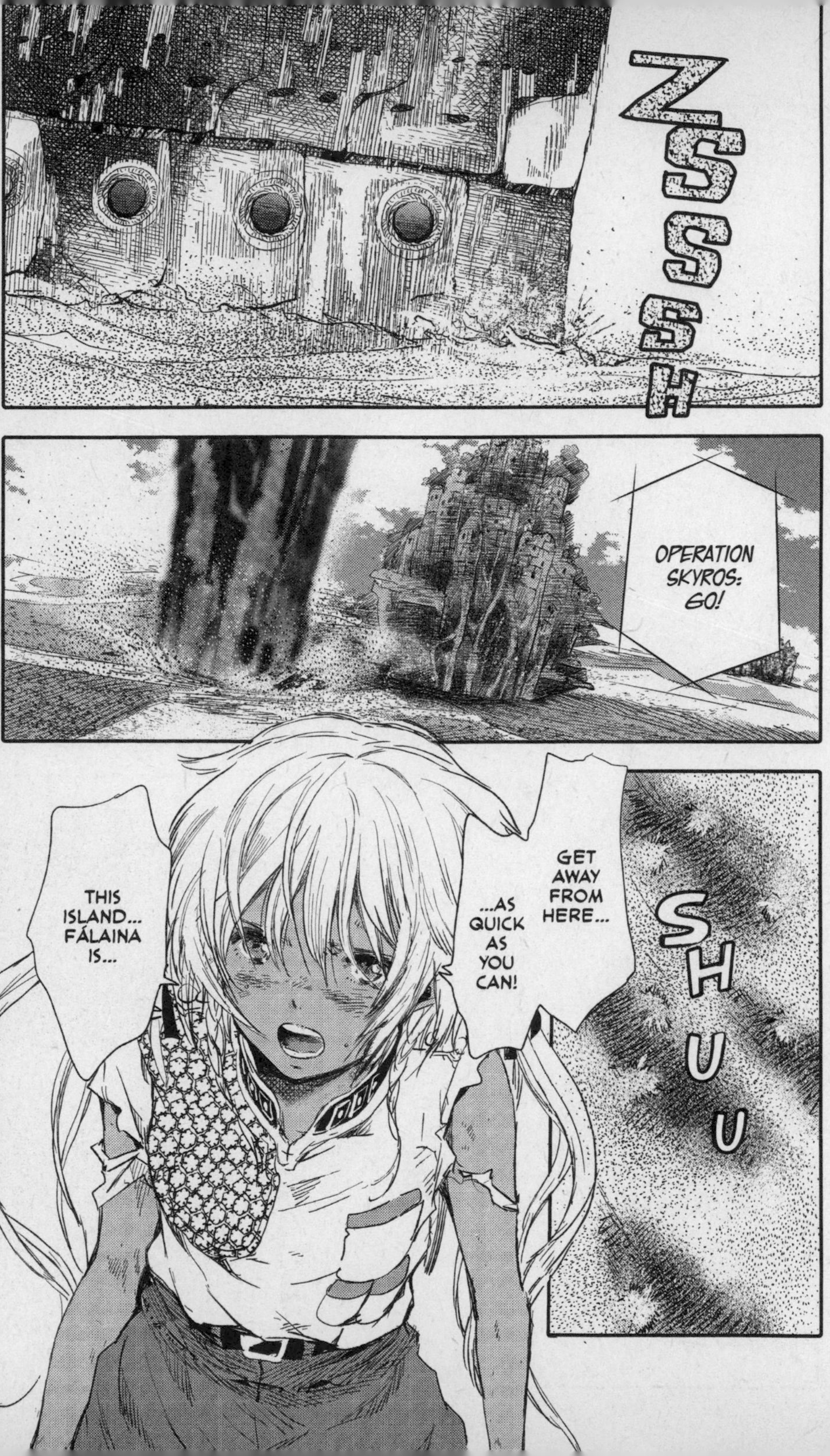
ZSSSH
OPERATION SKYROS: GO!
SHUU
GET AWAY FROM HERE...
...AS QUICK AS YOU CAN!
THIS ISLAND... FÁLAINA IS...

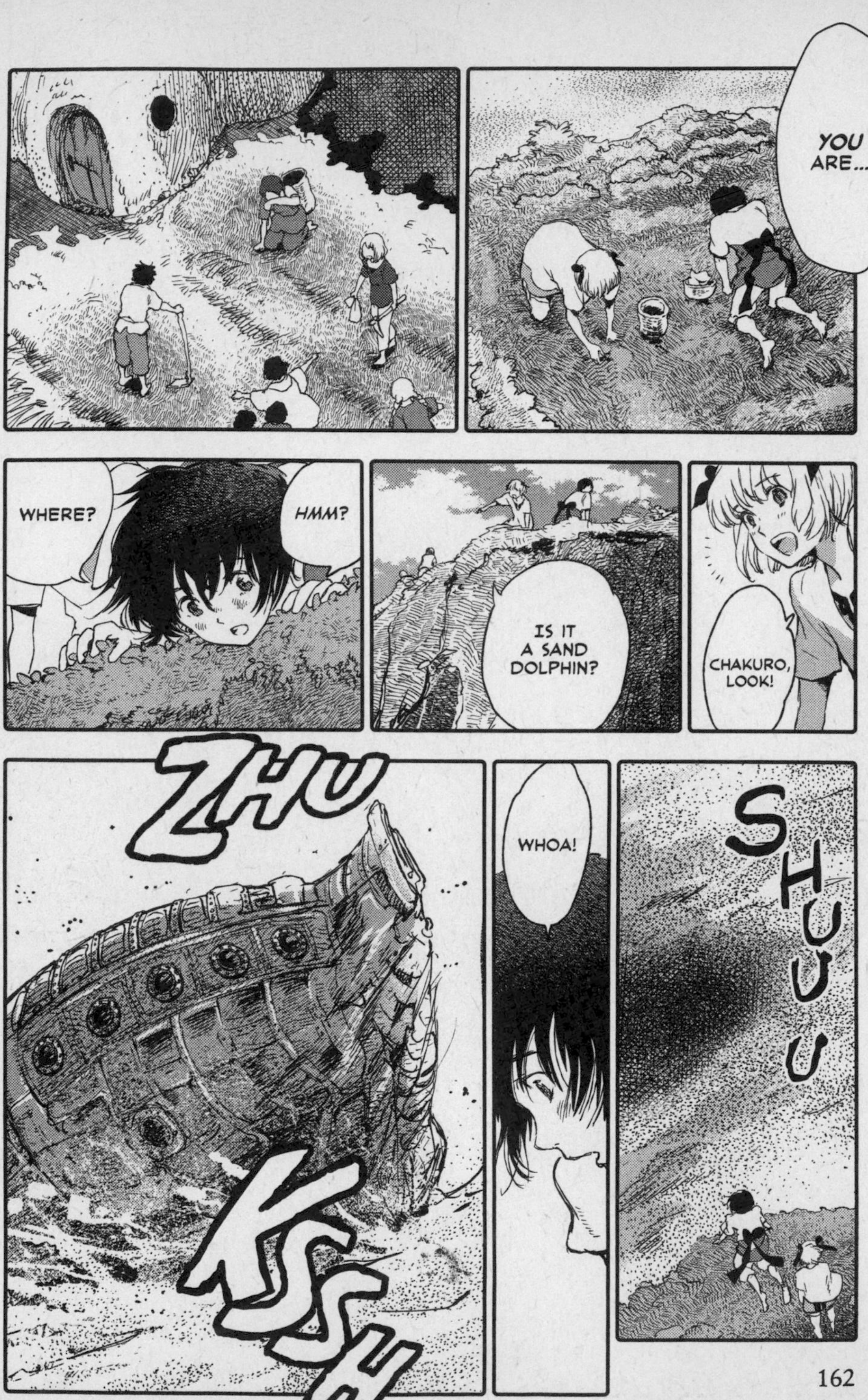
YOU ARE...
CHAKURO, LOOK!
IS IT A SAND DOLPHIN?
HMM?
WHERE?
SHUUU
WHOA!
ZHU
KSSH

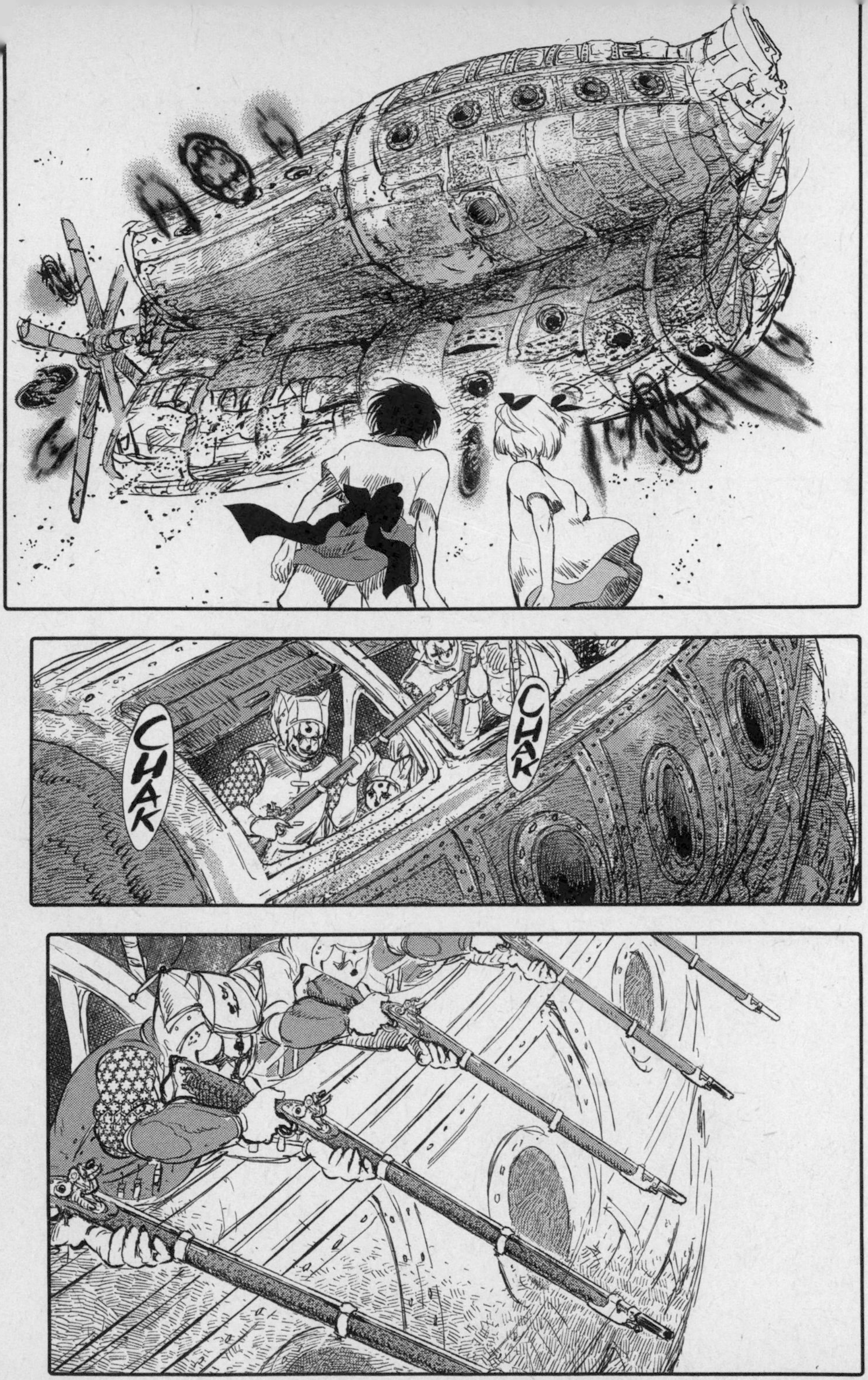
CHAK
CHAK

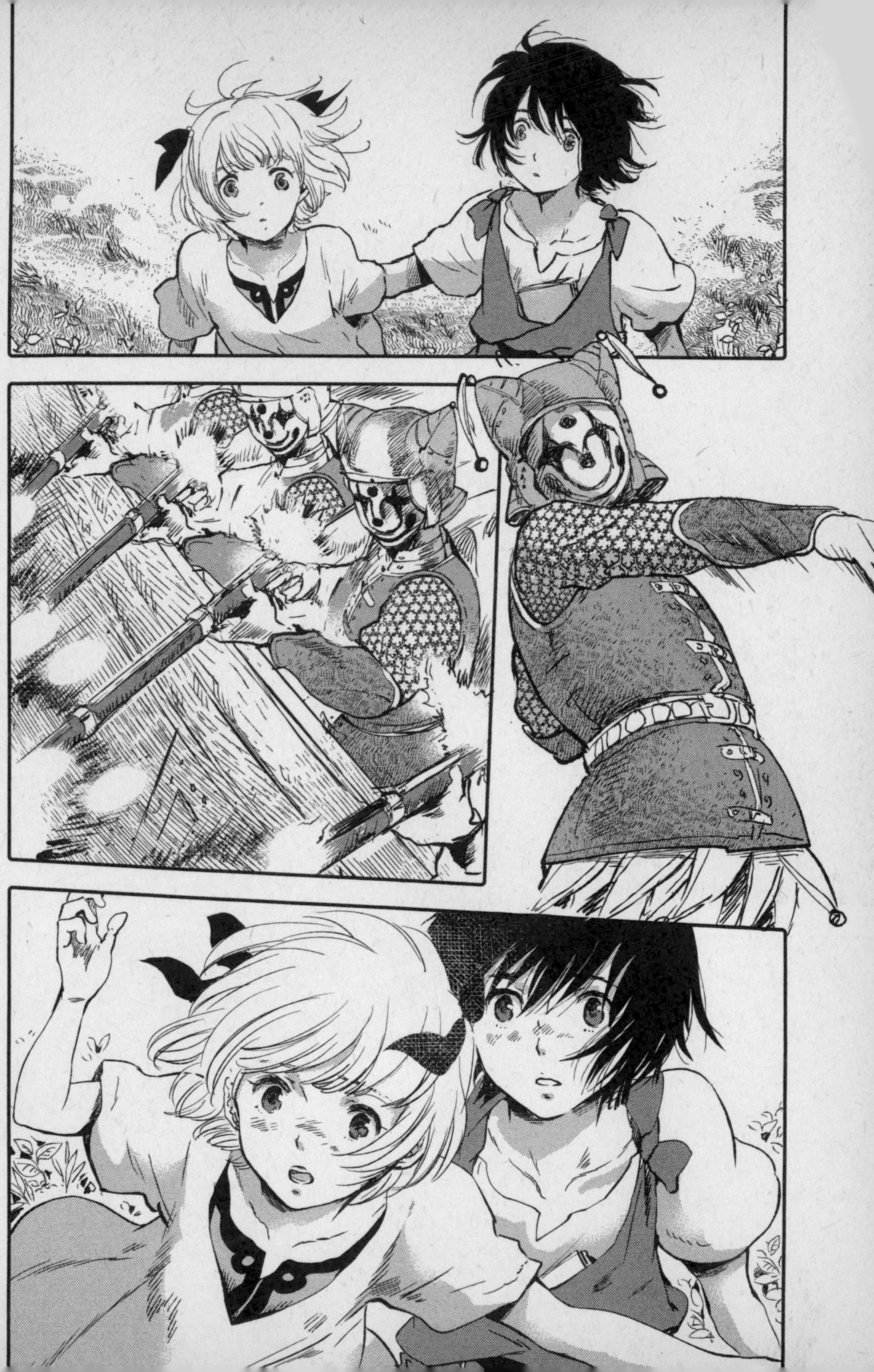

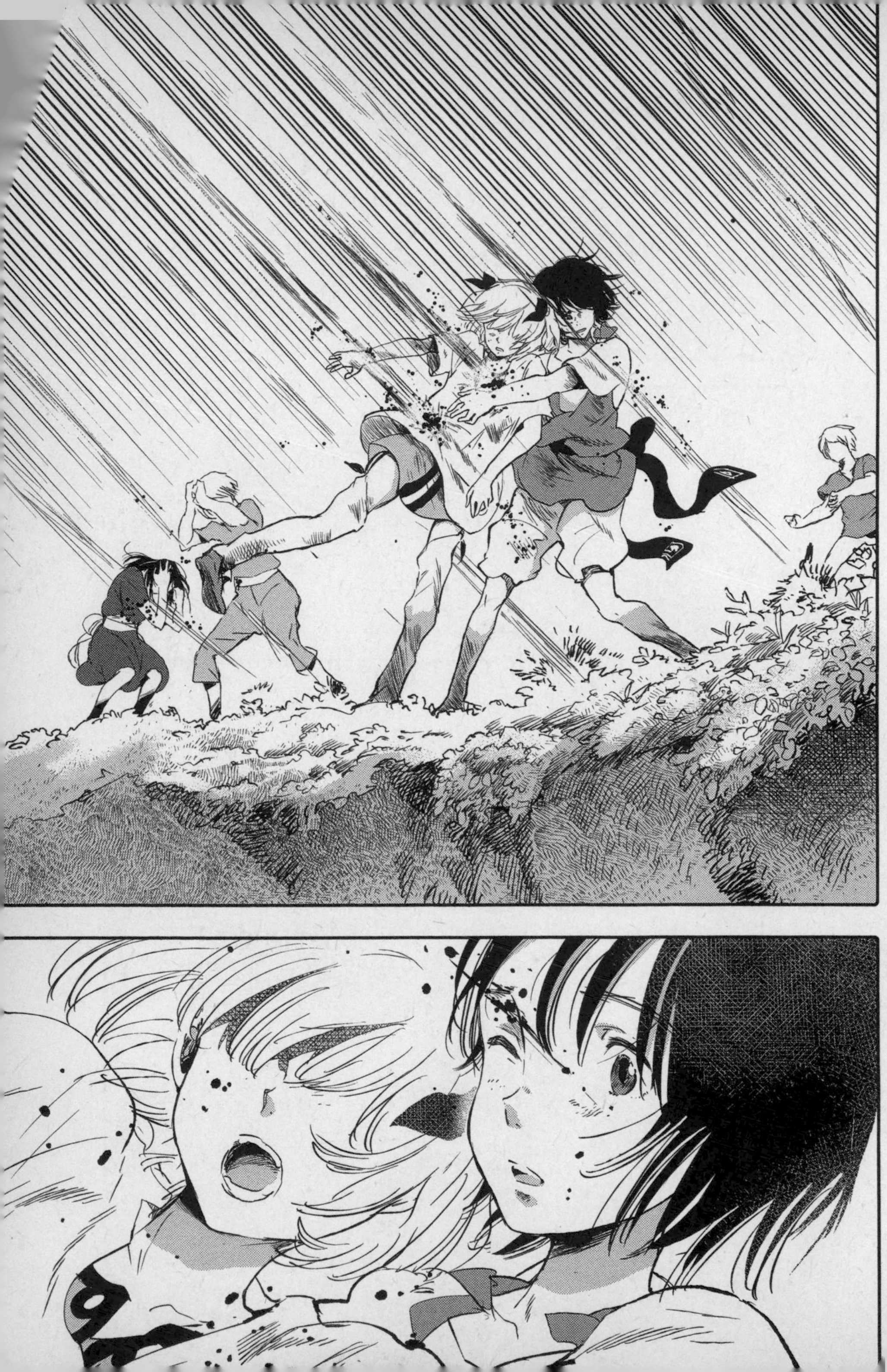

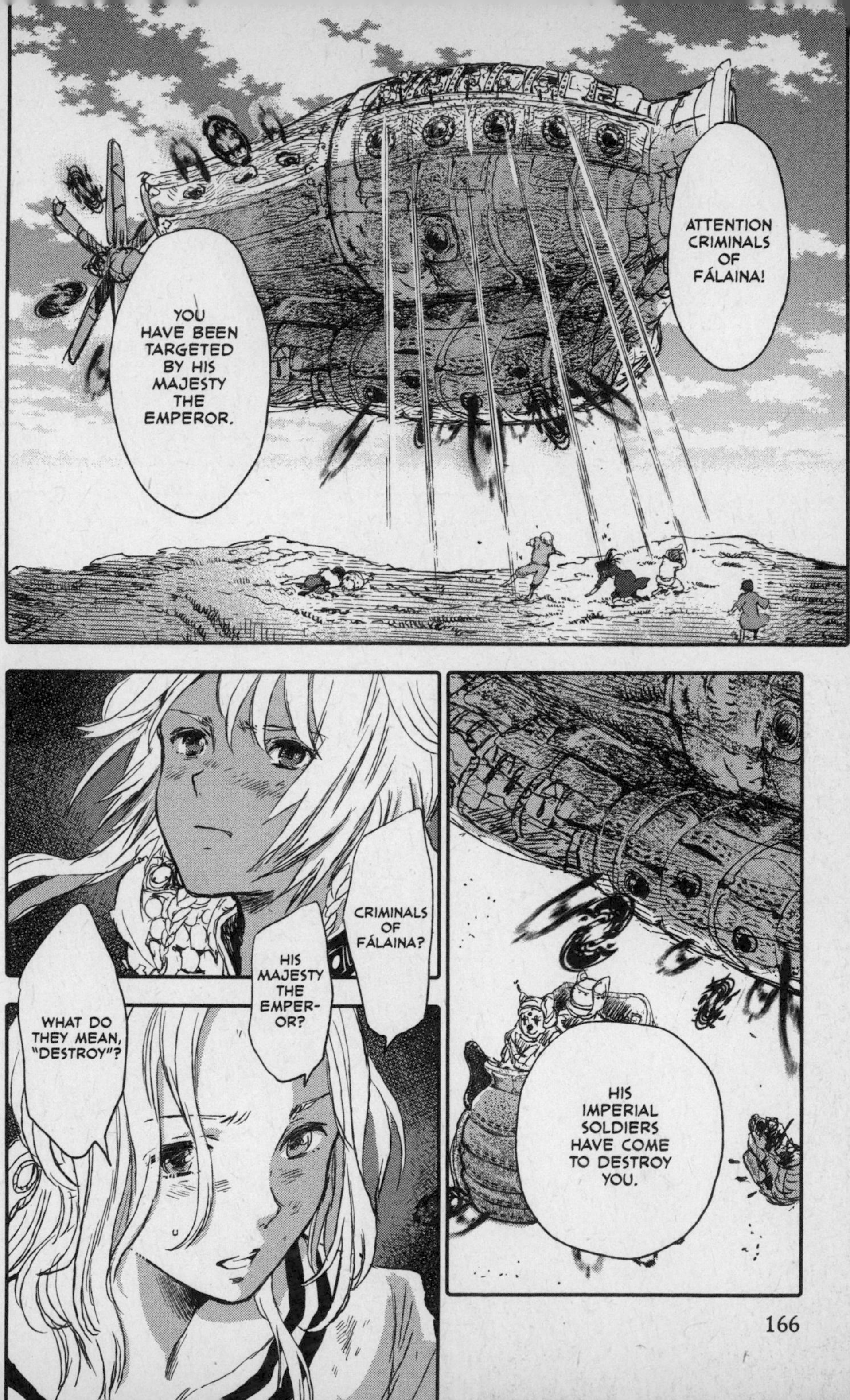
ATTENTION CRIMINALS OF FÁLAINA!
YOU HAVE BEEN TARGETED BY HIS MAJESTY THE EMPEROR.
HIS IMPERIAL SOLDIERS HAVE COME TO DESTROY YOU.
CRIMINALS OF FÁLAINA?
HIS MAJESTY THE EMPER-OR?
WHAT DO THEY MEAN, "DESTROY"?

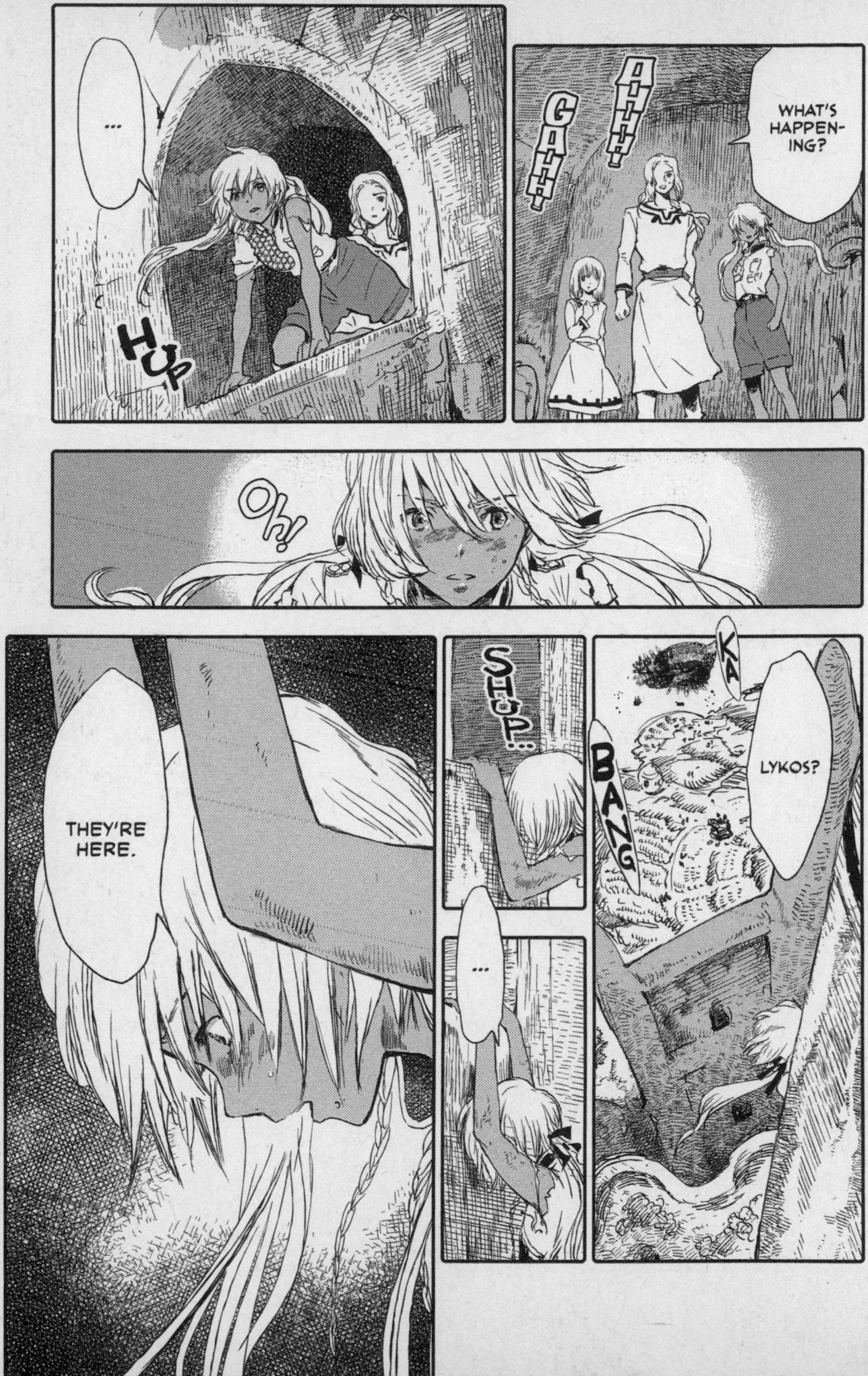
WHAT'S HAPPEN-ING?
AHHH!
GAHH!
...
HUP
Oh!
KA
BANG
LYKOS?
SHOP...
...
THEY'RE HERE.

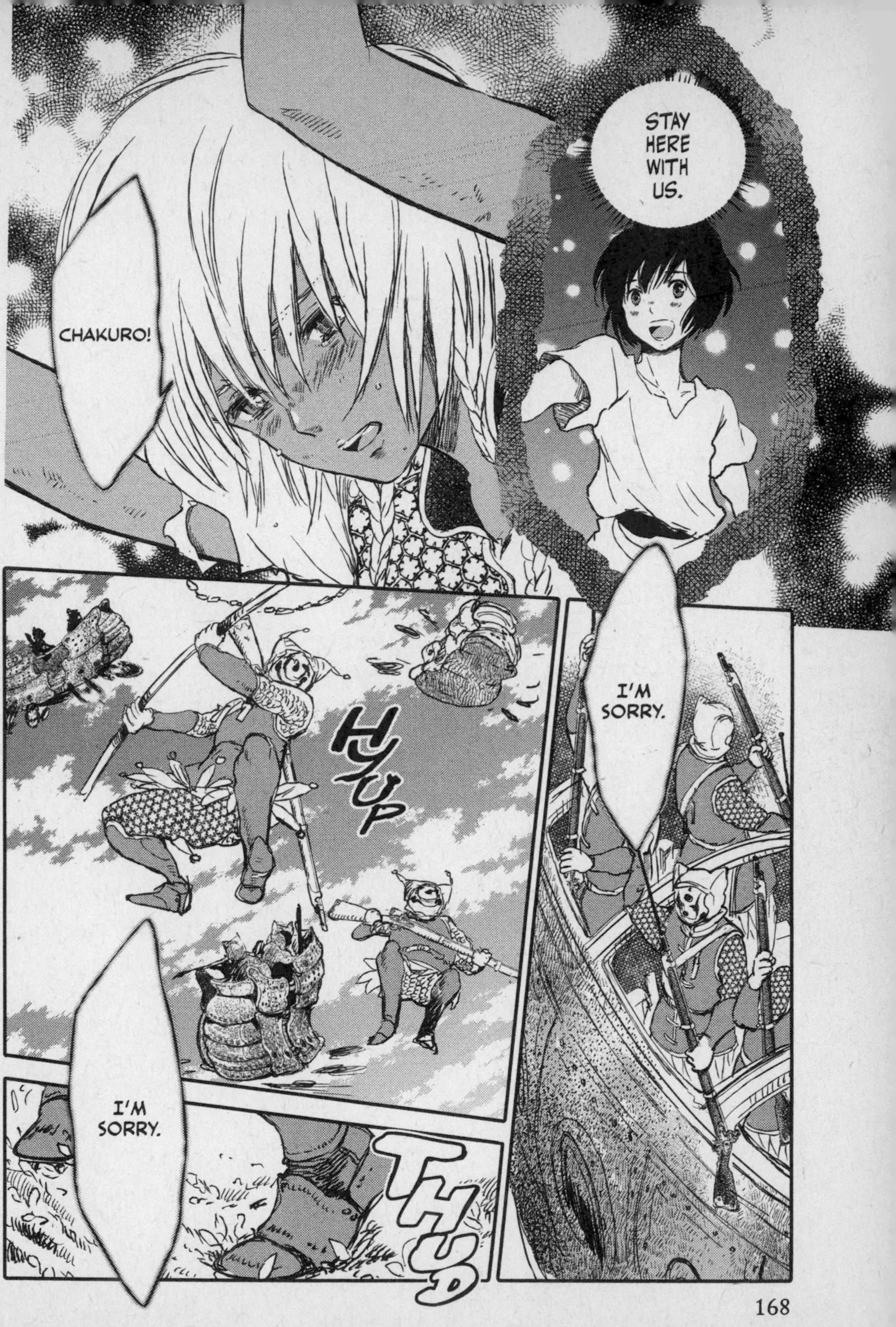
STAY HERE WITH US.
CHAKURO!
I'M SORRY.
HYUP
I'M SORRY.
THUD

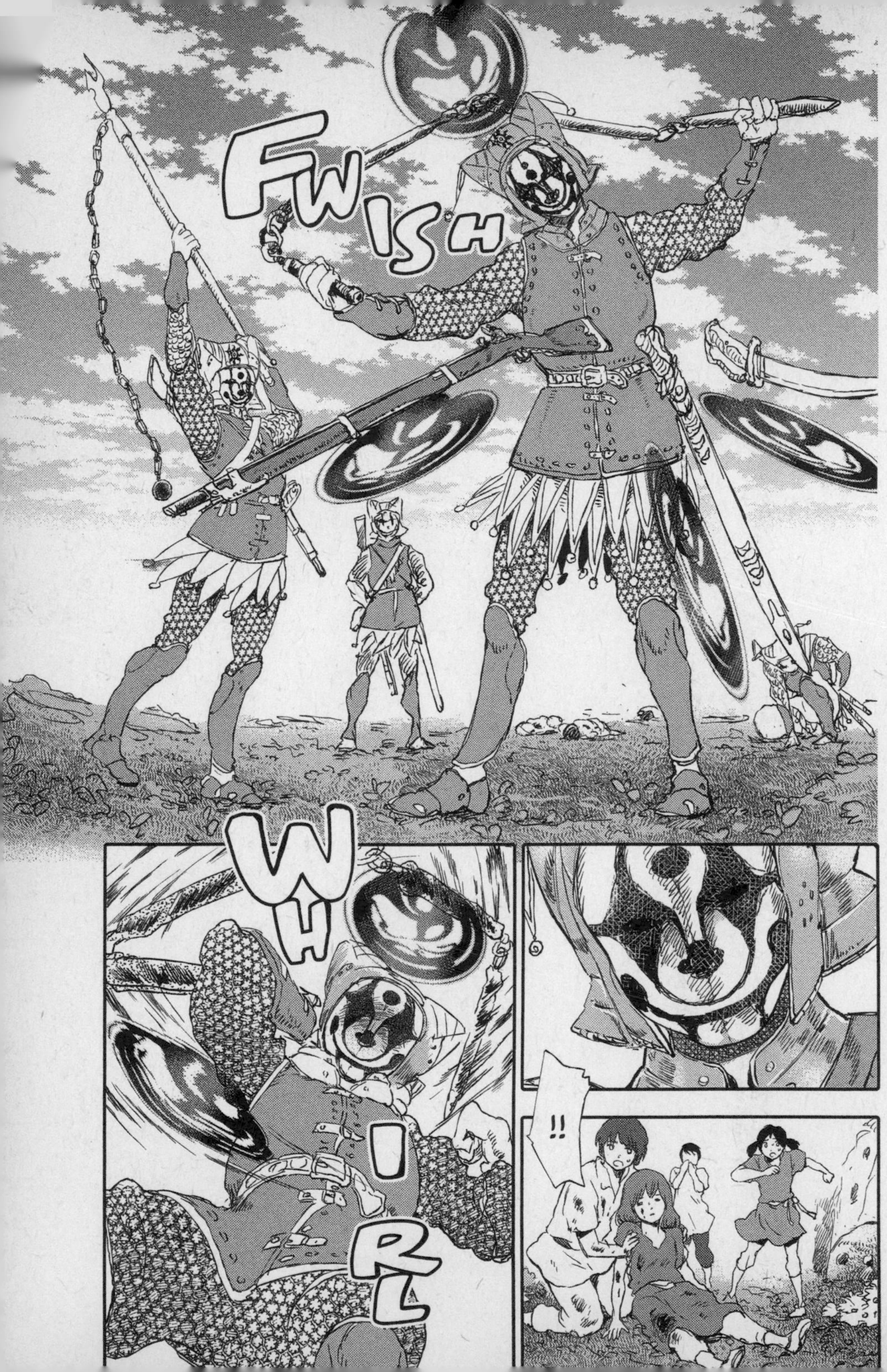
FWISH
!!
WHIRL

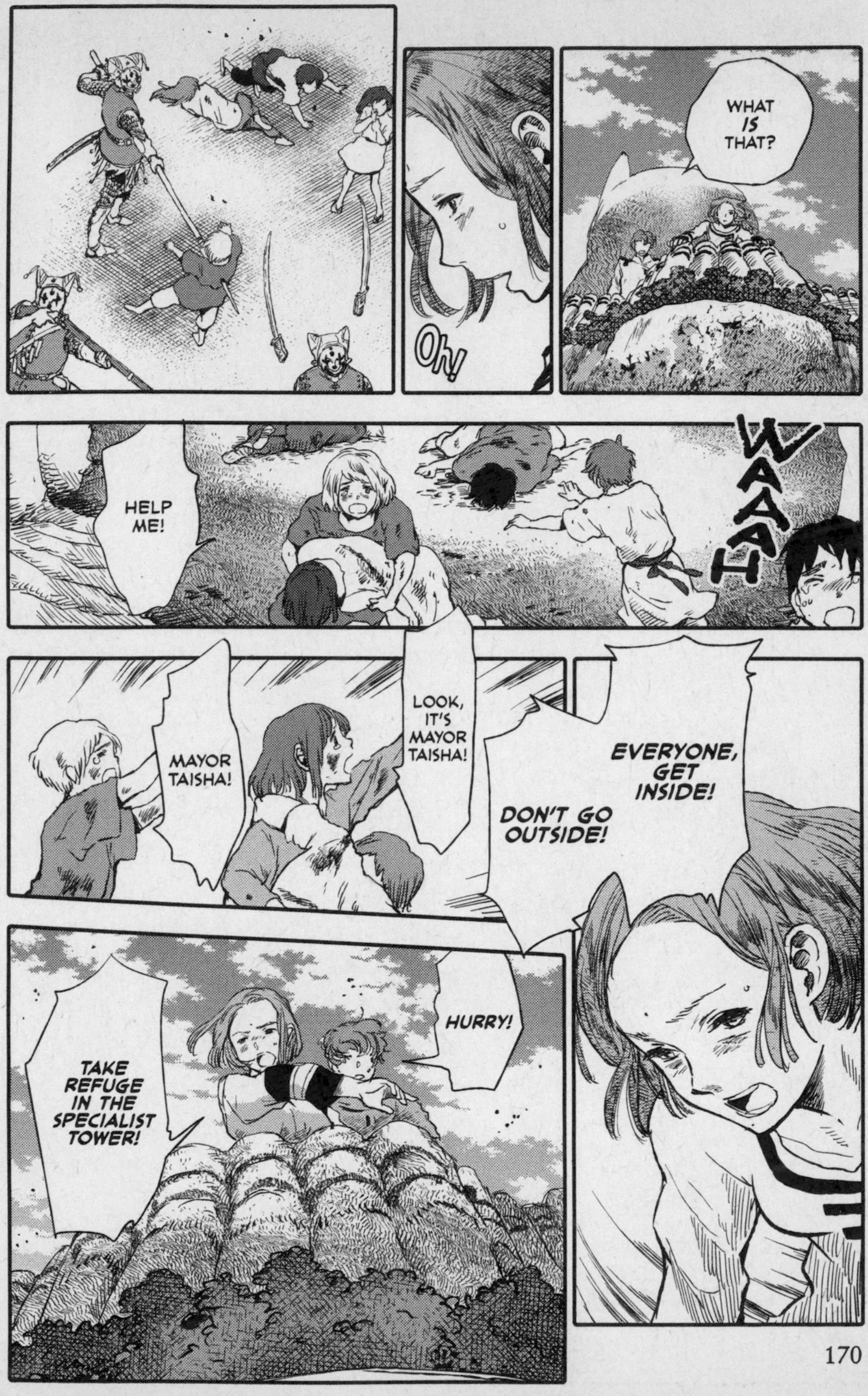
WHAT IS THAT?
Oh!
WAAAH
HELP ME!
EVERYONE, GET INSIDE!
DON'T GO OUTSIDE!
LOOK, IT'S MAYOR TAISHA!
MAYOR TAISHA!
HURRY!
TAKE REFUGE IN THE SPECIALIST TOWER!

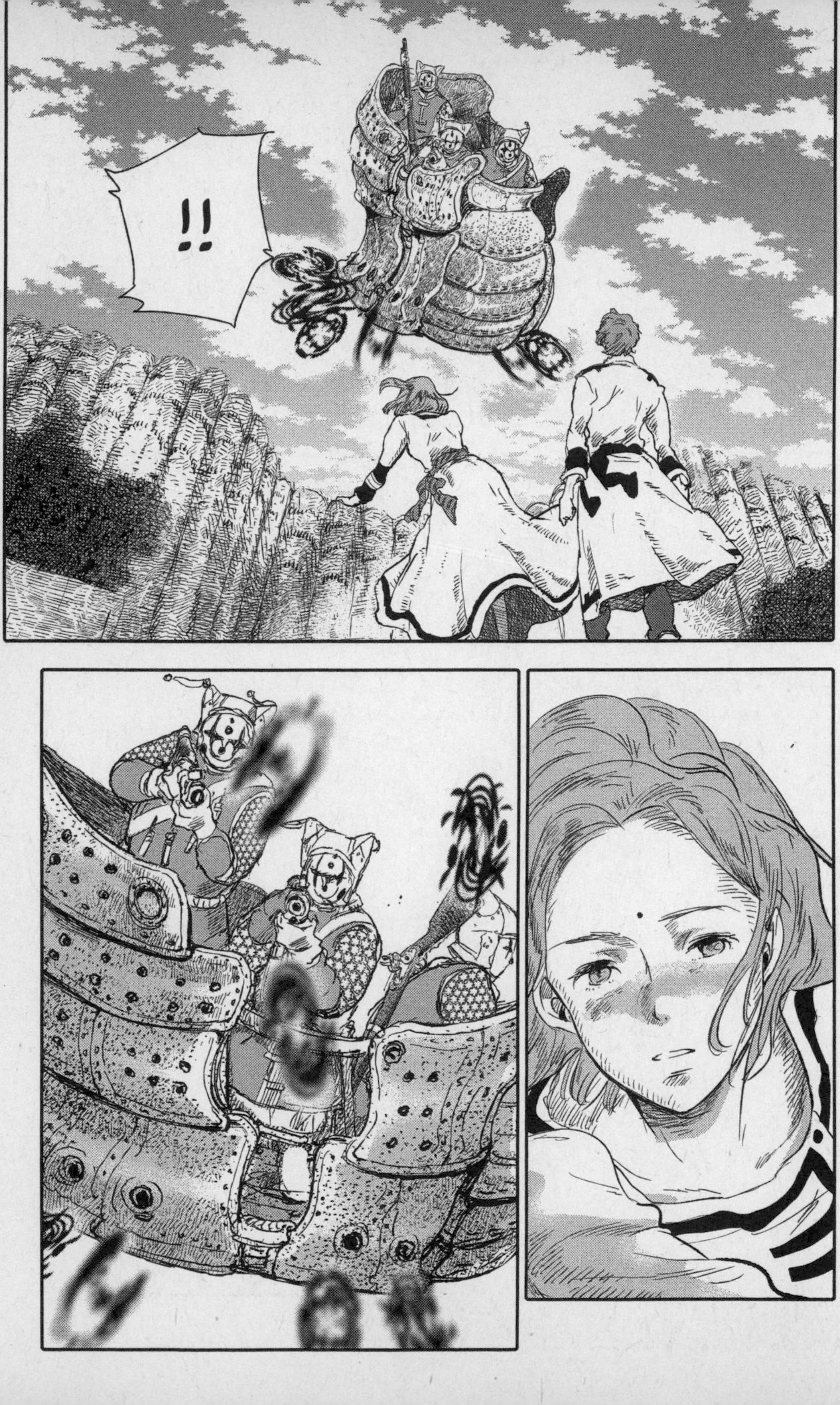
!!

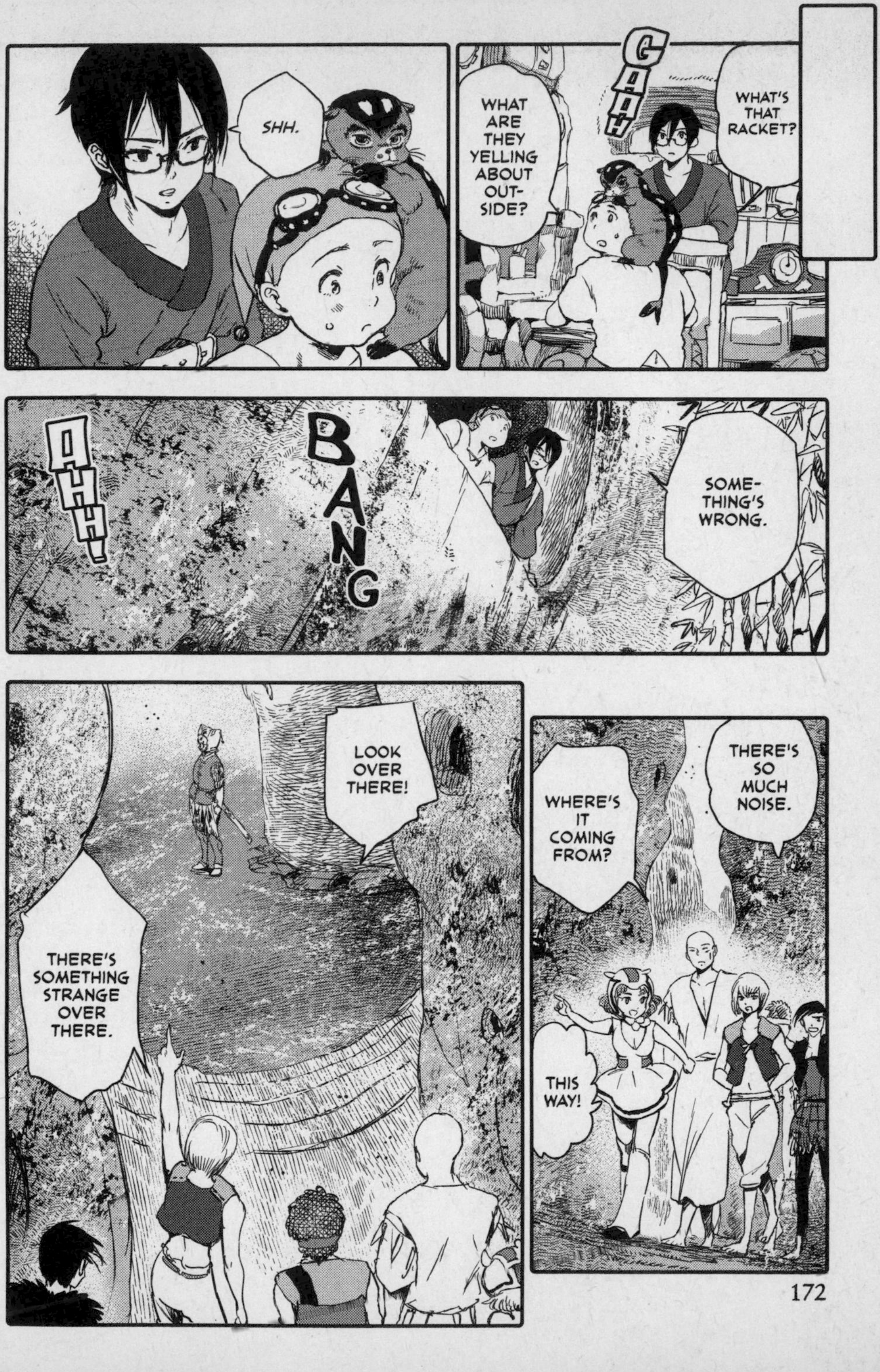
WHAT'S THAT RACKET?
GAAHH
WHAT ARE THEY YELLING ABOUT OUT-SIDE?
SHH.
SOME-THING'S WRONG.
BANG
AHHH!
THERE'S SO MUCH NOISE.
WHERE'S IT COMING FROM?
THIS WAY!
LOOK OVER THERE!
THERE'S SOMETHING STRANGE OVER THERE.

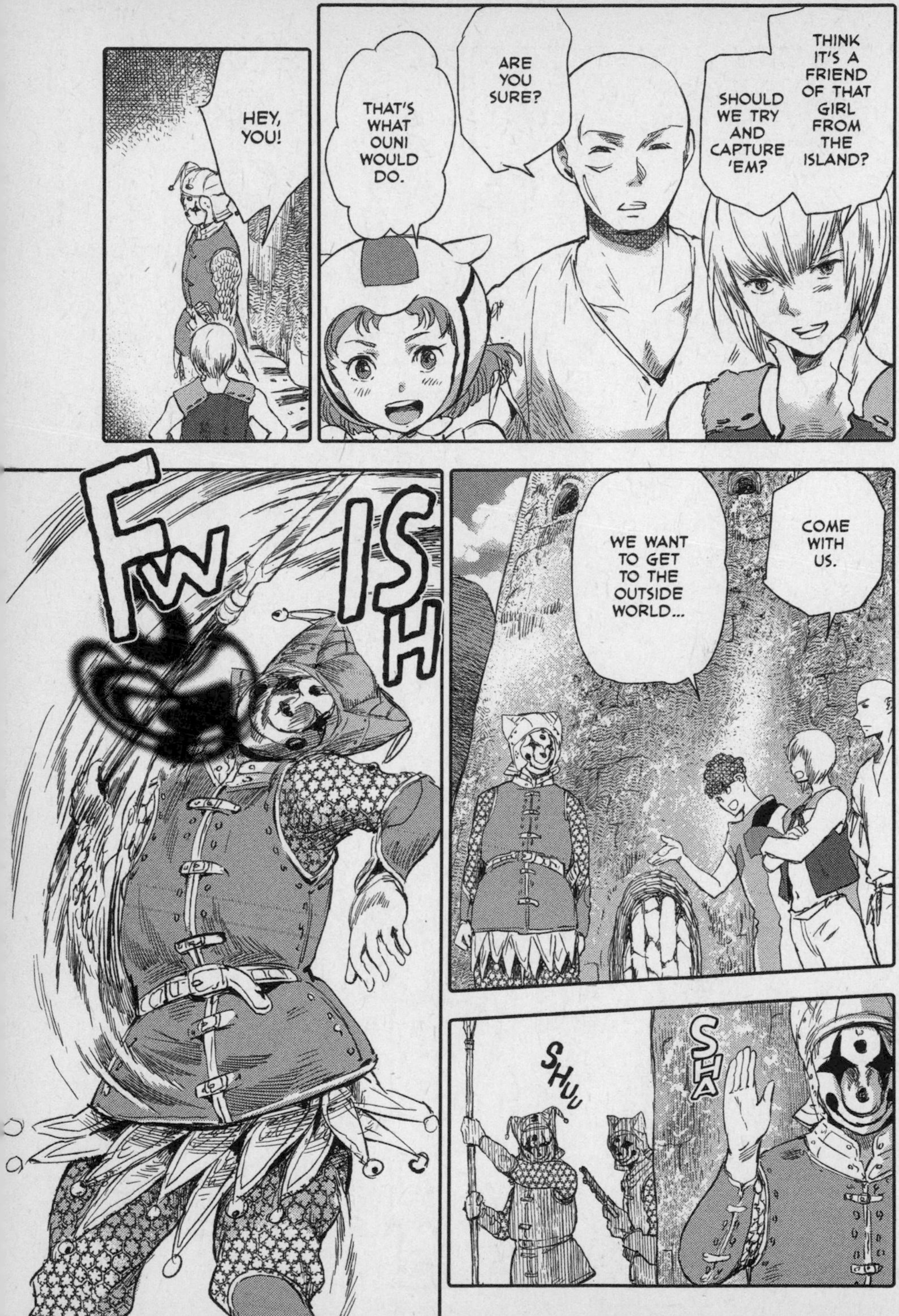
THINK IT'S A FRIEND OF THAT GIRL FROM THE ISLAND?
SHOULD WE TRY AND CAPTURE 'EM?
ARE YOU SURE?
THAT'S WHAT OUNI WOULD DO.
HEY, YOU!
COME WITH US.
WE WANT TO GET TO THE OUTSIDE WORLD...
SHA
SHUU
FWISH

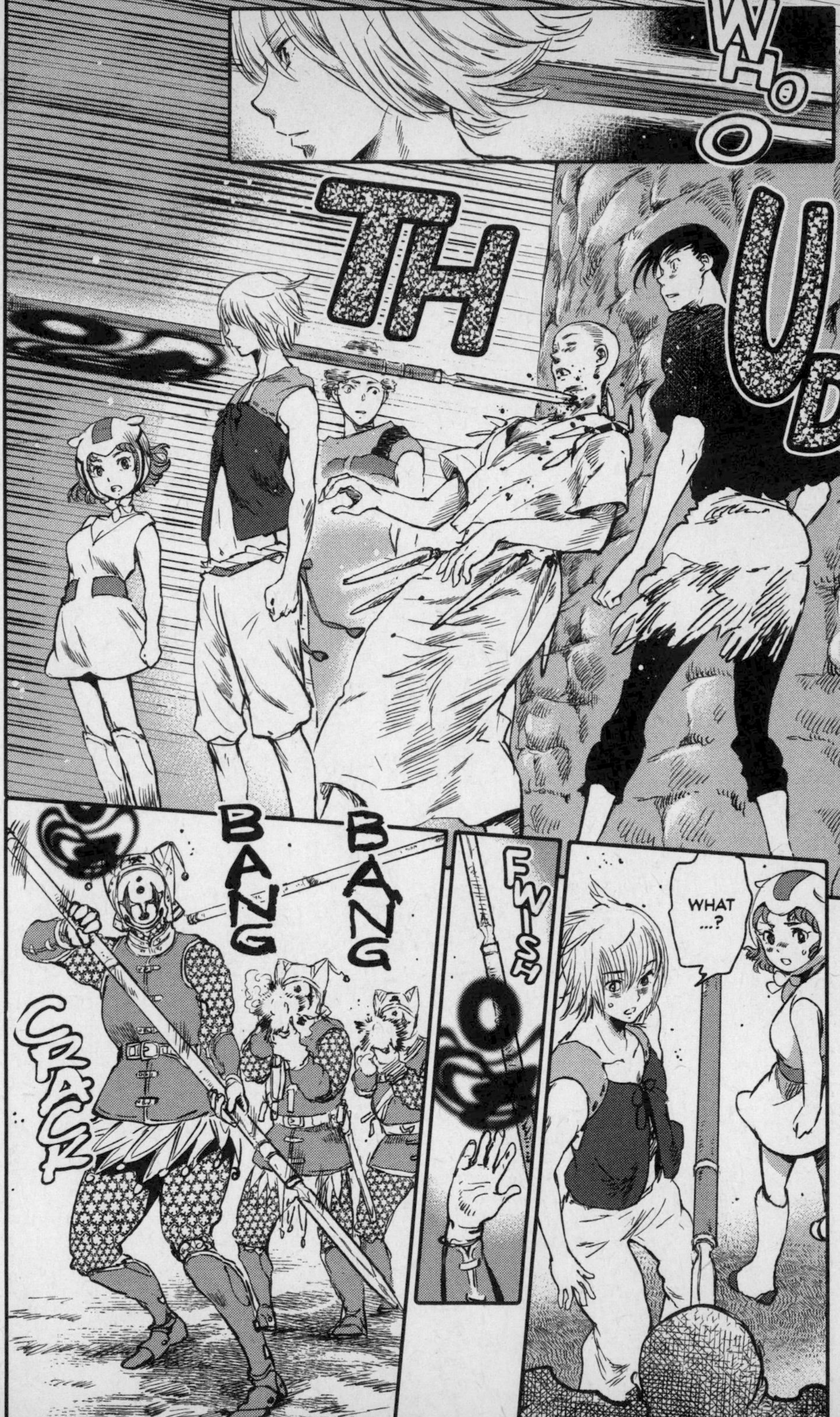
WHOO
THUD
WHAT ...?
FWISH
BANG BANG
CRACK

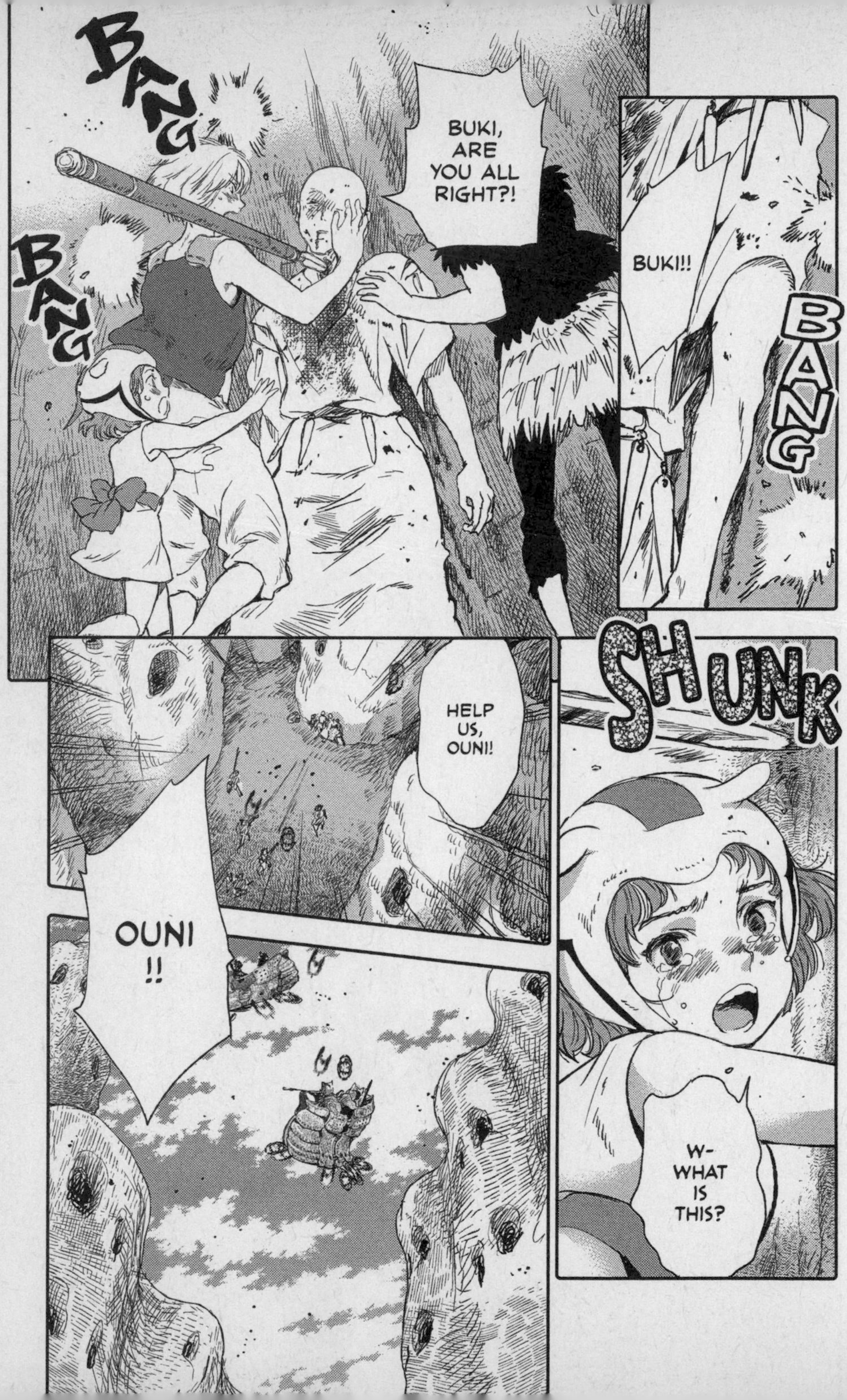
BUKI!!
BANG
BANG
BANG
BANG
BANG
BUKI, ARE YOU ALL RIGHT?!
SHUNK
W-WHAT IS THIS?
HELP US, OUNI!
OUNI!!

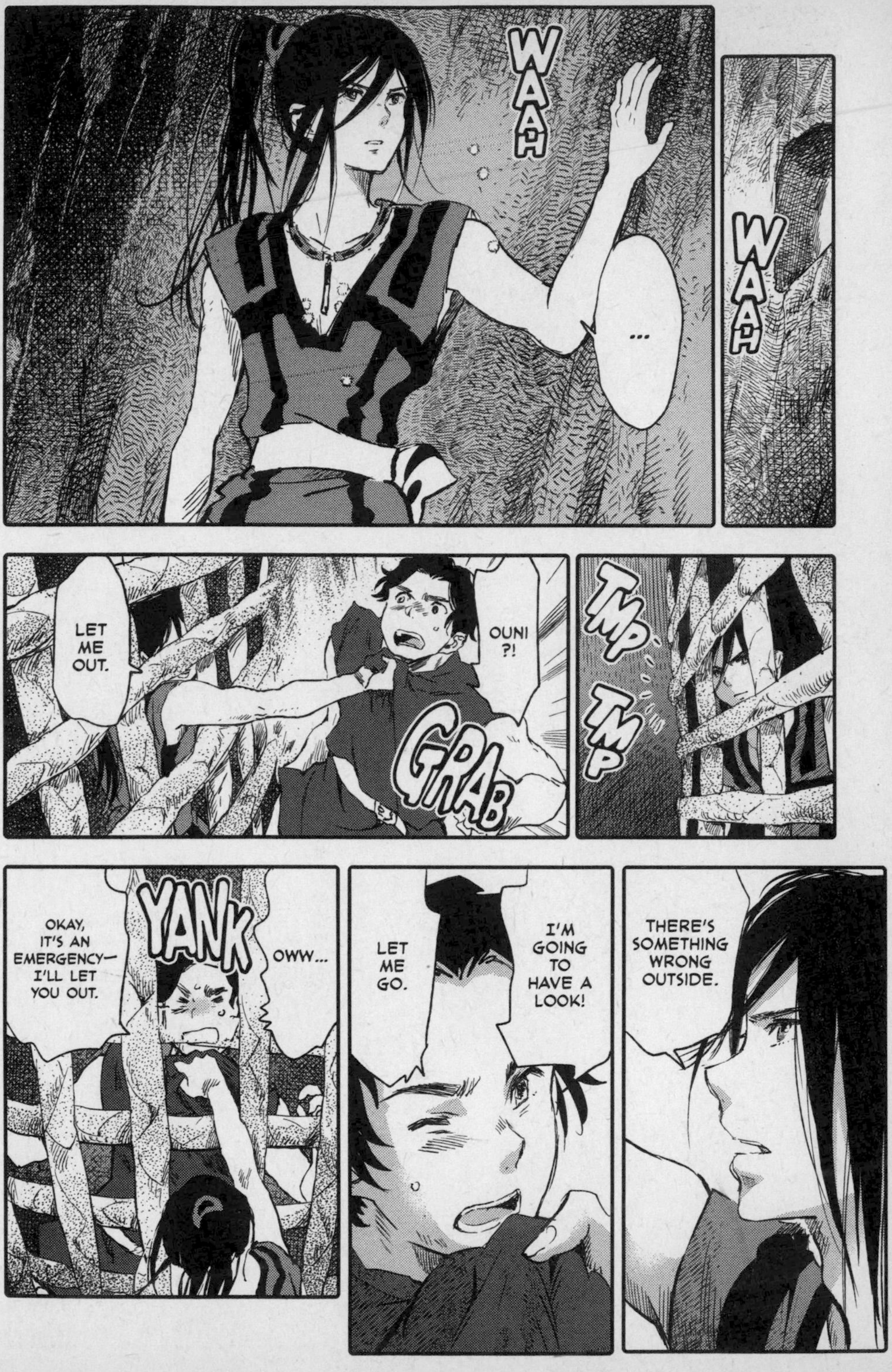
WAAH
WAAH
...
TMP TMP
OUNI?!
LET ME OUT.
GRAB
THERE'S SOMETHING WRONG OUTSIDE.
I'M GOING TO HAVE A LOOK!
LET ME GO.
OWW...
YANK
OKAY, IT'S AN EMERGENCY— I'LL LET YOU OUT.

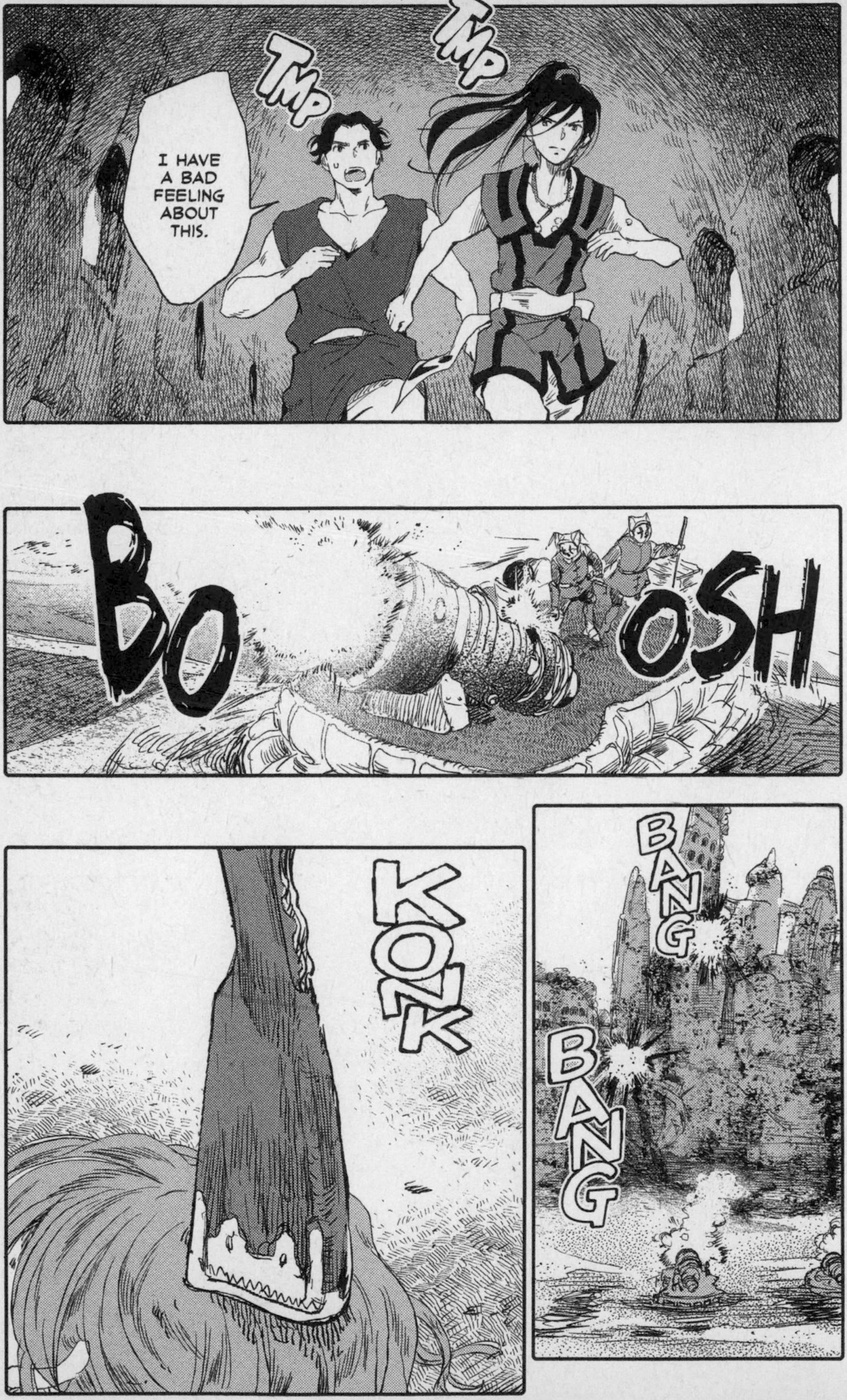
TMP
TMP
I HAVE A BAD FEELING ABOUT THIS.
BOOSH
BANG
BANG
BANG
KONK

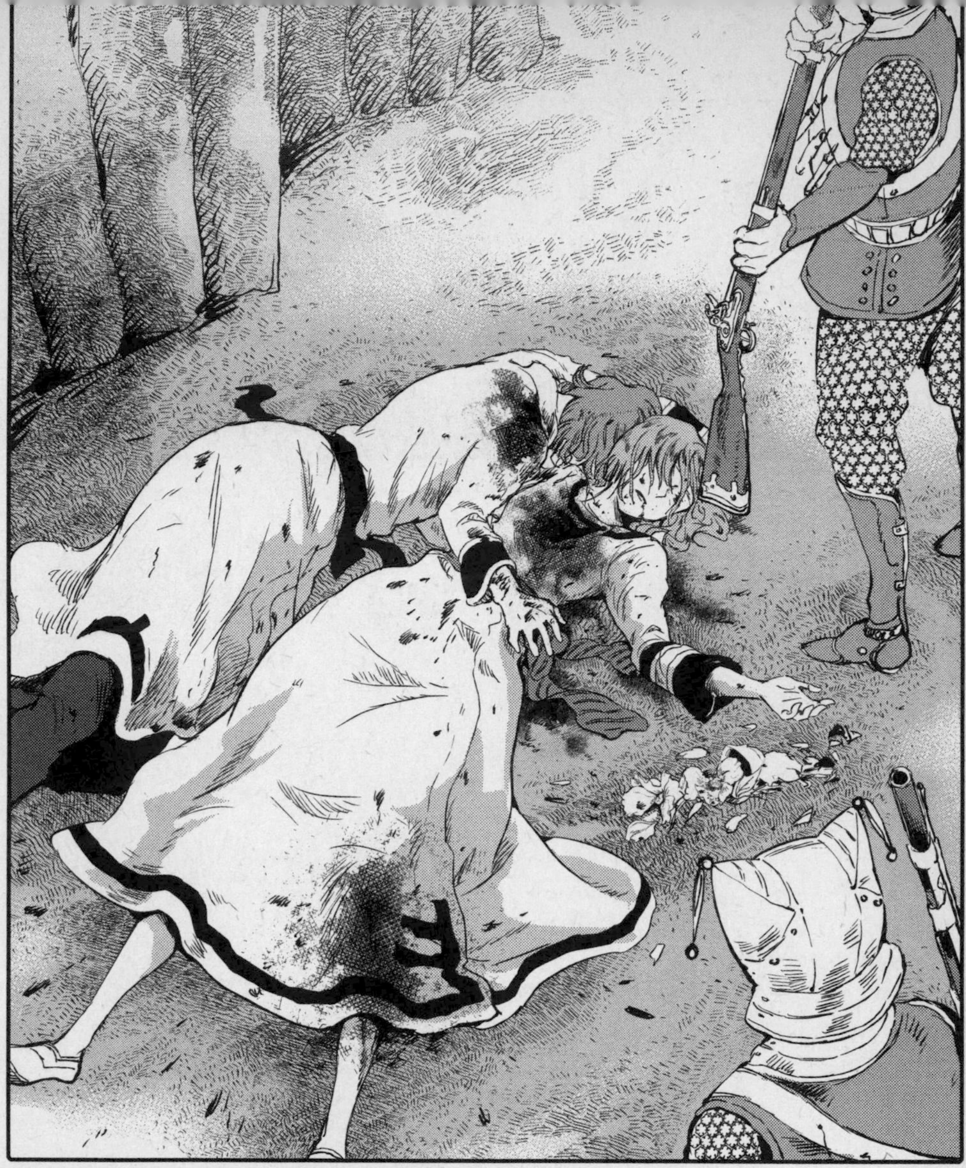

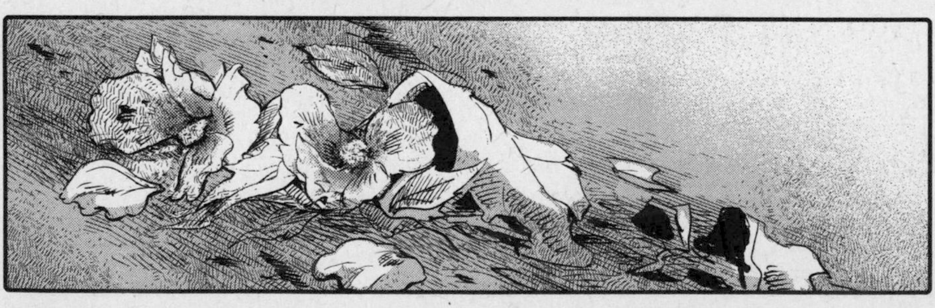

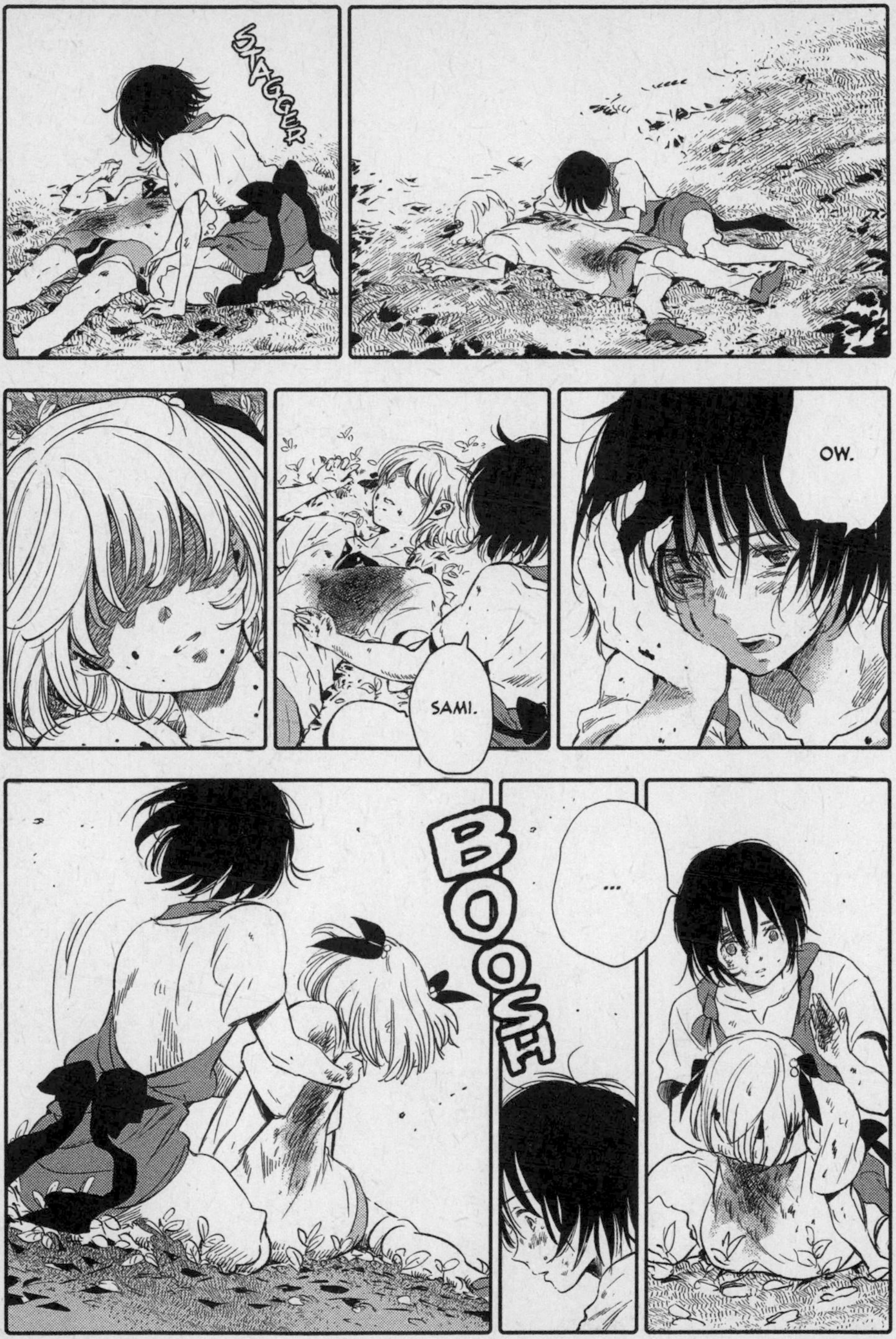
STAGGER
OW.
SAMI.
...
BOOSH

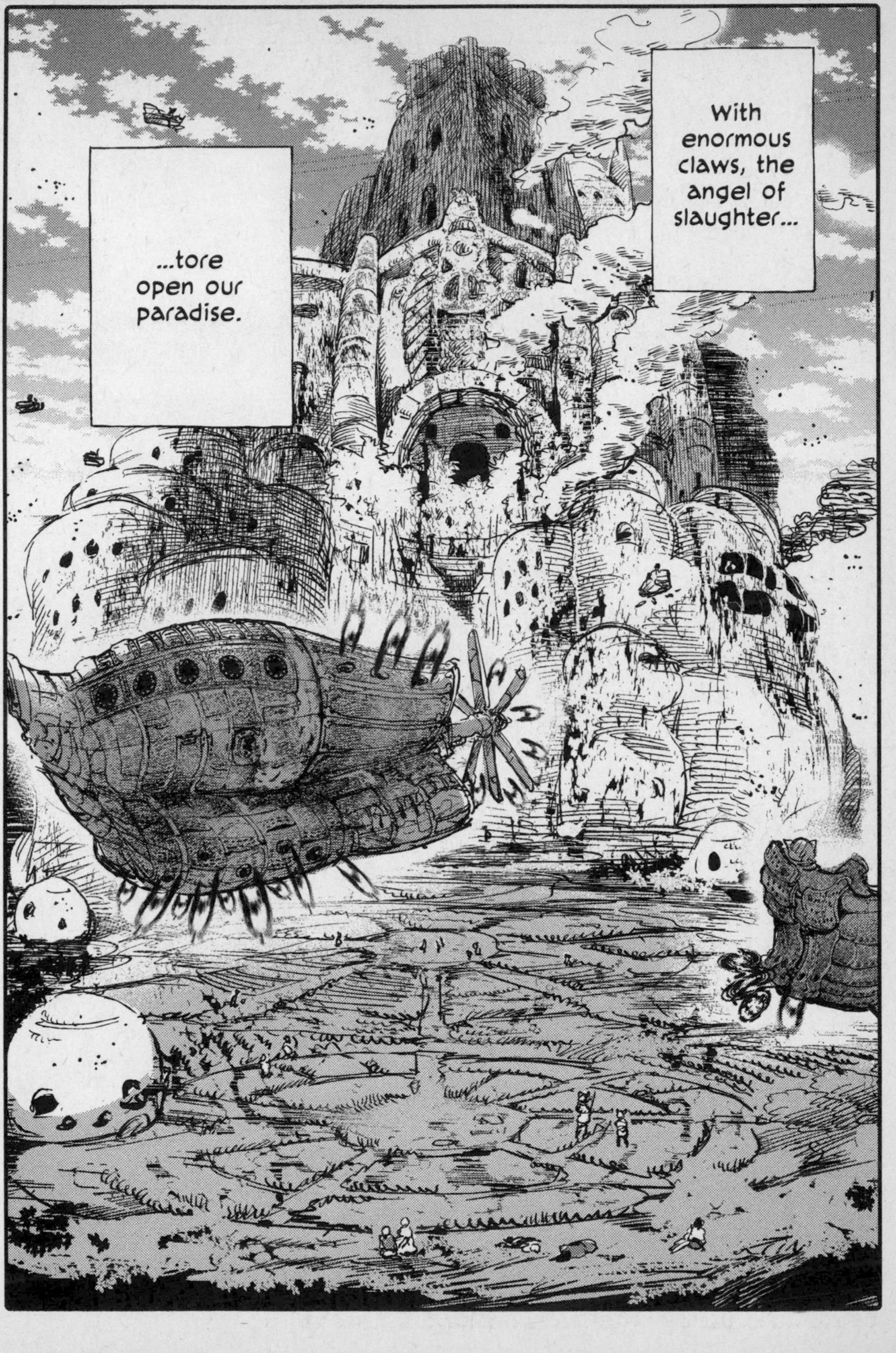
With enormous claws, the angel of slaughter...
...tore open our paradise.

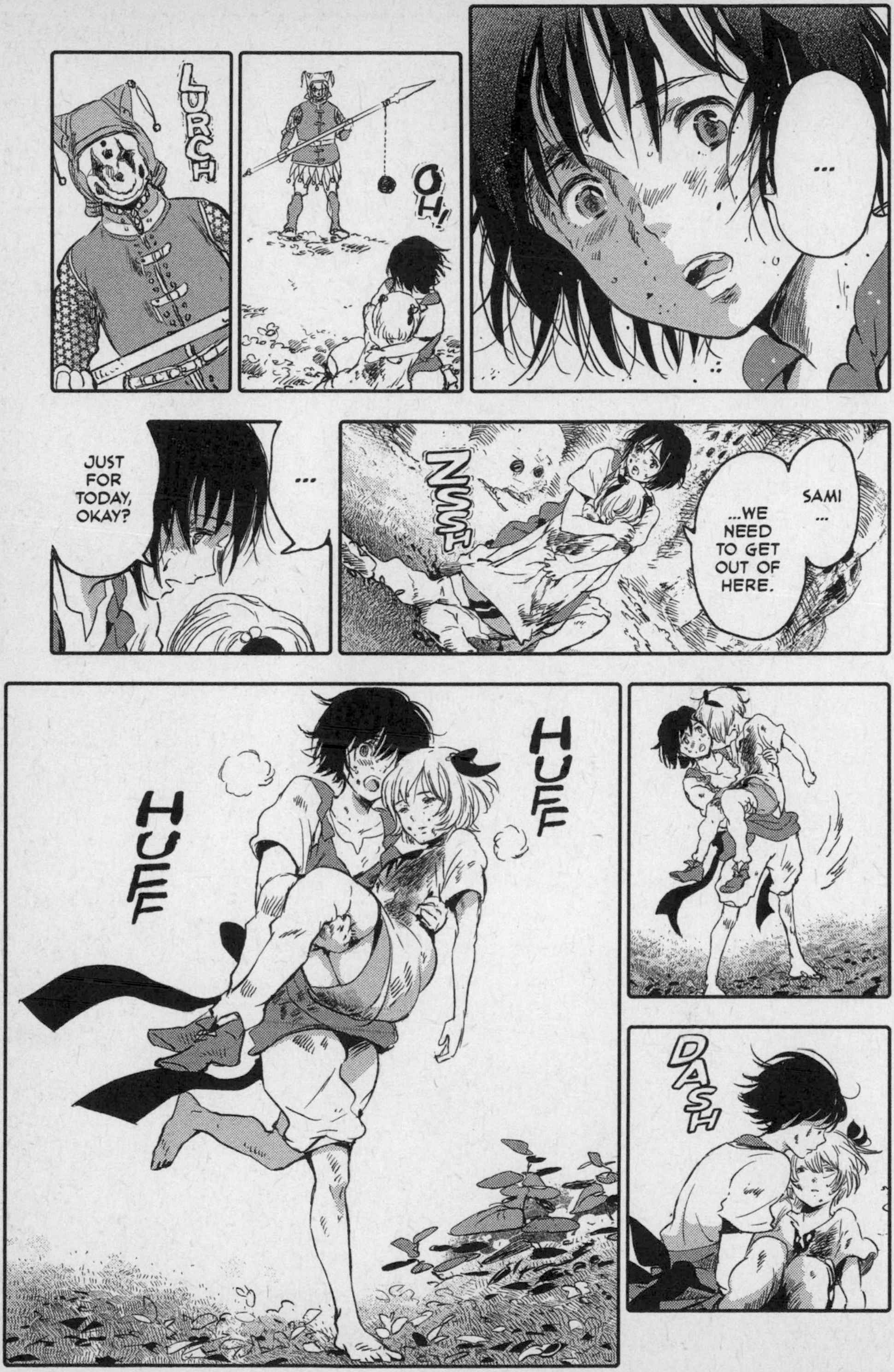
...
OH!
LURCH
SAMI ...
...WE NEED TO GET OUT OF HERE.
ZSSH
...
JUST FOR TODAY, OKAY?
DASH
HUFF
HUFF

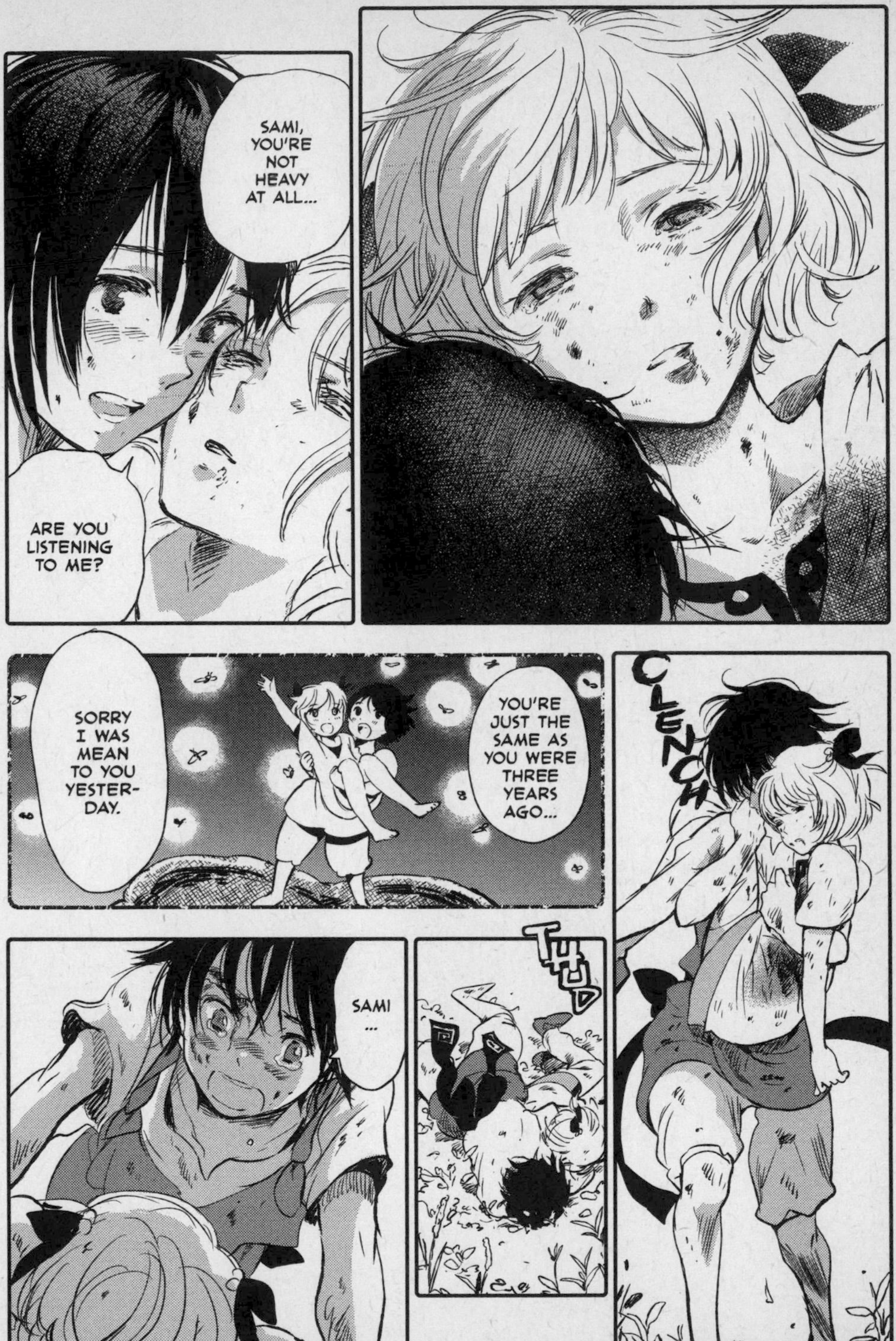
SAMI, YOU'RE NOT HEAVY AT ALL...
ARE YOU LISTENING TO ME?
CLENCH
YOU'RE JUST THE SAME AS YOU WERE THREE YEARS AGO...
SORRY I WAS MEAN TO YOU YESTER-DAY.
THUD
SAMI ...

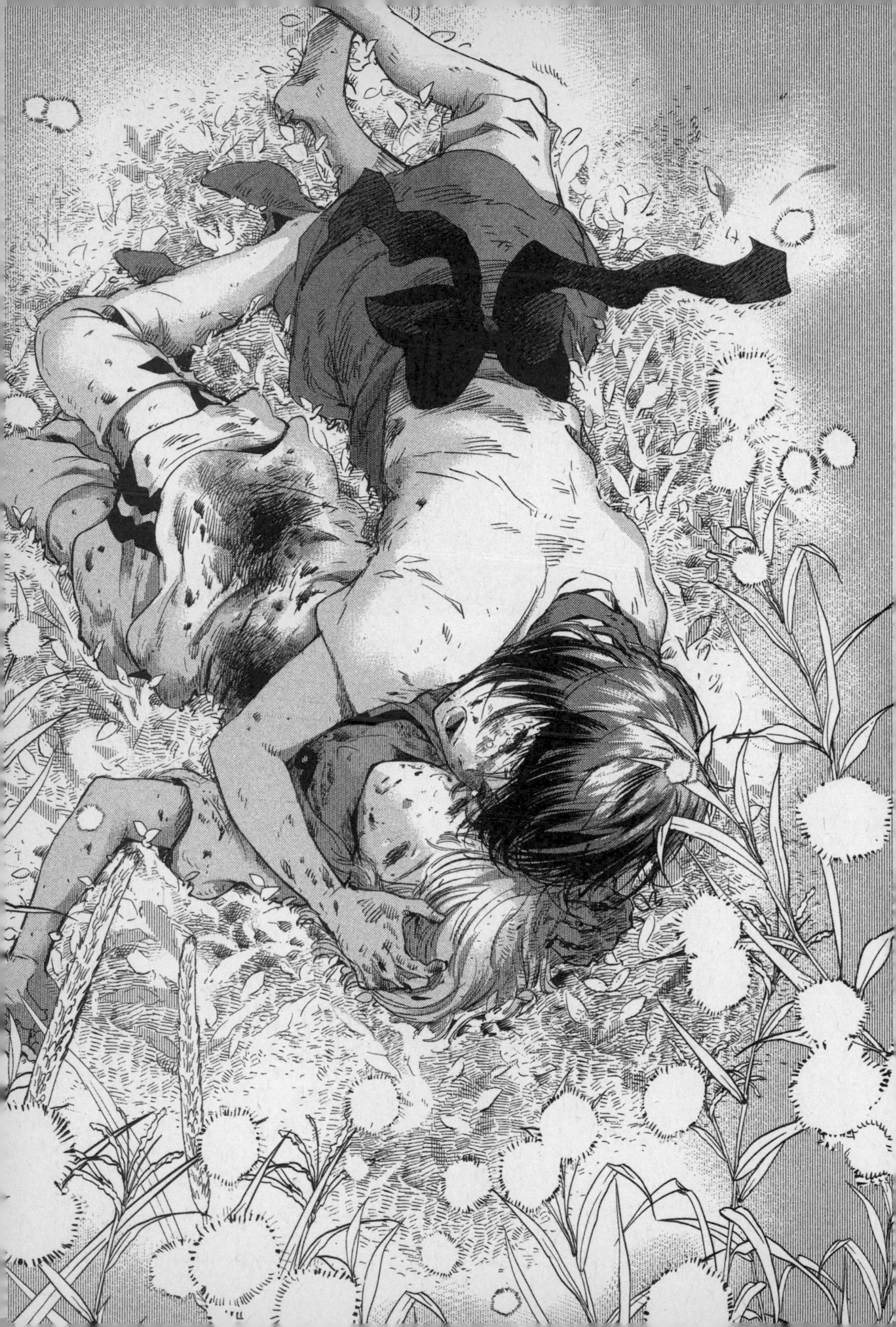

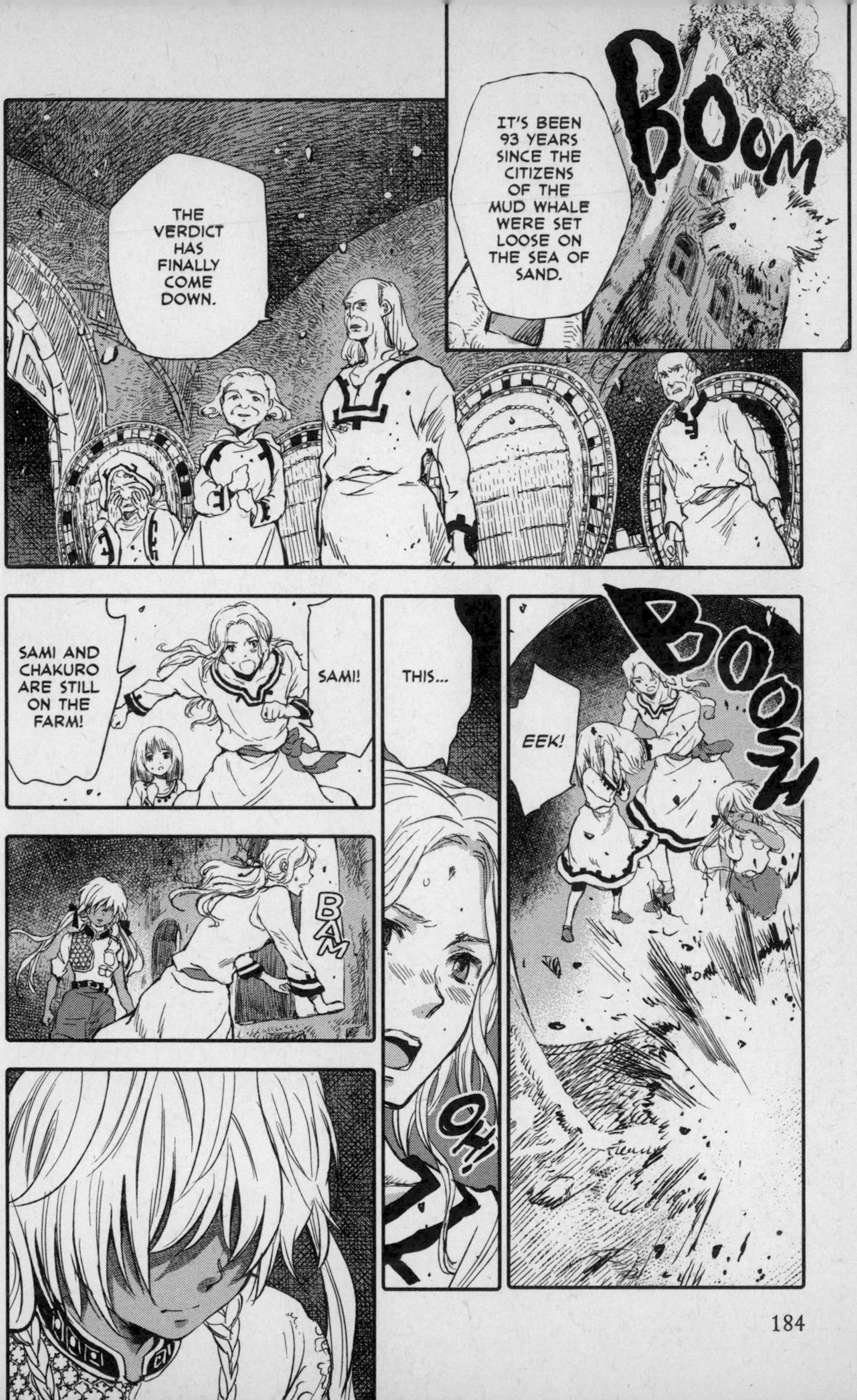
BOOM
IT'S BEEN 93 YEARS SINCE THE CITIZENS OF THE MUD WHALE WERE SET LOOSE ON THE SEA OF SAND.
THE VERDICT HAS FINALLY COME DOWN.
BOOOM
EEK!
THIS...
OH!
SAMI!
SAMI AND CHAKURO ARE STILL ON THE FARM!
BAM

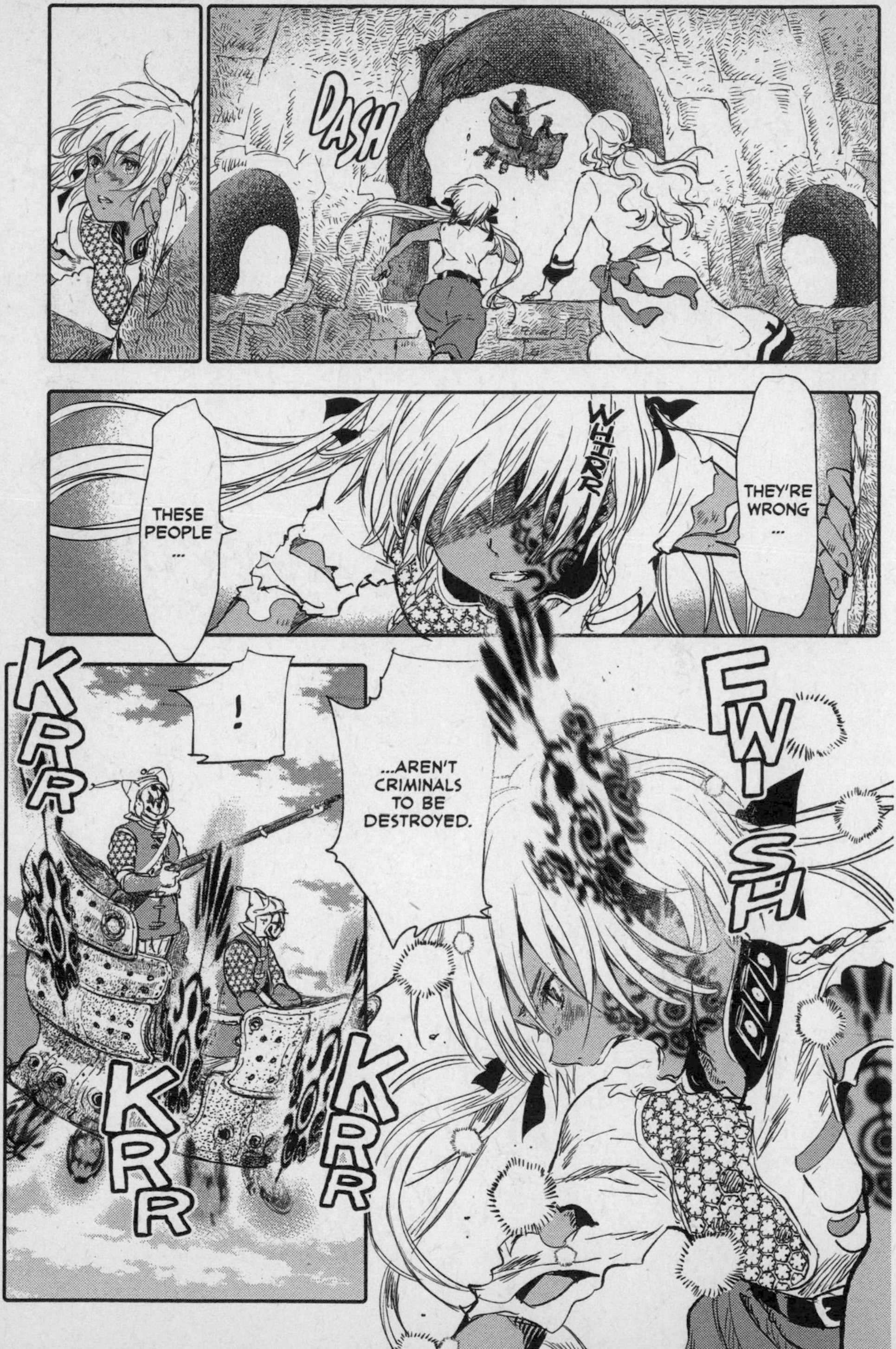
DASH
THEY'RE WRONG ...
WHIRR
THESE PEOPLE ...
FWISH
!
...AREN'T CRIMINALS TO BE DESTROYED.
KRRR
KRRR
KRRR

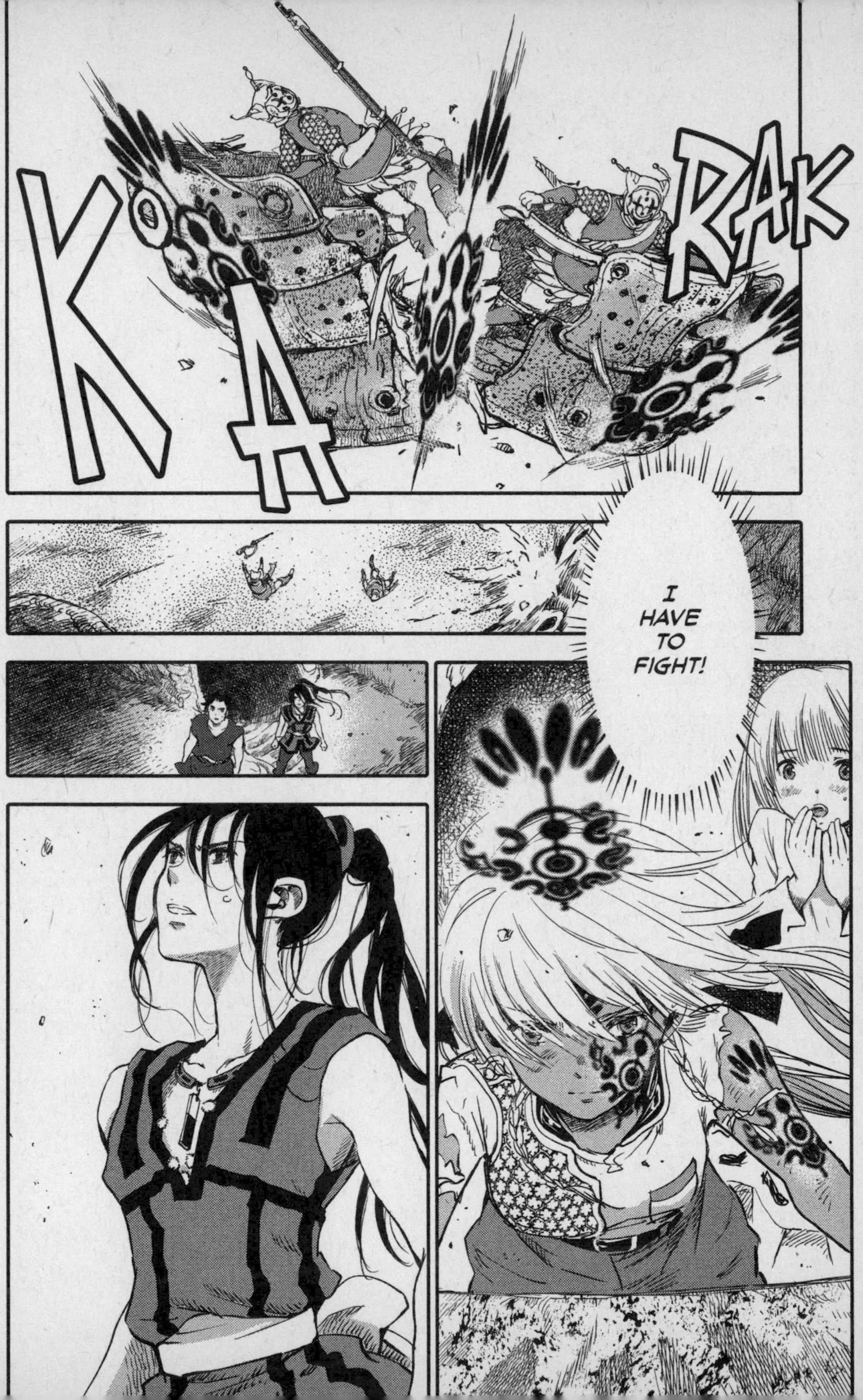
KA
RAK
I HAVE TO FIGHT!

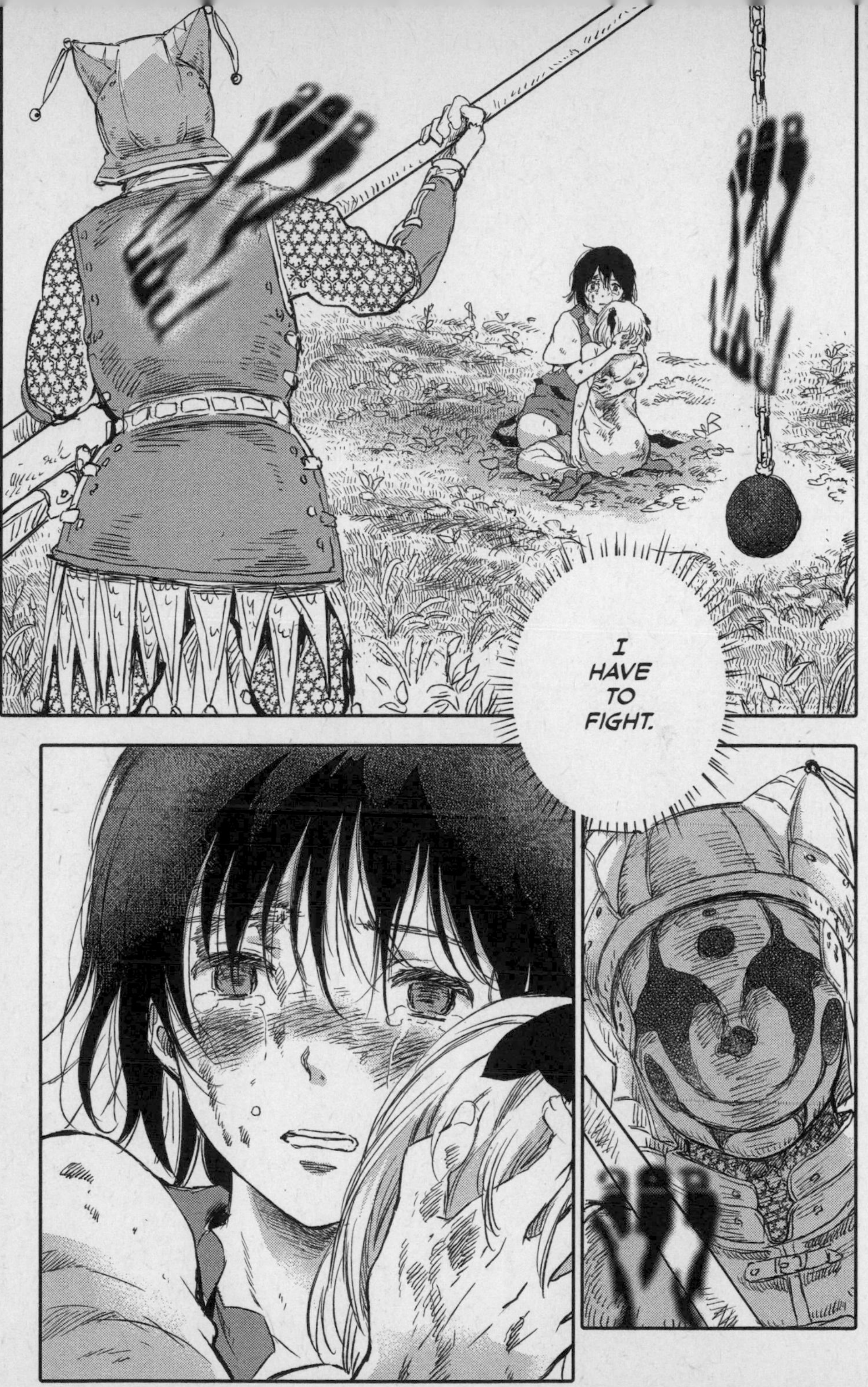
I HAVE TO FIGHT.

Toes of the Emissary -The End-

Children of the Whales volume 1 -The End-

How I Discovered Children of the Whales

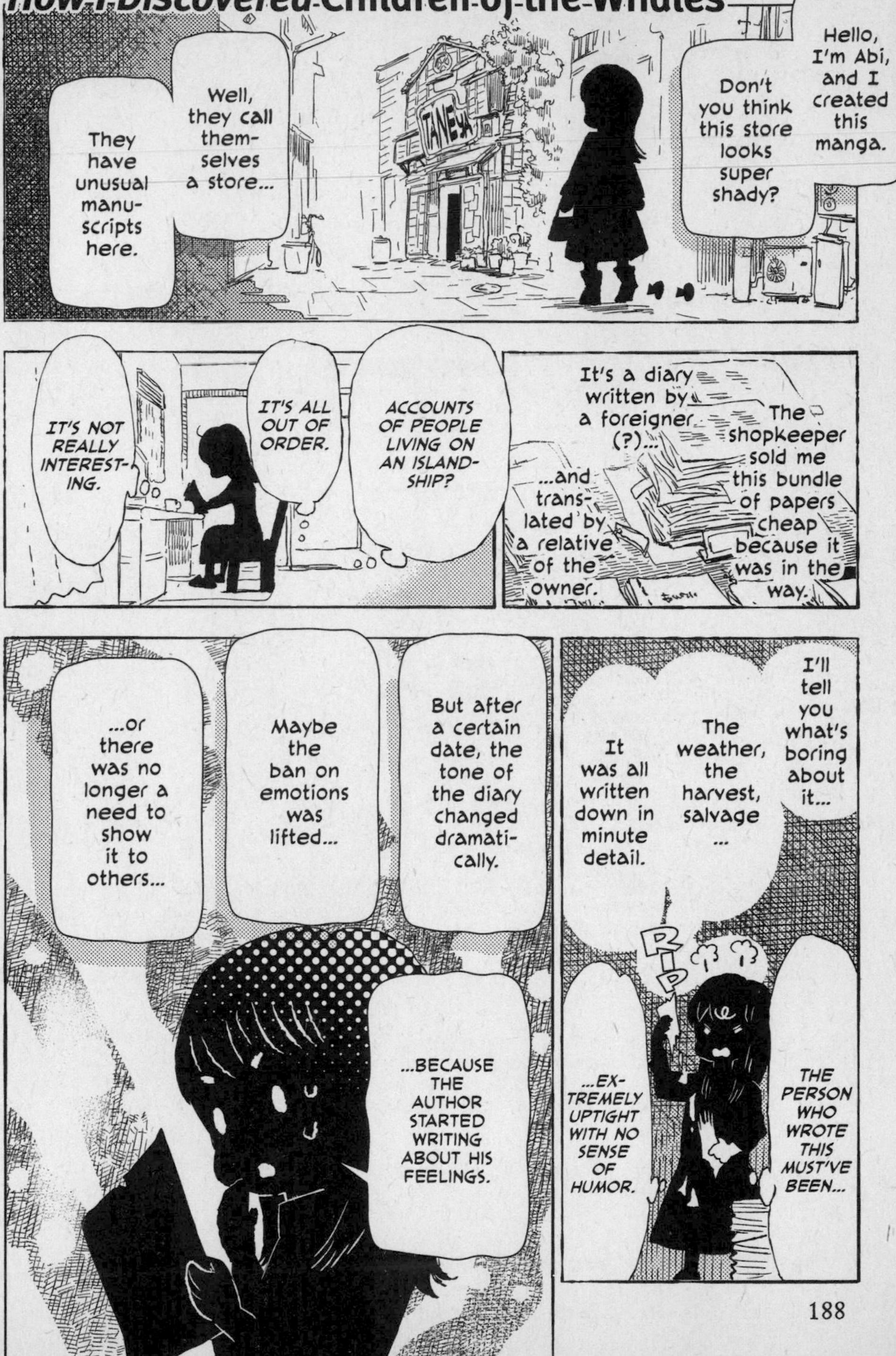
Hello, I'm Abi, and I created this manga.
Don't you think this store looks super shady?
TANEYA
Well, they call them-selves a store...
They have unusual manu-scripts here.
The shopkeeper sold me this bundle of papers cheap because it was in the way.
It's a diary written by a foreigner (?)...
...and trans-lated by a relative of the owner.
ACCOUNTS OF PEOPLE LIVING ON AN ISLAND-SHIP?
IT'S ALL OUT OF ORDER.
IT'S NOT REALLY INTEREST-ING.
I'll tell you what's boring about it...
The weather, the harvest, salvage ...
It was all written down in minute detail.
RIP
THE PERSON WHO WROTE THIS MUST'VE BEEN...
...EX-TREMELY UPTIGHT WITH NO SENSE OF HUMOR.
But after a certain date, the tone of the diary changed dramati-cally.
Maybe the ban on emotions was lifted...
...or there was no longer a need to show it to others...
...BECAUSE THE AUTHOR STARTED WRITING ABOUT HIS FEELINGS.

The afterward with a lot to dig into *How I Discovered* Children of the Whales

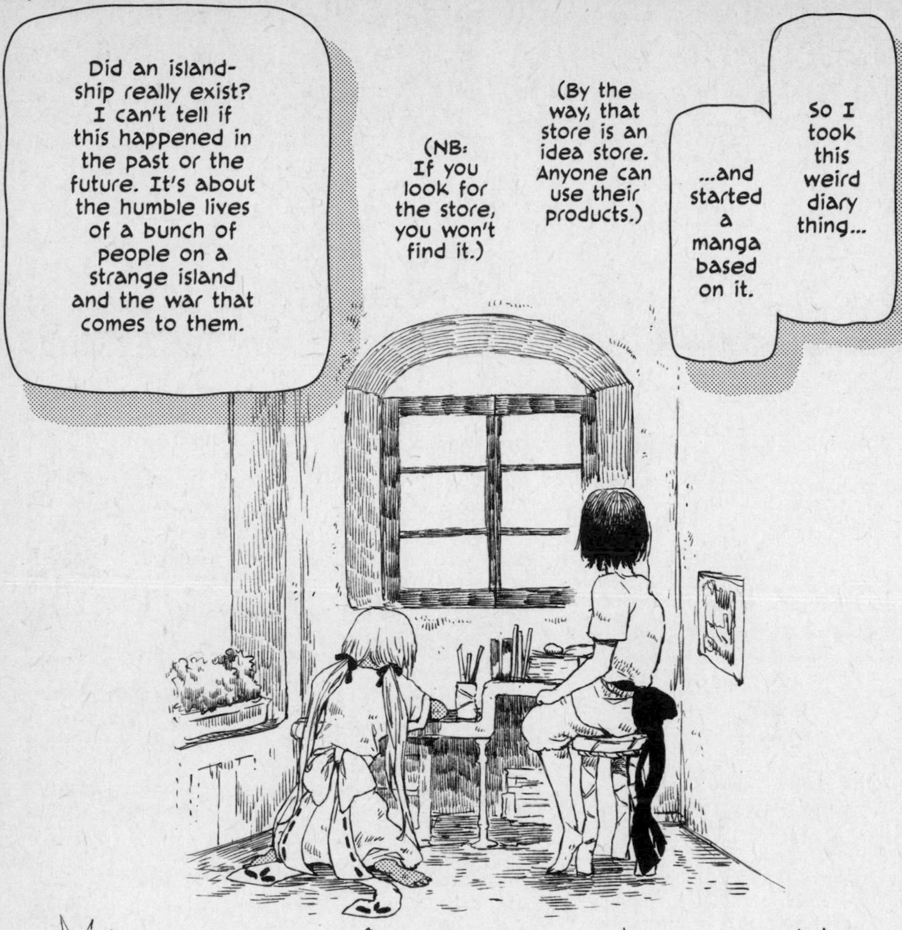

So I took this weird diary thing...
...and started a manga based on it.
(By the way, that store is an idea store. Anyone can use their products.)
(NB: If you look for the store, you won't find it.)
Did an island-ship really exist? I can't tell if this happened in the past or the future. It's about the humble lives of a bunch of people on a strange island and the war that comes to them.

- Since the diary of Chakuro (name changed) didn't contain any photos or drawings, I've had to imagine the setting and people.
- The names in the diary were strange and hard to pronounce. Since they were all based on colors, I decided to replace them with Japanese color names.
  (Ex.: *Chakuro* is blackish brown. *Taisha*, *suou* and *ouni* are shades of red.)
- The contents of the diary have been edited and rearranged for narrative flow.

On the next page, I will explain the setting for this story, the Mud Whale!

From the Archivist's Diary: An Illustration of the Mud Whale

*Some details, such as the shape of the Mud Whale, are speculation based on Chakuro's accounts.

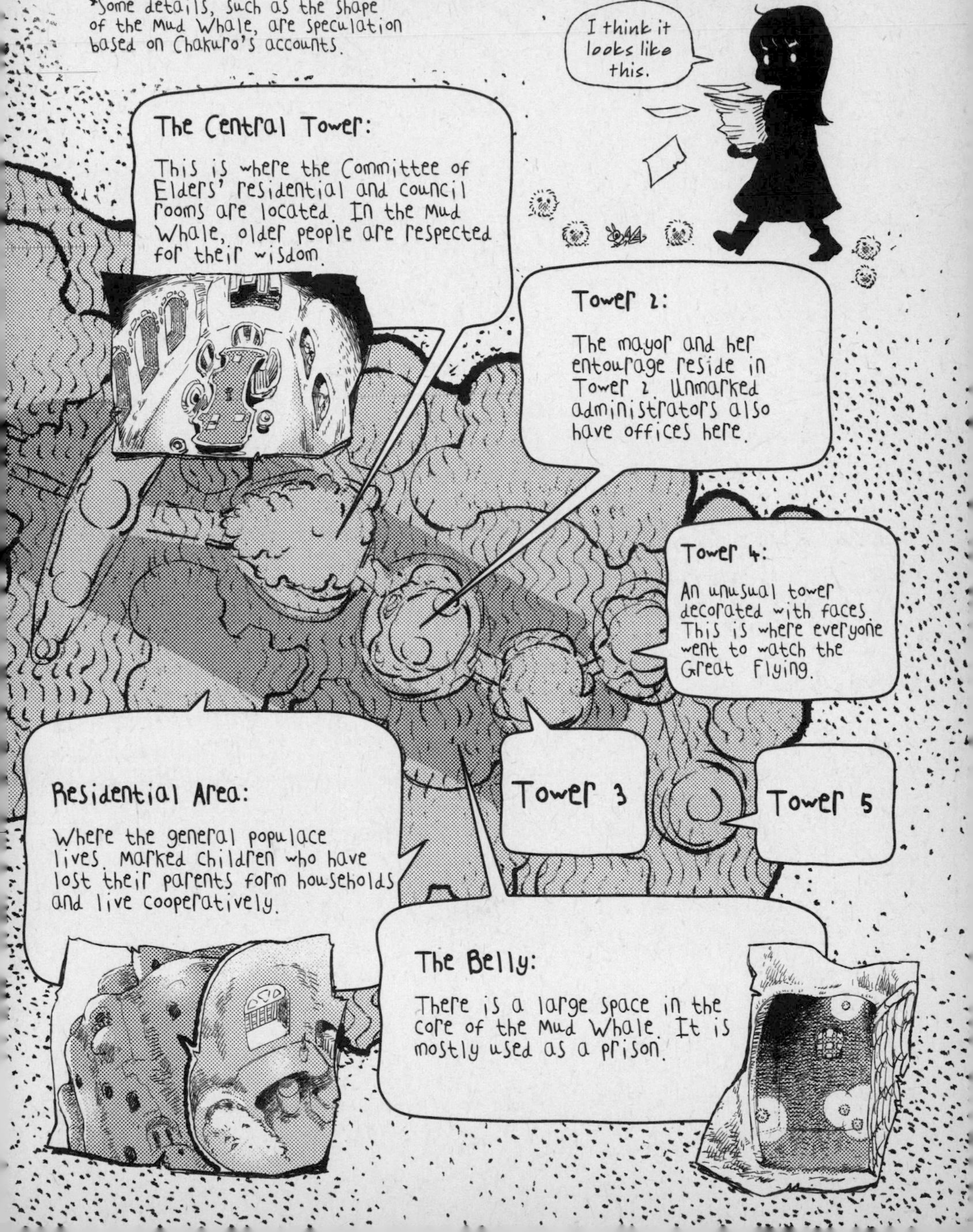
I think it looks like this.
The Central Tower:
This is where the Committee of Elders' residential and council rooms are located. In the Mud Whale, older people are respected for their wisdom.
Tower 2:
The mayor and her entourage reside in Tower 2. Unmarked administrators also have offices here.
Tower 4:
An unusual tower decorated with faces. This is where everyone went to watch the Great Flying.
Tower 3
Tower 5
Residential Area:
Where the general populace lives. Marked children who have lost their parents form households and live cooperatively.
The Belly:
There is a large space in the core of the Mud Whale. It is mostly used as a prison.

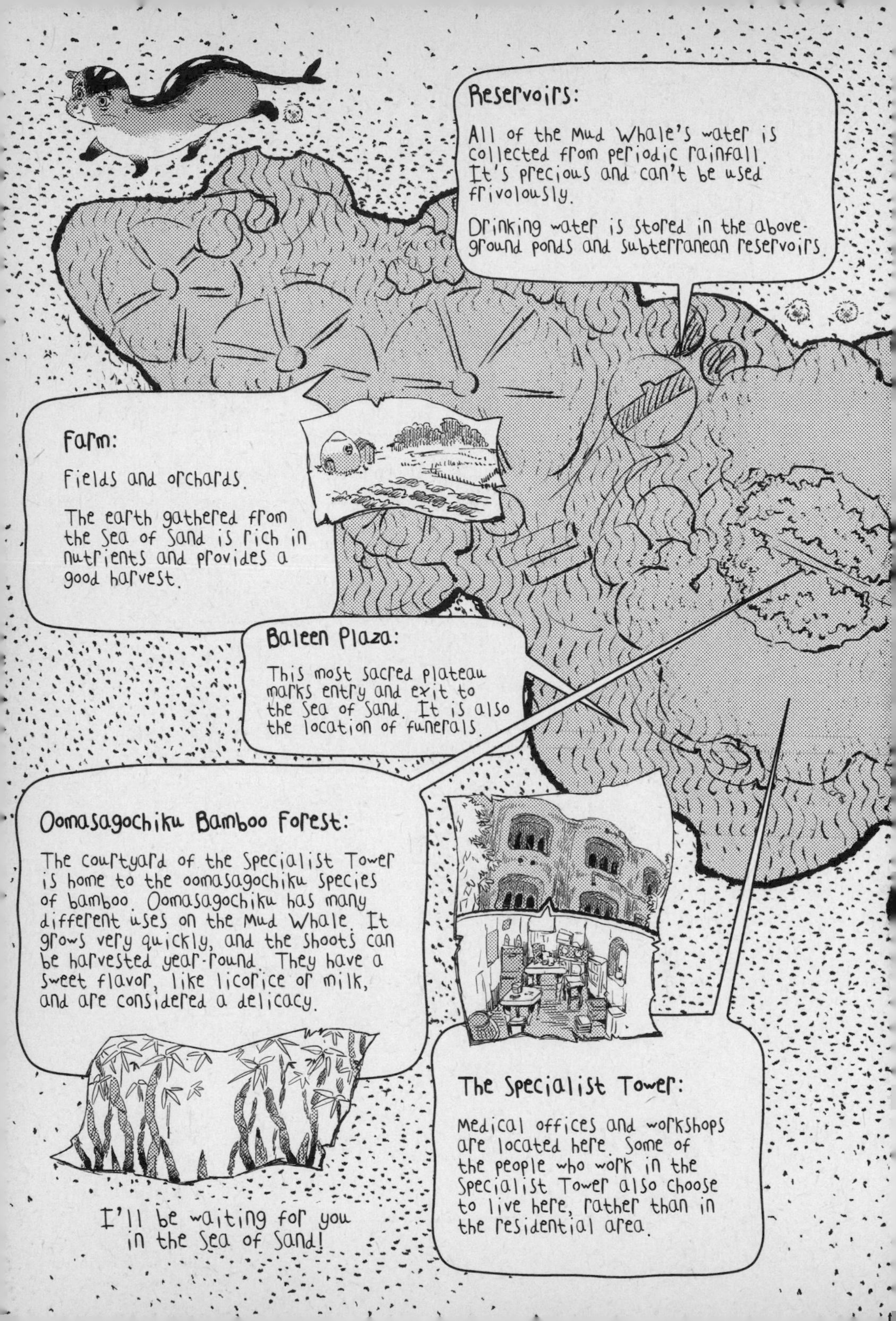

Reservoirs:

All of the Mud Whale's water is collected from periodic rainfall. It's precious and can't be used frivolously.

Drinking water is stored in the above-ground ponds and subterranean reservoirs.

Farm:

Fields and orchards.

The earth gathered from the Sea of Sand is rich in nutrients and provides a good harvest.

Baleen Plaza:

This most sacred plateau marks entry and exit to the Sea of Sand. It is also the location of funerals.

Oomasagochiku Bamboo Forest:

The courtyard of the Specialist Tower is home to the oomasagochiku species of bamboo. Oomasagochiku has many different uses on the Mud Whale. It grows very quickly, and the shoots can be harvested year-round. They have a sweet flavor, like licorice or milk, and are considered a delicacy.

The Specialist Tower:

Medical offices and workshops are located here. Some of the people who work in the Specialist Tower also choose to live here, rather than in the residential area.

I'll be waiting for you in the Sea of Sand!

A Note on Names

Those who live on the Mud Whale are named after colors in a language unknown. Abi Umeda uses Japanese translations of the names, which we have maintained. Here is a list of the English equivalents for the curious.

Benihi	scarlet
Buki	kerria flower (*yamabuki*)
Chakuro	blackish brown (*cha* = brown, *kuro* = black)
Kuchiba	decayed-leaf brown
Masoh	cinnabar
Neri	silk white
Nezu	mouse gray
Ouni	safflower red
Ro	lacquer black
Sami	light green (*asa* = light, *midori* = green)
Shinono	the color of dawn (*shinonome*)
Suou	raspberry red
Taisha	red ocher

Please spend some time relaxing on the Mud Whale.

—Abi Umeda

ABI UMEDA debuted as a manga creator with the one-shot "Yukokugendan" in *Weekly Shonen Champion*. *Children of the Whales* is her eighth manga work.

CHILDREN OF THE WHALES

VOLUME 1
VIZ Signature Edition

Story and Art by **Abi Umeda**

Translation / JN Productions
Touch-Up Art & Lettering / Annaliese Christman
Design / Julian (JR) Robinson
Editor / Pancha Diaz

KUJIRANOKORAHA SAJOUNIUTAU Volume 1
© 2013 ABI UMEDA
First published in Japan in 2013 by AKITA PUBLISHING CO., LTD., Tokyo
English translation rights arranged with AKITA PUBLISHING CO., LTD. through
Tuttle-Mori Agency, Inc., Tokyo

Printed in the U.S.A.

Published by VIZ Media, LLC
P.O. Box 77010
San Francisco, CA 94107

10 9 8 7 6 5 4 3 2 1
First printing, November 2017

viz.com

vizsignature.com

CHILDREN OF THE WHALES

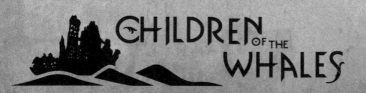

I'll tell you a story
about the sea.

It's a story that
no one knows yet.

The story of the sea
that only I can tell...

Children of the Sea

BY DAISUKE IGARASHI

Uncover the mysterious tale
with *Children of the Sea*—
BUY THE MANGA TODAY!

Available at your local bookstore and comic store.

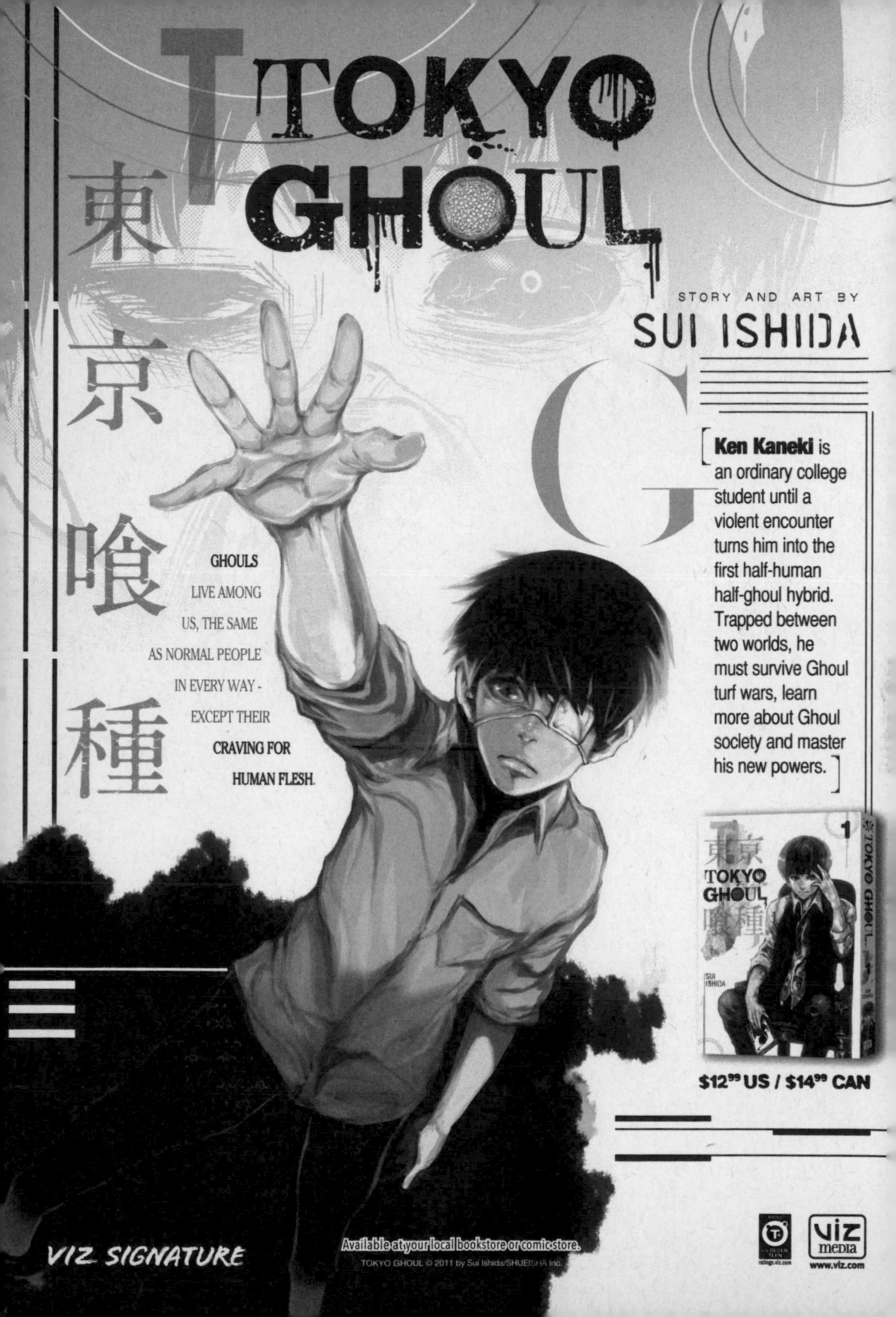
TOKYO GHOUL
東京喰種
STORY AND ART BY
SUI ISHIDA
GHOULS LIVE AMONG US, THE SAME AS NORMAL PEOPLE IN EVERY WAY - EXCEPT THEIR CRAVING FOR HUMAN FLESH.
Ken Kaneki is an ordinary college student until a violent encounter turns him into the first half-human half-ghoul hybrid. Trapped between two worlds, he must survive Ghoul turf wars, learn more about Ghoul society and master his new powers.
$12.99 US / $14.99 CAN
VIZ SIGNATURE
Available at your local bookstore or comic store.
TOKYO GHOUL © 2011 by Sui Ishida/SHUEISHA Inc.
viz media
www.viz.com

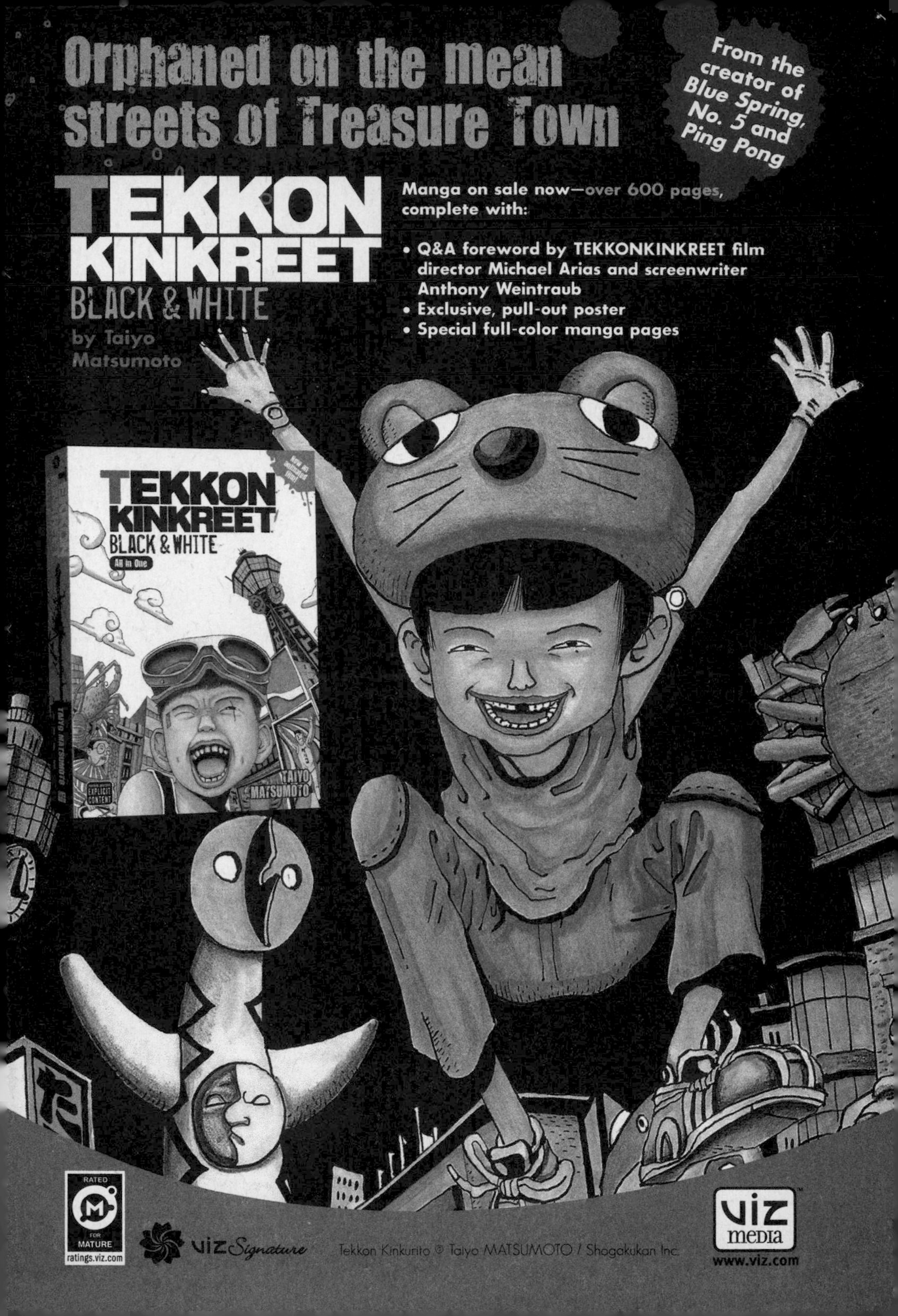
Orphaned on the mean streets of Treasure Town
From the creator of Blue Spring, No. 5 and Ping Pong
TEKKON KINKREET
BLACK & WHITE
by Taiyo Matsumoto
Manga on sale now—over 600 pages, complete with:
• Q&A foreword by TEKKONKINKREET film director Michael Arias and screenwriter Anthony Weintraub
• Exclusive, pull-out poster
• Special full-color manga pages
TEKKON KINKREET
BLACK & WHITE
All in One
TAIYO MATSUMOTO
EXPLICIT CONTENT
RATED M FOR MATURE
ratings.viz.com
VIZ Signature
Tekkon Kinkurito © Taiyo MATSUMOTO / Shogakukan Inc.
VIZ media
www.viz.com

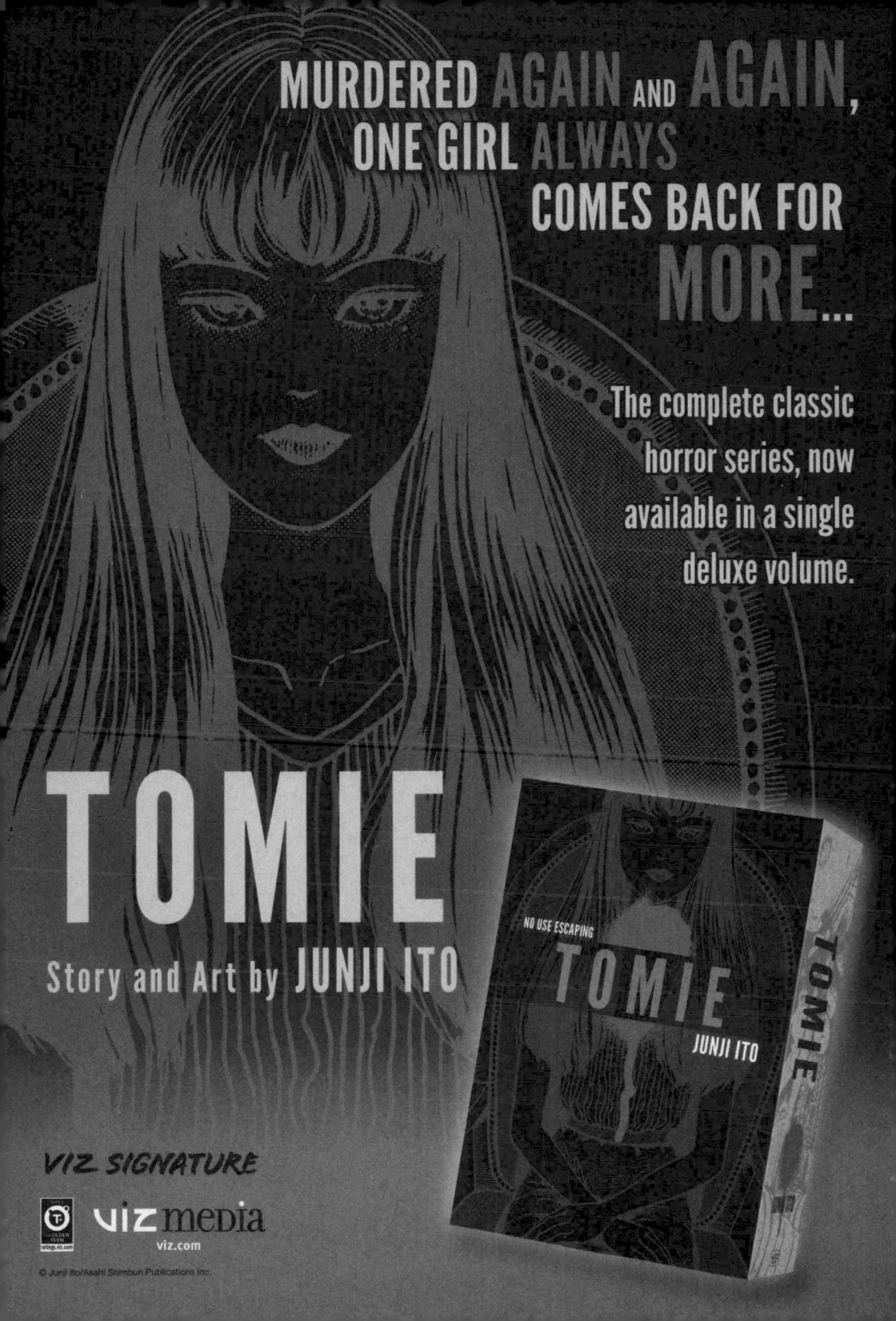
MURDERED AGAIN AND AGAIN,
ONE GIRL ALWAYS
COMES BACK FOR
MORE...
The complete classic horror series, now available in a single deluxe volume.
TOMIE
Story and Art by JUNJI ITO
NO USE ESCAPING
TOMIE
JUNJI ITO
TOMIE
VIZ SIGNATURE
OLDER TEEN
ratings.viz.com
VIZ media
viz.com
© Junji Ito/Asahi Shimbun Publications Inc.

THIS IS THE LAST PAGE!

Children of the Whales has been printed in the original Japanese format to preserve the orientation of the original artwork.